T0304655

Diversity and Precarious Work
during Socio-economic Upheaval

Existing research on the rise of precarious forms of employment has paid little attention to gender and diversity challenges. Yet precarious work has damaging effects for vulnerable demographics, with women, ethnic minorities, and people with disabilities more considerably affected. This volume unpacks this research and offers insights into the role of organisations in fostering inclusive change. It draws an awareness of precarious work and diversity in organisations in three ways:

(1) it uncovers and documents the variety of issues facing vulnerable demographic groups at work;
(2) it promotes greater scholarship on the link between precarious work and diversity during economic and social upheaval; and
(3) it develops a research program and agenda that sheds light onto new and important aspects of precarious work and diversity issues.

A group of international scholars come together to discuss ways to address these challenges and offer a way forward for the future.

ELINA MELIOU is Professor of Work and Organisation Studies at Brunel University London.

JOANA VASSILOPOULOU is Associate Professor at Brunel University London.

MUSTAFA F. ÖZBILGIN is Professor of Organisational Behaviour at Brunel University London.

Diversity and Precarious Work during Socio-economic Upheaval

Exploring the Missing Link

Edited by

ELINA MELIOU
Brunel University London

JOANA VASSILOPOULOU
Brunel University London

MUSTAFA F. ÖZBILGIN
Brunel University London

CAMBRIDGE
UNIVERSITY PRESS

CAMBRIDGE
UNIVERSITY PRESS

Shaftesbury Road, Cambridge CB2 8EA, United Kingdom

One Liberty Plaza, 20th Floor, New York, NY 10006, USA

477 Williamstown Road, Port Melbourne, VIC 3207, Australia

314–321, 3rd Floor, Plot 3, Splendor Forum, Jasola District Centre,
New Delhi – 110025, India

103 Penang Road, #05–06/07, Visioncrest Commercial, Singapore 238467

Cambridge University Press is part of Cambridge University Press & Assessment,
a department of the University of Cambridge.

We share the University's mission to contribute to society through the pursuit of
education, learning and research at the highest international levels of excellence.

www.cambridge.org
Information on this title: www.cambridge.org/9781108832113

DOI: 10.1017/9781108933070

© Cambridge University Press & Assessment 2024

First published 2024

A catalogue record for this publication is available from the British Library

Library of Congress Cataloging-in-Publication Data
Names: Meliou, Elina, editor. | Vassilopoulou,
Joana, editor. | Özbilgin, Mustafa F., editor.
Title: Diversity and precarious work during socio-economic upheaval :
exploring the missing link / edited by Elina Meliou, Brunel University, Joana
Vassilopoulou, Brunel University, Mustafa F. Ozbilgin, Brunel University.
Description: Cambridge, United Kingdom ; New York, NY : Cambridge
University Press, 2024. | Includes bibliographical references and index.
Identifiers: LCCN 2023021076 | ISBN 9781108832113 (hardback) |
ISBN 9781108933070 (ebook)
Subjects: LCSH: Precarious employment. | Discrimination in employment. |
Diversity in the workplace. | Personnel management.
Classification: LCC HD5857 .D58 2024 | DDC 331.25/729–dc23/eng/20230518
LC record available at https://lccn.loc.gov/2023021076

ISBN 978-1-108-83211-3 Hardback

Contents

Figures

Contributors

BASSANT ABDELMAGEED is an human resources project co-ordinator at booking.com in the Netherlands. She earned her master's degree in human resource management from Free University Amsterdam. Her master's thesis explored Syrian refugees' career behaviour and provided important insights for this chapter.

JAN AKALIN is a London-based serial entrepreneur and consultant in financial technology services. He has degrees in engineering and development studies. His areas of expertise include international relations, Europe, Middle East, and Africa economics, and fintech regulation.

DENIZ PALALAR ALKAN is Associate Professor of Organizational Behavior at Yeditepe University, Istanbul. She earned her baccalaureate degree from Florida Atlantic University, majoring in international business and trade. She received her master's degree from Lynn University and her PhD from Istanbul University. While attending Florida Atlantic University, she volunteered to work with students with disabilities. After obtaining her bachelor's degree, she began work at several international banks, including Citibank NA, and at global insurance brokerage firms. She has been an instructor since 2011 and currently teaches courses on areas such as leadership, business management, and entrepreneurship at Yeditepe University. Her areas of interest are organisational behaviour, leadership, and diversity.

KURT APRIL is the Allan Gray Chair, Endowed Professorship, specialising in leadership, diversity, and inclusion and director of the Allan Gray Centre for Values-Based Leadership at the Graduate School of Business, University of Cape Town, and is a faculty member of Duke Corporate Education, Duke University. He is series editorial board member of Palgrave (Springer) on *Equity, Diversity, Inclusion and Indigenization in Business* (Switzerland), associate editor of *Design Science*, editorial board member of the *European Management Review*, editorial review board member of the *Africa Journal of Management*, and editorial board member of *Good Governance, Ethics & Leadership*.

ERHAN AYDIN is Senior Lecturer at Liverpool John Moores University, Visiting Research Fellow at the Queen Mary University of London, and Affiliate Research Fellow at IPAG Business School (France). He earned his PhD at Brunel Business School, Brunel University London, and his MSc at Dokuz Eylul University. He was also Recognized Visiting Researcher at Said Business School, the University of Oxford, from October 2016 to April 2017. His research interests include diversity, equality, and inclusion at organisations, HRM, e-HRM, and entrepreneurship. He is acting as a member of the Academy of Management and the European Academy of Management. He is a regional editor of the *Journal of Organizational Change Management* and an associate editor of the *Management Decision* journal. Dr Aydin is also an editorial board member at Human Relations (CABS 4* and FT 50). His research has been published by well-known publication houses such as Sage and Edward Elgar and in journals such as the *Journal of Organizational Change Management*, the *Journal of Enterprise Information Management*, and *Production, Planning & Control*.

SUE CLAYTON is a fiction and documentary film writer and director, who also consults for *Channel 4 News* and *ITV News*. Her award-winning films include *The Stansted 15: On Trial* (2019), *Calais Children: A Case to Answer* (2017), and *Hamedullah: The Road Home* (2012). As a professor at Goldsmiths University of London, she co-authored *Unaccompanied Young Migrants: Identity, Care and Justice* (Policy Press) and recently published *The New Internationalists: Activist Volunteers in the European Refugee Crisis* (Goldsmiths Pres/ MIT Press, 2020).

ANNILEE GAME is Associate Professor in Organisational Behaviour and Business Ethics at Norwich Business School, University of East Anglia. She studies relational understandings of work, organisations and well-being, particularly the nature and effects of social dynamics in the workplace. Her work draws on perspectives from psychology, organisation studies, and sociology. Her research has been published in leading international journals including *Organizational Research*

Methods, Human Relations, the *British Journal of Management,* and the *Journal of Business Ethics.*

DIMITRIA GROUTSIS is Associate Professor in Work and Organisational Studies at the University of Sydney Business School. Dimitria is a leading scholar in the fields of migration, labour mobility, and cultural diversity in the business context. Her work has appeared in international peer-reviewed journals and book chapters, and she has co-edited and co-authored several books. She frequently works with industry and governmental and non-governmental organisations, developing evidence-based insights. Dr Groutsis has received a number of large competitive external research grants, with total funding in excess of $2 million. She is a frequent media contributor, and the director of the Migration, Ethno-Racial, Cultural and Intersectionality@Work Research Group (MERCI@WRG).

NUR GUNDOGDU is Research Fellow in Responsible Business at Birmingham Business School, University of Birmingham, and the founder of London Business and Sustainability Consulting Ltd. Her research focuses on artificial intelligence and digital transformation for sustainability; sustainable, responsible, and inclusive business; well-being and mental health at work; and gender equality. To study these phenomena, she usually uses a holistic system-level approach. Nur has carried out academic and professional careers together and collaborated with academia, government, industry, and non-governmental organisations in a national and international context. Her research and consultancy experience has been funded by UK Research and Innovation, the British Council, and EU Horizon 2020.

SOPHIE HENNEKAM is Professor in Organizational Behavior in Audencia Business School, Nantes. She studies invisible, stigmatised, precarious, and understudied populations, diversity, inclusion, and inequality with the aim to give them a voice. She is an editor of *Gender, Work and Organization* and has acted as a guest editor for *Human Resource Management* and the *International Journal of Human Resource Management.* She has published in journals such as the *Academy of Management Journal* and the *Journal of Applied Psychology.*

OSCAR HOLMES IV is Associate Dean of Undergraduate Programs, Associate Professor of Management, and RUSE Director at Rutgers

School of Business-Camden. Additionally, he is the founder of WH Consulting Firm LLC and creator and host of the *Diversity Matters* podcast. His research examines how leaders can maximise productivity and well-being through fostering more inclusive environments and has been published in several top-tier management journals and books.

RICHARD GREGGORY JOHNSON III is a tenured full professor and department chair for the Department of Public and Nonprofit Administration, School of Management, University of San Francisco. As a scholar, Professor Johnson's research centres on social equity within the fields of public policy, management, higher education, and human resources management. He has been teaching in higher education for twenty years and has published several peer-reviewed books and over three dozen peer-reviewed journal articles.

RIFAT KAMASAK is Professor of Management and Strategy at the University of the West of England. He also holds board membership positions in several companies listed on Istanbul Stock Exchange. He worked in the food, confectionery, carpet, textile, aluminium, metal, retailing, trading, and consulting industries for nearly twenty years. He has done research, consultancy, and training at a large number of organisations and run his family's traditional handmade carpet business. His primary interest areas are strategic management, knowledge and innovation, and diversity management.

SHIREEN KANJI is Professor of Work and Organisation at Brunel University London. She previously held positions at the University of Cambridge, the University of Leicester, the University of Basel, and the University of Birmingham. Her research lies at the intersections of gender, work, and social inequality, spanning investigations into precarious work, the working hours of men and women, and the way caring is organized impacts women's labour market outcomes across diverse country contexts. Her work has been published in leading journals. Her current research projects investigate the conditions of skilled workers under algorithmic control, how work and family arrangements impact transitions to self-employment, and visual representations of women in finance.

NOSHEEN JAWAID KHAN is Lecturer in Work and Employment at Newcastle University Business School. She has expertise in the areas of equality, diversity, and inclusion. Her research looks at the practices of social agents/agencies that promote women in employment through a critical realist lens. Further, Nosheen is interested in exploring the relationship between diversity and sustainability. She is also an associate fellow of the Higher Education Academy, United Kingdom.

LENA KNAPPERT is Assistant Professor at the department of Management and Organisation at Vrije Universiteit Amsterdam, the Netherlands. Her research interests are on the intersection of international HRM and diversity and inclusion in organizations, such as comparative perspectives on equality and diversity at work, global diversity and inclusion management in MNEs, and refugee employment and inclusion.

ANGELA KORNAU is Researcher and Lecturer at the Chair of Human Resource Management at Helmut Schmidt University Hamburg. Her research is concerned with context-sensitive, actor-centric perspectives on in/equality, diversity, and inclusion in different organizational and national contexts with a special emphasis on gender and migration. Currently, she is particularly interested in inclusion–exclusion dynamics in the context of alternative organisations and new work.

ANDREW KOZHEVNIKOV is Lecturer in Human Resource Management at Leeds University Business School. His research interests revolve around various aspects of people's careers, such as career projects, career resources, career boundaries, and career success. To study these phenomena, Andrew usually uses critical realist principles and, specifically, Archer's Realist Social Theory. His research has appeared in journals such as *Human Relations* and *Gender, Work and Organization*.

BRIGITTE KROON is Associate Professor of Human Resource Studies at Tilburg University. Her research interests are human resource management and decent work in non-standard organisations, such as small businesses, seasonal work, or temp agencies, with a special interest in vulnerable workers.

ANA LOPES is Senior Lecturer in Work and Employment at Newcastle University Business School. She has researched and written on diversity, gender, precarity, and employment relations. She has expertise in action-oriented and engaged research methods. She is an editorial board member of *Work, Employment and Society* and book reviews editor of *Gender, Work and Organization*.

RAMASWAMI MAHALINGAM is a cultural psychologist, award-winning researcher, teacher, mentor, artist, and filmmaker (www.mindfuldignity .com). Ram developed a social justice-focused mindfulness framework, Mindful Mindset, foregrounding dignity. His current research concerns nurturing a caring and compassionate workplace that treats its workers with dignity. He is committed to developing passionate leaders with a mindful commitment to promoting peace, dignity, and well-being while reducing invisibility and precarity. Recently, he received the Harold R. Johnson Award from the University of Michigan for his leadership and outstanding contribution to its DEI mission.

OLIVER MALLETT is Professor of Entrepreneurship at Stirling Management School, University of Stirling. Oliver's research focuses on the sociology of entrepreneurship, principally in terms of the experience of self-employment and employment relationships in small firms. He also researches the context for this activity in terms of enterprise policy and business support. His research has been published in journals including *Work, Employment and Society, British Journal of Management*, and *International Small Business Journal*.

ELINA MELIOU is Professor of Work and Organisation Studies at Brunel Business School, Brunel University London. Elina adopts a relational perspective to explore issues of gender, diversity, and leadership at work and in entrepreneurship. Her research has been funded by British and European funding bodies and has appeared in leading academic journals in the area of management and organisation studies. She has acted as a guest editor for journals and has coauthored and coedited several book chapters and books. She is a frequent writer for media outlets.

JULIE MONROE is an independent postdoctoral researcher and the principal investigator for an interinstitutional technology design project that shares knowledge between end-users of mobile technologies, designers, and researchers. Through interdisciplinary partnerships, a feminist codesign methodology underpins the exploration of digital well-being through design innovation. This work focuses on intersectional inequalities associated with gendered participation in the digital world, visible in new forms of interaction between the private and professional domains.

RACHEL MORGAN is a lecturer in HRM-Organisational Behaviour at Brunel University London. Her research broadly investigates the impact of inequality on the experiences of marginalized groups at work. Rachel has coauthored book chapters in *The Sage Handbook of Qualitative Research Methods* (2018) and *Stigmas in the Organizational Environment* (2018). She has coauthored articles in *Gender in Management: An International Journal* (2020) and *Population, Place and Space* (2021). Her current research focusses on structural inequalities and challenges to identity and subjectivity of working-class males in dirty occupations.

MARIAM MOHSIN is Assistant Professor at the Pakistan Institute of Development Economics, Islamabad. Her research focuses on the interplay of gender, social relations, and organisational systems. She completed her doctorate in organisational behaviour from the Suleman Dawood School of Business, Lahore University of Management Sciences.

MUSTAFA F. ÖZBILGIN is Professor of Organisational Behaviour at Brunel Business School, Brunel University London. He also holds two international positions: Co-Chaire Management et Diversité at Université Paris Dauphine and Visiting Professor of Management at Koç University, Istanbul. His research focuses on equality, diversity, and inclusion at work from comparative and relational perspectives. He has conducted field studies in the United Kingdom and internationally, and his work is empirically grounded. International and national scientific bodies support his research. His work focuses on changing policy and practice regarding equality and diversity at work. He is an engaged scholar, driven by values of workplace democracy, equality for all, and the humanisation of work.

EMIR OZEREN is Associate Professor of management and organisation studies in the Faculty of Tourism at Dokuz Eylul University. Dr. Emir Ozeren has published widely on comparative and interdisciplinary aspects of sexual orientation and gender identity discrimination, LGBTQ+ issues in tourism, and organisations in Turkey and the United Kingdom. His research has appeared in a number of scholarly outlets, including the *Journal of Organizational Behavior*, *Journal of Services Marketing*, *Tourism Management Perspectives*, and *Journal of Organizational Change Management*. His current research interests include equality, diversity, and inclusion in the workplace, queer and critical management studies, employee and organisational silence, social sustainability, Pride festivals, sociology of work and tourism, and qualitative research methods.

SARAH RICHARD is Associate Professor at EM Strasbourg Business School. She studies disability in the workplace looking at the micro-, meso-, and macro-level. She particularly focuses on identity choices, sheltered employment, and disability policies in different countries. Her work has been published in journals such as *Work, Employment and Society, International Journal of Human Resource Management, Journal of Vocational Behavior,* and *Journal of Management Studies.*

ESIN SAYIN works as a small and medium enterprise (SME) consultant at KOSGEB (SME Development Organization) in Tekirdag, Turkey. She conducts detailed analysis in SMEs and provides them with strategic advice in finance, knowledge, strategy, and planning for the last fifteen years. Dr Sayın, who also works as a project staff for Europe Enterprise Network and Euro Info Centre, holds a bachelor's degree in global administration and marketing and a PhD degree in management and organization from Bahcesehir University, Istanbul. Her primary interest areas are strategic management, knowledge management, SMEs, entrepreneurship including refugee and migrant entrepreneurship, and innovation.

NATALIA SLUTSKAYA is Reader in Work and Organization Studies at the University of Sussex. Her current research focuses on issues of recognition at work and stigma management. She has recent publications in journals such as *Work, Employment and Society, Organization, Gender, Work and Organization,* and *Organizational Research Methods.* Natasha co-authored the book *Gender, Class and Occupation: Working Class Men Doing Dirty Work* (Palgrave, 2016). She is also one of the editors of *Dirty Work: Concepts and Identities* (Palgrave, 2012).

JAWAD SYED is Professor of Organisational Behaviour and Leadership at the Suleman Dawood School of Business, Lahore University of Management Sciences. He has an extensive publishing record and has also edited several books. His research interests include diversity management, international HRM, business ethics, knowledge management, and leadership. He is Co-Chair of the European Academy of Management's Gender, Race and Diversity in Organisations Special Interest Group. He is a director of the Global Centre for Equality and Human Rights and a coordinator of the South Asian Academy of Management.

JOANA VASSILOPOULOU is Reader (Associate Professor) at Brunel Business School, Brunel University London. Her research focuses on diversity and inclusion at work, precarity, and migrant workers. She has an established academic and professional record in the field of diversity and inclusion, with over fifty peer-reviewed publications. She has successfully acquired grants in the field of diversity and inclusion with a total value of over £2 million. As a certified trainer in managing gender and diversity and HRM, she has developed and delivered training for organisations internationally. In 2022, she co-founded the Centre for Inclusion at Work in Athens, Greece.

STEVE VINCENT is Professor of Work and Organisation at Newcastle University Business School. His research covers a wide range of work and employment issues, and it is typically written using combinations of critical realist, labor process, political economy, and Bourdieusian perspectives. He has edited various books and special issues of peer-reviewed journals, and he has authored and coauthored more than thirty book chapters and peer-reviewed journal articles.

1 Introduction

ELINA MELIOU, JOANA VASSILOPOULOU,
AND MUSTAFA F. ÖZBILGIN

The idea for this book emerged from a number of conversations among colleagues in which observations were made surrounding changing political, economic, and societal circumstances, both in the countries in which we live and globally, and their differential impact on society, working conditions, and the diversity and inclusion of marginalised groups. These discussions were consolidated during meetings at the Academy of Management Conference over the years, highlighting the limited scholarly attention on precarious work and the ways it affects various socio-demographic groups. As such, while we started small, this edited volume is the result of a substantial community of scholars whose contributions spotlight the missing link between diversity and precarious work during times of socio-economic upheaval.

As a defining feature of contemporary life, precarity denotes a condition induced by socio-economic transformations, such as the introduction of 'flatter, leaner, more decentralized and more flexible forms of organization' (Jessop, 2002: 100) that result in the reduction of welfare provision and work rights (Standing, 2011). Precarious work is characterised by low pay, insufficient and variable hours, and short-term contracts rights, and is shaped by work–life balance considerations (Ayudhya et al., 2017) and the degree of regulatory protection (ILO, 2015; Kalleberg, 2011; Vallas, 2015). These characteristics are frequently found in what is known as part-time, temporary, and zero-hours contracts, and in dependent self-employment. At the same time, the concept of precarity captures the experiences of people and communities engendered by these existing conditions. In that sense, precarity is defined as 'the politically induced condition in which certain populations suffer from failing social and economic networks ... becoming differentially exposed to injury, violence, and death' (Butler, 2009: 25). Capturing how the 'objective insecurity gives rise to a generalized subjective insecurity' (Bourdieu, 1998: 83) is critical because while recent analyses of the precarity of work have unveiled certain aspects of labour market exclusion and marginality, scant attention has been paid to the gendered, racialised, and class-based challenges of these changes (Vincent, 2016). The rise of the gig economy, rooted in neo-liberal industrial relations, has sparked significant controversy due to its effects on labour conditions, wages, and the distributions of income and wealth, which have created a further surge in precarity among marginalised workers around the world.

The diversity-related challenges or the ways that precarity is experienced across various communities lie at the heart of this edited book. However, in line with Wacquant's (2022) critique of how communities that experience precarity are unjustly termed as an underclass, the contributors in this book purposely flesh out not only the precarity but also the agency of these groups in response to the limited choices and chances they are offered. Contrary to expectations of human development (Becker, 2009), there is an upsurge of precarity across sectors of work in developed countries and a deepening of precarity in less developed countries. Precarious work has deleterious effects on vulnerable demographic groups worldwide, with women, ethnic minorities, migrants and refugees, and people with disabilities, among others, experiencing in- and out-of-work poverty and being affected considerably more by precarious living. The purpose of this edited book is to unpack the research on the missing link between diversity and precarity and offer insights into the role of organisations and policymakers in fostering inclusive change and transformation. In doing so, it brings together international scholars in order to discuss ways to address the diversity challenges of precarious work and offer a way forward. Thus, we contribute to drawing awareness of precarious work and diversity in organisations by bringing together experts in an edited book designed to: (1) uncover and document the variety of issues facing vulnerable demographic groups at work, (2) promote greater scholarship on the link between precarious work and diversity during economic and social upheaval, and (3) develop a research programme and agenda that sheds light into new and important aspects of precarious work and diversity issues.

In the aftermath of the global financial crisis, recent policies of radical deregulation, technological change, and heterogeneous workforce have intensified shifts in the occupational structure, the place and the timing of work, and career patterns, putting a further strain on the standard employment relationship and promoting more commodified forms of labour (Stiglitz, 1982, 2000, 2016). Many countries have introduced neoliberal economic policies, including austerity measures in response to the 2008 financial crisis. The adoption and diffusion of neoliberal values worldwide, such as economic competition, individualism, and a lack of state-provided safety nets have led to significant uncertainty and deterioration of human rights in countries without social and economic safety nets (Kusku et al., 2021; Meliou and Özbilgin, 2023), due to an increasingly precarious mode of living for many in the world (Vassilopoulou et al., 2018). The energy crisis and the COVID-19 pandemic have created even more uncertainty, primarily due to policy choices driven by political interests rather than social safety concerns (Greenhalgh et al., 2022). Some counties, such as the United Kingdom, are again turning to austerity measures in response to the current crisis, which ultimately will lead to even more precarity.

The neoliberal austerity measures have exposed vulnerable demographic groups even more to precarity with, for example, women being disproportionally affected by the crisis and austerity measures (Vassilopoulou et al., 2016). Research has shown how such groups bear the brunt of the increase in the fragmentation of work and changes in the labour market. Women, ethnic minorities, people with disabilities, and LGBTQ+, among other groups, are more likely to experience precarity with regard to access to work opportunities and resource accumulation. Intersecting categories of exclusion such as ethnicity/race, class, sexual orientation, and age, as well as issues of migration embedded in life course trajectories, complicate those of gender and have widened class and race inequalities between and within communities (Acker, 2006; Walby, 2015). Intersectionality, a term and theory increasingly used by scholars and practitioners (e.g., Villesèche, Muhr, and Sliwa, 2018), refers to the intersecting, or a place of crossing, of two or more social categories, providing space for the connection and understanding across and within 'difference'. In her theorisation of intersectionality, Crenshaw (1991) identified that black women's experiences are not only shaped by gender or race alone, but also by gender and race together. Intersectionality theory has since expanded to include all forms of etic and emic diversity and difference at work (Tatli and Özbilgin, 2012a, 2012b; Sang et al., 2013), indicating the push for social movements to legitimate diversity and equality for all (Özbilgin and Erbil, 2021). Further, intersectionality is now used as a methodological and analytical tool (Kamasak et al., 2020). Kamasak et al. (2019) critique the individualisation of intersectionality theory when institutions and systems have intersections such as male, white, and cis gendered cultures and structures that can be more palpable to change when compared to individual intersections. Thus, the authors of this edited volume call for changing institutional intersections, with reflection on the intersectional precarities that individuals experience in their encounters with such institutions.

Intersectional precarities describe and highlight the subtle and insidious character of precarity that variously affects individuals at work and in life. The normalisation and all-encompassing character of precarity as a 'privileged engine of economic activity' (Bourdieu and Wacquant, 2001: 3) is promulgated by popular media and policy discourses of empowerment, flexibility, and choice (e.g., Villesèche et al., 2022). Such enabling discourses echo modern labour economics arguments of human capital (Becker, 1993) according to which people are induced to enhance their human capital and become responsible for their social and economic fate (Fleming, 2017). However, as the contributions in this book show, this is puzzling and bears consequences for those who lack access to necessary to material and symbolic resources. In this context, neoliberal politics on equality and diversity in organisations have significantly decreased the repertoire of interventions for diversity management in organisations in recent years (Kusku et al., 2022, 2021; Özbilgin and Slutskaya, 2017).

The interplay between precarity and diversity is often conflated with discussions of haves and have nots, leading to trivialising precarity by diversity and difference. Even when diversity is considered seriously in relation to precarity, this is not done in an even-handed way. There is a tendency to prioritise gendered forms of precarity or to use gender as an overarching framework through which other categories of difference could be considered. This approach highlights a pecking order and a hidden hierarchy among diversity categories, through which some marginalised diversity concerns, for example, of trans and/or refugee precarities, could be further sidelined. In order to counter this tendency and bias, in this volume, we present each salient diversity category and its concomitant form of precarity in each chapter. Table 1.1 outlines the kinds of precarity experienced by different diversity categories.

It seems, however, that in some cases, precarious forms of employment are for some people the only way to secure work. Studies have

Table 1.1 *Forms of precocity experienced by diversity categories*

Diversity category	Forms of precarity
Gender	Gender pay gap, lock in temporary, insecure, short term, part-time work, gendered organisation of work–life interface, labour market segmentation
Ethnicity and race	Ethnic pay gap, race discrimination, underrepresentation in positions of power and security, exposure to turbulent, unsafe, and insecure work
Class	Lack of class mobility, low pay, unsafe and insecure employment, stigma and devaluation, precarious working conditions affecting self-understanding
Sexual orientation and gender identity	Bars on and barriers to employment, closet, lack of representation on positions of power and security, voices silenced and marginalised in mainstream discussions
Migrants	Legal restrictions, health issues, and non-recognition of qualifications, ethnic pay gap, underrepresentation in positions of power and security, exposure to turbulent, unsafe, and insecure work, race discrimination, overrepresentation in the precarious gig economy, voices silenced and marginalised in mainstream discussions
Refugees	Legal restrictions, health issues, and non-recognition of qualifications, ethnic pay gap, underrepresentation in positions of power and security, exposure to turbulent, unsafe and insecure work, race discrimination, overrepresentation in the precarious gig economy, voices silenced and marginalised in mainstream discussions
Disability	Precarious position in the labour market, social and economic precarity for disabled people, unemployment and underemployment, discrimination, exclusion
Age	Age discrimination because of workplace cultures of youth, unemployment, low-paid positions, precarity arising from age–work-related exclusion faced during life course

demonstrated how, for example, in crisis economies, women have resisted a gender regime shift from public to domestic work by engaging in precarious labour market activities (Meliou, 2020). Kamasak et al. (2019) have shown how the gig economy had dual impact of widening precarity due to lower wages for workers, while at the same time allowing access to marginalised workers from ethnic and religious minorities to secure work, even if precarious. Given the limited opportunities for conventional forms of employment, precarious work, including through digital labour platforms may provide earning opportunities, allowing vulnerable groups to transcend local labour markets and secure employment during economic and social upheaval. The contributors in this edited volume discuss how diverse groups of workers resist and enact their agency under conditions of precarity. In turn, the analyses here highlight how for an emancipatory struggle to emerge, we must contest the self-evidence of precarity collectively, calling into question the legitimacy of precarity and enacting a 'demand for livable lives' (Butler, 2015: 218). Intersectional coalitions can open up possibilities for emancipatory transformation and solidarity in ways that precarity is no longer considered a personal shortcoming. Such initiatives should inform policy debates and actions by acknowledging the diversity of precarity experienced and inclusive policy solutions to address it.

1.1 Overview of the Chapters

The first chapter of this book introduces the topic of this edited book and sets the context for the following thirteen chapters, which examine how precarious work affects various socio-demographic groups. Each chapter is designated to a different socio-demographic and marginalised group. The following chapter, Chapter 2, titled 'Pandemic Precarities and Gendered Biopolitics within the Neoliberal University', explores the gendered biopolitics of the COVID-19 pandemic through an analysis of the UK's marketised higher education sector, by theoretically combining feminist political economy with labour market segmentation theory to develop a novel meso-level biopolitical analysis. Chapter 3, titled 'LGBTQ+ Individuals and Precarious Work', seeks to shed light on the missing link between diversity and precarious work from the viewpoint of sexual and gender identity minorities whose voices have been silenced and marginalised in mainstream discussions.

In Chapter 4, titled 'Age, Gender, and Precarity: The Experience of Late Career Self-Employment', the authors adopt an intersectional approach and discuss the experiences of older women engaged in self-employment to manage precarity arising from the age–work-related exclusion faced during their life course. Next, Chapter 5, which is titled 'How the (In)Ability of Using One's Disability Strategically Reinforces Inequality and Precariousness amongst Disabled Workers: The Case of France', presents three empirical studies on disabled individuals who use their disability strategically as they navigate their precarious position in the labour market. Chapter 6, titled 'Classed and Gendered Experiences of Precarity in Dirty Work', examines how precarity affects the experiences of low-skilled dirty workers – a group characterised by stigma and devaluation. Utilising Axel Honneth's ideas of mutual recognition and the normative significance of work for identity, the authors explore how precarious working conditions affect self-understanding at the intersection of class and gender. Subsequently, Chapter 7, titled 'Precarity and Diversity: The Intersectional Case of Female Christian Janitorial Workers', presents case studies of female Christian janitorial workers, working on a contractual basis in a public sector organisation in Pakistan where the typical employment format is full time and permanent. Chapter 8, titled 'Precarious Work in the Gig Economy: Diversity, Race, and Indigeneity Lenses', discusses how the meteoric growth of the platform economy, its economic underpinnings as well as the accompanying human practices, have provoked academic debates as well as shone a light on its praxis. The chapter highlights that many employees, migrants, and foreigners remain dependent on in-country structures to grant them rights – in many countries, though, they do not have the power to engage with those structures and have no way to build on and improve their rights. Chapter 9, titled 'Refugees' Vulnerability towards Precarious Work: An Intersectionality Perspective', highlights that refugees are particularly vulnerable to under-and unemployment and are more likely to find themselves in precarious working conditions compared to host country residents, with legal restrictions, health issues, and non-recognition of qualifications being the most discussed reasons for this. The authors draw on the concept of intersectionality and the psychology of working theory. Using four refugee accounts, this chapter illustrates how refugees' gender relates to their vulnerability towards precarious work and how this relationship is further complicated by

8 *Elina Meliou et al.*

refugees' economic status in their home country as well as by the societal expectations and protection in the host environment. Chapter 10, titled 'Trapped in Precarious Work: The Case of Syrian Refugee Workers in Turkey', drawing on a qualitative study, investigates the precarity experiences of Syrian refugees in Turkey. Chapter 11, titled 'How Precarity Is Threaded into Migration Rules: The Cases of the UK, Germany, and Australia', investigates the precarious arrangements embedded in the systems and processes of migration management across three different country contexts: the UK, Germany, and Australia. The chapter sheds light on the rules underscoring and the implications of the process of migrant worker acceptance, settlement, and integration in a new land and labour market.

Chapter 12, 'Culture, Precarity, and Dignity', draws on a case study of janitors in India to illustrate the gigification of cleaning and service jobs by theorising precarity and dignity. Importantly, the chapter outlines a mindfulness perspective to protect the dignity of precarious workers for a caring organisational culture. Chapter 13, titled 'Transforming Humanitarianism: Precarities at Work in the New Activist Volunteer Sector', illustrates how the refugee volunteer community – which intersects and has much in common with other new forms of humanitarian activism – has faced challenges which are not widely evidenced by the European governments or populist mainstream media: It has suited both to continue 'othering' the 'foreign invasion' of refugees and render invisible or play down the vital and challenging support role that the volunteers fulfil – a role that many argue should have been assumed by governments themselves. The final chapter, Chapter 14, titled 'Artificial Intelligence, the Gig Economy, and Precarity', explores the duality of the artificial intelligence (AI)-enabled gig economy in terms of the precarity and the promise it offers. The chapter focuses on underrepresented and disadvantaged groups of workers who found new homes in the AI-enabled gig economy.

References

Acker, J. (2006). Inequality regimes: Gender, class, and race in organizations. *Gender & Society*, 20(4), 441–464.
Ayudhya, U. C. N., Prouska, R., & Beauregard, T. A. (2017). The impact of global economic crisis and austerity on quality of working life and

work-life balance: A capabilities perspective. *European Management Review*, 16(4) Winter 2019, 847–862. DOI: 10.1111/imre.12128

Becker, G. S. (1993). Nobel lecture: The economic way of looking at behavior. *Journal of Political Economy*, 101, 385–409.

Becker, G. S. (2009). *Human Capital: A Theoretical and Empirical Analysis, with Special Reference to Education*. Chicago: University of Chicago Press.

Bourdieu, P. (1998). *Acts of Resistance: Against the New Myths of Our Time*. Cambridge: Polity Press.

Bourdieu, P., & Wacquant, L. (2001). Newliberalspeak: Notes on the planetary vulgate. *Radical Philosophy*, 105 (January/February): 2–5.

Butler, J. (2009). *Frames of War. When Is Life Grievable?* London: Verso.

Butler, J. (2015). *Notes toward a Performative Theory of Assembly*. Cambridge, MA: Harvard University Press.

Crenshaw, K. (1991). Mapping the margins: Identity politics, intersectionality, and violence against women. *Stanford Law Review*, 43(6), 1241–1299.

Fleming, P. (2017). The human capital hoax: Work, debt and insecurity in the ear of uberization. *Organization Studies*, 38(5), 691–709.

Greenhalgh, T., Özbilgin, M. F., & Tomlinson, D. (2022). How Covid-19 spreads: Narratives, counter narratives, and social dramas. *BMJ*, 378, 1–9.

ILO (International Labour Organization). (2015). *World Employment and Social Outlook: The Changing Nature of Jobs*. Geneva: ILO Publications.

Jessop, B. (2002). *The Future of the Capitalist State*. Cambridge: Polity Press.

Kalleberg, A. L. (2011). *Good Jobs, Bad Jobs: The Rise of Polarized and Precarious Employment Systems in the United States, 1970s–2000s. American Sociological Association Rose Series in Sociology*. New York: Russell Sage Foundation.

Kamaşak, R., Özbilgin, M. F., & Yavuz, M. (2020). Understanding intersectional analyses. In: King, E., Roberson, Q., & Hebl, M. (eds.), *Research on Social Issues in Management on Pushing Understanding of Diversity in Organizations* (pp. 93–115). Charlotte, NC: Information Age Publishing.

Kamasak, R., Özbilgin, M. F., Yavuz, M., & Akalin, C. (2019). Race discrimination at work in the United Kingdom. In Vassilopoulou, J., Brabet, J. and Showunmi, V. (eds.) *Race Discrimination and Management of Ethnic Diversity and Migration at Work* (pp. 81–105). London, UK: Emerald Publishing Limited.

Küskü, F., Araci, Ö., & Özbilgin, M. F. (2021). What happens to diversity at work in the context of a toxic triangle? Accounting for the gap between discourses and practices of diversity management. *Human Resource Management Journal*, 31(2), 553–574.

Küskü, F., Araci, Ö., Tanriverdi, V., & Özbilgin, M. F. (2022). Beyond the three monkeys of workforce diversity: Who hears, sees, and speaks up? *Frontiers in Psychology*, 13, 879862.

Meliou, E. (2020). Family as a eudaimonic bubble: Women entrepreneurs mobilizing resources of care during persistent financial crisis and austerity. *Gender, Work and Organization*, 27(2), 218–235.

Meliou, E. and Özbilgin, M. (2023). How is the illusio of gender equality in entrepreneurship sustained? A Bourdieusian Perspective. *Journal of Management Studies*, 0 (online first), 1–26.

Özbilgin, M. F., & Slutskaya, N. (2017). Consequences of Neo-liberal Politics on Equality and Diversity at Work in Britain: Is Resistance Futile? In Management and Diversity: Thematic Approaches. In Chanlat, J.-F. and Özbligin, M. F. (eds), Management and Diversity (International Perspectives on Equality, Diversity and Inclusion, Vol. 4). (pp. 319–334). London: Emerald Publishing Limited.

Özbilgin, M. F., Beauregard, T. A., Tatli, A., & Bell, M. P. (2011). Work–life, diversity and intersectionality: A critical review and research agenda. *International Journal of Management Reviews*, 13(2), 177–198.

Sang, K., Al-Dajani, H., & Özbilgin, M. F. (2013). Frayed careers of migrant female professors in British academia: An intersectional perspective. *Gender, Work & Organization*, 20(2), 158–171.

Standing, G. (2011). *The Precariat: The New Dangerous Class*. New York: Bloomsbury.

Stiglitz, J. (1982). The Inefficiency of the Stock Market Equilibrium. *Review of Economic Studies*, 49(2), 241–261.

Stiglitz, J. (2000). Democratic development as the fruits of labor. *Perspectives on Work*, 4(1), 31–37.

Stiglitz, J. E. (2012). *The Price of Inequality: How Today's Divided Society Endangers Our Future*. New York: W. W. Norton & Company.

Stiglitz, J. E. (2016). Nobel Prize-winning economist Stiglitz tells us why 'neoliberalism is dead'. www.businessinsider.com/joseph-stiglitz-says-neoliberalism-is-dead-2016-8?r=US&IR=T

Tatli, A. & Özbilgin, M. F. (2012a). An emic approach to intersectional study of diversity at work: A Bourdieuan framing. *International Journal of Management Reviews*, 14(2), 180–200.

Tatli, A. & Özbilgin, M. F. (2012b). Surprising intersectionalities of inequality and privilege: The case of the arts and cultural sector. *Equality, Diversity and Inclusion: An International Journal*, 31(3), 249–265.

Vallas, S. (2015). Accounting for precarity: Recent studies of labor market uncertainty. *Contemporary Sociology: A Journal of Reviews*, 44(4), 463–469.

Vassilopoulou, J., April, K., Da Rocha, J. P., Kyriakidou, O., & Özbilgin, M. F. (2016). Does the ongoing global economic crisis put diversity gains at risk?: Diversity management during hard times–international examples from the USA, South Africa, and Greece. In *Handbook of Research on Race, Gender, and the Fight for Equality* (pp. 424–452). Hershey, PA: IGI Global.

Vassilopoulou, J., Kyriakidou, O., Da Rocha, J. P., Georgiadou, A., & Mor Barak, M. (2018). International perspectives on securing human and social rights and diversity gains at work in the aftermath of the global economic crisis and in times of austerity. *European Management Review*, 16(4) Winter 2019, 837–845.

Villeseche, F., Meliou, E., & Jha, H. (2022). Feminism in women business networks: A freedom centred perspective. *Human Relations*, 75(10), 1903–1927.

Villesèche, F., Muhr, S. L., & Sliwa, M. (2018). From radical black feminism to postfeminist hashtags: Reclaiming intersectionality. *Ephemera*, 18(1), 1–17.

Vincent, S. (2016). Bourdieu and the gendered social structure of working time: A study of self employed human resources professionals. *Human Relations*, 69(5), 1163–1184.

Wacquant, L. (2022). *The Invention of the 'Underclass': A Study in the Politics of Knowledge*. Cambridge, UK/Hoboken, NJ: Polity Press/John Wiley & Sons.

Walby, S. (2015). *Crisis*. Cambridge: Polity Press.

2 | Pandemic Precarities and Gendered Biopolitics within the Neoliberal University

STEVE VINCENT, ANA LOPES, NOSHEEN JAWAID KHAN, ANDREW KOZHEVNIKOV, AND JULIE MONROE

2.1 Introduction

This chapter explores the COVID-19 pandemic (henceforth 'the pandemic') as a biopolitical issue within UK's marketised higher education (UKHE) sector. Our objective is to explain gendered aspects of *pandemic precarities*, a term which we use to describe workplace-precarities, either health-related or economic, that emerge with and developed through the pandemic. Workplace precarities occur where labour market institutions impel 'employment that is uncertain, unpredictable, and risky from the point of view of the worker' (Kalleberg, 2009, p. 2). They are a condition of vulnerability, social inequality, and labour-related insecurity in employment (Burton, 2018; Joseph–Salisbury et al., 2021; Standing, 2011; Vohlídalová, 2021). The concept is inherently biopolitical, as workplace precarity creates anxiety (Neilson, 2015) and job-stress (Godin et al., 2005). Precarious jobs are associated with more thoughts about suicide (Milner et al., 2018) and poorer health outcomes in general (Quinlan, 2017), and these outcomes can be amplified by the pandemic.

Whilst working class jobs typically experience greater precarity, health-based precarity is evidently not confined to the most disadvantaged workers. Presenteeism, or people working despite feeling unwell, transcends occupational classes (see Aronsson et al., 2000). 'Burnout', or exhaustion impelled by mentally demanding and stressful work, often accompanies professional employment (Schaufeli & Buunk, 1996). Specific professional jobs, including social work (Pentaraki & Dionysopoulou, 2019) and academic work (Ivancheva et al., 2019; Steinþórsdóttir et al., 2019), are associated with workplace precarity. It is thus important to consider how different types of precarity interact to affect different types of worker, as outcomes socially, economically and politically constructed, with some groups suffering more than others (Butler, 2009).

In what follows, we focus on gender rather than other protected characteristics due to the weight of evidence suggesting that women are more likely to be economically vulnerable, marginalised, and overlooked during the pandemic (GEO, 2020; WBG, 2020). For example, being employed in the UK as a 'key worker' within health sector or in essential services, which were obliged to work during the pandemic, increased health-related risks (Lally, 2020), and women are also overrepresented in these groups (TUC, 2020). Whilst men had higher morbidity than women and suffered more health-based complications (Klein et al., 2020; Wenham et al., 2020), women suffered more in the economic recession that followed the pandemic (Ro, 2020). Women were a third more likely to be employed in sectors that were 'shut down' over the first national lockdown in 2020 (Parliament, 2021). School closures during lockdown also disproportionately impacted working mothers (WBG, 2020). Also, concerns have been raised that pregnant women and women on maternity leave were refused furlough or were forced to take unpaid leave during the lockdown period (EHRC, 2020). Parallel to this, the pandemic inhibited specialist organisations and services supporting women (WRC, 2020), with many experiencing funding and operational challenges, as well as increased demand (WA, 2020). Consequentially, important questions have been raised regarding whether organisational responses to gendered pandemic precarities have been adequate.

To explore this area, we develop a novel approach to biopolitical analyses that explores the interactions of health-based issues – in this case, the pandemic – and gendered patterns in employment relations outcomes. It is known that workplace politics affect pandemic precarities (see James, 2021), and we contribute to this area by exploring and explaining variations in pandemic precarities by analysing how the actions of labour market institutions, or organisations that inform systems of rules which combine to shape labour market inequalities (see Rubery, 2007; Fleetwood, 2017), shaped pandemic precarities. Developing knowledge of this area is vital because it may impel a novel biopolitical struggles in the wake of the pandemic. This is because precarity is always a double-edged concept: it implies both a condition and a potential rallying point for biopolitical resistances (Waite, 2009).

Important questions relate to who holds responsibility for biopolitical issues, such as the pandemic. The State holds a good deal of responsibility for public health crises and their impacts on workers, but other groups, such as employers and worker representatives, also share responsibility for responses to crises. Doan and Harbin (2020) argue opportunities to improve health outcomes are shaped and constrained by organisations of different types (see also Sherwin, 2012). Organisations operate at different levels – the micro, meso, and macro – through the (re)creation of institutions (laws, rules, norms, guides, procedures, etc.) that are used to guide actions and decision-making, resulting in biopolitical discourses surrounding responsibility for public health issues. Ultimately, health is founded in a community of relations, of which the State is important but not the only actor in producing more or less favourable health-based outcomes. Consequentially, it becomes important to question how the interactions of organisations result in the tragic biopolitics of pandemic precarities – a question that we explore in what follows.

UKHE is taken as an exemplar case of outcomes under neoliberal capitalism, which tends to institutionalise precarity in a way that exacerbates existing global and local inequalities (McCormack & Salmenniemi, 2016). Approximately one-third of all UK workers experience workplace precarity, including poor pay and/or exclusion from statutory employment protections (de Ruyter, 2020). Neoliberalism is associated with, inter-alia, active labour market policies that push people into any job (Greer, 2015), forms of governance that hinder investments in people (Thompson, 2013), and constant workplace restructuring (Marchington et al., 2004). UKHE has been heavily affected by neoliberal policies associated with marketisation and new public management (McCann et al., 2020). Many academics have already fallen into precarious categories, such as the working poor (Courtois & O'Keefe, 2015; UCU, 2016, 2019). Precarious academics have reduced life chances in relation to buying a house, getting married, and having children (Bosanquet et al., 2017; Kinikoğlu & Can, 2021). Overall, whilst there has been a group of 'second-class citizens' within academia for some time (see Gappa and Leslie, 1993), this group has arguably grown into an 'army of workers' who endure precariousness (Ivancheva, 2015).

Our findings reveal that women employed in UKHE more typically suffered pandemic precarities. We argue that these vulnerabilities are catalysed by the marketisation of UKHE, and the defensive institutional response of powerful labour market institutions – the universities, as employers, and the Government. In contrast, the sector's main trade union – the University and Colleges Union (UCU) – was stridently in favour of actions to mitigate the gendered implications of pandemic precarities but was relatively powerless to affect outcomes. The chapter concludes that neoliberal policies within UKHE eroded ethical institutional responses to the pandemic, as a biological issue.

2.2 Theoretical Framework

Our objective is to consider and reveal gendered patterns within employment relations within UKHE, as the sector responded to pandemic precarities. An employment relations perspective considers the often-contested relations between and amongst different types of workers, and/or between workers and their supervisors and line-managers. Employment relations are always affected by or emergent from local labour market institutions that set the framework within which employment relations are negotiated (see Vincent et al., 2020). Our focus is novel because previous biopolitical studies have tended to be either Foucauldian, identity-based, and focussed on micro-level politics (see Campbell and Sitze, 2013), or macro-level Political Science analysis of political decision-making (see Somit and Peterson, 1998).

To focus on gendered aspect of employment relations, we combine feminist political economy (FPE) with labour market segmentation (LMS) theory (see Grimshaw et al., 2017). FPE encourages research to focus on gendered inequalities, and how women's labour market outcomes are limited by sexual discrimination, inequalities in domestic work and the interacting domains of work and life (see Federici, 2012, 2017). Domestic work, in particular, can be singled out as a historically specific form of work that emerges from the separation of production and reproduction, or paid and unpaid labour, in a way that disadvantages women (Federici, 2017). FPE is thus intimately associated with gendered biopolitics of social reproduction, which spills over into employment by affecting who gets 'good jobs' and 'bad jobs' (Rubery & Grimshaw, 2014).

To study variation on biopolitical employment relations issues, we combine FPE with LMS (see also Grimshaw et al., 2017). LMS rejects mainstream economic theories, which suggest labour market segmentation occurs due to supply-sided variations in skills and consequent variations in productivity. Instead, and in a way that is consonant with FPE, LMS focuses on the constitutions of employers, as collections of labour market institutions. This approach has demonstrated that employers actively shape the labour market, for example, by controlling access to training and opportunities (see Doeringer and Piore, 1971), undermining trade union organisations (Edwards et al., 1976) and pursuing low-skilled, low-road production strategies(Wilkinson, 1983). As a consequence of these strategies, labour markets become subdivided, with radically different experiences in different sections of the labour market.

Gendered inequalities are thus not merely supply-sided, labour market institutions combine to shape workplace experiences in gendered ways. In this regard, an important debate in LMS scholarship concerns labour market dualisation, which distinguishes between an arguably expanding 'precariat' group of workers, whose experiences can be separated from the core labour market 'salariat' (Standing, 2011), who experience relatively stable employment conditions. In times of crisis, such as during financial recessions or the pandemic, LMS theory argues that employers will seek to adapt by buffering core workers (Doeringer & Piore, 1971) who are often protected by labour market agencies, such as professional associations and trade unions (see Meardi, et al., 2021). As a consequence, peripheral or marginal groups will be disproportionately exposed to risks. Arguably, women, in particular, tend to find themselves in more marginal positions within the labour market because they are assumed to favour atypical employment, although this is not necessarily the case (Moore et al., 2018). We consequentially focus on the gendered patterns in the various segments of the UKHE labour market, and how these patinated experiences of pandemic precarities.

2.3 Studying the University Sector

Our analysis uses publicly available documents, including peer-reviewed academic journal articles, policy reports, online media sources, and organisation websites, which are all listed as references. The objective is to analyse the gendered experiences of academic employees and how these were affected by the actions of three dominant labour market institutions: universities, as employers; the Government; and the UCU. The analysis also benefits from our experiences and observations, as all the authors were teaching and/or researching within the sector during the pandemic. Our approach thus offers an example of 'barefoot' research, in which interested workers are motivated to explore and explain their own experiences and circumstances (see Ackroyd and Karlsson, 2014). In particular, we sought evidence of whether and how these dominant labour market institutions express a biopolitics of care for the self and others, and whether and how they express collective ethics and responsibilities for wellbeing (see McCormack and Salmenniemi, 2016), as they responded to perceived pandemic precarities.

2.3.1 Precarity in the UK Universities Context

Studies from various countries, including the UK, Ireland, Australia, Canada, Iceland, the Czech Republic, Finland, and Italy, identify increasing precarities in higher education. Marketisation has resulted in increasing corporate managerialism, which is motivated by profitability and performance (Ivancheva et al., 2019). As a consequence, the sector is increasingly bureaucratic and hierarchical (Rustin, 2016), secretive, arbitrary, and ruthless (Gill, 2010). The workforce has experienced casualisation, increasingly unmanageable workloads, and a proliferation of audit regimes (Burrows, 2012) aimed at increasing academics' 'accountability' (Gill, 2014). Yet, the proliferation of penalising audit cultures is arguably bound to fail. Not only is the intangible notion of 'academic excellence' impossible to quantify, but academic ethos and collegiality, upon which knowledge generation is founded, is corrupted by marketised organisational politics and competition for resources.

Universities are also increasingly demanding flexible and cheap labour (Ryan et al., 2013), with the portion of permanent or core employment reducing as part-time and casual work has increased. There are now more precarious research-only and teaching-only positions (Lynch, 2014) often filled by 'early career' academics employed on a non-standard short-term, part-time and/or zero-hour employment contracts (Courtois & O'Keefe, 2015). This casualisation has encouraged precarious workers to do 'hope labour', or to undertake voluntary or underpaid work with the assumption/speculation that it will result in better opportunities in the future (see Mackenzie and McKinlay, 2020), but, as precarity increases, such hopes will diminish (see also Ivancheva and O'Flynn, 2016).

This academic precarity is already also a feminist issue (Zheng, 2018). Women who opt-out of masculine ideas of competitive performance are more likely to suffer contractual precarity and become over-represented in atypical employment contracts (Ivancheva et al., 2019). Academia also demonstrates a strong tendency to promote academics who are White, male and middle-class, with those not fitting this profile concentrated in precarious roles (McKenzie, 2021). In this context, Yarrow (2021, p. 1) argues that inequality regimes and gendered power interact and are mutually reinforced through informal processes and gendered social networks.

Levels of precarity also depend on academics' relationships with family, partners, friends, students, and colleagues (Gill, 2010; Lynch, 2010; Reay, 2004), with the relative precarity of women's labour being a consequence of how these relations distribute domestic and caring labour (Ivancheva, 2015). Indeed, notions of care transcend the work-life boundary (Murray, 2018), with academic women perceiving themselves as channelled into feminised teaching and administrative roles that inhibit career progression (Ashencaen Crabtree & Shiel, 2019). Studies from Iceland, the Czech Republic, Australia, and Ireland all highlighted the gendered nature of precarity at all levels of universities, including PhD student, early academics, and established academics (Hogan et al., 2014; Ivancheva et al., 2019; McKenzie, 2021; Steinþórsdóttir et al., 2019; Vohlídalová, 2021). Female academics with caring responsibilities are at increased risk of precarity, as they are more likely to give up or reduce commitments to more prestigious research and publications in the effort to achieve a reasonable work-life balance (see Courtois and O'Keefe, 2015). Academic women also face difficulties in their personal and work lives, particularly around care, childbirth, and relocating with partners and family (Acker & Webber, 2017; Ivancheva et al., 2019; Lynch, 2010; McKenzie, 2017; Nikunen & Lempiäinen, 2020; Reay, 2004).

Overall, neoliberal labour market institutions, such as those impelled by the marketisation of UKHE and its associated metric control systems, both foster men's successes and deny women space (Morley, 2013), whilst they also enhance the precariousness of women, especially within the more feminised fields of research (Steinþórsdóttir et al., 2019, p. 124). Whilst precarious academic work is limiting to both men and women, arguably it impacts women's personal and professional trajectories more than men's (Hogan et al., 2014; Ivancheva et al., 2019; McKenzie, 2021; Reay, 2004). Consequentially, casualisation has exacerbated existing gender inequalities and unequal power relations, contradicting meritocracy, and reproducing White-male dominance in the UK academia (see Doharty et al., 2021).

2.3.2 Universities in the Pandemic

The universities' response to the pandemic appears to have exacerbated pre-existing inequalities. It was feared that the pandemic would be devastating for universities' incomes. The Institute for Fiscal Studies (IFS) estimated a reduction in income of £11 billion, which equated to a 25 per cent decline in annual income (Drayton & Waltmann, 2020). The report predicted that thirteen universities, which educate around 5 per cent of students, would have negative reserves as a consequence of the pandemic, and that these institutions may not be viable in the long run without a governmental bailout or debt restructuring. In this context, universities demanded and lobbied for students to return to campus in September 2020, even though it was unclear whether this would be safe or feasible. This resulted in a somewhat absurd situation where many students were present within their university towns and cities but being taught at a distance. This protected university incomes to an extent, but also increased health-based precarities for students and staff (Hall & Quinn, 2020).

The universities actions as employers reflected LMS theory, as core workers, who are more institutionally supported, were relatively protected, whilst other workers were treated more disposably (Doeringer and Piore, 1971). For example, the IFS report estimated that the sector could reduce the overall pay bill by £600 million, which accounted for around 6 per cent of the deficit, without redundancies, by sacking workers on precarious contracts. It has been reported that universities have not renewed contracts of fixed-term academics (Staton, 2020), which places the careers of ECRs, precarious and casualised academics at greater risk. By March 2021, at least twelve UK universities, including members of the prestigious Russell Group, were planning redundancies (Petrescu, 2021).

In part, these actions reflect declining demands for academic workers during the pandemic, with work opportunities for precarious academics, including self-funded PhD students and ECRs, being significantly eroded. Overall, this suggests a limited biopolitics of care, on the side of universities, as employers sought to defend incomes and cut costs via a mixture of limited redundancies and by axing precarious workers.

Simultaneously, as teaching and research resources have decreased, and in the context of erratic fluctuations between online and face-to-face teaching, university workers report increasingly intense teaching workloads (Ross & McKie, 2020). Our own estimate is that preparation time needed to place lecture materials online increased overall preparation time by approximately three times, per hour delivered, when compared to delivering previously prepared lecture material in person. Overall, whilst the number of teachers declined, owing to the shedding of precarious workers, the actual demand for academic labour has increased in many areas. This suggests universities have been responding to the pandemic by intensifying academic workloads, as an alternative to buying in additional support. Arguably, this situation will affect remaining precarious workers most acutely, as they are more likely to be paid for teaching time rather than for preparation time.

We know that women are more likely to be employed on precarious contracts and on teaching-only contracts (Baker, 2020), so it seems safe to conclude that women will be disproportionately affected by the sector's response to the pandemic. Evidence about academic research outputs demonstrates a telling pattern. Krukowski et al. (2021) provide evidence that only women with younger children reported a dip in productivity, in terms of academic authorship, due to the pandemic. Similarly, Duncanson et al. (2020) report that, whilst men's submissions to academic journals increased by 50 per cent, single-authored article submissions by women dropped (see also Flaherty, 2020).

2.3.3 The University and Colleges Union (UCU)

In contrast to the employers, who rushed to reopen following the first UK lockdown, the UCU consistently argued for caution. It systematically opposed the re-opening of university campuses and the return to face-to-face teaching. The UCU campaigned for a 'safe return' to campus, based on sustained reduction in Covid-19 cases and infection rates; social distancing; comprehensive testing and contact tracing; university-wide strategies for continuing health and safety; protection for those most vulnerable to Covid-19 (UCU, 2020e). This position is made clear by UCU's General Secretary, Dr Jo Grady, who addressed the Union's annual congress (the main policymaking body of the union):

From the start, the Government and employers pushed hard to maximise in-person working, even if it meant exposing staff, students and the wider community to the virus. But we have pushed back at every level: from our national press work, to our legal action against the Department for Education, to our extensive advice and guidance for members and branches, to the 700 reps we've trained throughout this pandemic, the staff who have spent countless hours studying risk assessments, the hundreds of activists who enrolled for our health and safety organising school, and to the branches that have organised for collective action on this issue. (UCU, 2021)

The UCU suspended existing industrial action to fight for workers' health and safety, and against redundancies and increasing workloads. It initiated legal action against the Government's decision to ignore advice from its own 'Scientific Advisory Group for Emergencies' committee of experts, concerning the opening university campuses to students in September 2020 (Grady, 2020). The UCU argued that the Government's failure to direct universities to move to online teaching was unlawful, unfair, unjust and irrational (Ferguson, 2020). It also advised members to use existing individual safety rights to protection from danger. In particular, the individual right in Section 44 of the Employment Rights Act 1996, as well as sections 68 and 132 of The Employment Rights (Northern Ireland) Order 1996, provide that individual employees (whether or not they are union members) are protected from detriment and dismissal if they leave the workplace – or tell their employer they plan to do so – because they believe there is 'serious and imminent danger'.

This focus on rights to health and safety and protection from 'imminent danger' is biopolitical and focussed on body politics, and the UCU has also highlighted and campaigned in relation to gendered aspects of pandemic precarities. For example, in 2020 UCU's Equality Representative's annual conference publicly asserted that 'Covid-19 has thrown the gendered division of work into sharp relief'. Several motions were passed at the 2020 National Congress, and other Union conferences, which emphasised the biopolitical aspect of the pandemic. For example, Congress noted that the lockdown disproportionally impacting women's work, and argued for adjustments for carers, parents and casualised workers, which the Union should campaign for (UCU, 2020a).

The UCU's Stamp Out Casualisation campaign also developed with the pandemic. As 'one of UCU's national priorities' (UCU, 2020d), this long-standing campaign highlights the extent and nature of casualisation in UKHE. This was extended during the pandemic, via a campaign for postgraduate researchers to be recognised as members of staff (UCU, 2020b). UCU's campaign around precarity has also highlighted how academics on casualised contracts are 'some of the most vulnerable to the effects of the Covid-19 crisis at work' (UCU, 2020c), and so their earnings should be protected (UCU, 2020c). As the Stamp Out Casualisation campaign argued:

The coronavirus crisis is highlighting some of the many flaws in this [UKHE] employment model. If employers had hired more of their staff on a more secure basis, they would now almost certainly be in a position to claim more support from the Government's wage replacement scheme. (UCU, 2020c)

The 2020 National Congress also passed motions that recognised that pandemic burden fell heavily on staff who were already precarious, but acknowledging that the UCU was 'ill prepared' for this eventuality (UCU, 2020a). As a consequence, it proposed to investigate the overall impact of the pandemic on different types of workers to guide future strategy. However, it is noteworthy that the union has been relatively powerless to protect the jobs of precarious academics. Arguably, this is because organising the types of industrial action that might counteract precarity has been made extremely difficult within a neoliberal policy regime.

2.3.4 Governmental Context and Response

The response of the UK Government and its agencies to the pandemic has been extensively questioned. Whilst the UK Government introduced strong laws preventing social gatherings, the regulation of health and safety at work appears much weaker (James, 2021), despite workplaces being the most likely setting for infection (see

Watterson, 2020). Guidance from the Health and Safety Executive, the governmental body responsible for regulating and enforcing health and safety at work, came in the form of sector-based advice for making workplaces 'Covid-safe'. This advice had no legal standing, and the enforcement of existing laws relating to health and safety at work was neglected (James, 2021). This lack is symptomatic of neoliberal employment regulation, which is predominantly supply-sided, or focused on the qualities of workers rather than the conditions of their employment (Grugulis, 2007).

To explore this area, we identify three areas of policy and regulation that appeared to be significant in affecting gendered experiences of pandemic precarities in UKHE. These include [1] regulation enabling marketisation of UKHE; [2] regulation of trade unions and employment contracts; and [3] regulation of gender equality and domestic care.

In relation to [1] the marketisation of UKHE, since the 1980s a series of Government Acts have commodified UKHE by transforming students into paying consumers of educational products, which are offered by institutions that are increasingly financially autonomous (Brown, 2015). The sector is now highly fragmented. The highest-ranking universities have significant cash reserves while the least selective institutions may fail to survive the pandemic without governmental bailouts.

In relation to [2] the regulation of work, since 1979 successive governments have argued that extensive employment rights and greater trade union involvement in decision making are counterproductive. The argument is that such interventions create rigidities and/or inefficient power resources that inhibit efficient operation of 'free' markets. The Conservative led Government (1979–97) significantly inhibited trade unions' ability to organise workers in defence or extension of their members' interests. Measures included the outlawing of secondary industrial actions and cumbersome balloting procedures that curbed the unions' ability to react to emerging issues (see Smith, 2009), such as those related to the pandemic.

Over the last forty years, the State has enabled a regulatory context that provides uneven protection for workers and favours employers prerogative: a context that promotes the use of more precarious atypical employment contracts (Forde & Slater, 2016). In common with other precarious workers, the work of the academic precariat is largely unregulated, with the employer holding power to determine future levels of employment.

In relation to [3] equality, whilst the State has legislated quite extensively for equality at work, important diversity initiatives were abandoned during the pandemic. For example, the requirement to report gender pay gap data in the UK was suspended in 2020, with the pandemic lockdown cited as the reason (GEO, 2020). During the same period, the National Institute for Health Research (NIHR) abandoned its requirement for academic partners to hold a Silver Athena SWAN award – a kitemark that demonstrates a significant commitment to equality. This was done order to 'reduce bureaucracy' (NIHR, 2020). Finally, State welfare institutions are important to individuals' ability to participate fully in the labour market, and yet these institutions have been negatively impacted by the steady withdrawal of UK Government from providing child and elder care support services (Tepe-Belfrage & Steans, 2016). Consequentially, whilst [gendered] equality is formally and legally enshrined, gendered inequalities associated with the work of social reproduction remain firmly in place (Steans & Tepe, 2010).

2.4 Discussion

While governmental responses to student concerns during the pandemic have been extensive, focusing, for example, on the circumstances in which tuition fees should be refunded and on student precarity due to loss of earnings (Government, 2020; HCPC, 2020), governmental focus on the impacts of precarity in academia and the welfare of precarious academics has been less evident (Collini, 2020). Indeed, amidst concerns over the viability of some HE institutions, a 'Restructuring Regime' strategy has emerged as a governmental response. This policy initiative, which has been designed to support academic providers to cope with the financial challenges of the pandemic (DfE, 2020), has been argued to be a tool that centralises control, so that cuts can be made to less profitable university courses (Adams, 2020). It seems the Government is very concerned with profitability of universities, and with the fair operation of markets for services to students, but it seems rather less concerned with the fair operation of labour markets. In this context, employers have divested precarious workers with impunity, and this will have disproportionately affected parts of the UKHE labour market in which women are more likely to be present.

Given this context, we must consider and highlight currently less visible and less rewarded forms of academic labour – such as the care of colleagues or other forms of 'academic housework' (Heijstra et al., 2017; Macfarlane & Burg, 2019). In this regard, we advocate the position of Pereira (2021), who is careful to separate pandemic asymmetries in gender equality which are either 'a consequence of asymmetries in *private* or *personal* labor, which are *external* to academia' or 'the many gender inequalities that result from asymmetries in *professional* labor, which are *internal* to academia' (Pereira, 2021, p. 6, emphasis in original).

Transforming academia during and after the pandemic will not be easy or quick. But if we approach academic labour differently, we can, hopefully, contribute both to reimagining that labour and to fighting the inequalities at the heart of it (Pereira, 2021, p. 8). Arguably, this implies a solidaristic politics that is both resistant to neoliberalism and seeks to realise material and social conditions conducive to universal 'ontological security' – both are necessary to reversing experiences of precarity (Nielson, 2015), within academic and beyond.

2.5 Conclusion

This chapter provides corroboration, from the academic labour market, for a large body of research which asserts that neoliberalism imposes forms of precarity within economic relations in ways that are not gender blind. Our objective has been to understand whether and how gendered and pandemic precarities interact, and how biopolitical employment relations potentially (re)frame societal responses to precarities, pandemic-related or otherwise. We found that existing gendered precarities within academic employment were exacerbated by the pandemic, and that this situation was impelled by a regulatory vacuum created by the UK's neoliberal institutional environment. This void arguably provides employers with tyrannical powers over their most vulnerable workers, which they are arguably currently bound to exploit in a manner that is blind to the gendered implications of decisions.

In this context, there may be scope for new biopolitical movements to emerge, based on the gendered nature of precarity and the severe impositions the pandemic has caused for an army of precarious workers in academia. Arguably, the UCU should continue to combine its fights *for* increased gendered equality within academic work with its fight *against* precarious academic employment, as the two are intimately related. For example, combining campaigning on these issues may be targeted at decision-making around employment contracts in the wake of the pandemic: arguments that having fewer precarious atypical contracts in the future is a pro-gender employment strategy appear very compelling.

Finally, further research in this area is urgently needed. Research into other sectors, which are likely to experience pandemic precarities in quite different ways, as well as how these sectors are differently regulated and impacted by employment relations agencies, could demonstrate which employment relations institutions result in better and/ or worse health-based outcomes. International comparative research that seeks to explore how different types of economy have responded to pandemic precarities could contribute similarly and inform policy debates at a supranational level. This chapter has contributed to the development of this work by starting to articulate a novel employment relations approach to biopolitical issues.

References

Acker, S., & Webber, M. (2017). Made to measure: Early career academics in the Canadian university workplace. *Higher Education Research & Development*, 36(3), 541–554. https://doi.org/10.1080/07294360.2017.1288704

Ackroyd, S., & Karlsson, J. C. (2014). Critical Realism, Research Techniques, and Research Designs. In P. K. Edwards, J. O'Mahoney, & S. Vincent (Eds.), *Studying Organizations Using Critical Realism: A Practical Guide (Vol. 17)*. Oxford University Press.

Adams, R. (2020). *English universities must prove 'commitment' to free speech for bailouts*. Guardian News & Media Limited. Retrieved 19 May 2021 from www.theguardian.com/education/2020/jul/16/english-universities-must-prove-commitment-to-free-speech-for-bailouts

Aronsson, G., Gustafsson, K., & Dallner, M. (2000). Sick but yet at work. An Empirical Study of Sickness Presenteeism. *Journal of Epidemiology and Community Health (1979-)*, 54(7), 502–509. www.jstor.org/stable/25569229

Ashencaen Crabtree, S., & Shiel, C. (2019). 'Playing Mother': Channeled careers and the construction of gender in academia. *SAGE Open*, 9(3), 2158244019876285. https://doi.org/10.1177/2158244019876285

Baker, S. (2020). Teaching-only contracts up again as REF approaches. *Times Higher Education* Retrieved 19 May 2021 from www.timeshigher education.com/news/teaching-only-contracts-again-ref-approaches

Bosanquet, A., Mailey, A., Matthews, K. E., & Lodge, J. M. (2017). Redefining 'early career' in academia: a collective narrative approach. *Higher Education Research & Development*, 36(5), 890–902. https://doi.org/10 .1080/07294360.2016.1263934

Brown, R. (2015). *The Marketisation of Higher Education: Issues and ironies.* www.uwl.ac.uk/sites/default/files/Departments/Research/new_vistas/ vol1_iss1/vol1_iss1_art1_23April2015.pdf

Burrows, R. (2012). Living with the H-Index? Metric assemblages in the contemporary academy. *The Sociological Review*, 60(2), 355–372. https://doi.org/10.1111/j.1467-954X.2012.02077.x

Burton, S. (2018). Writing Yourself In? The Price of Playing the (Feminist) Game in the Neoliberal Academy. In Y. Taylor & K. Lahad (Eds.), *Feeling Academic in the Neoliberal University: Feminist Flights, Fights and Failures.* (pp. 115–136). Palgrave Macmillan.

Butler, J. (2009). *Frames of War: When Is Life Grievable?* Cambridge University Press.

Campbell, T., & Sitze, A. (2013). *Biopolitics: A Reader* Duke University Press.

Collini, S. (2020). *Covid-19 shows up UK universities' shameful employment practices.* Guardian News and Media Limited. Retrieved 19 May 2021 from www.theguardian.com/education/2020/apr/28/covid-19-shows-up-uk-universities-shameful-employment-practices

Courtois, A., & O'Keefe, T. (2015). Precarity in the ivory cage: Neoliberalism and casualisation of work in the Irish higher education sector. *Journal for Critical Education Policy Studies*, 13(1), 43–66.

de Ruyter, A. (2020). Covid-19 and precarious work: time for end to the 'Gig Economy'. www.open-access.bcu.ac.uk/9680/

DfE. (2020). *Establishment of a Higher Education Restructuring Regime in Response to COVID-19.* (DfE-00121-2020). Retrieved from https:// assets.publishing.service.gov.uk/government/uploads/system/uploads/ attachment_data/file/902608/HERR_announcement_July_2020.pdf

Doan, M. D., & Harbin, A. (2020). Public health and precarity. *IJFAB: International Journal of Feminist Approaches to Bioethics*, 13(2), 108–130.

Doeringer, P. B., & Piore, M. J. (1971). *Internal Labor Markets and Manpower Analysis.* Heath Lexington Books.

Doharty, N., Madriaga, M., & Joseph-Salisbury, R. (2021). The university went to 'decolonise' and all they brought back was lousy diversity double-speak! Critical race counter-stories from faculty of colour in 'decolonial'

times. *Educational Philosophy and Theory, 53*(3), 233–244. https://doi
.org/10.1080/00131857.2020.1769601

Drayton, E., & Waltmann, B. (2020). Will universities need a bailout to
survive the COVID-19 crisis? Briefing note. *Institute for Fiscal Studies.*
Retrieved 12 April 2021 from www.ifs.org.uk/publications/14919

Duncanson, K., Weir, N., Siriwardhane, P., & Khan, T. (2020). *How
COVID is widening the academic gender divide.* The Conversation
Trust (UK) Limited. Retrieved 12 May from https://theconversation.com/
how-covid-is-widening-the-academic-gender-divide-146007

Edwards, R. C., Reich, M., & Gordon, D. M. (1976). *Labor Market Segmentation.* Lexington Books.

EHRC. (2020). *How coronavirus has affected equality and human rights.*
E. a. H. R. Commission. www.equalityhumanrights.com/en/publication-
download/how-coronavirus-has-affected-equality-and-human-rights

Federici, S. (2012). *Revolution at Point Zero: Housework, Reproduction
and Feminist Struggle.* PM Press.

Federici, S. (2017). Capital and Gender. In I. Schmidt & C. Fanelli (Eds.),
Reading Capital Today: Marx after 150 Years. Pluto Press.

Ferguson, D. (2020). *UK academics: opening of universities was illegal.* Guardian. Retrieved 19 May 2021 from www.theguardian.com/education/2020/
oct/24/uk-academics-opening-of-universities-was

Flaherty, C. (2020). *No Room of One's Own: Early journal submission data
suggest COVID-19 is tanking women's research productivity.* Retrieved 12
May 2021 from www.insidehighered.com/news/2020/04/21/early-journal-
submission-data-suggest-covid-19-tanking-womens-research-productivity

Fleetwood, S. (2017). From labour market institutions to an alternative
model of labour markets. In *Forum for social economics* (Vol. 46, No. 1,
pp. 78–103). Routledge.

Forde, C., & Slater, G. (2016). Labour market regulation and the 'competition state': an analysis of the implementation of the Agency Working
Regulations in the UK. *Work, Employment and Society, 30*(4), 590–606.
https://doi.org/10.1177/0950017015622917

Gappa, J. M., & Leslie, D. W. (1993). *The Invisible Faculty. Improving the
Status of Part-Timers in Higher Education.* Jossey-Bass Inc.

GEO. (2020). Employers do not have to report gender pay gaps. GOV.
UK. Retrieved 19 May 2021 from www.gov.uk/government/news/
employers-do-not-have-to-report-gender-pay-gaps

Gill, R. (2010). Breaking the Silence: the Hidden Injuries of the Neo-
liberal Academia. In Ryland-Flood, R. and Gill, R. (eds.) *Secrecy and
Silence in the Research Process: Feminist Reflections* (pp. 228–244).
Routledge.

Gill, R. (2014). Academics, cultural workers and critical labour studies. *Journal of Cultural Economy, 7*(1), 12–30. https://doi.org/10.1080/175 30350.2013.861763

Godin, I., Kittel, F., Coppieters, Y., & Siegrist, J. (2005). A prospective study of cumulative job stress in relation to mental health. *BMC Public Health, 5*(1), 67. https://doi.org/10.1186/1471-2458-5-67

Government. (2020). The impact of Covid-19 on university students: Government Response to the Committee's Second Report. UK Parliament Retrieved from https://publications.parliament.uk/pa/cm5801/cmselect/cmpetitions/780/78002.htm

Grady, J. (2020). The government must support students stuck in Covid nightmare at universities. *Guardian.* Retrieved 19 May 2021 from www.theguardian.com/commentisfree/2020/oct/24/the-government-must-support-students-stuck-in-covid-nightmare-at-universities

Greer, I. (2015). Welfare reform, precarity and the re-commodification of labour. *Work, Employment and Society, 30*(1), 162–173. doi.org/10.1177/0950017015572578

Grimshaw, D., Fagan, C., Hebson, G., & Tavora, I. (2017). A new labour market segmentation approach for analysing inequalities: introduction and overview. In *Making Work More Equal: A New Labour Market Segmentation Approach.* Manchester University Press.

Grugulis, I. (2007). *Skills, Training and Human Resource Development: A critical text.* Palgrave Macmillan.

Hall, R., & Quinn, B. (2020, 19 October 2020). England campus lockdowns creating 'perfect storm' for stressed students. *Guardian.* Retrieved 19 May 2021 from www.theguardian.com/education/2020/nov/06/england-campus-lockdowns-perfect-storm-students-mental-health-covid-restrictions

HCPC. (2020). *The impact of Covid-19 on university students: Second Report of Session 2019–21.* House of Commons Petitions Committee Retrieved from https://committees.parliament.uk/publications/1851/documents/18140/default/

Heijstra, T. M., Einarsdóttir, Þ., Pétursdóttir, G. M., & Steinþórsdóttir, F. S. (2017). Testing the concept of academic housework in a European setting: Part of academic career-making or gendered barrier to the top? *European Educational Research Journal, 16*(2–3), 200–214. doi.org/10.1177/1474904116668884

Hogan, V., Hogan, M., Hodgins, M., Kinman, G., & Bunting, B. (2014). An examination of gender differences in the impact of individual and organisational factors on work hours, work-life conflict and psychological strain in academics. *The Irish Journal of Psychology 35*(2–3), 133–150. https://doi.org/-10.1080/03033910.2015.1011193y1–2014

Ivancheva, M., & O'Flynn, M. (2016). Between Career Progression and Career Stagnation: Casualisation, tenure, and the contract of indefinite duration in Ireland. In *Academic Labour, Unemployment and Global Higher Education* (pp. 167–184). Palgrave Macmillan.

Ivancheva, M., Lynch, K., & Keating, K. (2019). Precarity, gender and care in the neoliberal academy. *Gender, Work & Organization*, 26(4), 448–462. https://doi.org/10.1111/gwao.12350

Ivancheva, M. P. (2015). The Age of Precarity and the New Challenges to the Academic Profession. *Studia Universitatis Babes-Bolyai. Studia Europaea*, 60(1), 39–47. www.proquest.com/scholarly-journals/age-precarity-new-challenges-academic-profession/docview/1676465185/se-2?accountid=12753

James, P. (2021). *HSE and Covid at Work: A Case of Regulatory Failure* (P. James, Ed. Vol. 2021). Institute of Employment Rights. www.ier.org.uk/product/hse-and-covid-at-work-a-case-of-regulatory-failure/

Joseph–Salisbury, R., Connelly, L., & Wangari-Jones, P. (2021). 'The UK is not innocent': Black Lives Matter, policing and abolition in the UK. *Equality, Diversity and Inclusion: An International Journal*, 40(1), 21–28. https://doi.org/10.1108/EDI-06-2020-0170

Kalleberg, A. L. (2009). Precarious work, insecure workers: Employment relations in transition. *American Sociological Review*, 74(1), 1–22.

Kinikoğlu, C. N., & Can, A. (2021). Negotiating the different degrees of precarity in the UK academia during the Covid-19 pandemic. *European Societies*, 23(sup1), S817–S830. https://doi.org/10.1080/14616696.2020.1839670

Klein, S. L., Dhakal, S., Ursin, R. L., Deshpande, S., Sandberg, K., & Mauvais-Jarvis, F. (2020). Biological sex impacts COVID-19 outcomes. *PLoS pathogens*, 16(6), e1008570–e1008570. https://doi.org/10.1371/journal.ppat.1008570

Krukowski, R. A., Jagsi, R., & Cardel, M. I. (2021). Academic productivity differences by gender and child age in science, technology, engineering, mathematics, and medicine faculty during the COVID-19 pandemic. *Journal of Women's Health*, 30(3), 341–347.

Lally, C. (2020). *COVID-19 and Occupational Risk*. POST: UK Parliament Retrieved from post.parliament.uk/covid-19-and-occupational-risk/

Lynch, K. (2010). Carelessness: A hidden doxa of higher education. *Arts and Humanities in Higher Education*, 9(1), 54–67. https://doi.org/10.1177/1474022209350104

Lynch, K. (2014). New managerialism: The impact on education. *Concept*, 5(3), 11–11.

Macfarlane, B., & Burg, D. (2019). Women professors and the academic housework trap. *Journal of Higher Education Policy and Management*, 41(3), 262–274. https://doi.org/10.1080/1360080X.2019.1589682

Mackenzie, E., & McKinlay, A. (2020). Hope labour and the psychic life of cultural work. *Human Relations, 0*(0). https://doi.org/10.1177/0018726720940777

Marchington, M., Grimshaw, D., Rubery, J., & Wilmott, H. (2004). *Fragmenting Work: Blurring Organizational Boundaries and Disordering Hierarchies*. Oxford University Press. https://doi.org/10.1093/acprof:oso/9780199262236.001.0001

McCann, L., Granter, E., Hyde, P., & Aroles, J. (2020). 'Upon the gears and upon the wheels': Terror convergence and total administration in the neoliberal university. *Management learning, 51*(4), 431–451. https://doi.org/10.1177/1350507620924162

McCormack, D., & Salmenniemi, S. (2016). The biopolitics of precarity and the self. *European Journal of Cultural Studies, 19*(1), 3–15. https://doi.org/10.1177/1367549415585559

McKenzie, L. (2017). A Precarious Passion: Gendered and Age-based Insecurity Among Aspiring Academics in Australia. In R. Thwaites & A. Preslland (Eds.), *Being an Early Career Feminist Academic* (pp. 31–49). Palgrave Macmillan.

McKenzie, L. (2021). Un/making academia: gendered precarities and personal lives in universities. *Gender and Education, 34*(3), 1–18. https://doi.org/10.1080/09540253.2021.1902482

Meardi, G., Simms, M., & Adam, D. (2021). Trade unions and precariat in Europe: Representative claims. *European Journal of Industrial Relations, 27*(1), 41–58. https://doi.org/10.1177/0959680119863585

Milner, A., LaMontagne, A. D., Spittal, M. J., Pirkis, J., & Currier, D. (2018). Job stressors and employment precarity as risks for thoughts about suicide: An Australian study using the ten to men cohort. *Annals of Work Exposures and Health, 62*(5), 583–590. https://doi.org/10.1093/annweh/wxy024

Moore, S., Tailby, S., Antunes, B., & Newsome, K. (2018). 'Fits and fancies': the Taylor Review, the construction of preference and labour market segmentation [Article]. *Industrial Relations Journal, 49*(5/6), 403–419. https://doi.org/10.1111/irj.12229

Morley, L. (2013). The rules of the game: women and the leaderist turn in higher education. *Gender and Education, 25*(1), 116–131. https://doi.org/10.1080/09540253.2012.740888

Murray, Ó. M. (2018). *Feel the Fear and Killjoy Anyway: Being a Challenging Feminist Presence in Precarious Academia*. In (pp. 163–189). Cham: Springer International Publishing.

Neilson, D. (2015). Class, precarity, and anxiety under neoliberal global capitalism: From denial to resistance. *Theory & Psychology, 25*(2), 184–201. https://doi.org/10.1177/0959354315580607

NIHR. (2020). *NIHR respond to the Government's call for further reduction in bureaucracy with new measures.* National Institute for Health Research. Retrieved 19 May 2021 from www.nihr.ac.uk/news/

Nikunen, M., & Lempiäinen, K. (2020). Gendered strategies of mobility and academic career. *Gender and Education, 32*(4), 554–571. https://doi.org/10.1080/09540253.2018.1533917

Parliament, U. (2021). *Unequal impact? Coronavirus and the gendered economic impact.* UK Parliament. Retrieved 19 May 2021 from https://committees.parliament.uk/work/319/unequal-impact-coronavirus-and-the-gendered-economic-impact/publications/

Pentaraki, M., & Dionysopoulou, K. (2019). Social workers: a new precariat? Precarity conditions of mental health social workers working in the non-profit sector in Greece. *European Journal of Social Work, 22*(2), 301–313. https://doi.org/10.1080/13691457.2018.1529664

Pereira, M. d. M. (2021). Researching gender inequalities in academic labor during the COVID-19 pandemic: Avoiding common problems and asking different questions. *Gender, work, and organization. 28,* 498–509. https://doi.org/10.1111/gwao.12618

Petrescu, I. (2021). UK universities and colleges escalate attacks on jobs and pay as Johnson government reopens unsafe campuses. WSWS. Retrieved 12 May 2021 from www.wsws.org/en/articles/2021/03/10/unuk-m10.html

Quinlan, M. (2017). Precarity and Workplace Well-Being: A General Review. In T. Nichols & D. Walters (Eds.), *Safety or Profit? International Studies in Governance, Change and the Work Environment* (pp. 17–31). Routledge.

Reay, D. (2004). Cultural capitalists and academic habitus: Classed and gendered labour in UK higher education. *Women's Studies International Forum, 27*(1), 31–39. https://doi.org/10.1016/j.wsif.2003.12.006

Ro, C. (2020, 27 October 2020). *Why this recession disproportionately affects women.* BBC. Retrieved 19 May 2021 from www.bbc.com/worklife/article/20201021-why-this-recession-disproportionately-affects-women

Ross, J., & McKie, A. (2020, 19 October 2020). Will Covid kill off the teaching-research employment model? *Times Higher Education.* www.timeshighereducation.com/news/will-covid-kill-teaching-research-employment-model

Rubery, J. (2007). Developing segmentation theory: A thirty years perspective. *Economies et sociétés, 41*(6), 941–964.

Rubery, J., & Grimshaw, D. (2014). The 40-year pursuit of equal pay: a case of constantly moving goalposts. *Cambridge journal of economics, 39*(2), 319–343. https://doi.org/10.1093/cje/beu053

Rustin, M. (2016). The neoliberal university and its alternatives. *Soundings (London, England)* (63), 147. https://doi.org/10.3898/136266216819377057

Ryan, S., Burgess, J., Connell, J., & Groen, E. (2013). Casual Academic Staff in an Australian University: Marginalised and excluded. *Tertiary Education and Management, 19*(2), 161–175. https://doi.org/10.1080/1 3583883.2013.783617

Schaufeli, W. B., & Buunk, B. P. (1996). Professional Burnout. In M. Schabracq, J. Winnubst, & S. Cooper (Eds.), *Handbook of Work and Health Psychology* (Vol. 1, pp. 383–425). John Wiley and Sons Ltd.

Sherwin, S. (2012). Relational Autonomy and Global Threats. In J. Downie & J. Lewellyn (Eds.), *Being Rational: Reflections on Relational Theory and Health Law and Policy* (Vol. 27). UBC Press. www.proquest .com/trade-journals/being-rational-reflections-on-relational-theory/ docview/919036102/se-2?accountid=12753

Smith, P. (2009). New Labour and the commonsense of neoliberalism: trade unionism, collective bargaining and workers' rights [Article]. *Industrial Relations Journal, 40*(4), 337–355. https://doi.org/10.1111/j.1468-2338 .2009.00531.x

Somit, A., & Peterson, S. A. (1998). Biopolitics after three decades – A balance sheet. *British Journal of Political Science, 28*(3), 559–571.

Standing, G. (2011). *The Precariat.* Bloomsbury Academic.

Staton, B. (2020). *Universities to Cut Thousands of Academics on Short Contracts.* Financial Times. Retrieved 19 May 2021 from www.ft.com/ content/67f89a9e-ac30-47d0-83e7-eba4d1284847

Steans, J., & Tepe, D. (2010). Introduction – Social reproduction in international political economy: Theoretical insights and international, transnational and local sitings. *Review of International Political Economy, 17*(5), 807–815. https://doi.org/10.1080/09692290.20 10.481928

Steinþórsdóttir, F. S., Brorsen Smidt, T., Pétursdóttir, G. M., Einarsdóttir, Þ., & Le Feuvre, N. (2019). New managerialism in the academy: Gender bias and precarity [Article]. *Gender, Work & Organization, 26*(2), 124–139. https://doi.org/10.1111/gwao.12286

Tepe-Belfrage, D., & Steans, J. (2016). The new materialism: Re-claiming a debate from a feminist perspective. *Capital & Class, 40*(2), 305–326. https://doi.org/10.1177/0309816816653892

Thompson, P. (2013). Financialization and the workplace: extending and applying the disconnected capitalism thesis. *Work, Employment & Society, 27*(3), 472–488.

TUC. (2020). Key workers report: Decent pay and secure work for key workers through coronavirus and beyond. www.tuc.org.uk/research-analysis/ reports/key-workers-report

UCU. (2016). *Precarious work in higher education: A snapshot of insecure contracts and institutional attitudes.* www.ucu.org.uk/media/7995/

Precarious-work-in-higher-education-a-snapshot-of-insecure-contracts-and-institutional-attitudes-Apr-16/pdf/ucu_precariouscontract_hereport_apr16.pdf

UCU. (2019). *Counting the costs of casualisation in higher education: Key findings of a survey conducted by the University and College Union.* UCU. www.ucu.org.uk/media/10336/Counting-the-costs-of-casualisation-in-higher-education-Jun-19/pdf/ucu_casualisation_in_HE_survey_report_Jun19.pdf

UCU. (2020a). *Congress motions 2020.* University and College Union. Retrieved 19 May 2021 from www.ucu.org.uk/article/11075/Congress-motions-2020

UCU. (2020b). *PGRs as staff, not students.* University and College Union. Retrieved 19 May 2021 from www.ucu.org.uk/article/11206/PGRs-as-staff-not-students?list=7268

UCU. (2020c). *Protecting precarious workers.* University and College Union. Retrieved 19 May 2021 from www.ucu.org.uk/article/10736/Protecting-precarious-workers

UCU. (2020d). *Stamp out casual contracts.* University and College Union. Retrieved 19 May 2021 from www.ucu.org.uk/stampout

UCU. (2020e). *UCU tests for safe returns to on-campus working in HE.* University and College Union. Retrieved 19 May 2021 from www.ucu.org.uk/media/10935/UCU-HE-on-campus-return-tests/pdf/ucu_covid19_hetests.pdf

UCU. (2021). *Staff in post-16 education are having to fight UK government and employers throughout Covid crisis, says Jo Grady.* University and College Union. Retrieved 19 May 2021 from www.ucu.org.uk/article/11404/Staff-in-post-16-education-are-having-to-fight-UK-government-and-employers-throughout-Covid-crisis-says-Jo-Grady

Vincent, S., Bamber, G.J., Delbridge, R., Doellgast, V., Grady, J. and Grugulis, I., 2020. Situating human resource management in the political economy: Multilevel theorising and opportunities for kaleidoscopic imagination. *Human Resource Management Journal*, 30(4), 461–477.

Vohlídalová, M. (2021). Early-Career Women Academics: Between Neoliberalism and Gender Conservatism. *Sociological Research Online*, 26(1), 27–43. https://doi.org/10.1177/1360780420914468

WA. (2020). *A Perfect Storm: The Impact of the Covid-19 Pandemic on Domestic Abuse Survivors and the Services Supporting Them.* W. s. Aid. www.womensaid.org.uk/a-perfect-storm-the-impact-of-the-covid-19-pandemic-on-domestic-abuse-survivors-and-the-services-supporting-them/

Waite, L. (2009). A place and space for a critical geography of precarity? *Geography Compass*, 3(1), 412–433. https://doi.org/10.1111/j.1749-8198.2008.00184.x

Watterson, A. (2020). *Coronavirus is spreading rapidly through work-places – here's what is needed to make them safer*. The Conversation. Retrieved 19 May 2021 from https://theconversation.com/coronavirus-is-spreading-rapidly-through-workplaces-heres-what-is-needed-to-make-them-safer-149333

WBG. (2020). Crises Collide: Women and Covid-19. Examining gender and other equality issues during the Coronavirus outbreak. wbg.org.uk/wp-content/uploads/2020/04/FINAL.pdf

Wenham, C., Smith, J., & Morgan, R. (2020). COVID-19: The gendered impacts of the outbreak. *The Lancet, 395*(10227), 846–848. https://doi.org/10.1016/S0140-6736(20)30526-2

Wilkinson, F. (1983). Productive systems. *Cambridge journal of economics, 7*(3–4), 413–429. https://doi.org/10.1093/cje/7.3-4.413

WRC. (2020). *The Crisis of COVID-19 and UK Women's Charities: Survey responses and findings*. W. s. R. Centre. www.wrc.org.uk/the-impact-of-the-covid-19-crisis-on-the-uk-womens-sector

Yarrow, E. (2021). Knowledge hustlers: Gendered micro-politics and networking in UK universities. *British Educational Research Journal. 47*(3), 579–598. https://doi.org/10.1002/berj.3671

Zheng, R. (2018). Precarity is a feminist issue: Gender and contingent labor in the academy. *Hypatia, 33*(2), 235–255.

3 | *LGBTQ+ Individuals and Precarious Work*

OSCAR HOLMES IV, ERHAN AYDIN, RICHARD
GREGGORY JOHNSON III, AND EMIR OZEREN

3.1 Introduction

Precarious work refers to employment conditions that include 'uncertainty,' 'instability,' and 'insecurity' and is often characterized by low pay, inadequate and variable hours, and short-term/temporary contracts (Kalleberg & Hewison, 2013; Vallas, 2015). Precarious work arrangements have exploded due to globalization, technological advancements, decreases in manufacturing, and increases in service and gig economies (Campbell & Price, 2016; Kalleberg & Vallas, 2017). In the United States, nearly one in two workers (46.2 percent) are considered to be in some form of precarious work (Albelda et al., 2020). At a slightly lesser rate, 40 percent of workers in Turkey are engaged in precarious work. As such, the United States and Turkey represent a stark contrast to the 4.8 percent of workers in precarious employment within European Union countries, making the United States and Turkey interesting case studies (Emre et al., 2017).

Understanding the factors contributing to and outcomes of precarious work is important. Precarious work creates severe challenges for workers as they have limited protections yet bear significant economic, physical, and social risks due to their working conditions (Okulicz-Kozaryn et al., 2014; Vosko, 2010). Typically, precarious work rate participation is higher for people with stigmatized or marginalized identities (Campbell & Price, 2016; Kalleberg & Vallas, 2017). In this chapter, we will focus on the experiences lesbian, gay, bisexual, transgender, and queer (LGBTQ+) workers have with precarious work by juxtaposing a US and Turkey case study to outline the macro- and micro-level factors and outcomes of precarious work. To conclude the chapter, we present a research agenda for scholars further to uncover LGBTQ+ individuals' experiences with precarious work.

As a group, LGBTQ+ people are among the most marginalized and stigmatized people in the world. In fact, in many countries, LGBTQ+ people still experience enormous levels of government-sanctioned discrimination rooted largely in heteronormativity, heterosexism, and transphobia (Holmes, 2019, 2020). For example, seventy-two jurisdictions criminalize same-sex sexual relations among men, forty-four jurisdictions criminalize same-sex sexual relations among women, eleven jurisdictions can impose the death penalty, and fifteen jurisdictions criminalize transgender identity expression (Human Dignity Trust, 2021). In the United States, sexual orientation made up 16.7 percent of the 2019 hate crimes reported ranking third only to hate crimes based on race and religion (Ronan, 2020). The number of US hate crimes explicitly based on gender identity was 2.7 percent in 2019 (Ronan, 2020). In Turkey, violence committed against people based on sexual orientation, gender identity, and sex characteristics is not even considered a judicial hate crime. However, in a study surveying 150 LGBTQ+ individuals in Turkey, 123 reported their attacks were motivated based on sexual orientation, and 61 said they were based on gender identity (Kaos GL Association, 2020). Considering how vulnerable LGBTQ+ people are in society, it is widely believed that violence committed against LGBTQ+ people is chronically underreported to authorities, which further contributes to their precarity (Friedman et al., 2011; Holmes et al., 2016).

In the past two decades, LGBTQ+ people have organized impressively to pass pro-LGBTQ+ legislation and have won consequential pro-LGBTQ+ legal victories. Same-sex marriage is now legal in 29 countries, with the Netherlands becoming the first country to grant such rights in 2001. While same-sex marriage became legal nationwide in the United States in 2015, same-sex marriage and civil unions are still illegal in Turkey (Out Leadership, 2019). However, in Turkey, transgender people are permitted to legally change their gender if they undergo sex reassignment surgery (Out Leadership, 2019). Considering the importance healthy adult romantic relationships have on employment, health, and social outcomes, marriage equality plays a central role in LGBTQ+ individuals' workplace experiences and wealth attainment (Holmes, 2020; Pichler & Holmes, 2017).

Concerning employment discrimination, the United States Supreme Court made it illegal to discriminate against LGBTQ+ employees on June 15, 2020. However, 20 percent of LGBTQ+ workers still admit to having experienced workplace discrimination and over 50 percent admit to having experienced microaggressions (Catalyst, 2020). In Turkey, employment discrimination against LGBTQ+ workers is legal and openly LGBTQ+ people are not permitted to serve in the military (Kaos GL Association, 2014; Out Leadership, 2019). As such, a significant number of LGBTQ+ employees in both countries had experienced being fired or demoted when their LGBTQ+ or partner identity became known to employers (Badgett et al., 2007; Meyer, 2003; Ozturk & Tatli, 2016; Ragins, 2004). Since no legal protections exist for LGBTQ+ employees in Turkey, there is no legal recourse for LGBTQ+ employees who are dismissed or demoted because of their sexual orientation or gender identity. Although legal recourse is now possible in the United States, unsuccessful or unchallenged involuntary separation or demotion cases far outweigh the number of successful legal cases (Eckes, 2007; Holmes, 2019; Kollen, 2016; Rabelo & Cortina, 2013). These types of negative career occurrences not only interrupt employees' career trajectories and tenure within organizations, but also these involuntary workplace separations create, at least temporarily, financial, emotional, and social instability for LGBTQ+ workers and can derail otherwise promising careers (Albelda et al., 2020; Griffin & Lopez, 2005; Kessler et al., 1999; Meyer, 2003). The necessity to quickly earn replacement income forces a significant number of LGBTQ+ employees experiencing this type of discrimination into underemployment or other precarious work arrangements (Bidwell et al., 2013; McKee-Ryan & Harvey, 2011; Wang & Wanberg, 2017).

Due to the persistently high levels of workplace discrimination LGBTQ+ people experience, many do not disclose their LGBTQ+ identities to workplace supervisors and colleagues until they feel it is safe to do so. In some cases, LGBTQ+ employees never disclose their identities and go to great lengths to project a cis-heterosexual identity to prevent experiencing negative workplace outcomes (Guittar & Rayburn, 2016; Holmes et al., 2019; Ragins et al., 2007). Although this identity concealment strategy may prevent one from experiencing LGBTQ+ bias and discrimination, research has found that this strategy typically takes a psychological and emotional toll on LGBTQ+ people and can result in their reduced job performance and engagement (Holmes, 2019; Hwahng & Lin, 2009; Lindsey et al., 2020; Ragins & Cornwell, 2001). Ironically, even when LGBTQ+ workers experience positivity in the workplace, their careers can still be stifled as they may be reluctant to pursue new opportunities because they cannot be sure of the support they would receive in their new workplace environments (Pichler, 2007; Pichler & Holmes, 2017). This is particularly the case when the opportunities require the employees to take on roles in which their significant other is expected to be visible and explicitly or tacitly facilitate or support their partner's success in that role (Holmes, 2020). Due to these employment constraints, it is no surprise that research has identified the *lavender ceiling* as a unique employment barrier for LGBTQ+ workers that contributes to their experience with precarious work arrangements (Anteby & Anderson, 2014; Gedro, 2010; Hill, 2009).

Borrowing from the glass ceiling metaphor, the lavender ceiling is a term that has been used to describe employers' reluctance to promote their LGBTQ+ employees into leadership or highly visible roles within their organizations (Gedro, 2010; Hill, 2009). The term has also expanded to describe the overrepresentation of LGBTQ+ employees in specific industries (e.g., beauty/fashion or airline industry for gay men, sex work/entertainment industry for transgender women, trade work for lesbian women, etc.) (Hill, 2009; Pichler & Holmes, 2017; Ragins, 2004). Research has found that lesbian and gay workers employ an identity-protection strategy wherein they systematically self-segregate into occupations that provide them with increased levels of task independence, social perceptions, or both (Tilcsik et al., 2015). Entertainment and artistic industries are notoriously precarious careers since employment is often project-specific. Thus, income, health, retirement, and other employment-related benefits are often sporadic, particularly if one is not a union member (Curtin & Sanson, 2016). Albeit, some LGBTQ+ celebrities and jobs in these industries pay LGBTQ+ employees respectably or above median income levels. Nonetheless, it remains true that LGBTQ+ people remain underrepresented in leadership positions and typically do not enjoy the same level of success as their cis-heterosexual counterparts within the same industries (Holmes, 2019, 2020). For example, there have only been five openly gay or lesbian world leaders; currently, only three are openly gay or lesbian Fortune 500 CEOs (Holmes, 2020). To date, there have been zero openly bisexual or transgender world leaders or Fortune 500 CEOs. However, some bisexual and transgender individuals are currently in executive-level positions and hold political offices within the United States. Only time will tell if any of these bisexual or transgender leaders will make history by reaching the pinnacle of their respective careers. Notwithstanding the amazing success of these LGBTQ+ trailblazers, the fact remains that employment discrimination, bias, and barriers that LGBTQ+ people experience in the workplace leave them overrepresented in precarious work environments and susceptible to a number of negative professional, psychological, social, and emotional outcomes (Hill, 2009; Ragins et al., 2007).

3.2 Theorizing Sexual Orientation, Gender Identity, and Precarious Work

Work is a component of society that has a central role in creating an individual identity, linking individuals to each other, and locating them within the stratification system. However, social, economic, and political forces can make work more precarious. The concept of precarious work refers to a type of employment that the workers recognize as uncertain, unpredictable, and risky (Kalleber, 2009). The growth of precarious work comes from neoliberal globalization that creates intensified economic integration, increased competition among companies, and provides access to workers from lower-wage countries. Additionally, immigration to developed countries expands new labor pools for companies (Kalleberg, 2011). For this reason, such situations produce an important rate of surplus for the labor force that comes from different strands of diversity such as culture, ethnicity, sexual orientation, and gender identity.

Recently, we have witnessed significant changes and transformations in the nature of employment caused by the proliferation of precarious work. One of the major theoretical explanations leading to the proliferation of precarious work has rooted in the field of sociology. The dark side of economic growth comes to light with the emergence of the 'risk society' in which many individuals encounter numerous difficulties and ambiguities impacting their daily lives. This economic growth driven by the industrial capitalism paved the way for a new period called 'liquid modernity' by Bauman (2000), in which the state of 'precariousness', 'instability,' and 'vulnerability' is the most common characteristics of social life (Bauman, 2000, p. 160–161). Along with the waves of neoliberalism, being 'insecure' has been so strong and deeply felt by the workers (not only by the blue-collar workers but also by white-collar workers) that those who are subject to various forms of precarity are less likely to engage in collective action and resistance (Bourdieu, 1998, p. 82). Particularly, white-collar workers tend to internalize the precarious working conditions by branding and comporting themselves with market logics, adopting career management ideologies (Lane, 2011), embracing an entrepreneurial mindset and assuming individual responsibility in the workplace (Vallas & Cummins, 2015). Thus, in the reign of uncertainties created by neoliberalism, precarity has an extended meaning of being insecure; it is rather 'a mode of domination' of a new kind (Bourdieu, 1998, p. 85) or a new instrument of governance that holds enduring hegemony and oppression over the masses of working class. In other words, precariousness is not a temporary, passing, or episodic condition. Instead, it seems like a long-lasting structural phenomenon, precisely a new form of regulation described by Butler (2015, p. vii).

In the extant literature, the proliferation of precarious work is explained by several interdependent dynamics: 'de-unionization,' 'financialization,' 'globalization,' and, more recently, 'digital transformation' (Kalleberg 2009, 2011). However, we know relatively little about the gendered understanding of the phenomenon as there has been little emphasis on the entrenched inequalities concerning diversity. Much of the current literature that focuses on relatively privileged, white men's experiences (Kalleberg and Vallas, 2017: 13) does not seek to go beyond the binary categories of gender without addressing these issues from sexual orientation and gender identity perspective. Therefore, we can argue that the work precarity literature relies heavily on heterosexist/cisgender assumptions and, to a great extent, remains silent on various forms of experiences that LGBTQ+ people are subject to in precarious work settings.

Research (e.g., Mirowsky and Ross, 2003; Wilson and Ebert, 2013) demonstrates that precarious work has increased both the level of distress and the vulnerabilities from the micro-individual to the macronational level. However, the level of welfare in countries impacts precarious work conditions since it can remove the risks of work (Westergaard-Nielsen, 2008). This situation demonstrates that social, political, and economic institutions shape the nature of precarious work for employees. For instance, since social institutions adopt institutionalized gender norms and heterosexist perspectives, LGBTQ+ individuals face various types of discrimination at work, such as being pushed into low-wage jobs or being passed over for promotions

(Pichler & Holmes, 2017). Also, the Movement Advancement Project (2013) report highlights that LGBTQ+ individuals of color face additional difficulties in securing health insurance access and social security spousal and survivor benefits. Given the socio-economic upheaval in the transforming nature of work (Mor Barak, 2019), among several minority groups in organizations, LGBTQ+ individuals, in particular, experience various vulnerabilities, causing them to experience a high level of poverty (Walby, 2015).

Given the briefly described theoretical background of precarity, studying LGBTQ+ in precarious work arrangements can facilitate our understanding in two ways: first, to extend the theory of precarity in the light of unique experiences, barriers and challenges faced by LGBTQ+ subjects; second, to illuminate the political and social mechanisms explaining how and why the participation of such stigmatized and marginalized identities is high in precarious work settings.

3.3 LGBTQ+ and Precarious Work: The Turkish Context

LGBTQ+ individuals in Turkey face institutionalized discrimination in the social and organizational domains (Ozeren and Aydin, 2016). The main reason is due to political and social institutions that shape the living conditions of LGBTQ+ individuals in Turkey. In this section, we create a link between sexual and gender identity minorities and precarious work by considering a critical perspective from scholarly research and the report of LGBTQ+ Non-Governmental Organizations (NGOs) in Turkey. We introduce the Turkish context by considering macro-national and meso-organizational levels, respectively.

3.3.1 Macro-National Level: Role of Political and Social Institutions

At a macro-national level, political institutions include legislative structure, competition among political parties, and the types of government (Kim, 2011). The institutions create a social structure that has either inclusionary or exclusionary approaches to minority groups such as LGBTQ+ individuals by adopting discourses of political leaders in a ruling party. The positive or adverse discourses contribute to the institutionalization of equality among sexual and gender minority identities or discrimination against these groups. Also, religion and prejudicial beliefs play a critical role in shaping the aforementioned political discourses when the majority of individuals in society believe in certain religions. In the context of Turkey, the macro-national structure dominated by a pro-Islamic perspective has a conservative ruling party called Justice and Development Party *AK Parti in Turkish*. Even though Turkey has no official religion and has a secular state structure constitutionally, the current governmental regime adopts a religious perspective to interpret rights for LGBTQ+ individuals in Turkey (Uygur and Aydin, 2020). For instance, based on the report of Kara et al. (2020), there was a hate speech broadcast on April 24, 2020, during the Friday khutba in response to social media activism regarding LGBTQ+ children with the hashtag #thereareLGBTQ+children. Also, the report shows that even though there were criticisms of the Khutba, the government authorities supported the religious affairs administration. Thus, this situation contributed to the institutionalization of discrimination through discourses against LGBTQ+ individuals and the movement.

Research on human rights violations in Turkey (Kaos GL et al., 2014) demonstrates that state authorities adopt discriminative discourses on LGBTQ+ individuals in two ways: First, they consider sexual minorities as a group who have a sickness. Second, the sexual minorities are perceived as immoral against the commonly shared values of a society that comes from its traditional cultural and religious beliefs.

The macro-national context of Turkey has an exclusionary approach to sexual minorities, even though being an LGBTQ+ individual is not a crime under Turkish Law (Göçmen and Yılmaz, 2017). However, as Yilmaz (2013) states, the policy practitioners and judges use some legal phrases such as 'acts incompatible with public morality' against LGBTQ+ individuals. Such an interpretation of law creates a context that avoids recruiting LGBTQ+ individuals in governmental organizations that are in the control of the ruling party. However, the main opposition party, Republican People's Party ('Cumhuriyet Halk Partisi' in Turkish), raises equal rights for LGBTQ+ individuals and supports the movement by showing solidarity, such as publishing messages on social media during the month of Pride via the municipalities that belong to the main opposition party. Another wing of the opposition side, the Peoples' Democratic Party ('Halkların Demokratik Partisi' in Turkish), officially declares in its party program that discrimination against LGBTQ+ individuals is no different than a form of racism by raising the voice of the community and standing against hate crimes and violence against the LGBTQ+ people.

In order to legitimize the inclusion of LGBTQ+ individuals in social and political institutions, there are LGBTQ+ organizations in Turkey. They create a resistance to the current heterosexual dominance in social and political institutions (Aydin, 2017). This situation demonstrates that the macro-national level includes heterosexual dominance by having resistance from the LGBTQ+ movement. Thus, the current conditions result in precarious work for LGBTQ+ individuals in Turkey. This macro setting shapes the meso-organizational level that consists of the inclusion and exclusion of sexual minorities at work that we discuss in the following section.

3.3.2 Meso-Organizational Level: LGBTQ+ and Precarious Work in Organizations

Political and social institutions shape the employment of LGBTQ+ individuals who are visible because the institutions can create exclusionary mechanisms that prevent the employment of these individuals (Yılmaz and Göçmen, 2016). Since the Turkish context has adverse political and social discourses regarding the inclusion of LGBTQ+ individuals in work and social life, this situation creates a discriminative approach to sexual and gender identity minorities in the workplace (Aydin and Ozbilgin, 2019). As a result, many private companies do not prefer to employ LGBTQ+ individuals even though there are no legal restrictions (Duman, 2017). Instead, they raise some unrelated concerns such as lack of experience not to employ the individuals.

In Turkey, LGBTQ+ individuals face precarious work conditions when they prefer to become visible in public. For instance, the individuals who work in governmental institutions face the risk of being fired as the judges, practitioners, and managers in institutions consider it immoral behavior and against the cultural values of society (Kaos Gl et al., 2015). Unfortunately, some companies employ these same tactics against their LGBTQ+ employees, as it is common for conservative owners of such companies in Turkey to fire LGBTQ+ individuals (Ozduzen and Korkut, 2020).

The Pembe Hayat report (2019) shows that LGBTQ+ individuals face violence and discrimination in companies. For instance, the report tells a story of an individual who started to work for a well-known company in 2013. After becoming a transwoman in 2015, she faced verbal harassment at work by her colleagues. Thus, she was forced to resign from the organization. Such examples demonstrate the precarious nature of work conditions for sexual and minorities in Turkey. However, the LGBTQ+ movement created some areas of freedom for themselves because LGBTQ+ organizations, as NGOs, provide employment opportunities for sexual minorities (Hernik, 2008). The organizations create their budgets through organizing events and the funding opportunities that come from European Union projects. Since the budgets of such organizations do not come from the national budget, they can operate the NGOs and recruit LGBTQ+ individuals. The 'safe zones' provided by LGBT NGOs enable LGBTQ+ workers to cope to some degree with precarious work conditions within LGBTQ+ friendly workplaces.

The Turkish context indicates macro-national and meso-organizational dimensions that create both inclusionary and exclusionary societal approaches. While political parties (against LGBTQ individuals or support them) and religious perspectives have dominance in society for minority groups at the macro national level, NGOs, private and public organizations as a workplace are considered for meso-organizational level. Within the Turkish context, macro-national shapes meso-organizational level. For this reason, the dominance of exclusionary approaches, including discrimination against LGBTQ+ individuals in society, mostly leads these individuals to work in LGBTQ+ NGOs. However, since there are limited NGOs and employment opportunities, the Turkish context demonstrates many LGBTQ+ individuals tend to work in precarious work settings.

3.4 LGBTQ+ and Precarious Work: The US Context

The history of modern LGBTQ+ rights has been accompanied by great challenges and victories, such as the federal legalization of same-sex marriage in 2015 in the United States. Bell Hooks (2009) called transversal politics and coalition building anchored in engaging multiple group standpoints to advance social justice through intersectional knowledge projects. This was indeed the case with the advancement of the LGBTQ+ movement within the last several decades. However, while the US legalization of same-sex marriage is monumental, and allies of all types have assisted in the movement, there are still many issues that the LGBTQ+ community must work to overcome.

There is no doubt that the workplace can be a place of pride or heartache for most workers. Human Resources Management began to flourish as a field during the turn of the twentieth century in the United States and Europe. For the most part, employees were regarded primarily as parts of an assembly line for how work could be carried out in the most efficient ways. During this time period, LGBTQ+ workers had to remain closeted and invisible. Policies that governed workers did not, for the most part, consider them as important or essential. In fact, it is doubtful that workplaces considered their employees' economic well-being and safety until much later in the twentieth century. Though the presence of workplace unions was starting to appear as early as 1869 with the Knights of Labor, Fedrick Winslow Taylor's 1916 Principles of Scientific Management dominated workplace practices and policies (Shafritz, Ott & Yang, 2011). Taylor devised a theory that explained precisely how long a worker should take to do one task. Indeed, Taylor believed that workers could be used interchangeably. In other words, he thought that if workers were trained properly, they could do any job their coworkers were doing. This was a unique idea at the time since his theory assumed that workers were expendable and could be terminated at any point because another employee could do their job.

During the second half of the twentieth century, HRM developed with attention to employees and employee rights. Many rights were obtained due to unions and movements of the day. Today, there are several agreed-upon functions of HR in the United States. The most widely agreed-upon functions of Human Resource Management include: (1) Find and hire employees; (2) Ensure fairness and compliance; (3) Drive productivity and results; (4) Drive productivity and results; (5) Keep employees healthy and safe; (6) Optimize the organizational structure; (7) Coach, train, and develop staff; and (8) Promote best practices. These functions were centered on employees more ostensibly than previous management principles and practices. This fact is undoubtedly observable compared with the preceding decades. The Occupational Safety and Health Administration (OSHA) was formed on April 28, 1971, and is the US regulatory agency charged with overseeing employee rights (Rosner and Markowitz, 2020). OSHA ensures the physical well-being of all employees at work sites.

Despite the improvement in working conditions and the existence of federal agencies to oversee working conditions, many employees, particularly LGBTQ+ employees, still work in precarious work situations. LGBTQ+ individuals continue to face widespread discrimination in the workplace. Studies show that anywhere from 15 to 43 percent of gay people have experienced some form of discrimination and harassment in the workplace. Moreover, a staggering 90 percent of transgender workers report some form of harassment or mistreatment on the job. These workplace abuses pose a real and immediate threat to the economic security of LGBTQ+ workers (Burns and Krehely, 2011).

Many discrimination lawsuits are rooted in Title VII. For example, the EEOC, or Equal Employment Opportunity Commission, lists the following statement on their website. Title VII prohibits discrimination because of an 'individual's ... sex' 42 U.S.C. § 2000e-2(a)(1). In *Bostock v. Clayton County, Georgia,* No. 17–1618 (S. Ct. June 15, 2020)[1], the Supreme Court held that firing individuals because of their sexual orientation or transgender status violates Title VII's prohibition on discrimination because of sex. The Court reached its ruling by focusing on the plain text of Title VII and did not adopt other theories – such as sex stereotyping and associational discrimination – to reach its conclusion. As the Court explained, 'discrimination based on homosexuality or transgender status necessarily entails discrimination based on sex; the first cannot happen without the second.' For example, suppose an employer fires an employee because she is a woman married to a woman but would not do the same to a man married to a woman. In that case, the employer is taking action because of the employee's sex because the action would not have taken place but for the employee being a woman. Similarly, suppose an employer fires an employee because that person was identified as male at birth, but uses feminine pronouns and identifies now as a female. In that case, the employer is taking action against the individual because of sex since the action would not have been taken. Still, for the fact, the employee was originally identified as male (EEOC, 2021).

In 1988, Anne Hopkins sued her employer, Price Waterhouse, for denying her a promotion for two years in a row. Hopkins's lawsuit was that her employer alleged that she might consider acting more femininely and dressing in more feminine attire. This would include items such as wearing makeup and high-heel shoes. Hopkins was well qualified for the promotion having both a bachelor's degree and a master's degree in mathematics. In most years, she also outperformed her male colleagues at Price Waterhouse. In 1989 the Supreme Court ruled in Hopkins's favor as Price Waterhouse could not prove how gender positively or negatively impacted a person's employment. But equally as important, the courts articulated that Price Waterhouse could not prove without a reasonable shadow of a doubt that social psychological harm regarding sex-role stereotyping did not lead to sex discrimination under Title VII. Though Hopkins won the lawsuit, the entire experience traumatized her, and she never fully bounced back in her professional or personal life (Goldstein, 2006).

Another issue of workplace precarity for LGBTQ+ employees is a lack of access to workplace benefits. For example, some insurance companies do not cover the much-needed benefits such as hormone therapy or sex reassignment surgery for transgender employees. In 2020, Gee and Waldrop (2021) stated that workplace insurance covered around 49 percent of adults living in the United States, though other sources indicate that this amount is probably closer to 60 percent. This fact creates an even more challenging situation when LGBTQ+ workers have difficulty accessing healthcare needs via employer-provided coverage that is typically limited to full-time employees. In the United States, employer HR departments often negotiate insurance coverage for their organizations. To save money, many organizations opt out of insurance benefits often used by LGBTQ+ workers, thus leaving LGBTQ+ individuals to cover certain health-related medical expenses on their own.

The LGBTQ+ community has been the hardest hit by the HIV/AIDS virus, and even in the twentieth century, having and treating HIV is still stigmatized in the workplace. Precarious work disproportionately exacerbates the negative health outcomes for LGBTQ+ workers living with HIV/AIDS. Though there is currently no cure for HIV/AIDS, antiretroviral medications can suppress the virus and, in recent cases, keep the virus at long-term undetectable levels. However, these lifesaving medications are costly and are not always covered by employer-provided workplace health insurance plans. This can be detrimental to LGBTQ+ workers who need these drugs and cannot obtain them for free or at affordable prices via other programs or sources (Halkitis, 2013). Additionally, HIV/AIDS is now considered a chronic condition. Therefore, the challenging aspect of care and treatment becomes even more difficult for LGBTQ+ employees who do not have adequate workplace benefits or who have no benefits at all because they work in precarious jobs.

Despite recent advancements for LGBTQ+ individuals in the United States, the US workplace remains a precarious environment for far too many LGBTQ+ persons. Structural biases and institutionalized homophobia, and heterosexism remain embedded within the culture of many US organizations. As long as this is the case, LGBTQ+ workers will continue to suffer from precarious work arrangements in disproportionate numbers.

3.5 Conclusion

In this chapter, we discussed the unique challenges that LGBTQ+ workers face with precarious work conditions. Despite the incidences of precarious work arrangements skyrocketing for all workers in the United States and Turkey, LGBTQ+ workers are disproportionately represented in these labor conditions due to the widespread discrimination, bias, and lack of legal protections these communities notoriously face. Though some recent legal victories have proved employment protections for LGBTQ+ workers in the United States, such achievements do not appear to be on the horizon for LGBTQ+ workers in Turkey. Indeed, suppose countries are to remedy the disparate impact LGBTQ+ workers experience with precarious work. In that case, they must focus on passing vast and robust pro-LGBTQ laws in every aspect of human life, not simply concerning employment law.

At a macro-national level, the role of political and social institutions in creating exclusionary practices and discourses against LGBTQ+ employment, promotion and visibility in the workplace is so evident that many LGBTQ+ individuals in Turkey are compelled to develop a wide variety of identity management tactics (concealing own identities at work, passing as cis-heterosexual, etc.) to cope with precarious and vulnerable workplace conditions. For example, being an openly gay or lesbian in a public sector profession (such as a gay teacher or a police officer) is almost impossible. Due to the limited availability of permanent, secure job opportunities and tenure positions in the job market that LGBTQ+ people can apply for, they are likely to be employed in precarious work settings with short-term, temporary contracts. At a meso-organizational level, professional NGOs working in the field of human rights and LGBTQ+ activism, several private companies, and multinational corporations in Turkey that value equality, diversity, and inclusion in their policies (albeit very limited) create so-called 'safe zones' and LGBTQ+ friendly workplace atmosphere.

Despite the long-standing contested history of LGBTQ+ rights and recognitions in the United States (such as federal legalization of same-sex marriage) and relative progress made so far in terms of working conditions for sexual and gender identity minorities, LGBTQ+ people still continue to work in precarious situations without discrimination-free practices. One major issue that deepens their precariousness is that LGBTQ+ persons in the USA lack access to workplace benefits typically granted to full-time employees. Particularly, LGBTQ+ individuals of color experience additional challenges and vulnerabilities in securing health insurance access and social security spousal and survivor benefits. As the significant policy implication of this chapter, these benefits should be granted equally to LGBTQ+ employees as well as cis-heterosexual people in the workplace.

Given the fact that the level of employability of LGBTQ+ people is relatively high in particular sectors (such as beauty/cosmetics/fashion/sex work/entertainment) (Hill, 2009; Pichler & Holmes, 2017; Ragins, 2004), we argue that those careers are mostly precarious considering the nature of such work arrangements characterized by short-term/temporary contracts and insecure, unstable, and uncertain work conditions. However, the extant literature has not identified to what extent and why LGBTQ+ individuals are mostly engaged in precarious work arrangements. Examining LGBTQ+ in precarious work in this chapter sheds some light on the factors, processes, and underlying mechanisms leading to the higher participation of such stigmatized and marginalized identities in precarious work settings.

The existing literature on the theory of precarity mainly emphasizes the nature of work rather than the unique characteristics of the individuals. For this reason, the theory defines the context and the scope of precarious work based on workplace characteristics. This creates a lack of perspective on individuals who live in precarious working conditions. Thus, within the context of the present study, we highlight LGBTQ+ individuals as a strand of diversity that commits to considering precarious work in order to avoid the challenges that come from political, social, and economic contexts. Also, by adopting LGBTQ+ individuals as a strand of diversity that mostly lives in precarious working conditions, we demonstrate the characteristics and the factors that lead individuals to consider precarious working conditions. Furthermore, in this chapter, we unpack the underexplored characteristics of individuals in precarious working conditions who belong to a minority group in society. Thus, we demonstrate a missing link between diversity and the theory of precarity by highlighting the main drivers for committing to consider precarious work for individuals who belong to a minority group.

We suggest EDI (equality, diversity, and inclusion) scholars scrutinize empirically why and how LGBTQ+ individuals are engaged in precarious work by also taking into account the contextual challenges and dynamics as a potentially relevant research topic for future studies. This chapter highlights that LGBTQ+ individuals, to a great extent, suffer negatively due to precarious work arrangements in both country contexts. However, we still need to know in-depth about personality and individual differences, structural conditions, cultural issues and situational factors that moderate the relationship between precarious work and negative outcomes. Further research is suggested to examine the degree to which these factors converge and diverge with respect to LGBTQ+ workers and their cis-heterosexual counterparts. Finally, we encourage researchers to investigate the macro- and micro-level factors that would impact policy adoption of precarious work mitigation initiatives for LGBTQ+ communities.

References

Albelda, R., Bell-Pasht, A., & Konstantinidis, C. (2020). Gender and precarious work in the United States: Evidence from the contingent work supplement 1995–2017. *Review of Radical Political Economics, 52*(3), 542–563. https://doi.org/10.1177/0486613419891175

Anteby, M., & Anderson, C. (2014). The shifting landscape of LGBT organizational research. *Research in Organizational Behavior, 34*, 3–25. https://doi.org/10.1016/j.riob.2014.08.001

Aydin, E. (2017). 'Problems and suggestions': Non-governmental organisations of sexual orientation minorities in the context of Turkey and United Kingdom. In Potocan, V., Üngan M. C., Nedelko, Z. (eds.) *Handbook of Research on Managerial Solutions in Non-Profit Organizations* (pp. 232–252). IGI Global.

Aydın, E., & Ozbilgin, M. F. (2019). Exploring the interplay between the aims and the context of LGBTI+ organising: The case of LGBTI+

organisations in Turkey and the UK. *LGBT+ Studies Turkey, Transnational Press, London, 1*, 9–32.

Badgett, M. V. L., Lau, H., Sears, B., & Ho, D. (2007). Bias in the Workplace: Consistent Evidence of Sexual Orientation and Gender Identity Discrimination. In *The Williams Institute on Sexual Orientation Law and Public Policy*. The Williams Institute. https://escholarship.org/content/qt5h3731xr/qt5h3731xr.pdf

Bauman, Z. (2000). *Liquid Modernity*. Cambridge: Polity Press.

Beck, U. (1992). *The Risk Society: Toward A New Modernity*. London: Sage.

Bidwell, M., Briscoe, F., Fernandez-Mateo, I., & Sterling, A. (2013). The employment relationship and inequality: How and why changes in employment practices are reshaping rewards in organizations. *Academy of Management Annals, 7*(1), 61–121. https://doi.org/10.1080/19416520.2013.761403

Bourdieu, P. (1998). *Acts of Resistance: Against the Tyranny of the Market* (R. Nice, Trans.). Cambridge: Polity Press.

Burns, C., & Krehely, J. (2011). Gay and transgender people face high rates of workplace discrimination and harassment. *Center for American Progress, 1*(1), 1–4.

Butler, J. (2015). Foreward. In Lorey I. (Ed.), *State of Insecurity: Government of the Precarious* (pp. vii–xi). London: Verso.

Campbell, I., & Price, R. (2016). Precarious work and precarious workers: Towards an improved conceptualisation. *Economic and Labour Relations Review, 27*(3), 314–332. https://doi.org/10.1177/1035304616652074

Catalyst. (2020). *Lesbian, gay, bisexual, and transgender workplace issues: Quick take*. www.catalyst.org/research/lesbian-gay-bisexual-and-trans gender-workplace-issues/

Curtin, M., & Sanson, K. (2016). Precarious creativity: Global media, local labor. In Curti (Ed.), *Precarious Creativity: Global Media, Local Labor*. University of California Press.

Duman, E. (2017). Ayrımcılık Yasağı ve Türkiye İnsan Hakları ve Eşitlik Kurumu Raporu. Pembe Hayat and Kaos GL.

EEOC (2021) Knowing your rights. EEOC website: www.eeoc.gov/laws/guidance/what-you-should-know-eeoc-and-protections-lgbt-workers.

Eckes, S. E. (2007). The legal 'rights' of LGBT educators in public and private schools. *Texas Journal on Civil Liberties & Civil Rights, 23*(1), 29–54.

Emre, O., Polat, V., & Duman, Y. S. (2017). Precarious work in Turkey: A comparison with EU member countries. *Journal of Business Research Turk, 9*(4), 436–454. https://doi.org/10.20491/isarder.2017.340

Friedman, M. S., Marshal, M. P., Guadamuz, T. E., Wei, C., Wong, C. F., Saewyc, E. M., & Stall, R. (2011). A meta-analysis of disparities in childhood sexual abuse, parental physical abuse, and peer victimization among sexual minority and sexual nonminority individuals. *American Journal of Public Health*, *101*(8), 1481–1494. https://doi.org/10.2105/AJPH.2009.190009

Gedro, J. (2010). The lavender ceiling atop the global closet: Human resource development and lesbian expatriates. *Human Resource Development Review*, *9*(4), 385–404. https://doi.org/10.1177/1534484310380242

Gee and Waldrop (2021). Policies to improve health insurance coverage as America recovers from COVID-19. Center for American Progress.

Goldstein, L. (2006). Gender stereotyping and the workplace: Price Waterhouse v.

Griffin, R. W., & Lopez, Y. P. (2005). 'Bad Behavior' in Organizations: A Review and Typology for Future Research. *Journal of Management*, *31*(6), 988–1005. https://doi.org/10.1177/0149206305279942

Guittar, N. A., & Rayburn, R. L. (2016). Coming out: The career management of one's sexuality. *Sexuality and Culture*, *20*(2), 336–357. https://doi.org/10.1007/s12119-015-9325-y

Halkitis, P.N. (2013). *The AIDS Generation: Stories and Survival of Resilience*. The AIDS Generation: Stories and Survival of Resilience.

Hayat, P. (2019). 2019 yılında Translara Yönelik Gerçekleşen Hak İhlalleri Raporu. Pembe Hayat LGBTI Derneği.

Hernik, J. (2008) Polish Non-Governmental Organisations (NGOs) as workplace resources: from the point of view of provinces with the highest unemployment. *International Journal of Trade and Global Markets*, *1*(3), 298–305.

Hill, R. J. (2009). Incorporating queers: Blowback, backlash, and other forms of resistance to workplace diversity initiatives that support sexual minorities. *Advances in Developing Human Resources*, *11*(1), 37–53. https://doi.org/10.1177/1523422308328128

Holmes IV, O. (2019). The antecedents and outcomes of heteronormativity in organizations. In *Oxford Encyclopedia of Business and Management* (pp. 1–21). Oxford University Press. https://doi.org/10.1093/acrefore/9780190224851.013.57

Holmes IV, O. (2020). Sexuality blindness: A new frontier of diversity resistance. In K. M. Thomas (ed.), *Diversity Resistance in Organizations* (2nd ed., pp. 34–57). Lawrence Erlbaum Associates.

Holmes IV, O., Lopiano, G., & Hall, E. V. (2019). A review of compensatory strategies to mitigate bias. *Personnel Assessment and Decisions*, *5*(2), 23–34.

Holmes IV, O., Whitman, M. V., Campbell, K. S., & Johnson, D. E. (2016). Exploring the social identity threat response. *Equality, Diversity*

and Inclusion: An International Journal, 35(3), 205–220. https://doi
.org/10.1108/EDI-08-2015-0068

Hooks, B. (2009). *Belonging: A Culture of Place.* New York: Taylor and
Francis Press.

Hopkins, 1989. *The Constitutional and Legal Rights of Women,* 3rd ed.
Los Angeles:Roxbury, 2006. 167–175.

Human Dignity Trust. (2021). *Maps of Countries that Criminalise LGBT People.* www.humandignitytrust.org/lgbt-the-law/map-of-criminalisation/

Hwahng, S. J., & Lin, A. J. (2009). The health of lesbian, gay, bisexual,
transgender, queer, and questioning people. In C. Trinh-Shevrin, N. Islam,
& M. Rey (Eds.), *Asian American Communities and Health: Context,
Research, Policy, and Action.* (Vol. 7, pp. 226–282). Jossey-Bass. https://
doi.org/10.1016/B978-0-12-373580-5.50043-0

Kalleberg, A. L. (2009). Precarious work, insecure workers: Employment
relations in transition. *American Sociological Review, 74*(1), 1–22.

Kalleberg, A. L. (2011). *Good Jobs, Bad Jobs: The Rise of Polarized and
Precarious Employment Systems in the United States, 1970s to 2000s.*
New York, NY: Russell Sage Foundation.

Kalleberg, A. L., & Hewison, K. (2013). Precarious work and the challenge for Asia. *American Behavioral Scientist, 57*(3), 271–288. https://
doi.org/10.1177/0002764212466238

Kalleberg, A. L., & Vallas, S. P. (2017). Probing precarious work: Theory, research, and politics. *Research in the Sociology of Work, 31,* 1–30.
https://doi.org/10.1108/S0277-283320170000031017

Kaos GL Association. (2014). *Human Rights Violations of LGBT Individuals in Turkey.* https://ilga.org/wp-content/uploads/2016/02/Shadow-report-16.pdf

Kaos GL Association. (2020). *Homophobia and transphobia based hate
crimes in Turkey.* https://kaosgldernegi.org/images/library/2020nefret-suclari-raporu-2019-eng.pdf

Kaos, GL, LGBT News, and IGLHRC. (2015). *Türkiye'deki LGBT Yurttaşlara Yönelik İnsan Hakları İhlalleri.* Ayrıntı Basımevi.

Kara, Y., Kır, H., Özgün, Y. & Okumuş, E. (2020). *Pandemi Sürecinde
LGBTİ+'Ların Sosyal Hizmetlere Erişimi Araştırma Raporu.* Sosyal Politika, Cinsiyet Kimliği ve Cinsel Yönelim Çalışmaları Derneği, İstanbul.

Kessler, R. C., Mickelson, K. D., & Williams, D. R. (1999). The prevalence,
distribution, and mental health correlates of perceived discrimination in
the United States. *Journal of Health and Social Behavior, 40*(3), 208–230.
https://doi.org/10.2307/2676349

Kim, J. (2011). Political institutions and public R&D expenditures in democratic countries. *International Journal of Public Administration, 34*(13),
843–857.

Kollen, T. (2016). *Sexual Orientation and Transgender Issues in Organizations: Global Perspectives on LGBT Workforce Diversity*. (T. Kollen (ed.)). Springer International Publishing. https://doi.org/10.1007/978-3-319-29623-4

Lane, C. (2011). *A Company of One: Insecurity, Independence and the New World of White Collar Unemployment*. Ithaca, NY: ILR Press.

Lindsey, A., King, E., Gilmer, D., Sabat, I., & Ahmad, A. (2020). The benefits of identity integration across life domains. *Journal of Homosexuality*, 67(8), 1164–1172.

McKee-Ryan, F. M., & Harvey, J. (2011). 'I have a job, but …': A review of underemployment. *Journal of Management*, 37(4), 962–996. https://doi.org/10.1177/0149206311398134

Meyer, I. H. (2003). Prejudice, social stress, and mental health in lesbian, gay, and bisexual populations: Conceptual issues and research evidence. *Psychological Bulletin*, 129(5), 674–697. https://doi.org/10.1037/a0039906

Mirowsky, J. and Ross, C. E. (2003). *Social Causes of Psychological Distress*. Hawthorne, NY: Transaction Publishers, Aldine de Gruyter.

Mor Barak, M. E. (2019). Erecting walls versus tearing them down: Inclusion and the (false) paradox of diversity in times of economic upheaval. *European Management Review*, 16(4), 937–955. https://doi.org/10.1111/emre.12302

Movement Advancement Project. (2013). '2013 National LGBT Movement Report: A Financial Overview of Leading Advocacy Organizations in the LGBT Movement.' www.lgbtmap.org/file/2013-national-lgbt-movement-report.pdf

Okulicz-Kozaryn, A., Holmes IV, O., & Avery, D. R. (2014). The subjective well-being political paradox: Happy welfare states and unhappy liberals. *Journal of Applied Psychology*, 99(6), 1300–1308. https://doi.org/10.1037/a0037654

Out Leadership. (2019). *LGBT+ Business Climate Score. CEO Brief*. https://outleadership.com/wp-content/uploads/2018/10/OL-CEO-Brief_Turkey.pdf

Ozduzen, O., & Korkut, U. (2020). Enmeshing the mundane and the political: Twitter, LGBTI+ outing and macro-political polarisation in Turkey. *Contemporary Politics*, 26(5), 493–511.

Ozeren, E., & Aydin, E. (2016). What does being LGBT mean in the workplace? A comparison of LGBT equality in Turkey and the UK. In *Research Handbook of International and Comparative Perspectives on Diversity Management*. Edward Elgar Publishing.

Ozturk, M. B., & Tatli, A. (2016). Gender identity inclusion in the workplace: Broadening diversity management research and practice through the case of transgender employees in the UK. *International Journal of Human Resource Management, 27*(8), 781–802. https://doi.org/10.1080/09585192.2015.1042902

Pichler, S. (2007). Heterosexism in the workplace. *Sloan Work and Family Research Network, Work-Family Encyclopedia.* Chestnut Hill, MA: Sloan Work and Family Research Network. www.researchgate.net/profile/Shaun-Pichler/publication/323384558_Heterosexism_in_the_Workplace/links/5a91b0f745851535bcd79ec9/Heterosexism-in-the-Workplace.pdf

Pichler, S., & Holmes IV, O. (2017). An investigation of fit perceptions and promotability in sexual minority candidates. *Equality, Diversity and Inclusion: An International Journal, 36*(7), 628–646. https://doi.org/10.1108/EDI-02-2017-0037

Rabelo, V. C., & Cortina, L. M. (2013). Two sides of the same coin: Gender harassment and heterosexist harassment in LGBTQ work lives. *Law and Human Behavior, 38,* 1–22.

Ragins, B. R. (2004). Sexual orientation in the workplace: The unique work and career experiences of gay, lesbian, and bisexual workers. *Research in Personnel and Human Resources Management, 23,* 35–120.

Ragins, B. R., & Cornwell, J. M. (2001). Pink triangles: Antecedents and consequences of perceived workplace discrimination against gay and lesbian employees. *Journal of Applied Psychology, 86*(6), 1244–1261.

Ragins, B. R., Singh, R., & Cornwell, J. M. (2007). Making the invisible visible: Fear and disclosure of sexual orientation at work. *Journal of Applied Psychology, 92*(4), 1103–1118. https://doi.org/10.1037/0021-9010.92.4.1103

Ronan, W. (2020). *New FBI hate crime reports shows increase in anti-LGBTQ attacks.* Human Rights Campaign Press Releases. www.hrc.org/press-releases/new-fbi-hate-crimes-report-shows-increases-in-anti-LGBTQ-attacks

Rosner, D., & Markowitz, G. (2020). A short history of occupational safety and health in the United States. *American Journal of Public Health, 110*(5), 622–628.

Shafritz, J. M., Ott, J. S., and Yang, J. S. (2011). *Classics of Organization Theory. Wadsworth Cengage Learning* (7th ed.). Boston: Wadsworth Cengage Learning.

Tilcsik, A., Anteby, M., & Knight, C. R. (2015). Concealable stigma and occupational segregation: Toward a theory of gay and lesbian occupations. *Administrative Science Quarterly, 60*(3), 446–481. https://doi.org/10.1177/0001839215576401

Uygur, S., and Aydin, E. (2020). Religious diversity in the workplace. In Syed, J. and Ozbilgin, M. (eds.) *Managing Diversity and Inclusion: An International Perspective* (pp. 261–282). Sage.

Vallas, S. (2015). Accounting for precarity. *Contemporary Sociology: A Journal of Reviews, 44*(4), 463–469. https://doi.org/10.1177/00943061 15588484a

Vosko, L. (2010). *Managing the Margins: Gender, Citizenship, and the International Regulation of Precarious Employment*. Oxford University Press.

Walby, S. (2015). *Crisis*. Cambridge: Polity Press.

Wang, M., & Wanberg, C. R. (2017). 100 years of applied psychology research on individual careers: From career management to retirement. *Journal of Applied Psychology, 102*(3), 546–563. https://doi.org/10.1037/apl0000143

Westergaard-Nielsen, N., ed. (2008). *Low-Wage Work in Denmark*. New York: Russell Sage Foundation.

Wilson, S. and Ebert, N. (2013). Precarious work: economic, sociological and political perspectives. *The Economic and Labour Relations Review, 24*(3), 263–278. https://doi.org/10.1177/1035304613500434

Yılmaz, V. (2013). The new constitution of Turkey: a blessing or a curse for LGBT citizens? *Turkish Policy Quarterly, 11*(4), 131–140.

Yılmaz, V., & Göçmen, İ. (2016). Denied citizens of Turkey: experiences of discrimination among LGBT individuals in employment, housing and health care. *Gender, Work & Organization, 23*(5), 470–488.

4 | Age, Gender, and Precarity
The Experience of Late Career Self-Employment

ELINA MELIOU AND OLIVER MALLETT

4.1 Introduction

As the populations of the world's largest economies age, such as in Japan, the UK, and Germany (United Nations, 2019), extending lifespans are leading to significant pension shortfalls, accelerating a worsening pension crisis (Zalewska, 2018; Flood, 2020), and resulting in many people choosing or needing to work longer (Krekula and Vickerstaff, 2020; Ekerdt, 2010). Yet, older workers are frequently excluded from work altogether or moved into relatively low-skill jobs that contain little scope for financial and other rewards (Rudman and Aldrich 2021; Riach, 2007). The challenges can be heightened further for some older workers with differential social markers and resources. Research has shown how the experiences of older women have been discussed in terms of the 'double jeopardy' of gender discrimination and ageism (Duncan and Loretto, 2004), producing intersectional inequalities related to the quality and possibility of extended work (Bowman et al., 2017). These trends, in a context of increasingly individualised risk and responsibility, have led older workers to constitute a part of the modern 'precariat' where precarity in everyday life is marked by insecurity, instability, and lack of time control (Standing, 2011). This emphasises the importance of understanding the sense of precariousness experienced by older people in the context of increased pressures to continue working (Lain et al., 2019).

Self-employment has been proposed as a way for older workers to escape discrimination and disadvantage in the workplace, to maximise the potential for flexibility and as part of the changing nature of work that can support the extension of working lives (OECD, 2019). Self-employment can offer older women the potential for autonomy, empowerment, and self-fulfilment (Meliou and Mallett, 2021).

However, self-employment can also be an experience of precarity, self-exploitation, and struggle where many businesses fail (Meliou et al, 2019; MacDonald, 1996). The shift of the responsibility for ensuring adequate work and financial resources for later life onto older workers (Phillipson, Shepherd, Robinson, and Vickerstaff, 2018; Riach and Loretto, 2009) has ignored deeply embedded social structures and asymmetrical power relations that produce and legitimise social inequality (McKie, Biese and Jyrkinen 2013; Ogbor, 2000). An intersectional perspective attuned to 'the problem of sameness and difference and its relation to power' (Cho, Crenshaw and McCall, 2013: 795) is, therefore, axiomatic in order to understand the experiences of late career self-employment.

In this chapter, we first offer a background to the precarity in employment that older workers experience and provide insights into the societal and organisational structures and norms that shape ageing in employment and everyday life. We then adopt an intersectional perspective to theorise the precarity experienced by older self-employed women. Previous studies of self-employed women have tended to focus on women as parents (e.g., deriving the compound 'mumpreneur') and often at an earlier stage of their lives. Studies of self-employed older people have tended to focus on men (Mallett and Wapshott, 2015a). This has left self-employed older women invisible in the literature and our study addresses this by stressing the significance of considering the intersection of age and gender to study the experiences of older women in self-employment. Our theorisation enables us to simultaneously consider the interplay between individual agency and context to shed light on privileges and disadvantages that shape precarity employment for older self-employed women. To illustrate our arguments, we present three biographical cases of older self-employed women in the United Kingdom. Finally, we discuss the implications of age, gender, and self-employment and conclude with a call for inclusive policy to tackle precarity in this context.

4.2 Background on Age, Ageing, and Precarity in Employment

Precarity is defined as the development of working situations that lack predictability and security and is extended into life worlds characterised by uncertainty and increased vulnerability (Hewison, 2016;

Kalleberg, 2011; Waite, 2009). This chapter adopts the general term 'older workers' to encompass those in their fifties and beyond engaged in paid work (Department for Work and Pensions, 2017). It is this group that, whether through choice or as a reaction to the challenges it faces, stands to radically reinvent assumptions about retirement. In many wealthy economies' improvements in health, longevity, and the transitions from physical labour to sedentary, white-collar work may permit people to work beyond traditional limits imposed by physical change (Adler and Hilber, 2009). However, there are also pressures to work longer for those insecure and concerned about the afford-ability of a longer life (Johnson, 2009). The transition to retirement is best considered as not being a discrete event but as a complex process that is experienced very differently across society (Zissimopoulos and Karoly, 2007)

However, despite the practical possibility and availability of a will-ing older workforce, employers resistant to engaging or retaining these workers will limit the prospects for this form of employment (Harris et al, 2017). Age discrimination creates an unfavourable environment for older workers (Johnson, 2009; Adler and Hilber, 2009; Neumark, 2009). For example, recruitment and selection processes, along with training and development opportunities, have been identified as major sites for discrimination. In her analysis of recruitment literature from 'Foodmall' targeting the over-50s, Riach (2007) found that older workers were cast exclusively in low-paid service roles. The discourse that surrounds the creation and recruitment of these types of roles contribute to the social construction of limited/limiting stereotypes of older workers. Riach argues that, in this way, older workers are marginalised from other, more engaging employment opportunities available to their younger colleagues. There are fears that exclusion in the workplace will leave many older people 'too old to work and too young to die' (Freedman, 2007: 43).

The traditional business case for employing older workers has proven problematic (Duncan, 2003). Previous forms of equal opportu-nities legislation have demonstrated that legal enforcement is unlikely to bring about significant changes in the mindsets of businesses (Beck, 2011). Instead, it may simply prompt superficial compliance and quota filling (Neumark, 2009). Some employers actively encourage older workers to join their workforce, but their approach has been criticised for reinforcing the boundaries to equal participation in the labour market (Riach, 2007). In the healthcare sector, the desire to retain older workers has been found to be driven primarily by a need to address staff shortages with older workers, therefore, considered as marginal or non-integral (Moore, 2009).

Discrimination and disadvantage in the workplace, combined with other powerful factors, has led to 'increased insecurity in later life [...] associated with economic pressures on public services, precarious forms of employment, and negative perceptions about the implications of population aging' (Grenier et al., 2020: 620). Focusing in particular on the unemployed, Ainsworth and Hardy (2008) explored how age implies a negative characteristic in relation to employment and enterprise, even among those charged with helping the older unemployed find work. Ageing has become characterised as a 'problem' (Ainsworth and Hardy, 2009: 1200) and older workers are thrust into an identity constructed around a 'deficit model' (Loretto and White, 2006) of ageing and, restrained by the discourses surrounding this type of model, finding themselves in an 'identity cul-de-sac' (Ainsworth and Hardy, 2009: 1200). Factors relating to capital such as qualifications, income level, occupational level, and gender all have a bearing on late career employment (McNair, 2006; Moore, 2009). These factors are clustered in such a way that both the affluent and the poor may remain in work but, crucially, for different reasons.

'Older women' are continuing their working lives beyond their fifties as a result of the demographic and pension changes that increasingly defer retirement (Kerr and Miftari, 2017; Bohlinger and van Loo, 2010). However, government policies and efforts to prolong working lives may contrast with the realities that older women encounter in the workplace (Atkinson et al, 2015). Studies of age and gender have demonstrated how labour market structures (Moore, 2009), age norms of retirement (Radl, 2012), and standardised transition patterns (Kohli, 2007) constrain women's late career employment prospects. Duncan and Loretto (2004) discuss 'gendered ageism' in reference to their finding that older women disproportionately experience ageist attitudes and age discrimination in employment compared to older men, reflecting the established gender segregation of the workforce as a whole (Foweracker and Cutcher, 2015). In turn, unsympathetic organisational cultures to those perceived as lacking youthful vigour (Ainsworth and Hardy, 2008) reflect the significance of aesthetic labour (Witz et al, 2003) as 'the "right" look relies on a display of

the culturally approved characteristics [...] within and upon the body'
(Cutcher and Riah, 2017:165). Invariably, the increased importance
of image and appearance in the workplace represent a real barrier for
older women (Hockey and James, 2003).

To understand the experiences of older women it is important
not to simply consider people in a fixed state of being 'older' but to
consider their experiences in the context of the ageing process. This
understanding challenges the dominant view of growing older as a
break with the past (Dumas and Laberge, 2005). It moves us towards
an understanding of the different developments and changes in the
body's functions over time: the losses, the gains, and the perceptions
resulting from these changes (Austad, 1997). Ageing takes place at the
site of the body and embodiment necessarily brings with it the social
experience of ageing (Hockey and James, 2003). We reflect on who we
are as 'embodied agents' (Crossley, 2006) and communicate to others
through our embodied practices (Shilling, 2007). Ageing thus may be
viewed as an ongoing process of accumulation of gender scripts, class
experiences, ethnicity, and organisational values that are mapped onto
the body (Riach and Cutcher, 2014).

Without a viable model of what is appropriate for accessing or
remaining in challenging job roles, older women might struggle to see
past the 'choice' of total retirement or Foodmall-style top-up jobs. One
proposed solution to the precarity arising from the age discrimination
and exclusion older women face in the workplace is for them to pursue self-employment (Lewis and Walker, 2011; Hitachi Capital, 2017;
Jones, 2017; OECD, 2019; Abraham, Hershbein and Houseman,
2020; Whiting and Pritchard, 2020). Older workers pursuing self-
employment at this stage of their careers have increased in prominence
and come to be known by a variety of terms including olderpreneurs
(Mallett and Wapshott, 2015a), senior entrepreneurs (Perenyi, Zolin
and Maritz, 2018), grey entrepreneurs (Weber and Schaper, 2004),
or 'Wearies' (working entrepreneurial and active retirees, in discourse
analysed by Whiting and Pritchard, 2020).

Self-employment has, in many economies, grown in economic and
social significance, constituting an important proportion of employment. Policy agendas have extended to target those under-represented
in the statistics; they are the 'missing entrepreneurs' (OECD, 2019)
from social groups that are less engaged in self-employment than
might be expected. This missing entrepreneur agenda has identified

a lack of older self-employed women where there are lower rates of self-employment amongst the over-50s compared with younger age groups (Levesque and Minniti, 2006) and women reportedly make up only 25 per cent of the over-50s in self-employment (Bachelor, 2013). To date, studies of older women at work have mostly explored their careers and experiences within traditional organisational settings (Jyrkinen and McKie, 2012; Moore, 2009). It is, however, recognised that 'individual experiences of the workplace can be qualitatively very different, reflecting unique, spatially and temporally situated combinations of the intertwining systems of age and gender' (Spedale et al, 2014). Through the association of self-employment with a specifically youthful energy and optimism and the presumption that women are in their reproductive age during their working lives, many women and their experiences are left out (Meliou et al, 2019).

While some accounts of the potential for self-employment are positive and have emphasised the potential for flexibility, autonomy, and self-fulfilment it is important to note that, for many of those seeking self-employment in response to unemployment, marginalisation or social exclusion, they are not running to enterprise but away from a lack of alternatives as a means of survival (MacDonald, 1996). In this way, it is vital that precarity is a central part of debates about older women and self-employment.

4.3 Theorizing Precarity for Self-Employed Older Women

The experiences of older women have been discussed in terms of the 'double jeopardy' of gender discrimination and ageism, including in studies of self-employed older women. However, the positionality involved in intersections such as that of age and gender are not simply additive (ageism + sexism). An additive approach can lead to studies where women's 'experiences of phenomenon, such as retirement, are interpreted in relation to assumptions based on men' (Krekula, 2007: 160). It is important that we do not simply add to studies of self-employed women other forms of experience or discrimination identified in relation to age (and often to self-employed older men).

Intersectional approaches have sought to treat, for example race and gender, not as mutually exclusive but to bring intersectional positions, such as 'black women', in from the margins (Crenshaw, 1991).

An intersectional approach engages with the multidimensionality of experience, acknowledging the simultaneity of privilege and oppression, therefore going beyond additive considerations of analytical distinctions. It understands age and gender as mutually constitutive and often intertwined with class or race/ethnicity, attending to the heterogeneity of experiences in relation to multiple structural and cultural elements that produce specific social outcomes (Anthias, 2013) while also solidifying the structural and cultural barriers, raising broader issues of social organisation and representation. It leads us to explore how individuals 'do' being an older woman in self-employment with more nuanced attention to what this positionality might involve in terms of resources: that is, resources that enable (or hinder) access to opportunities or actual material goods – and experiences of work (Risman, 1998).

Notwithstanding the structural inequalities self-employed women face (Ahl, 2006; Ahl and Marlow, 2012), it has been argued that being older may be an advantage, due to experience, resources, and networks and that the 'entrepreneurship domain appears somewhat liberated from the age-related discrimination compared to the domain of occupational employment' (Perenyi, Zolin and Maritz, 2018: 85). However, it is important not to assume that all older women have the skillsets and resources applicable to self-employment. For example, some women may not have the financial independence, freedom from caring responsibilities or the experiences necessary to contribute to their human capital (Jayawarna et al., 2014; Tomlinson and Colgan, 2014). Such life circumstances may be seen as entrepreneurial resources unequally distributed across society. Some older women, especially those with less prominent businesses, who do not seek business support services or whose businesses fail, risk 'invisibility' (Krekula, 2007: 158) in theory and research on self-employment. It is not enough to identify an intersection of age and gender amongst a section of the self-employed, an intersectional analysis must tackle 'the problem of sameness and difference and its relation to power' (Cho, Crenshaw and McCall, 2013: 795).

An intersectionality approach to understanding precarity and self-employed older women is important due to its highlighting 'how single-axis thinking undermines legal thinking, disciplinary knowledge production, and struggles for social justice' (Cho, Crenshaw and McCall 2013: 787). In their review of research on ageing and precarity, Grenier et al. (2020) highlight articles that emphasise 'the detrimental effects of low educational attainment, working conditions, and low-paid work carried out by visible minority women' (p. 626). There is a risk of 'blind spots' in research on self-employment, especially if minority women are not included in sampling frames. Further, the limited research on self-employed older women focuses predominantly on their motivations and hopes of entering self-employment (e.g., Hodges, 2012; McKie, Biese and Jyrkinen, 2013; Tomlinson and Colgan, 2014), lacking an understanding of the day-to-day realities of self-employment and the potential for precarity.

Motivation studies have highlighted the push factor of discrimination in employment experienced by older women driving them towards self-employment where they identify greater possibilities of autonomy and personal success (see, e.g., Tomlinson and Colgan's (2014) study of older women considering the transition into self-employment). This has been built upon by Meliou and Mallett (2021) who identify the emancipatory and empowering potential of self-employment for older women's longer-term experience of the practice of self-employment. Meliou and Mallett (p. 21) identify the 'the possibility of achieving forms of expression, learning and solidarity' through self-employment.

However, there are potential dangers in such accounts of marginalising those self-employed older women who experience precarity and insecurity. In empirically identifying the potential available in self-employment for some older women it is important that this does not become generalised into a policy solution for the challenges many older women may face. For example, while Tomlinson and Colgan's research produces invaluable insights into motivations for self-employment it is worth noting that, when the researchers followed up on the women's progress several years later, none of them had been successful in establishing a sustainable business. As Tomlinson and Colgan (2014: 1673) state, 'it is inappropriate to make generalised statements about their needs, or about the particular advantages or disadvantages [their participants] share'. Other, potentially exclusionary positionalities, such as class, may compound particular challenges while limiting certain opportunities (McMullin and Cairney, 2004; Moore, 2009). The degree these barriers are able to be addressed varies greatly and may lead to a very different experience in self-employment for older women.

Focusing on the successes and obscuring the experiences of others is particularly dangerous in an existing context of individualisation and responsibilisation of the risks increasingly associated with older age. As Whiting and Pritchard (2020) emphasise, 'the construction of retirement as a period of self-sufficient productivity means older people are on their own now'. While we must attend to agency and not theorise self-employed older women, or other older workers within the precariat, as passive (Lain et al., 2019), nor should we over-state the potential for the individual to overcome all obstacles as is sometimes represented in discourses surrounding self-employment and entrepreneurship. The 'privileged entrepreneur' (Parry and Mallett, 2016) can be seen as 'pushed' into self-employment, not out of economic necessity, but rather from a lack of self-fulfilment from their employed work. For those individuals with a successful career behind them, a strong financial imperative may not be present. For such individuals the pursuit of financial gain may not be a sufficient motivation, and they will be seeking to fulfil other personal goals.

However, contrary to a dominant view of older entrepreneurs as advantaged by financial resources, limited family responsibilities, accumulated stocks of human capital and experience (Jayawarna et al., 2014; Kautonen et al., 2008; Singh and DeNoble, 2003), the existence and interaction of the challenges faced by many older people highlight how the processes of entrepreneurship in the context of pending retirement can be messy, complex and highly emotional (Mallett and Wapshott, 2015b; Meliou and Mallett, 2021). Importantly, those most precarious due to discrimination, social isolation, fears of pension poverty and insecurity may be those least likely to be equipped to succeed in self-employment.

Drawing on a qualitative study of older women in the United Kingdom, in this chapter, we explore how older women with different life histories negotiate ageing and enact self-employment. We selected three cases to illustrate how older women experience and manage precarity leading to the realisation of self-employment while seeking to satisfy concerns emergent from their life stage: that is, the exclusion at work they face during their life course (Radl, 2012). The three case studies presented below extend existing research by showing how the multifaceted experience of ageing, as an experiential, embodied process across the life course variously shapes self-employment activity, experiences, and outcomes.

4.4 Methodology

Drawing on a qualitative study of older women in the United Kingdom, in this chapter, we explore how older women with different life histories negotiate ageing and enact self-employment. We selected three cases to illustrate how older women, who started their business at the age of fifty and beyond, experience and manage precarity leading to the realisation of self-employment while seeking to satisfy concerns emergent from their life stage: that is, the exclusion at work they face during their life course (Radl, 2012). The biographical interviews were conducted as part of a larger project focusing on the lives of self-employed women. For this larger project, access was gained through a UK university business network and formal and informal women entrepreneurs' networks. Additionally, we used snowball techniques to identify and acquire suitable interview participants. Interviews were in-depth, recorded and transcribed verbatim. Participants reflected upon themselves in relation to their work and life situations explaining how they made decisions and their current understanding of employment and personal life in the context they reside. The three case studies presented below extend existing research by showing how the multifaceted experience of ageing, as an experiential, embodied process across the life course variously shapes self-employment activity, experiences, and outcomes.

4.5 Three Case Studies

Case 1 Jessie- 'Nobody Is Going to Employ a Woman of My Age, with a Criminal Record'

Jessie, a black, working class, London-born woman, with no formal education, was in her sixties when she started her current company – a social enterprise that 'helps women out of prison'. Following forty years in corporate organisations in 'a semi-management roles', she was made redundant and started a property company with the aim 'to retire on that money or build a house'. A market crash and untrustworthy client relationships resulted in Jessie's incarceration for conspiracy to defraud 'at 50-odd years'. During the four years following the arrest and prior to trial, Jessie found a job in the hospitality industry and 'worked my way up to Operations Manager'. Jessie, who had no previous convictions, finally spent twelve months in prison.

She recounted how her positionality and life situation made her reflex-ive regarding future employment, as 'nobody is going to employ a woman of my age, with a criminal record, so I have to go back to self-employment'.

This situation seemingly provoked a move to negotiate precarity arising from paid employment through self-employment. She started studying women in prison and by the time she was sentenced she 'wrote the beginning of a business plan [...] literally wrote my own thesis [laughter] on women in prison, 110 pages it was'. Following her release, Jessie decided to pursue her idea and start a social enterprise 'to make lingerie so that women could sell it', but 'that's when the struggle started'. Her story depicts the personal concerns pertaining to the lack of skills and knowledge that she feels 'all the time', as well as legal and financial challenges. As Jessie 'knew that banks don't lend money anymore, not least because of my criminal record'. She started a crowd funding campaign, which failed as she 'didn't understand how much you have to put into it, it cannot be done by one person'. Throughout, Jessie reflexively invoked and contested her struggles as a self-employed older woman with limited resources.

Nonetheless, Jessie expressed her persistence and resilience to make this work, whilst at the same time feeling physically over-whelmed, 'totally exhausted'. During this tough period, working part time at a supermarket and having appointments up and down the country in order to support her social enterprise, Jessie 'came up with the idea of inviting people to hear me talk about my experiences to get corporate sponsorship' to fund training for women. At the time of our interview, she had featured in national newspapers, TV shows and prison radio and had collaborated with the Government to recruit undergraduates to be the next prison officers. Ultimately, Jessie reflected on her situation as a self-employed older woman and the emotional tension she experiences as a mother and grandmother, as 'My family would prefer me to just pack shelves, so therefore I don't discuss the hard things that go on in my life ... I hardly see my family, or my grandchildren'. At sixty-four, Jessie is a social entre-preneur and a public speaker and as an older woman and ex-offender has been empowering women in their transition out of prison. While self-employment has been a positive response to the precarity and upset brought about by life circumstances at an older age, it was not without challenges.

Case 2 Karen – 'It's Because of My Grey Hair'

Karen, a white, middle-class, London-born woman, became self-employed after a long career in the publishing industry as 'she was going nowhere; the books couldn't get bigger'. To manage the transition to the marketing and branding industry, Karen decided to re-train and completed an MBA degree in one of the most prestigious universities in the country for people who 'reached a brick wall or they needed revitalising, or they needed to learn new skills'. She recalled, however, how her 'grey hair' shaped the employment opportunities available because 'Everyone was very nice to me and was willing to talk to me. Nobody offered me a job. Some people said to me it's because of my age [...] they would say things like oh we couldn't put you with the youngsters, the beginners [...] I was grey-haired already'. When Karen finally worked for a year in branding for a publisher and had the required experience, they then said 'well you haven't got very much experience [...] you just can't win'. Karen described feeling that 'the world I was trying to get into, was actually very rigid' and this was 'very depressing'. Despite her persistence, she explained that 'there is a point when you have to say it's not working'.

These events and past experiences made Karen realise that the 'MBA was my big steppingstone ... I learnt how to talk the talk ... it was a revelation'. Karen started developing and running workshops on networking skills and selling them at organisations and universities. In her story she recounted her fear and uncertainty due to the lack of experience but also how she turned her disadvantage into an advantage. 'The fact that I had grey hair was an advantage because it meant I had gravitas. Nobody ever has asked me what my qualifications are for running workshops [...] I think it's very powerful [...] think talking the talk is terribly important, particularly perhaps in a very commercial organisation'.

At sixty-five, Karen doesn't feel old and continues to run workshops 'as I'm doing something I enjoy'. Karen acknowledged that being 'reasonably secure', not having familial responsibilities and a mortgage to pay meant that 'the earning is not the big thing ... I don't need much'. Karen's story shows a continuing effort to manage precarity in employment as an older woman, particularly to satisfy 'lookism' by embracing ageing and combining her skills and knowledge to extend the solutions available to her to start her own business.

Case 3- Wendy – 'I Just Need that Extra Money'.

Wendy, a white, working class woman, and the sole carer of three children, started offering cleaning services, following early retirement from the military in her late forties. In her story she reflected on the male dominated environment that shaped her career prospects as 'I wasn't being recognised; I was never going to get promoted because I couldn't do the things that men were doing. Like on a Sunday, they could sit around and read the newspapers and be all knowledgeable about the world. I didn't have time for that'. Despite her management skills 'previously managing three of four different sections with regiment, with the physical training, with education', Wendy started working part-time as a PA before 'it was literally a month before Christmas that I got made redundant from that. I thought, "Oh my God, this is tough […] I just need that extra money."'

Watching a TV programme about chemicals, Wendy started looking 'at what was in my washing powders, what was in the shampoos, and I was horrified. I started doing more research because I had time on my hands'. She started making up and using her own ways of cleaning 'basically learn[ing] about vinegar, sodium bicarb, citric acid and things like that'. She set up a cleaning ecological business using her products, 'just do it part time just to make up the amounts'. Wendy entered a business competition and 'beat a multimillion-pound company because they liked what I was trying to do'. Ever since, she has been trying to build on this success. She recounted the challenges faced because 'I didn't really have a great lot of business knowledge'. In turn, her health problems and caring responsibilities curtailed the growth of the business 'as I didn't really have a great lot of business knowledge […] I've not had the time because in that time; I've had both my hips replaced and then last year I had fourteen months out having to take over the care of my father and helping my mum with all their finances and everything'.

Wendy, however, expressed her resilience to make the business succeed. She took a business degree and with the help of her now-adult children, she developed her digital skills to promote her products and services online. She is reflexive of the challenges of digital entrepreneurship; yet 'I'm succeeding, I've got some really good things that are good for the environment, good for our own homes to make them more healthy for us to live in'.

4.6 Concluding Discussion

In a context of increasingly individualised risk and responsibility, Thomas et al. (2014:1573) argue that 'there is a need for research that elucidates the differentiated experiences of ageing and gender in different industries and organisations'. In this chapter, we adopted an intersectional approach and discussed the experiences of older women engaged in self-employment as a way to manage precarity arising from the age-work related exclusion faced during their life course (Moore, 2009, Radl, 2012). While self-employment can be an inclusive activity, allowing older women to offset the ill-effects of a challenging period, it can also be precarious, marked by insecurity and a sense of lack of control in employment and everyday life.

Ageism and other intersecting forms of discrimination experienced in the workplace, combined with prolonged working lives and dwindling pension incomes, have led to increased precarity in later life. The cases discussed illustrate how this precarity can be further heightened through the ways in which changes in the body influenced older women's legitimacy and in some cases their perception of their abilities. Bowman et al. (2017) highlight how concerns about ageing reflect the obsolescence of older workers knowledge and skills wrought by 'age cultures' (De Vroom, 2004: 8) in which experience and loyalty are increasingly devalued (Roberts, 2006).

Our theorisation demonstrated how social positionality affects the capacity to apply privilege to self-employment. The range of diversity and difference *within* the group of older women are apparent in the three cases presented in this study. Life trajectories and experiences enabled them to combine a variety of resources at hand in ways that allowed them to embrace the challenges encountered and thus, extend the solutions available to them. What is important here is how the interplay of actions and resources for actions is shaped by social positionality and life trajectories reflecting arguments on the impact of life course pathways on self-employment activity (Jayawarna et al., 2014). However, despite these challenges, older women's active negotiation of ageing motivated self-employment activity, eliciting feelings of increased empowerment and offering a solution to material challenges.

Given the policy emphasis on the extended working life agenda to tackle the challenges and opportunities of older people, it is imperative to re-think self-employment as a potential solution to the precarity older workers face. The 'missing entrepreneurs' agenda that highlights the promotion of self-employment for older women, is a policy priority internationally (OECD, 2019). As the evidence provided in this chapter shows, in economies such as the UK, self-employment can be a route to self-exploitation and struggle, and opportunities of self-employment for older women may differ significantly due to their social position within social hierarchies. We suggest that a more informed policy debate that fully acknowledges the barriers facing older women and the diversity of the 'entrepreneur' is required to avoid the risk of producing precariousness for older self-employed women. While self-employment can provide opportunities for empowerment and change, older women's actions are influenced by various intersecting structural and cultural contexts in which they are embedded during their life course and, as such, negotiating self-employment and ageing might be harder to negotiate for those with less resources.

Future research could explore the interplay of policy and business support for self-employment to provide an in depth understanding of the views and transitioning experience of older workers. Further, longitudinal analyses of self-employment among older women could identify life experience and drivers for transitioning into self-employment in later life including, motivations, resources available, formal, and informal support, societal and economic pressure, and ecosystem support. Cross country comparative analyses could further shed light on the ways precarity and later-career self-employment is experienced.

References

Abraham, K.G., Hershbein, B. and Houseman, S. (2020). Contract work at older ages (No. w26612). *National Bureau of Economic Research*. Available at: www.nber.org/programs-projects/projects-and-centers/retirement-and-disability-research-center/center-papers/nb19-19a Accessed 01/02/21.

Adler, G. and Hilber, D. (2009). Industry hiring patterns of older workers. *Research on Aging*, 31(1), 69–88.

Ahl, H. (2006). Why research on women entrepreneurs needs new directions. *Entrepreneurship Theory and Practice*, 30(5), 595–621.

Ahl, H. and Marlow, S. (2012). Exploring the dynamics of gender, feminism and entrepreneurship: advancing debate to escape a dead end? *Organization*, 19(5), 543–562.

Ainsworth, S. and Hardy, C. (2008). The enterprising self: an unsuitable job for an older worker. *Organization*, 15(3), 389–405.

Ainsworth, S., & Hardy, C. (2009). Mind over body: physical and psychotherapeutic discourses and the regulation of the older worker. *Human Relations*, 62(8), 1199–1229.

Anthias, F. (2013). Hierarchies of social location, class and intersectionality: towards a translocational frame. *International Sociology*, 28(1), 121–138.

Atkinson, C., Ford, J., Harding, N. and Jones, F. (2015). The expectations and aspirations of a late-career professional woman. *Work, Employment and Society* 29(6), 1019–1028.

Austad, S. N. (1997). *Why We Age: What Science Is Discovering About The Body's Journey Through Life*. New York: Wiley.

Bachelor, L. (2013). Self-employed worker numbers soar in the UK. Available at: www.theguardian.com/money/2013/feb/06/self-employed-worker-numbers-soar-uk.

Beck, V. (2011). Extending Working Life: The Retention of Older Workers. In *Managing an Age-Diverse Workforce*, E. Parry and S. Tyson (Eds). London: Palgrave Macmillan, pp. 173–188.

Bohlinger, S., van Loo, J. (2010). Lifelong Learning for Ageing Workers to Sustain Employability and Develop Personality. In: *CEDEFOP, Working and Ageing: Emerging Themes and Empirical Perspectives*. Luxembourg: Publications Office of the European Union, pp. 28–57.

Bowman D., McGann M., Kimberley H. and Biggs S. (2017). Rusty, invisible and threatening: ageing, capital and employability. *Work, Employment and Society*, 31, 465–482.

Cho, S., Crenshaw, K. W. and McCall, L. (2013). Toward a field of intersectionality studies: theory, applications, and praxis. *Signs: Journal of Women in Culture and Society*, 38 (4), 785–810.

Crenshaw, K. (1991). Mapping the margins: identity politics, intersectionality, and violence against women. *Stanford Law Review*, 43(6), 1241–1299.

Crossley, N. (2006). *Reflexive Embodiment In Contemporary Society: The Body In Late Modern Society*. Maidenhead: Open University Press.

Cutcher, L., and Riach, K. (2017). Age in the City: Embodied Ageing in Financial Services Ageing, Organisations and Management: Constructive Discourses and Critical *Perspectives*; Sydney: Palgrave Macmillan, 161–182.

Department for Work and Pensions. (2017). *Automatic Enrolment Review 2017: Maintaining the Momentum*. London, UK: Department of Work and Pension. Available at: www.gov.uk/government/publications/automatic-enrolment-review-2017-maintaining-the-momentum. Accessed: 11/02/2020.

De Vroom, B. (2004). Age-arrangements, Age-culture and Social Citizenship: A Conceptual Framework for an Institutional and Social Analysis.

In *Ageing and Transition to Retirement. A Comparative Analysis of European Welfare States*, Maltby, T., De Vroom, B., Mirabile, M. and Overbye, E. (Eds). Aldershot: Ashgate, pp. 6–17.

Dumas, A. and Laberge, S. (2005) Social class and ageing bodies: understanding physical activity in later life. *Social Theory and Health* 3(3), 183–205.

Duncan, C. (2003). Assessing anti-ageism routes to older worker re-engagement. *Work, Employment and Society*, 17(1), 101–120.

Duncan, C. and Loretto, W. (2004). Never the right age? Gender and age-based discrimination in employment. *Gender, Work & Organization*, 11(1), 95–115.

Ekerdt, D. J. (2010). Frontiers of research on work and retirement. *Journal of Gerontology: Social Sciences*, 65B(1), 69–80.

Flood, C. (2020). Toxic side effects of coronavirus weaken global pension systems. *Financial Times*. Available at: www.ft.com/content/d1fce3e7-428b-4b8a-ab6a-119a38fa1e7d Accessed 01/02/21.

Foweraker, B., and Cutcher, L. (2015). Work, age and other drugs: exploring the intersection of age and masculinity in a pharmaceutical organization. *Gender, Work and Organization*, 22 (5), 459–473.

Freedman, M. (2007). *Encore: Finding Work That Matters in the Second Half of Life*. New York: PublicAffairs.

Grenier, A., Hatzifilalithis, S., Laliberte-Rudman, D., Kobayashi, K., Marier, P. and Phillipson, C. (2020). Precarity and aging: a scoping review. *The Gerontologist*, 60(8), e620-e632.

Harris, K., Krygsman, S., Waschenko, J., & Laliberte Rudman, D. (2017). Ageism and the older worker: a scoping review. *The Gerontologist*.

Hewison, K. (2016). Precarious Work. In *The Sage Handbook of the Sociology of Work and Employment*, S. Edgell, H. Gottfried, and E. Granter (Eds). Thousand Oaks, CA: Sage, pp. 428–443.

Hitachi Capital. (2017). The Economic Impact of the Silver Pound. Centre for Economics and Business Research. Available at: www.hitachicapital.co.uk/media/1393/hitachi-capital-uk-silver-pound-report.pdf Accessed 01/21/21.

Hockey, J. and James, A. (2003) *Social Identities across the Life Course*. Basingstoke: Palgrave Macmillan.

Hodges, J. (2012). The transition of midlife women from organisational into self-employment. *Gender in Management: An International Journal*, 3(27), 186–201.

Jayawarna, D., Rouse, J. and Macpherson, A. (2014). Life course pathways to businessstart-up. *Entrepreneurship & Regional Development* 26(3–4), 282–312.

Johnson, R. W. (2009). Employment opportunities at older ages: introduction to the special issue. *Research on Aging*, 31(1), 3–16.

Jones, D. (2017). Gig economy: time to shift the spotlight to older self-employed workers. Centre for Ageing Better. Available at: www.ageing-better.org.uk/news/gig-economy-time-shift-spotlight-older-self-employed-workers Accessed 01/02/21.

Jyrkinen, M. and McKie, L. (2012) Gender, age and ageism: experiences of women managers in Finland and Scotland. *Work, Employment and Society* 26(1), 61–77.

Kalleberg, A. L. (2011) *Good Jobs, Bad Jobs: The Rise of Polarized and Precarious Employment Systems in the United States, 1970s-2000s.* New York: Russell Sage Foundation.

Kautonen, T., Down, S. and South, L. (2008) Enterprise support for older entrepreneurs: the case of PRIME in the UK. *International Journal of Entrepreneurial Behavior & Research* 14(2), 85–101.

Kerr, J. and Miftari, D. (2017). The age of the older entrepreneur, Institute of Directors, policy report.

Kohli, M. (2007). The institutionalization of the life course: looking back to look ahead. *Research in Human Development* 4(3), 253–71.

Krekula, C. (2007). The intersection of age and gender: reworking gender theory and social gerontology. *Current Sociology*, 55(2), 155–171.

Krekula, C., and Vickerstaff, S. (2020). The 'older worker' and the 'ideal worker': A critical examination of concepts and categorizations in the rhetoric of extending working lives. In A. Ni Leine, et al. (Eds.), *Extended working lives policies* (pp. 29–45). Switzerland: Springer. https://doi.org/10.1007/978-3-030-40985-2_2

Lain, D., Airey, L., Loretto, W. and Vickerstaff, S. (2019). Understanding older worker precarity: the intersecting domains of jobs, households and the welfare state. *Ageing & Society*, 39(10), 2219–2241.

Lévesque, M. and Minniti, M. (2006). The effect of aging on entrepreneurial behaviour. *Journal of Business Venturing* 21, 177–194.

Lewis, K. and Walker, E. A. (2011). Self-employment: policy panacea for an ageing population? *Small Enterprise Research* 18, 143–151.

Loretto, W. and White, P. (2006). Work, more work and retirement: older workers perspectives. *Social Policy and Society*, 5(4), 495.

MacDonald, R. (1996). Welfare dependency, the enterprise culture and self-employed survival. *Work, Employment and Society*, 10(3), 431–447.

Mallett, O. and Wapshott, R. (2015a). Making sense of self-employment in late career: understanding the identity work of olderpreneurs. *Work, Employment and Society*, 29(2), 250–266.

Mallett, O. and Wapshott, R. (2015b). Entrepreneurship in a Context of Pending Retirement: The Lived Experience of Older Entrepreneurs. In: *Entrepreneurship, Self-Employment and Retirement* N. Sappleton and F. Lourenço (Eds). Palgrave Macmillan, London, pp. 67–89.

McKie, L., Biese, I. and Jyrkinen, M. (2013). 'The best time is now!': the temporal and spatial dynamics of women opting into self-employment. *Gender, Work & Organization*, 20(2), 184–196.

McMullin, J. A. and Cairney, J. (2004). Self-esteem and the intersection of age, class, and gender. *Journal of Aging Studies*, 18(1), 75–90.

McNair, S. (2006). How different is the older labour market? Attitudes to work and retirement among older people in Britain. *Social Policy & Society*, 5(4), 485–494.

Meliou, E. and Mallett, O. (2021). Negotiating gendered ageing: intersectional reflexivity and experiences of incongruity of self-employed older women. *Work, Employment and Society*, 36(1), 101–118, OnlineFirst.

Meliou, E., Mallett, O. and Rosenberg, S. (2019). Being a self-employed older woman: from discrimination to activism. *Work, Employment and Society*, 33(3), 529–538.

Moore, S. (2009). 'No matter what I did I would still end up in the same position' age as a factor defining older women's experience of labour market participation. *Work, Employment and Society* 23(4), 655–671.

Neumark, D. (2009). The Age Discrimination in Employment Act and the challenge of population aging. *Research on Aging*, 31(1), 41–68.

OECD. (2019). *The Missing Entrepreneurs 2019: Policies for Inclusive Entrepreneurship*. Paris, FR:OECD Publishing. Available at: www.oecd .org/industry/the-missing-entrepreneurs-43c2f41c-en.htm

Ogbor, J. O. (2000). Mythicizing and reification in entrepreneurial discourse: ideology-critique of entrepreneurial studies. *Journal of Management Studies*, 37(5), 605–635.

Parry, S. and Mallett, O. (2016). Motivation for later-life entrepreneurship: An examination of 'privileged entrepreneurs. *39th Institute for Small Business and Entrepreneurship Conference*, Paris on 27–28 October 2016.

Perenyi, A., Zolin, R. and Maritz, A. (2018). The perceptions of Australian senior entrepreneur on the drivers of their entrepreneurial activity. *International Journal of Entrepreneurial Behavior and Research* 24(1), 81–103.

Phillipson, C., Shepherd, S., Robinson, M. and Vickerstaff, S. (2018). Uncertain futures: organisational influences on the transition from work to retirement. *Social Policy & Society*, 18(3), 335–350, 1–6.

Radl, J. (2012). Too old to work, or too young to retire? The pervasiveness of age norms in Western Europe. *Work, Employment and Society*, 26(5), 755–771.

Riach, K. (2007). 'Othering' older worker identity in recruitment. *Human Relations*, 60(11), 1701–1726.

Riach, K. and Cutcher, L. (2014) Built to last: ageing, class and the masculine body in a UK hedge fund. *Work, Employment and Society*, 28(5), 771–787.

Riach, K. and Loretto, W. (2009). Identity work and the 'unemployed' worker: age, disability and the lived experience of the older unemployed. *Work, Employment & Society*, 23, 102–118.

Risman, B. (1998). *Gender Vertigo: American Families in Transition*. New Haven, CT: Yale University Press.

Roberts, I. (2006). Taking age out of the workplace: putting older workers back in? *Work, Employment and Society*, 20(1), 67–86.

Rudman, D. L. and Aldrich, R. (2021). Producing precarity: the individualization of later life unemployment within employment support provision, *Journal of Aging Studies*, 57, 100924.

Shilling, C. (2007). Sociology and the body: classical traditions and new agendas. *The Sociological Review*, 55, 1–18.

Singh, G. and DeNoble, A. (2003). Early retirees as the next generation of entrepreneurs. *Entrepreneurship Theory and Practice*, 27(3), 207–226.

Spedale, S., Coupland, C. and Tempest, S. (2014) Gendered ageism and organizational routines at work: the case of day-parting in television broadcasting. *Organization Studies*, 35(11), 1585–1604.

Standing, G. (2011). *The Precariat: The Dangerous New Class*. London: Bloomsbury.

Thomas, R., Hardy, C., Cutcher, L. and Ainsworth, S. (2014). What's age got to do with it? On the critical analysis of age and organisations. *Organization Studies*, 35(11), 1569–1584.

Tomlinson F and Colgan F (2014). Negotiating the self between past and present: narratives of older women moving towards self-employment. *Organization Studies* 35(11), 1655–1675.

United Nations. (2019). *World Population Prospects 2019*. Department of Economic and Social Affairs, Population Division, Report ST/ESA/SER.A/444. Available at: www.un.org/en/sections/issues-depth/ageing/ Accessed 01/02/21.

Waite, L. (2009). A place and space for a critical geography of precarity? *Geography Compass*, 3(1), 412–433.

Weber, P. and Schaper, M. (2004). Understanding the grey entrepreneur. *Journal of Enterprising Culture*, 12(2), 147–164.

Whiting, R. and Pritchard, K. (2020). Reconstructing retirement as an enterprising endeavor. *Journal of Management Inquiry*, 29(4), 404–417.

Witz, A., Warhurst, C. and Nickson, D. (2003). The labour of aesthetics and the aesthetics of organization. *Organization*, 10(1), 33–54.

Zalewska, A. (2018). Huge pension fund deficits are a global crisis in waiting. *The Conversation*. Available at: https://theconversation.com/huge-pension-fund-deficits-are-a-global-crisis-in-waiting-88420 Accessed 01/02/21.

Zissimopoulos, J. M. and Karoly, L. A. (2007). Transitions to self-employment at older ages: the role of wealth, health, health insurance and other factors. *Labour Economics*, 14(2), 269–295.

5 | How the (In)Ability of Using One's Disability Strategically Reinforces Inequality and Precariousness amongst Disabled Workers
The Case of France

SARAH RICHARD AND SOPHIE HENNEKAM

5.1 Introduction

The awareness of and interest in disability in the workplace is growing. According to the Convention on the Rights of Persons with Disabilities, disabled individuals are defined as individuals with "long-term physical, mental, intellectual or sensory impairments which in interaction with various barriers may hinder their full and effective participation in society on an equal basis with others" (CRPD, 2006, article 1). Indeed, there are many barriers for disabled individuals to participate in society fully and effectively. Disability is a stigmatizing condition and can lead to marginalization, discrimination, and precarity at work. Globally, there are 1.1 billion disabled individuals, making up around one-sixth of the world's population (Schur et al., 2013). Although the Convention on the Rights of Persons with Disabilities (2006) has increased global awareness of disability rights including those in a workplace context, individuals with disabilities continue to experience a range of challenges at work and often precarious working conditions. Firstly, the employment rate of individuals with a disability is half of that of non-disabled workers and underemployment in which individuals work below their educational level is frequent amongst disabled workers (World Health Organization, 2011). In addition, disabled workers tend to earn less compared to non-disabled workers (Baldwin and Johnson, 2006), are more likely to lose their jobs, experience exclusion, and are less likely to be offered training or other career development opportunities (Schur et al., 2009; Schur et al., 2013), making their long-term inclusion into the labour market often precarious. Secondly, despite anti-discrimination legislation (Corby et al., 2019), discrimination is common, which has many negative outcomes related to their own well-being and their careers (Beatty et al., 2019). Moreover, the negative stereotypes about disabled workers influence the way they are perceived by others and are sometimes internalized by disabled workers themselves (Elraz, 2018; Jammaers et al., 2016; Santuzzi and Waltz, 2016).

Despite the general patterns outlined above, disabled workers are a heterogeneous population. Indeed, disabled individuals are far from being passive victims, but do express agency as they enhance their own attractiveness and employability in the labour market by making strategic use of existing legislation, by positioning their characteristics as an asset for their job or by comparing themselves with other disabled workers who they perceive to have a disability that is more stigmatizing than theirs. By doing so, they are able to get jobs in which they have more control over their work, experience better working conditions, greater job stability and more opportunities for advancement for example, fighting as such precarious employment that is common amongst disabled workers. This chapter provides a range of empirical studies on disabled individuals that strategically use their disability identity as they navigate the world of work. First, we show how disabled workers in France reflect on factors on societal level, such as the legislation surrounding disability and more specifically a quota system and how they can use this to their own advantage (Richard and Hennekam, 2021a). Second, we reveal that disabled workers take into consideration factors on organizational or sectoral level as they make their career choices. More precisely, through an international sample of 257 individuals with mental health conditions, we highlight how they self-select into sectors in which their characteristics can be turned into an advantage (Hennekam et al., 2021). Third, we report on a study in which disabled individuals compare several characteristics of their disability with other disabled workers. When this comparison is positive, in that they perceive their disability to be less stigmatizing than that of other disabled workers, they use their identity as disabled worker strategically in that it has a positive impact on their careers (Richard and Hennekam, 2021b). Together, these empirical findings reveal a range of factors on macro-societal, meso-organizational and micro-individual level that led to, sustain and reinforce a situation in which not all disabled workers are equal as they navigate the world of work. The French case is particularly interesting because on the one hand employers struggle to recruit disabled workers (Perotte, 2013) and on the other hand disabled workers still suffer from a lower level of labour market participation (Insee, 2020). Indeed, their precarious position in the workplace is visible through higher levels and longer periods of unemployment and their overrepresentation in low-skilled jobs (Aubin and Daniel, 2019–2020). We end the chapter by a reflection on the implications of these findings and present an overview of suggestions to take this line of study forward.

5.2 Context

Worldwide, there is an increasing awareness of the importance to improve the integration of people with disabilities in the labour market. The majority of European countries have signed conventions that guaranty the rights of individuals with disability, such as the Convention on the Rights of Persons with Disabilities of the United Nations. In addition, many European countries have established anti-discrimination legislation that includes disability. Despite a certain level of convergence on terms of legislation, two broad approaches regarding disabled workers can be identified (Corby et al., 2019): the self-regulation approach and the command-and-control approach. In the self-regulation approach, we find general and disability-specific anti-discrimination laws, but the state does not intervene to guarantee that these laws are respected. In a command-and-control approach, a disability quota system forces companies to employ a minimum percentage of disabled individuals. The quota varies depending on the country, ranging from 2 per cent in Spain to 7 per cent in Italy (Vornholt et al., 2018). In some cases, the company can pay a fee that fully or partially releases them from fulfilling the quota. Quota systems have been largely criticized because it may convey the idea that the protected group (disabled workers) is inferior (Sargeant et al., 2018). Nevertheless, the six European countries with the lowest activity gaps between disabled and non-disabled individuals have implemented this approach (Grammenos, 2013).

The various empirical studies discussed in this chapter are either exclusively based in France or have a sample in which French disabled workers make up the majority of the subjects under study. In France, employers are required to provide reasonable accommodations for disabled workers, which implies that they have to take appropriate measures to enable disabled workers to obtain or keep a job corresponding to their qualifications. France has a quota system that stipulates that organizations with 20 employees or more need to have a workforce in which 6 per cent consists of disabled workers. In addition, disabled individuals need to be legally recognized as disabled workers, under legislation known as Reconnaissance de la Qualité de Travailleur Handicapé [Recognition of the Quality of Disabled Workers] (RQTH), in order to be counted in the French quota system. However, having this legal recognition does not imply that they are obliged to inform their employer of their disability status. Employers who fail to fulfil their quota have to pay a fine. French companies struggle to attract and recruit qualified disabled workers (Perotte, 2013), which is paradoxical as individuals with a legal recognition of their disability have a lower labour market participation than individuals without a disability. Forty-four per cent of disabled individuals of working age are employed, compared to 72 per cent for the working population as a whole (Insee, 2020). Similarly, nearly 28 per cent of disabled workers have been unemployed for more than three years, which is double the percentage of the non-disabled unemployed population (Insee, 2020). Apart from their lower level of labour market participation, French disabled individuals are also more likely to be employed in low-skilled occupations. More specifically, 65 per cent of disabled workers are considered to be blue-collar workers, against 47 per cent of the population as a whole (Insee, 2020).

5.3 Case Studies

Below we draw on three empirical studies to show how the (in)ability of disabled individuals to use their disability strategically as they navigate the workplace reinforces the inequality and precariousness within the population of disabled workers.

Methods Case 1

We draw on a sample of thirty-nine disabled individuals who recently entered or were seeking to enter the labour market in France. A call for participation was sent through a charitable organization for disabled individuals in France that aims to facilitate their professional integration. A snowball technique was adopted, a sampling method that is commonly used in studies that involve sensitive and hard-to-reach individuals (Hennekam, 2019). The participants' average age was 25.54 years (ranging from 20 to 42 years), and the sample included 22 men and 17 women. Twenty-eight per cent had a sensory disability, another 28 per cent a physical disability, 13 per cent a learning disability, 5 per cent a mental illness, 3 per cent a neurological disability, and 23 per cent reported a debilitating condition. Further, 54 per cent had a master's degree, 28 per cent a bachelor's degree, 10 per cent a PhD, and 8 per cent had received short-cycle tertiary education.

Participants were invited to present themselves and tell their stories about the disclosure of their disability. The researcher only intervened when the participant no longer spoke on a topic related to the disclosure decision and used probing to encourage the participants to develop their answers further in order to obtain more information. The process of data collection was completed once saturation point was reached, and all interviews were recorded, transcribed and translated. The interviewees were informed that participation was voluntary and anonymous. A thematic analysis was used to analyse the data following an inductive approach of open coding. Some codes were based on the existing literature, whereas others emerged naturally from the data. NVivo software was used to analyse the data.

Case 1: The Empowering Effect of Disability Identity Disclosure in a Quota System

This study reveals how the macro-societal context in the form of the legal context can be perceived as an opportunity to strategically use one's identity as disabled worker. The decision whether to reveal or conceal one's disability is a dilemma that disabled people face when entering the workforce (Von Schrader et al., 2014). We examined whether and how a quota system influences an individual's decision to disclose his or her disability at work. Drawing on thirty-nine life story interviews with highly qualified disabled individuals who had recently entered or were seeking to enter the labour market in France, we reveal that a quota system can be empowering for disabled individuals. Earlier studies have looked into the effects of quota systems on the employment of disabled workers (e.g., Sargeant et al., 2018), but few studies have investigated their impact on disabled individuals themselves (Vornholt et al., 2018).

The decision whether to disclose one's identity as disabled worker at work involves an individual risk–benefit analysis that includes possible positive and negative consequences of (non)-disclosure (Jans et al., 2012). Positive outcomes could include social support and workplace adaptations that can contribute to higher performance and greater well-being (Böhm et al., 2013), whereas negative consequences include stigma or negative career outcomes that can result in a decrease in well-being (Santuzzi et al., 2014) and an increase in precariousness. Indeed, disclosing one's disability can lead to negative attitudes, hindering their career progression for example. Similarly, making one's disability known might increase their chances to have jobs in which they have less control over their working hours, less autonomy and are more likely to experience challenging working conditions.

Disabled workers are often depicted as powerless, passive victims. However, we show that individuals with disabilities can also perceive their environment to be empowering. Empowerment is a process of transitioning from a state of powerlessness to one of relative control over one's life, destiny, or environment. According to Barnes and Mertens (2008), when applied to disability, empowerment consists of revealing social barriers, changing perceptions of disability, and stimulating political action. Empowerment through regulation is called "legal empowerment" (Golub, 2010: 13) and involves legislation and regulations that are designed to empower the disadvantaged. A disability quota system is a form of legal empowerment.

A quota system puts pressure on organizations and disabled individuals alike to disclose and declare disability. HR, colleagues, and friends seem to encourage disabled workers to disclose their disability by making them aware that their disability can be an asset rather than a liability. Instead of focusing on the potential stigmatizing nature of their disability (Santuzzi et al., 2014), the disabled workers in this study realized that their status could be an advantage in a country with a quota system (Vornholt et al., 2018), providing agency and empowerment. A quota system can thus be used strategically in order to facilitate the labour market integration of disabled workers.

Apart from the macro-legal environment in the form of the quota system, disabled workers also took into consideration their personal attributes and organizational environment. First, the visibility of their disability influenced the disclosure process as only disabled workers with less visible or invisible disabilities can choose whether they want to disclose their condition. Their need for workplace accommodations was another personal attribute they took into account. Individuals with disabilities that require significant adaptations at work were forced to reveal their status. They were conscious that the fewer accommodations they needed, the more choice they had in their disclosure decision. They also reported that needing only minor adjustments increased their value in the labour market. On the contrary, participants with impairments that required extensive accommodations highlighted that they perceived themselves to be less employable. Finally, highly qualified participants seemed to be aware that many organizations in France struggle to hire qualified disabled workers (Perotte, 2013), which encouraged them to disclose their disability identity.

Participants also observed and analysed the organizational environment, with a specific focus on the attitude and commitment to diversity and disability. They adopted a pro-active attitude by looking for concrete actions that reflect an organization's commitment to diversity. Organizations that seemed truly committed to diversity issues encouraged participants to be open about their condition.

To summarize, this study reveals that a disability quota system makes disabled workers more aware of their rights and strengthens their ability to exercise those rights in the form of workplace support that is legally available to them upon legal disclosure. In addition, we highlight that disabled individuals carefully reflect on how they compare with others on some personal attributes. Although it has been argued that governments use differences between disabled individuals to cut overall welfare provision with the intention of giving more to those who are severely impaired (Oliver, 2013), the findings of this study show that disabled workers themselves also use such differences to their own advantage. Therefore, a quota system does not promote general inclusion, but further marginalizes disabled workers with lower educational attainments and visible disabilities that require workplace adaptations. Consequently, such a system decreases precarious work only for some disabled individuals but enhances inequality within the general population of disabled workers. Those workers who perceive themselves to be less employable and present more constraints for employers are more likely to end up in jobs with for example irregular working hours, fluctuating income and/or physically demanding work.

Methods: Case 2

A mix of networks and professional associations related to mental health/illness as well as social media and forums, were used to invite individuals who self-identified as someone with a mental illness to complete an online survey. The sample consisted of 8 per cent males and 92 per cent females. The average age of the participants was 34.8 years, ranging from 16 to 64 years. The participants lived in different areas of the world: 55 per cent were European; 29 per cent North American; 11 per cent Oceanian; 3 per cent African; and 2 per cent Asian. The participants worked in a variety of sectors, and 91 per cent reported being diagnosed with more than one mental illness.

We analysed 257 qualitative surveys. The survey started with easy questions to break the ice and make participants feel at ease. Moreover, participants were asked to provide examples to illustrate their perceptions, feelings, or experiences. The qualitative surveys were analysed with the aid of NVivo software. A thematic analysis was employed to describe, understand, and interpret the experiences of individuals with mental illness as they navigate the labour market.

Case 2: Individual with Mental Illness Navigating the Labour Market

This study focuses on the specific case of individuals with mental health conditions who face particular difficulties as they navigate the workplace. A mental illness is a diagnosable psychological disorder that can be "characterized by dysregulation of mood, thought, and/or behavior" (Center for Disease Control and Prevention, 2016). There is relatively small body of knowledge on this population (Follmer and Jones, 2018), despite the growing number of individuals who struggle with mental health conditions (Weissman et al., 2017). Individuals with mental health conditions do not only face exclusion and stigmatization, but also encounter difficulties in obtaining and maintaining employment (Corbière et al., 2011). The unemployment rate of this population is higher than average (Harris et al., 2014), underemployment is a serious issue (Levinson et al., 2010) and they struggle to integrate at work (Elraz, 2018). Drawing on 257 qualitative surveys with individuals with mental health conditions in twenty-three countries worldwide, this study aimed to understand how this population navigates the world of work. We reveal that individuals with mental health condition have a particularly difficult position in the labour market. First, we show that the capital endowments of individuals with mental illness are devalued in the labour market. The participants with mental health conditions involved in the study reported finding it challenging to socialize, build, and maintain relationships at work. Moreover, they explained perceiving themselves to lack social understanding and social skills and highlighted being sensitive to stress and having difficulties to control their emotions. Second, the findings highlight how individuals with mental illness internalize, legitimize, and normalize their disadvantaged positions in the labour market, blaming themselves rather than questioning the social structures that lead to their challenging position in the labour market. They often had employment with low job security, making them vulnerable to job loss, irregular income and work, little autonomy over their tasks, schedule as well as few opportunities for training and career development. Third, our findings highlight how social norms constrain even the opinion that individuals with mental illness have of themselves and show how this affects how they navigate the labour market.

Despite these difficulties, even this highly stigmatized population showed agency as they made career choices. Indeed, people with mental illness may adopt empowering beliefs and attitudes, rejecting the negative stereotypes about mental illness (Corrigan and Watson, 2002). Using the same data, we show that individuals with mental illness reflect on the positive and negative characteristics of their conditions and purposefully select jobs and sectors in which their characteristics are perceived to be an asset. More specifically, the participants reported that they perceived themselves to possess some unique skills that helped them to develop and excel in their careers. The participants explicitly related their mental illness to certain qualities they possessed and explained that being perfectionistic, organized, and having eye for detail were helpful in their work. They also outlined that the characteristics of their mental illness positively shaped their work attitudes and work ethic, leading to a tendency to overdeliver, which made them high-achieving valuable employees. For others, their condition enabled them to uniquely perceive and process information, leading them to see things differently and propose alternative solutions or ideas. In addition, they mentioned that their mental illness helped them be more empathetic and understanding which allowed them to relate broadly to others and stressed that their empathy, patience, and understanding were especially valuable in interactions with their co-workers. When individuals with mental illness worked in sectors in which there was a good fit between their characteristics and the needs or demands of the job or organization, they could thus turn their mental health condition into a strength. This also helped them manage their own mental health and increased their own well-being, satisfaction, and feelings of self-worth. By working in sectors or occupations that fulfil their need to feel valued and useful through the positive characteristics of their mental illness, they achieved a good fit between their needs and desires on the one hand and the outcomes or rewards supplied by the job on the other hand. Person-job fit, defined as the relationship between a person's characteristics and those of the job or tasks that are performed at work (Kristof, 1996) can thus help individuals with mental illness to turn their particularities into an advantage as they navigate the workplace. Being able to use one's personal strengths has been found to be positively related to work engagement, feelings of self-efficacy, self-esteem, well-being, and job performance, while it is negatively related to stress and absenteeism (van Woerkom et al., 2016; van Woerkom and Meyers, 2015; Wood et al., 2011).

To summarize, individuals with mental illness are in a disadvantaged position in the labour market as their skills and characteristics tend to be devalued by individuals without mental health conditions. This lack of worth is often internalized, leading to a vicious circle that makes the integration into the workforce a challenging process. They tended to have precarious employment characterized by temporary contracts, having few or no union coverage, no pension, social rights, or medical protection. Despite the challenges they face as they navigate the world of work, individuals with mental illness self-selected into job sectors that allowed them to capitalize on the strengths of their mental illness. By working in sectors that aligned with their preferences and need to feel valued or recognized for what they do and to obtain meaningful work are being met.

Methods Case 3

The sample consisted of 36 disabled individuals: 24 women (67 per cent) and 12 men (33 per cent). Average age was 32 years, ranging from 23 to 60 years. Sixty per cent was French, 17 per cent was American, 14 per cent was Dutch, 6 per cent was British, and 3 per cent Australian. Individuals reported a range of disabilities including mental illness (51 per cent), physical disabilities (17 per cent), sensory disabilities (14 per cent), neurological disabilities (6 per cent), learning disabilities (6 per cent), and debilitating conditions (6 per cent).

Interviews were conducted face-to-face or over Skype. All interviews were audio-recorded, fully transcribed, and translated when needed. An interview guide was used, but we also let the interviewees elaborate on themes we had not anticipated. The interview guide consisted of four blocks of questions: general information about the interviewee; questions about their functioning at work; questions about workplace adaptations; and finally questions about their identity and stigma. The analysis was inductive and iterative in nature and was conducted by hand without the use of a software package.

Case 3: Social Comparison between Disabled Workers and Its Impact on the Ability to Construct a Positive Work-related Identity
This study shows how factors on micro-individual level can reinforce the inequality between disabled individuals in the workplace. Drawing on thirty-six semi-structured in-depth interviews with individuals with a variety of disabilities in the workplace in multiple countries, the study sheds light on how disabled individuals construct a positive work-related identity. The disabled workers involved in this study reflected on the characteristics of their disability. More specifically, we found that disabled workers compare themselves with others and that these comparisons, as a stigma identity management strategy, affect their sense of self. Four characteristics of their disability, the (in)visibility of their condition, the severity of their disability, its controllability and whether they need workplace adaptations seemed to influence the extent to which their condition was perceived to be stigmatized. Indeed, the visibility of a disability affects how individuals are viewed by others (Mik-Meyer, 2016) in the sense that more visible impairments tend to be more stigmatizing (Sabat et al., 2019). While uncontrollable disabilities are more stigmatizing, individuals with such disabilities are simultaneously more positively perceived by others (Reilly et al., 2006). Regarding disability severity, research shows that access to employment decreases as the severity of one's impairment increases (Carrieri et al., 2014). Finally, the need for workplace adaptations is a constraint for employers as organizations are obliged to provide "reasonable accommodations" for individuals with disabilities (Nardodkar et al., 2016) in many countries. Reasonable accommodations are defined as "changes that are made in a particular workplace environment or in the way things are usually done that make it possible for a person with a disability to do the job" (Kirsh

et al., 2009, p. 396). Disabled individuals seem well aware of the fact
that needing adaptations at work puts them in a disadvantaged position and are therefore reluctant to ask for such adaptations (Wang
et al., 2011). The perception of stigma related to their disability influenced how they positioned themselves compared to other disabled
workers. When they perceived themselves to have a less stigmatizing
condition, they tended to engage in downward in-group social comparison, by comparing themselves with other disabled workers who
they considered to have more stigmatizing conditions. For example,
individuals with invisible, mild, controllable conditions for which no
workplace adaptations were needed compared themselves with those
who were less well-off, which made them feel good about themselves
and made them reveal or even emphasize their disability identity. The
level of stigma related to one's disability was used in this social comparison process. The participants in this study used a range of stigma
identity management strategies as they tried to construct a positive
work-related identity. Some participants used downward social comparison and positioned themselves as "the perfect disabled worker"
consisting of a well-crafted identity that excludes the negative aspects
of having a disability. Their disability tended to be mild, invisible,
and controllable and did not require any adaptations for organizations. Those individuals integrated their identity as disabled worker
into their professional identity, using their disability as a professional
advantage. This helped them to secure jobs with greater social protection, benefits and medical coverage for example. On the contrary,
participants with disabilities that were more stigmatizing could not
easily engage in downward comparisons. Those individuals either
downplayed or dis-identified with their identity as disabled worker.
To downplay their identity as a disabled worker, participants tended
to highlight their professional identity and insisted on their ambition,
expertise, and competencies. Apart from downplaying their disability identity, dis-identification was another way in which they dealt
with their stigmatized identity. When doing so, disabled individual
detached their identity as professional from their identity as disabled
individual.

To summarize, this study reveals that disabled individuals do not
only compare themselves with non-disabled individuals, but also
engage in social comparisons with other disabled workers. They strategically reflect on their disability characteristics as they determine the

level of stigma attached their condition. When they perceive their disability to be less stigmatizing and less constraining for employers, they highlight their identity as disabled worker as they are "easy" to integrate the workplace. In today's neoliberal labour market in which disabled are put in a disadvantageous position, being an "easy" disabled worker is a competitive advantage and helps to gain employment. However, disabled workers who were unable to engage in downward social comparison seemed to have more difficulties to construct positive work-related identities, reinforcing once more the marginalization and exclusion of individuals with visible, severe, and uncontrollable conditions that require extensive workplace adaptations.

5.4 Conclusion

This chapter discusses three empirical studies to explain how disabled individuals tend to take into account factors on macro-societal, meso-organizational, and micro-individual level as they reflect on their identity as disabled worker. More specifically, through observation and reflection, disabled workers seem to decide whether they can use their disability identity in a strategic way, differentiating themselves either from other disabled workers or from their non-disabled peers as they navigate a discriminatory labour market. While this is empowering for some disabled individuals, these processes and mechanisms simultaneously reinforce the marginalization of other disabled individuals, especially in the light of the prevailing neoliberal labour market logic. Below we outline the practical implications of the studies presented in this chapter.

First, governments around the world should be aware that there is great diversity and inequality within the population of disabled workers. Measures and tools that take these differences into account are necessary to provide much-needed support for the most marginalized, stigmatized, and vulnerable individuals with disabilities. Without such measures, the most vulnerable individuals will move further to the margins, leading to even more exclusion or precarious employment. Research has shown that having employment has a range of positive outcomes for individuals with disabilities. It provides them a sense of meaning and belongingness, provides structure to their lives, gives them a sense of identity, and enhances the inclusion in the wider community (Leufstadius et al., 2009). Given that social exclusion from the labour market is one of the main challenges that disabled individuals face, more insights in the factors, processes and mechanisms that play a role are important for policy makers in order to develop an inclusive workplace for all. However, the issue is not only about getting access to employment, but also about what kind of employment they are able to secure and maintain over time. Nowadays, disability tends to be viewed as an individual concern and responsibility, rather than an issue the state and the welfare system needs to tackle. As a consequence of the free market system in which it is believed that everyone can thrive in a competitive market, disabled individuals are overrepresented in sectors in which precarious work is common. Therefore, rules and legislation on societal level as well as policies and practices on organizational level could be developed and implemented to combat the structural nature of their precarious position in the labour market.

Second, the studies presented in this chapter have implications for organizations, HR professionals or managers of disabled workers. Our findings showed that when individuals with mental illness perceive a match between their personal characteristics and the requirements of the job, they report positive workplace outcomes. Organizations could therefore provide disabled workers the opportunity to engage in job crafting, so that they can make changes to their jobs to align it with their preferences, motives, and passions (Tims et al., 2016) and use the characteristics of their disability as a strength or asset for the organization. Moreover, this is likely to lead to greater feelings of self-worth and self-efficacy, which leads to a more positive perception of themselves. We recommend an individualized approach that allows disabled workers to reach their full potential. In addition, we find that disabled individuals are unequal in their capacity to construct a positive identity at work and that this depends on their disability characteristics as well as their national, organizational, and personal context. Employment agencies, HR practitioners and managers should be aware of how disability characteristics affect the level of perceived stigma attached to a particular disability when supporting or working with disabled workers. More tailored support that acknowledges the heterogeneous nature of this population is needed to attract, retain, and develop their careers (Brzykcy et al., 2019; Kulkarni, 2016). Furthermore, support groups or networks, where people can meet other disabled workers so that they can share their experiences, exchange ideas, provide support and demand accommodations might be useful to combat the social exclusion they may experience at work. Moreover, whether one needs workplace adaptations seemed to play an important role in the disclosure decision of disabled workers and influenced their capacity to construct a positive work-related identity. Raising awareness about existing policies and the provision of accommodations without stigmatizing the individual are therefore of utmost importance.

Third, several implications for disabled individuals themselves can be outlined. Disability is a stigmatizing attribute and individuals can internalize these negative beliefs, which might prevent them from seeking professional help or asking for workplace adaptations needed to fully function (Talebi et al., 2016). One recommendation relates to building self-confidence amongst these individuals in order to prevent the internationalization of negative attitudes and beliefs. This can be done by making disabled workers more aware of their strengths through strengths inventories for example which should also reduce the issue that individuals self-select themselves in precarious jobs.

We end this chapter by presenting a range of ideas to take this line of research further in the future. It is important to stress that disabled individuals are not passive victims that have nothing to contribute but are pro-active analytical actors as they craft their own career paths and identities. More research is needed to further understand under which circumstances disabled workers are able to express agency to combat their precarious and disadvantaged position in the labour market.

For example, more research on the diversity within the population of disabled workers is needed as recent research has stressed the different experiences of multiple sub-populations (Beatty et al., 2019; Richard et al., 2021). Studies could for example examine degenerative illnesses, in order to consider agency in a context where the condition is going to get worse. What strategies do individuals use in this specific case? How can such individuals be supported to maintain a positive identity or develop their careers?

Another avenue for future research relates to intersectionality in which individuals have more than one stigmatizing attribute. Recent research shows that there might not always be an additional effect, but that this can lead to qualitative different outcomes that include opportunities of agency and empowerment (Smith et al., 2019). Future research should not only include disabled individuals with multiple conditions, but also study disabled workers who possess other stigmatized social identities. Another area that merits more attention is the overall context in which disabled individuals evolve. Our empirical work shows that one needs to take into account factors on societal, sectoral, organizational, and individual level if we want to fully grasp the complexities of the experiences of disabled individuals. Multi-level studies are well suited to capture the contextually sensitive nature of the experiences of this population.

Furthermore, research should investigate alternative form of employment as disabled individuals are not only employed in the mainstream sector. They can have entrepreneurial trajectories that are either chosen or being pursued by constraints. They may also find jobs in the sheltered sector, which employs more than 50 per cent of disabled individuals (European Commission, 2016). However, sheltered employment is stigmatized because it provides jobs with for which few skills are required and that have few possibilities for career advancement (Hemphill and Kulik, 2017), which provides little agency for workers in this sector.

A longitudinal perspective to the empowerment and agency of disabled workers provides another interesting avenue for future research. Is agency something that stays or can one lose it? Under which circumstances can disabled individuals gain or lose agency? Are there specific career stages or events that put disabled individuals at risk as they navigate their careers?

References

Aubin, C., & Daniel, C. (2019–2020). Handicaps et emploi. Rapport thématique 2019–2020 de l'Inspection générale des affaires sociales. www.igas.gouv.fr/IMG/pdf/rapport_igas-2020handicapsetemploi_interactif.pdf.

Baldwin, M. L. & Johnson, W. G. (2006). A critical review of studies of discrimination against workers with disabilities. In W. M. Rodgers (Ed.), *Handbook on the economics of discrimination* (pp. 119–160). Northampton, MA: Edward Elgar Publishing.

Barnes, C., & Mertens, D. M. (2008). An Ethical Agenda in Disability Research: Rhetoric or Reality. In D. M. Mertens and P. E. Ginsberg (eds.) *The Handbook of Social Research Ethics*. London: Sage, 485–473.

Beatty, J. E., Baldridge, D. C., Boehm, S. A., Kulkarni, M. & Colella, A. J. (2019). On the treatment of persons with disabilities in organizations: A review and research agenda. *Human Resource Management, 58*(2), 119–137.

Böhm, S., Baumgärtner, M. K., & Dwertmann, D.J. (2013) *Berufliche Inklusion von Menschen mit Behinderung: Best Practices aus dem ersten Arbeitsmarkt.* Berlin, Heidelberg: Springer-Verlag.

Brzykcy, A. Z., Boehm, S. A., & Baldridge, D. C. (2019). Fostering sustainable careers across the lifespan: The role of disability, idiosyncratic deals and perceived work ability. *Journal of Vocational Behavior, 112,* 185–198.

Carrieri, L., Sgaramella, T. M., Bortolon, F., Stenta, G., Fornaro, L., Cracco, A., & Soresi, S. (2014). Determinants of on-the-job-barriers in employed persons with multiple sclerosis: The role of disability severity and cognitive indices. *Work, 47*(4), 509–520.

Center for Disease Control and Prevention. (2016). *"Mental illness".* Available at: www.cdc.gov/mentalhealth/basics/mental-illness.htm.

Convention on the Rights of Persons with Disabilities (CRPD). (2006). United Nations. Retrieved from www.un.org/development/desa/disabilities/convention-on-the-rights-of-persons-with-disabilities.html (accessed 15 April 2019).

Corbière, M., Zaniboni, S., Lecomte, T., Bond, G., Gilles, P. Y., Lesage, A. & Goldner, E. (2011). Job acquisition for people with severe mental illness enrolled in supported employment programs: A theoretically grounded empirical study. *Journal of Occupational Rehabilitation, 21*(3), 342–354.

Corby, S., William, L. & Richard, S. (2019). Combatting disability discrimination: A comparison of France and Great Britain. *European Journal of Industrial Relations, 25*(1), 41–56.

Corrigan, P. W., & Watson, A. C. (2002). The paradox of self-stigma and mental illness. *Clinical Psychology: Science and Practice, 9*(1), 35–53.

Elraz, H. (2018). Identity, mental health and work: How employees with mental health conditions recount stigma and the pejorative discourse of mental illness. *Human Relations, 7*(5), 722–741.

European Commission. (2016). Disability and labour market integration. Employment, social affairs and inclusion. *Publications Office of the European Union.*

Follmer, K. B., & Jones, K. S. (2018). Mental Illness in the Workplace: An Interdisciplinary Review and Organizational Research Agenda. *Journal of Management, 44*(1), 325–351.

Golub, S. (2010). *Legal Empowerment: Practitioners' Perspectives.* Rome: International Development Law Organization.

Grammenos, S. (2013). *European Comparative Data on Europe 2020 and People with Disabilities.* Ithaca NY: Cornell University ILR School.

Harris, L. M., Matthews, L. R., Penrose-Wall, J., Alam, A. & Jaworski, A. (2014). Perspectives on barriers to employment for job seekers with mental illness and additional substance-use problems'. *Health and Social Care in the Community*, 22(1), 67–77.

Hemphill, E., & Kulik, C. T. (2017). The tyranny of fit: Yet another barrier to mainstream employment for disabled people in sheltered employment. *Social Policy & Administration*, 51(7), 1119–1134.

Hennekam, S. (2019). How to Adapt a Research Design to the Particularities of a Vulnerable Group of Workers Under Study. SAGE Research Methods Cases. DOI: 10.4135/9781526474391.

Hennekam, S., Follmer, K., & Beatty, J. E. (2021). The paradox of mental illness and employment: A person-job fit lens. *The International Journal of Human Resource Management*, 32(15), 3244–3271.

INSEE, (2020). *Emploi, chômage, revenus du travail*. Institut National de la Statistique et des Etudes Economiques.

Jammaers, E., Zanoni, P. & Hardonk, S. (2016). Constructing positive identities in ableist workplaces: Disabled employees' discursive practices engaging with the discourse of lower productivity. *Human Relations*, 69(6), 1365–1386.

Jans., L. H., Kaye, H. S. & Jones., E. C. (2012). Getting hired: Successfully employed people with disabilities offer advice on disclosure, interviewing, and job search. *Journal of Occupational Rehabilitation*, 22(2), 155–165.

Kirsh, B., Stergiou-Kita, M., Gewurtz, R., Dawson, D., Krupa, T., Lysaght, R., & Shaw, L. (2009). From margins to mainstream: what do we know about work integration for persons with brain injury, mental illness and intellectual disability? *Work*, 32(4), 391–405.

Kristof, A. L. (1996). Person-organization fit: An integrative review of its conceptualizations, measurement, and implications. *Personnel Psychology*, 49(1), 1–49.

Kulkarni, M. (2016). Organizational career development initiatives for employees with a disability. *The International Journal of Human Resource Management*, 27, 1662–1679.

Leufstadius, C., Eklund, M., & Erlandsson, L. (2009). Meaningfulness in work: Experiences among employed individuals with persistent mental illness. *Work*, 34(1), 21–32.

Levinson, D., Lakoma, M. D., Petukhova, M., Schoenbaumn M., Zaslavsky, A. M., Angermeyer, M. ... Gureje, O. (2010). Associations of serious mental illness with earnings: results from the WHO World Mental Health surveys. *The British Journal of Psychiatry*, 197(2), 114–121.

Mik-Meyer, N. (2016). Othering, ableism and disability: A discursive analysis of co-workers' construction of colleagues with visible impairments. *Human Relations*, 69(6), 1341–1363.

Nardodkar, R., Pathare, S., Ventriglio, A., Castaldelli-Maia, J., Javate, K., Torales, J. & Bhugra, D. (2016). Legal protection of the right to work and employment for persons with mental health problems: A review of legislation across the world. *International Review of Psychiatry*, 28(4), 375–384.

Oliver, M. (2013). The social model of disability: Thirty years on. *Disability and Society*, 28(7), 1024–1026.

Perotte, D. (2013). Handicapés: les entreprises manquent de candidats diplômés. *Les Echos*, 21 novembre, p. 4.

Reilly, N. P., Bocketti, S. P., Maser, S. A., & Wennet, C. L. (2006). Benchmarks affect perceptions of prior disability in a structured interview. *Journal of Business and Psychology*, 20, 489–500.

Richard, S., & Hennekam, S. (2021a). When Can a Disability Quota System Empower Disabled Individuals in the Workplace? The Case of France. *Work, Employment and Society*, 35(5), 837–855.

Richard, S., & Hennekam, S. (2021b). Constructing a positive identity as a disabled worker through social comparison: The role of stigma and disability characteristics. *Journal of Vocational Behavior* 125.

Richard, S., Lemaire, C., & Church-Morel, A. (2021). Beyond identity consciousness: Human resource management practices and mental health conditions in sheltered workshops. *The International Journal of Human Resource Management*, 32(15), 3218–3243.

Sabat, I. E., Lindsey, A. P., King, E. B., Winslow, C., Jones, K. P., Membere, A. & Smith, N. A. (2019). Stigma Expression Outcomes and Boundary Conditions: A Meta-Analysis. *Journal of Business and Psychology*, 35, 171–186.

Santuzzi, A. M., & Waltz, P. R. (2016). Disability in the workplace: A unique and variable identity. *Journal of Management*, 42(5), 1111–1135.

Santuzzi, A.M., Waltz, P.R, Finkelstein, L.M., & Rupp, D. (2014) Invisible Disabilities: Unique Challenges for Employees and Organizations. *Industrial and Organizational Psychology*, 7(2), 204–219.

Sargeant, M., Radevich-Katsaroumpa, E., & Innesti, A. (2018). Disability quotas: Past or future policy? *Economic and Industrial Democracy*. 39(3), 404–421.

Schur, L., Kruse, D. & Blanck, P. (2013). *People with disabilities: Sidelined or mainstreamed*. New York: Cambridge University Press.

Schur, L., Kruse, D., Blasi, J. & Blanck, P. (2009). Is disability disabling in all workplaces? Workplace disparities and corporate culture. *Industrial Relations*, 48(3), 381–410.

Smith, A. N., Watkins, M. B., Ladge, J. J., & Carlton, P. (2019). Making the invisible visible: Paradoxical effects of intersectional invisibility on the career experiences of executive Black women. *Academy of Management Journal*, 62(6), 1705–1734.

Talebi, M., Matheson, K., & Anisman, H. (2016). The stigma of seeking help for mental health issues: Mediating roles of support and coping and the moderating role of symptom profile. *Journal of Applied Social Psychology*, 46(8), 470–482.

Tims, M., Derks, D., & Bakker, A. B. (2016). Job crafting and its relationships with person–job fit and meaningfulness: A three-wave study. *Journal of Vocational Behavior*, 92, 44–53.

van Woerkom, M., & Meyers, M. C. (2015). My strengths count! Effects of a strengths-based psychological climate on positive affect and job performance. *Human Resource Management*, 54(1), 81–103.

van Woerkom, M., Oerlemans, W. G. A., & Bakker, A. B. (2016). Strengths use and work engagement: A weekly diary study. *European Journal of Work and Organizational Psychology*, 25(3), 384–397.

Von Schrader, S., Malzer, V., and Bruyere, S. (2014). Perspectives on disability disclosure: the importance of employer practices and workplace climate. *Employee Responsibilities and Rights Journal*, 26(4), 237–255.

Vornholt, K., Villotti, P., Muschalla, B., Bauer, J., Colella, A., Zijlstra, F. et al. (2018). Disability and employment–overview and highlights. *European Journal of Work and Organizational Psychology*, 27(1), 40–55.

Wang, J. L., Patten, S., Currie, S., Sareen, J. & Schmitz, N. (2011). Perceived needs for and use of workplace accommodations by individuals with depressive and/or anxiety disorder. *Journal of Occupational and Environmental Medicine*, 53(11), 1268–1272.

Weissman, J., Russell, D., Jay, M., Beasley, J. M., Malaspina, D., & Pegus, C. (2017). Disparities in health care utilization and functional limitations among adults with serious psychological distress, 2006–2014. *Psychiatric Services*, 68(7), 653–659.

Wood, A. M., Linley, P. A., Maltby, J., Kashdan, T. B., & Hurling, R. (2011). Using personal and psychological strengths leads to increases in well-being over time: A longitudinal study and the development of the strengths use questionnaire. *Personality and Individual Differences*, 50(1), 15–19.

World Health Organization. (2011). World Report on Disability: Summary, 2011. Geneva, Switzerland. Available at: www.who.int/disabilities/world_report/2011/report.pdf.

6 | Classed and Gendered Experiences of Precarity in Dirty Work

RACHEL MORGAN, ANNILEE GAME,
AND NATALIA SLUTSKAYA

6.1 Introduction

The aim of this chapter is to examine how precarity affects the experiences of those involved in 'dirty work' (jobs or roles that are seen by others as distasteful or 'undesirable') (Ashforth & Kreiner, 1999, p. 416). In particular, we focus on physically tainted occupations that involve direct contact with physical dirt or working conditions that are deemed dangerous (Ashforth and Kreiner, 1999). Dirt refers both to the cleanliness of a particular space or object and to its symbolic link to the social rules set by societies; namely, that which deviates from the preferred order should be removed or avoided (Douglas, 1966). People occupying tainted positions undergo experiences of devaluation that often threaten their positive identities. Thus, seeking self-respect and establishing individual self-worth is potentially challenging for those fighting against stigmatisation (Ashforth and Kreiner, 1999; Hughes 1951, 1958). Moreover, there is a significant overlap between tainted categories of dirty work and stigmatised categories of socioeconomic status, class, racioethnicity, and gender (see, e.g., Anderson and Anderson, 2000; Mendonca and D'Cruz 2021). In this sense, 'dirt' gestures towards power differentials, and correspondingly speaks to how exclusion and oppression are produced (Elias and Scotson, 1994).

Physical menial work is largely performed by working class men. Reflecting this gender composition, most participants in the present study were male and working class. We understand class as 'a set of power relations, rather than simply a difference in income or occupations' (Todd, 2021, p. 3). As McDowell (2012) notes, classed and gendered identities might usefully be connected in analyses of disadvantage and exclusion among working class people as gender and class inform unjust experiences in precarious workplaces. Research so far has uncovered distinct values, attitudes and motivations that working class men attach to waged work, valuing it for the recognition and respect it affords in a context where primacy is awarded to effort and longevity of employment (Sennett and Cobb, 1972; Willis, 1977; Charlesworth, 2000; Sayer, 2005). Workers in physical, menial work invest in 'waged work' as a resource to create dignity and moral worth (Charlesworth, 2000). Hence, growing precarity and the erosion of access to stable work is likely to affect workers' gendered and classed identities.

Existing literature on dirty work has mainly focused on how precarity aggravated the economic struggles of those involved in these jobs. For example, in the cleaning industry a recent move towards professionalisation, accompanied by implementation of outsourcing measures, has led to deteriorating working conditions amongst cleaners (Tomic et al., 2006; Larsen et al. 2019). The freedom with which private organisations can enter the market and charge lower costs exacerbates the difficulties faced by unions acting on behalf of cleaning workers (Ryan and Herod, 2006; Eichhorst and Marx, 2015). As a result, the limited power of trade unions has rendered cleaners in a state of job insecurity with lower wages (Rowbotham, 2006; Ryan and Herod, 2006; Dube and Kaplan, 2010, Grimshaw et al., 2015, Keune and Pedaci, 2019), perpetuating a rise in precarious work (Kalleberg and Vallas, 2018), and work which is insecure (impacting on an employee's accessibility to social benefits and legal protection; Rodgers, 1989; Kalleberg et al., 2000; Vosko, 2010; Hewison, 2016).

In this literature, less attention has been paid to individual experiences of precarity and how precarious conditions might limit forms of gendered and classed self-understanding. What is also missing is a rethinking of how fear and anxiety caused by precarity (Neilson, 2015) might undermine the potential for social solidarity. Consequently, more attention needs to be paid to examining how conditions of precarity might shape, or confine the forms of resistance that are accessible to workers (Hyman and Gumbrell-McCormick, 2017).

In this chapter, we seek to address these concerns by drawing on Axel Honneth's ideas of mutual recognition and the normative significance of work for identity. In particular, we explore how precarity affects self-understanding at the intersection of class and gender, and what impact it has on class-related solidarity.

6.2 Precarity, Masculinity, and Class

Prior studies have drawn attention to the relationships between class, masculinity, and precarity (Sennett, 2008; Mole, 2010; Giorgi, 2013). Scholars including Sennett (2008) have highlighted how increasing precarity not only poses unfavourable objective conditions such as low pay and higher job insecurity, but also harms a person's character by inhibiting one's opportunity to construct and draw on their work contributions. As such, experiencing precarity challenges meanings of the self, and poses struggles for self-understanding due to the loss of symbolic recognition (Giorgi, 2013) that is afforded by access to stable work. The importance of attaining and retaining stable employment for dignity and moral worth, and the impact precarity can have on one's sense of self, is apparent through Muehlebach's (2011) investigation of factory workers in Milan who lost their jobs through organisational restructuring. For these men, self-construction is built on useful contribution through stable work, the loss of which has a more profound effect than any material damage. Similarly, Choi (2018) explores the working experiences of male migrant taxi drivers in China, arguing that despite long working hours, their wages limit their ability to provide for their families, which is perceived by them as a failure of their working class masculinity. Turgo (2021) examines how Filipino seafarers manage increasing precarity at work through 'masculinity shift', that is, performing different types of masculinity to suit a particular place and time. While the seafarers exhibited behaviours such as obedience, this did not displace their sense of masculinity, since by doing so, they were more likely to gain additional work that was deemed to represent a true form of masculinity (pp. 1569–1572). Furthermore, a link has been established between increased precarity and gun ownership amongst white men in America, since gun ownership compensates for their inability to provide financially by becoming the 'protector' of the family (Carlson, 2015).

Scholars have paid less attention to the potential implications of increasing precarity for working class solidarity. The rise of unstable work has promoted an internal conflict within individuals as they grapple with on the one hand the value of individualisation, and on the other hand the de-humanising effects of exclusion and alienation from the job market, which perpetuates affective experiences of angst and marginalisation (Molé, 2010). Neilson (2015) is concerned that growing precarity leads to existential anxiety (i.e., physically and mentally overwhelming fear through fragility) as well as blame and denial, which limit the potential for social solidarity in a complex and divided class system. Other examples suggest that there might be new emerging forms of solidarity due to the precarious market conditions. In exploring experiences of precarity amongst Chinese migrant workers, Smith and Pun (2018) argue, 'they may lack secure employment contracts, legal labour rights with an employer, but they can band together along lines of common class interest in cultures of solidarity' (p. 612). Similarly, Hyman and Gumbrell-McCormick (2017) note that while labour insecurity poses constraints such as difficulties in organising precarious workers for resistance action, it can also provide opportunities. Yet those opportunities are determined by social relations which differ depending on the position in which we find ourselves in the social hierarchy. Arguably, current accounts pay insufficient attention to ever-changing labour movements (Munck, 2013), and give limited consideration to the potential of precarity to obstruct and/or open new paths to resistance (Neilson, 2015).

6.3 Self-Respect and Self-Understanding in Physically Tainted Dirty Work

Involvement in physically tainted work, with its close proximity to dirt, devalues occupational identities of workers resulting in their stigmatisation and dehumanisation (Crocker and Quinn, 2001, Goffman, 1963). The ways in which workers manage devalued identity has been extensively researched, with the key arguments focusing on the strategies workers employ to neutralise stigma, including reframing, recalibrating, and refocusing (Ashforth and Kreiner, 1999). For example, care aides provide descriptions of themselves as honorable and worthy since they relish completing tasks that others would struggle to do, such as cleaning up human excrement (Stacey, 2005). While firefighters engage in recalibrating techniques by focusing on the dangerous aspects of their work (Tracy and Scott, 2006).

Members of physically tainted occupations also draw on narrative resources such as masculinity (e.g., emphasising toughness and strength) and heroism/self-sacrifice to reaffirm a positive self-identity (Ashforth and Kreiner, 2014; Johnston and Hodge, 2014). For example, street cleaners and refuse withstand work-related hardship to provide a better life for their families (Simpson et al., 2014a). Similarly, butchers display fortitude, which reinforces their positive working class masculinity through a process of self-value and, in turn, increases their tolerance of the unpleasant and dirty tasks (Simpson et al., 2011). Turning to selective social comparisons is another means by which workers in physically tainted occupations seek to affirm a positive identity through work (Ashforth and Kreiner, 1999). For example, street cleaners and refuse workers engage in comparisons with migrant workers and women to seek esteem enhancement (Slutskaya et al., 2016). Similarly, domestic cleaners make downward comparisons between themselves and the unemployed, as well as drawing on working class or masculine norms that enhance value (Bosmans et al., 2015).

Existing work on precarity has noted the importance of trade union membership amongst those involved in physically tainted work. This shared membership is thought to aid workers in constructing occupational dignity as well as providing material benefits (Soni-Sinha and Yates, 2013). Indeed, unions have attempted to improve the visibility of cleaners through development of campaigns, such as 'Justice for Cleaners' in 2006, which focused on building a collective identity amongst cleaning operatives and promoting recognition of the occupation (Keune and Pedaci, 2019, p. 149). However, market changes including the turn towards outsourcing labour and a more general decline in trade union power weaken the prospect of building a strong collective culture, further fuelling workers' feelings of vulnerability (Atkinson et al., 2012). The cleaning industry is characterised by higher staff turnover and growth in the use of agency workers, leading to higher levels of isolation and a weaker collective culture amongst workers (Simpson et al., 2014b). In addition, the increasingly solitary nature of industrial cleaning work, as well as the ease at which workers can be replaced poses challenges regarding collective action as well as the formation of a positive collective identity (Keune and Pedaci, 2019).

Similarly, ethnographic research on meat inspectors in a UK slaughterhouse demonstrates that changes to the structure of the workforce, such as increased use of agency workers, has led to limited opportunities for group cohesion (McCabe and Hamilton, 2015). The workers in these industries show a reluctant acceptance of changing work practices due to greater job insecurity (Slutskaya et al., 2016). Indeed, for those lower in the hierarchy, value is placed on job stability, rather than the nature and conditions of the work (Lene, 2019).

In sum, the increasingly precarious nature of the work appears to hinder the opportunity for low-skilled physically tainted workers to affirm a positive identity at work. In addition, this enhanced precarity might potentially limit available sources of solidarity. While previous research has demonstrated how greater precarity has increased feelings of vulnerability, and lessened opportunities to affirm a positive identity at work (McCabe and Hamilton, 2015), little research has examined how precarity is impacting workers' self-perception, or how this might impact forms of solidarity.

6.4 Honneth: Self-Respect, and Solidarity

To gain further understanding of the impact of increasing precarity at work on self-understanding, and on forms of solidarity available to those occupying positions in low-skilled physically tainted work, we now turn to Axel Honneth's conceptualisation of recognition.

Honneth invites attention to individual experiences of misrecognition and, as importantly, the moral feelings that are evoked (Zurn, 2015). For Honneth, these experiences have a common 'normative core' (Fraser and Honneth, 2003, p. 131) – all such experiences result from the violation of expectations about recognition (Thompson, 2006). If our personhood depends on recognition from others, the threat exists that those who constantly encounter refusal of recognition will suffer a debilitating injury (Honneth, 1996, 2012, Laitinen, 2012, Taylor, 1989). Thus, recognition is a necessary condition to develop a positive self-concept.

Honneth (1996) proposes three modes of self-relation that are dependent on intersubjective relations: self-confidence, self-respect, and self-esteem, all of which influence our ability to form as an autonomous self (Honneth, 1996). Each mode of self-relation is connected to a sphere of recognition: the love sphere, the legal sphere, and the solidarity sphere respectively. The love sphere refers to close relationships and attachments with family, friends and spouses (Honneth, 2014), while the legal sphere encompasses recognition as an equal and autonomous participating member of society, from a legal and moral standpoint (Honneth, 1996). The esteem sphere concerns skills and attributes that are legitimatised by ever-changing societal norms

(Honneth, 1996). In his writings, Honneth is particularly insightful in his attention to work, portraying it as the most important social practice. Social esteem is seen as closely connected to work and labour, and to what Honneth calls the 'achievement principle' (Honneth, 2003, p. 140). This is the key to the normative ideal of recognition, in which everyone gets an opportunity for self-realisation through work. Employment, according to Honneth, therefore remains a major source of recognition.

Recognition also appears to be a useful concept for a deeper understanding of the continuing importance of work in times of precarity (Motakef, 2019). For the purposes of this chapter, we therefore focus on Honneth's (1996) ideas about work in order to consider how the precarious nature of work might affect a worker's ability to attain self-respect. In so doing, we firstly aim to respond to calls to advance understanding of the conceptual relationship between precarity and recognition. Secondly, we aim to explore how this struggle for recognition could potentially be exacerbated by the historically gendered and classed meanings that those involved in low-skilled physically tainted jobs attach to their working lives.

6.5 Methodology

The chapter draws on ethnographic data collected in summer 2011, summer 2015, and spring 2017 from street cleaners and refuse workers across four London Borough councils. Participants included both permanent employees contracted by the council and agency workers. The length of time participants had worked at the councils spanned six months to twenty-five years. The majority of participants were male (9 per cent female). Participants were a mix of white British and migrants, generally reflecting the diversity profiles of each borough.

The research combined participant observation and semi-structured interviews. Participant observation was recorded through field notes (Silverman, 2001). In total, 32 interviews and 128 hours of participant observation were conducted by two female researchers. The identity of the researchers and their purpose was communicated to the street cleaners and refuse workers that participated in the research. Anonymity was assured to all participants. As part of the in-situ field notes, the researchers included reflections on personal experiences and feelings, not solely observations of the work and experiences of the participants. This enabled deeper consideration of any differences between the perspectives of the researchers as participant observers and those of the participants. Best efforts were made to ensure field notes reflected the language used by the street cleaners/refuse workers themselves (Riemann, 2011), to provide more authentic and robust findings. Interviews followed a conversational approach while also being led by theoretical underpinnings (Kvale and Brinkmann, 2009). Topics included current role, previous work, changes in work, parents' occupations, interests and hobbies and future plans. Additionally, participants were free to discuss anything else that they felt was relevant to their own work experiences.

Data analysis was an iterative process, conducted simultaneously with data collection. Hence, reading of interview transcriptions and preliminary field notes informed further discussion points for the data collection process. Two researchers read all transcriptions and field notes to familiarise themselves with the data before discussing their own interpretations of the data and clarifying emergent themes. Thereafter, a more comprehensive thematic analysis was conducted using NVivo software. Both researchers initially completed analysis individually, followed by collaborative discussions on interesting interpretations. This analytical method enabled the researchers to identify recurring patterns based on interpretation of meanings and language (Taylor and Bodgan, 1984). Adopting Strauss and Corbin's (1998) coding techniques, specific codes and concepts from the data were identified. At this stage, several codes were identified regarding how market changes had led to an increase in social and economic struggles for the workers. The next stage of coding involved a process of axial coding whereby initial codes were grouped and linked into various sub-categories. Key themes identified at this stage were an increased sense of job insecurity and difficulties in attaining an acceptable standard of living due to council budget cuts. Finally, a process of relational coding took place involving consolidation of relationships that arose from the data (Taylor and Bodgan, 1984).

6.6 Findings

Three overarching themes were identified: (1) Precarity and economic struggles. (2) The effect of precarity on self-worth. (3) Precarity and the limits of solidarity. Each theme is elaborated below with illustrative extracts from the interviews and observations. Most themes were not specific to occupational groups. In general, our participants' accounts were remarkably similar.

6.6.1 Experiences of Precarity in Low-Skilled Physically Tainted Dirty Work

Increased precarity has encroached on the opportunity of secure work and respectable standards of living for the workers. Market changes such as a movement towards outsourcing has led to alterations in working practices including a loss of jobs due to restructuring leading to redundancies and/or fewer roles and increasing use of agency workers, resulting in the feeling of replaceability.

Most participants were directly affected by the growing precarity. Many underwent the embarrassment of being laid off, the distress of low wages and the threat of poverty. All the participants described their experience of being made redundant multiple times:

Um, I went and worked for Spillers down Houghton Road there, delivering flour.... It done us proud ..., I got a day job and was working for Spillers, Monday to Friday, home weekends.... There for seven years, got made redundant, went to Allied Mills and walked out of a job on a Friday and went into a job on a Monday ... I left there nineteen years later when I got made redundant and, um.... It's quite upsetting, you know...

For many, the strong adherence to a gendered and classed preference 'to have a job for life' and aspirations for more stable and secure employment (Bernard, 1995; Hayward and Mac An Ghaill, 2003) fashioned the decision to join the local councils. However, the funding cuts of local authorities and the continuous introduction of 'market discipline' through commercialisation and privatisation undermined the security of public sector jobs:

You know, you've got all the councils doing different cut backs and all this sort of thing now. You know, it's horses for courses, isn't it, you know, you could come in ... I've been made redundant twice thinking, you know, you're sound enough sort of thing.

Since the recession of the early 1990s, key employers in the industry have increasingly been contracting their workforce on a temporary basis. Workers expressed their frustration with the resulting changes (new monitoring systems, lower pay, less overtime). One of the loaders talked about the costs of competitive tendering highlighting the deteriorated pay and the decline in job security due to the increased number of agency workers:

competitive tendering brought in place during the 90s progressed later made easier through legislation to go out to tender, less consultation time with the workforce to do so, far less trade union rights.

Concurring with previous scholars (Simpson et al., 2014b, McCabe and Hamilton, 2015), the street cleaners and refuse workers in this study repeatedly acknowledged that the market changes to the cleaning industry negatively affected their working experiences and produced new vulnerabilities and anxieties related to their employment:

Cuts in the councils budget for the start, I mean we lost a hell of a lot, a hell of a lot of money and they had to make it somewhere and a lot of it was frontline staff went and one stage we lost 53 members of staff.

Participants also remarked on the impact agency workers have had on the status of permanent working positions:

when I first started there was no such thing as an agency worker, so if I went on strike, tomorrow they'd make a phone call and get another driver in from the agency, the work would still get done, so what's the point in striking, we're not achieving nothing accept losing a day's pay.

The decline in trade union membership and the power has enhanced the feelings of helplessness and vulnerability amongst the workers (Gallie et al., 2016). For Honneth (2007) such feelings of vulnerability result in moral injury fuelling a continuous struggle to regain respect (Honneth, 1996). However, the market changes and decline in trade union power were perceived by these workers as limiting opportunities for resistance (Keune and Pedaci, 2019), thus creating a sense of unattainability of equal recognition.

6.6.2 *Precarity and Self-Worth*

For Honneth (1996), esteem is gained on the basis of the social usefulness of one's achievements – the more useful one is perceived to society, the higher the social esteem they are expected to enjoy.

According to Honneth (1996, 2014), the world of work remains the central place where social esteem is distributed. In other words, social usefulness is directly linked to the work you do and to how legitimate your expectation of respect is. It is particularly pertinent for working class masculinities that remain centred around paid work. For working class men, social esteem can potentially be experienced outside of paid work, but it can never replace the absence of the social esteem earned through and by it (Charlesworth, 2000; Walkerdine and Jimenez, 2012).

In the study, workers' understandings of worth were both classed and gendered; participants heavily relied on traditional notions of working class masculinities – finding and retaining secure employment, creating value for their families and ensuring their children's future (McClelland, 1991; Archer et al., 2001). Being employed and supporting one's family were central to participants' identity and a source of self-respect. In the following quote, one of the road sweepers highlighted the importance of stable employment for the sense of well-being and self-respect:

I'm not the sort of person to sit around, sponging off the dole, I found it all the time I was out of work I was just tired out all the time, it's just the boredom and I kept going to the Job Centre signing on, hated it, so I see this agency, the money was low but I thought, I've got to take it and I did, and I'm glad I did in the end 'cos it led onto a permanent job with the council which is, you know, quite amazing really.

Precarity exacerbated workers' struggle to support their families and undermined participants' sense of self-worth:

I need this to get by because this, without this job then I don't know, I probably wouldn't be able to live because it's just too hard. I need this, this job is just my main priority so if I ever lost my job, I don't know what'd happen because it's a big part of me.

Well put it this way, no, there's been no hope for years, it's been that way, money's just not there. The wages are not there basically to give you a comfy life. It's not there. You're struggling every week, you're struggling to pay things, so life's one big pressure basically.

No, never in a million years. I'm in debt up to my eyeballs at the moment basically. It's very difficult to do on the wages you get, running a home.

Here we see not only feelings of vulnerability but also feelings of frustration due to the changes in overtime rates and the impact it has had on earning a living wage. What follows is a more descriptive account of how this would impact living standards for the workers:

You wouldn't be able to have a mortgage or if you were renting you wouldn't be able to afford to rent, you wouldn't be able.... Now if I was young doing this job, trying to start out a family, wouldn't be able to afford it, no way on earth, no way. –

Men in the study described not being able to get a permanent job as 'not being given a chance to prove their worth'.

if you give me a chance and I mess it up I can't come back to you and say give me another chance, but obviously if you don't give me a chance how can I show what I'm worth.

As secure employment has a huge normative significance for attainment of self-esteem among working class men, precarity can become a real threat to their identities. For these workers, the importance of work is not only related to self-realisation but also to their positive identification with working class masculinity (Slutskaya et al., 2016). Growing precarity perpetuates struggles to retain secure employment and provide for one's family, and therefore exacerbates moral injuries and undermines the sense of self-worth. As such, the centrality of work for self-realisation is classed and gendered.

6.6.3 Precarious Working Conditions, the Limits of Resistance, and the Perpetuated Divisions

The participants' experiences of precarity and uncertainty were projected onto figures and objects that were perceived as signs of unwelcome change, namely foreign workers and managers. Angst and hopelessness in relation to the precarious nature of the work appeared to be dividing workers into 'them' and 'us'.

it's always been the same, it's about who you are and who your supervisor is, I'm not saying it's a racist thing, but if you've got a Hungarian supervisor and you're a Hungarian and you are chatting, you're gonna get the contract before the English person, that's the way it goes.

There were multiple mentions of job centres that were full of migrants/immigrants queuing for jobs (according to dustcart teams). Workers felt that the uncertainty of their jobs was due to the influx of foreign labour. For them it was the most obvious explanation of their struggles. Most unwanted job-related changes were attributed to 'the mass migration … and immigration'. Immigration was blamed for job loss, for the demise of trade unions and for difficulties with management.

groups at work like to stay with their own race, religion, creed, whatever, you know, I mean here (in Hayes) a lot of Polish or Eastern European, a lot of Somalian, a lot of Indian … they still talk about Poland as their home, Somalia as their home, the cafes that they have they don't come here, they go there.

A growing divide was felt between the frontline workers themselves, particularly amongst migrant agency workers:

Certainly there seems to be a lot of animosity towards migrants. They felt that people in this work lose jobs because they come over and work for cheaper money. They clearly didn't feel valued by the management as they informed me 'don't worry, if we left they'd soon replace us with cheap poles'. – Field notes 9.11.16

In-line with Slutskaya et al. (2016), animosity towards migrant agency workers can be interpreted as a way of expressing insecurities manifested through the increasingly precarious nature of the work, and as reflecting a sense of loss of 'what was' (e.g., when a job at the council was a job for life). Additionally, the increasing animosity and divisions between frontline workers, and frontline workers and management, correspond to previous research arguing that an increase in agency workers evokes the threat of being easily replaced, fuelling workers' isolation and, in turn, inhibiting the formation of a positive collective identity (Keune and Pedaci, 2019; Simpson et al., 2014b, McCabe and Hamilton, 2015). In other words, precarity weakens one of the key benefits of work groups – a collective culture where workers can shield themselves against stigma (Ashforth and Kreiner, 1999) – by eroding the space for positive identity formation at work (Rosso et al., 2010). According to Honneth (1996), structures which promote individualisation, implicated in the production of a highly competitive labour market and insecure forms of work inhibit the emergence of a collective understanding of the injustices perpetuated by this very organisation of work (Honneth, 1996).

6.7 Discussion and Conclusion

The aim of this chapter was to examine how rising precarity impacts attainment of self-respect amongst those in low-skilled dirty work by drawing on an ethnographic study conducted with street cleaners and refuse workers in London. Utilising Honneth's recognition theory and his assertion of significance of work for self-realisation, it sought to explore how precarity affects self-understanding at the intersection of class and gender, and how this impacted class-related solidarity. In-line with previous research, our findings have demonstrated that increasing precarity resulted in deteriorating economic and social conditions for workers, such as low pay, job insecurity, and poorer standards of living (Rowbotham, 2006; Ryan and Herod, 2006; Dube and Kaplan, 2010, Grimshaw et al., 2015, Keune and Pedaci, 2019). In accordance with Honneth (1996, 2014), we emphasise the centrality of work for self-esteem by demonstrating that lack of secure employment has resulted, for street cleaners and refuse workers, in experiences of self-doubt and diminished sense of self-worth (Honneth, 2007).

Our findings also suggest that although work is central to everybody's self-realisation, the intensity with which one experiences precarity might differ significantly. For those involved in occupations that are stigmatised and devalued, the accessibility of secure employment is crucial in terms of survival and of identity. In addition, the centrality of work remains classed and gendered. Our findings highlight how secure employment and the ability to provide for one's family is imperative to these workers, due to the heavy reliance on working class masculinity norms for affirming identity (Archer et al. 2001).

Finally, we also show how the vulnerabilities created by the increasingly precarious nature of work undermine opportunities for class solidarity. Concurring with Slutskaya et al. (2016), the ease of being replaced, and the accompanying feelings of nostalgia and hopelessness amongst these workers, have given way to fragmentation of the workforce as well as animosity towards migrant workers. As such, rising precarity has raised barriers to conforming with a positive collective identity (Ashforth and Kreiner, 1999), underpinned by masculine and working class ideals (Simpson et al. 2014b, McCabe and Hamilton, 2015). Indeed, precarity has perpetuated competition amongst workers, thus inhibiting the propensity to collective action in the face of moral injury for working class men (Honneth, 1996).

To further enhance our understandings of how precarity impacts self-respect at work through the intersection of class and gender, future research could seek to explore other contexts such as female-dominated occupations. Current scholarship has identified a strong link between femininity and precarity consequent upon traditional gendered roles, such as women as the caregiver, that force women into insecure employment (De Ruyter and Warnecke, 2008; Webber and Williams, 2008). Yet the intersection between precarity in female-dominated occupations and self-understanding amongst women could benefit from more detailed research. For instance, it would be interesting to examine care work in order to address the nuances of gendered identity, self-respect, and precarious employment. Additionally, a cross-sectoral comparison of the impact of precarity on workers' self-respect amongst self-employed professional occupations (often deemed as 'freelance') and low-skilled dirty work may increase understandings regarding the interplay between classed position, precarity, and subjectivity.

References

Anderson, B. and Anderson, B. L., (2000). *Doing the Dirty work?: The Global Politics of Domestic Labour*. Palgrave Macmillan.

Archer, L., Pratt, S. D. and Phillips, D. (2001). Working-Class Men's Constructions of Masculinity and Negotiations of (Non) Participation in Higher Education. *Gender and Education*, 13(4), pp. 431–449.

Ashforth, B. E., and Kreiner, G. E. (1999). 'How can you do it?': Dirty Work and the Challenge of Constructing a Positive Identity. *Academy of Management Review*, 24(3), pp. 413–434.

Ashforth, B. E., and Kreiner, G. E. (2014). Dirty work and Dirtier Work: Differences in Countering Physical, Social and Moral Stigma. *Management and Organization Review*, 10(1), pp. 81–108.

Atkinson, W., Roberts, S. and Savage, M. (2012). *Class Inequality in Austerity Britain: Power, Difference and Suffering*. Springer.

Bernard, J. (1995) The Good Provider. In Kimmel, M. S. and Messner, M. A. (eds.) *Men's Lives*. Boston, MA: Allyn and Bacon, pp. 149–163.

Bosmans, K., Mousaid, S., De Cuyper, N., Hardonk, S., Louckx, F., & Vanroelen, C. (2015). Dirty Work, Dirty Worker? Stigmatisation and Coping Strategies Among Domestic Workers. *Journal of Vocational Behavior*, 92, pp. 54–67.

Carlson, J., (2015). Mourning Mayberry: Guns, Masculinity, and Socioeconomic Decline. *Gender & Society*, 29(3), pp. 386–409.

Charlesworth, S. (2000). *A Phenomenology of Working Class Experience.* Cambridge: Cambridge University Press.

Choi, S. Y. (2018). Masculinity and Precarity: Male Migrant Taxi Drivers in South China. *Work, Employment and Society,* 32(3), pp. 493–508

Crocker, J. and Quinn, D. M., (2001). Psychological Consequences of Devalued identities. In Brown, R. and Gaertner, S. (eds.) *Blackwell Handbook of Social Psychology: Intergroup Processes.* Blackwell Publishing, pp. 238–257.

De Ruyter, A. and Warnecke, T. (2008). Gender, Non-Standard Work and Development Regimes: A Comparison of the USA and Indonesia. *Journal of Industrial Relations,* 50(5), pp. 718–735.

Douglas, M. (1966). *Purity and Danger: An Analysis of Concepts of Pollution and Taboo.* London, England: Routledge & Kegan Paul.

Dube, A. and Kaplan, E. (2010). Does Outsourcing Reduce Wages in the Low-Wage Service Occupations? Evidence from Janitors and Guards. *Industrial and Labor Relations Review,* 63(2), pp. 287–306.

Eichhorst, W. and Marx, P. (2015). *Non-standard Employment in Post-industrial Labour Markets.* Cheltenham: Edward Elgar.

Elias, N. and Scotson, J. L. (1994). *The Established and the Outsiders: A Sociological Enquiry into Community Problems.* (2nd ed.). Sage.

Fraser, N. and Honneth, A. (2003). *Redistribution or Recognition?: A Political-Philosophical Exchange.* London: Verso.

Gallie, D., Gebel, M., Giesecke, J., Halldén, K., Van der Meer, P. and Wielers, R. (2016). Quality of Work and Job Satisfaction: Comparing Female Part-time Work in Four European Countries. *International Review of Sociology,* 26(3), pp. 457–481.

Giorgi, G. (2013). Improper Selves: Cultures of Precarity. *Social Text,* 31(2), pp. 69–81.

Goffman, E. (1963). *Stigma: Notes on the Management of Spoiled Identity.* Englewood Cliffs, NJ: Prentice-Hall.

Grimshaw D., Rubery J., and Anxo D. (2015). Outsourcing of Public Services in Europe and Segmentation Effects. *European Journal of Industrial Relations,* 21(4), pp. 295–313.

Hayward, C. and Mac An Ghaill, M. (2003) *Men and Masculinities.* Buckingham: Open University Press.

Hewison, K. (2016). Precarious work. In Edgell, S. Gottfried H. & Granter E. (eds.) *The Sage Handbook of the Sociology of Work and Employment,* Thousand Oaks, CA: Sage, pp. 428–443.

Honneth, A. (1996). *The Struggle for Recognition: The Moral Grammar of Social Conflicts.* Cambridge MA: MIT Press.

Honneth, A. (2003). 'Redistribution as Recognition: A response to Nancy Fraser.' In Fraser, N. and Honneth, A. (eds.) *Redistribution or*

Recognition? A Political-Philosophical Exchange. London: Verso, pp. 110–197.

Honneth, A. (2007). *Disrespect: The Normative Foundations of Critical Theory.* Polity Press.

Honneth, A. (2012). *The I in We: Studies in the Theory of Recognition.* Polity Press.

Honneth, A. (2014). *Freedom's Right: The Social Foundations of Democratic Life.* Cambridge: Polity Press.

Hughes, E. (1951) Work and The Self. In: Rohrer, J. and Sherif, M. (eds.) *Social Psychology at the Crossroads.* New York: Harper & Brothers, pp. 313–323.

Hughes, E. (1958) *Men and Their Work.* Glencoe, IL: Free Press.

Hyman, R. and Gumbrell-McCormick, R. (2017). Resisting Labour Market Insecurity: Old and New Actors, Rivals or Allies? *Journal of Industrial Relations,* 59(4), pp. 538–561.

Johnston, M. S., & Hodge, E. (2014). 'Dirt, Death and Danger? I Don't Recall Any Adverse Reaction...': Masculinity and the Taint Management of Hospital Private Security Work. *Gender, Work & Organization,* 21(6), pp. 546–558.

Kalleberg, A. L. and Vallas, S. P. (2018). Probing Precarious Work: Theory, Research, and Politics. *Research in the Sociology of Work,* 31(1), pp. 1–30.

Kalleberg, A. L., Reskin, B. F. and Hudson, K. (2000). Bad Jobs in America: Standard and Nonstandard Employment Relations and Job Quality in the United States. *American Sociological Review,* 65(2), pp. 256–278.

Keune, M. and Pedaci, M. (2019). Trade Union Strategies Against Precarious Work. *European Journal of Industrial Relations,* 26(2), pp. 139–155.

Kvale, S. and Brinkmann, S. (2009). *Interviews: Learning the Craft of Qualitative Research Interviewing.* Sage.

Laitinen, A. (2012). Mis recognition, Mis recognition, and Fallibility. *Res Publica,* 18(1), pp. 25–38.

Larsen, T. P., Mailand, M. and Schulten, T. (2019). Good Intentions Meet Harsh Realities: Social Dialogue and Precarious Work in Industrial Cleaning. *Economic and Industrial democracy,* 43(1), pp. 1–25.

Léné, A. (2019). Job Satisfaction and Bad Jobs: Why are Cleaners so Happy at Work? *Work, Employment and Society,* 33(4), pp. 666–681.

McCabe, D., & Hamilton, L. (2015). The Kill Programme: An Ethnographic Study of 'Dirty Work' in a Slaughterhouse. *New Technology, Work and Employment,* 30(2), pp. 95–108.

McClelland, K. (1991). Masculinity and the 'Representative Artisan' in Britain, 1850–80, in Roper, M. and Tosh. J. (eds.) *Manful Assertions.* London, Routledge, pp. 74–91.

McDowell, L., (2012). Post-crisis, Post-Ford and Post-gender? Youth Identities in an Era of Austerity. *Journal of Youth studies*, 15(5), pp. 573–590.

Mendonca, A. and D'Cruz, P. (2021). Workplace Bullying, Emotional Abuse and Harassment in the Context of Dirty Work. In D'Cruz, P., Noronha, E., Keashly, L., Tye-Williams, S. (eds.) *Special Topics and Particular Occupations, Professions and Sectors*. Springer, pp. 551–586.

Molé, N. J. (2010). Precarious Subjects: Anticipating Neoliberalism in Northern Italy's Workplace. *American Anthropologist*, 112(1), pp. 38–53.

Motakef, M. (2019). Recognition and Precarity of Life Arrangement: Towards an Enlarged Understanding of Precarious Working and Living Conditions. *Distinktion: Journal of Social Theory*, 20(2), pp. 156–172.

Muehlebach, A. (2011). On Affective Labor in Post-Fordist Italy. *Cultural Anthropology*, 26(1), pp. 59–82.

Munck, R. (2013). The Precariat: A View from the South. *Third World Quarterly*, 34(5), pp. 747–762.

Neilson, D. (2015). Class, Precarity, and Anxiety Under Neoliberal Global Capitalism: From Denial to Resistance. *Theory & Psychology*, 25(2), pp. 184–201.

Riemann, G. (2011). Self-reflective Ethnographies of Practice and their Relevance for Professional Socialisation in Social Work. *International Journal of Action Research*, 7(3), pp. 262–293.

Rodgers, G., (1989). Precarious Work in Western Europe: The State of the Debate. In Rodgers, G. and Rodgers, J. (eds.) *Precarious Jobs in Labour Market Regulation: The Growth of a Typical Employment in Western Europe*. Geneva: International Institute for Labour Studies.

Rosso B. D., Dekas K. H. and Wrzesniewski A. (2010). On the Meaning of Work: a Theoretical Integration and Review. *Research in Organizational Behavior*, 30, pp. 91–127.

Rowbotham, S. (2006). Cleaners' Organizing in Britain from the 1970s: A Personal Account. *Antipode*, 38(3), pp. 608–625.

Ryan, S. and Herod, A. (2006). Restructuring the Architecture of State Regulation in the Australian and Aotearoa/New Zealand Cleaning Industries and the Growth of Precarious Employment. *Antipode*, 38(3), pp. 486–507.

Sayer, A. (2005). *The Moral Significance of Class*. Cambridge: Cambridge University Press.

Sennett, R. (2008). *The Craftsman*. London: Allen Lane.

Sennett, R. and Cobb, J. (1972). *The Hidden Injuries of Class*. Cambridge: Cambridge University Press.

Silverman, D. (2001). *Interpreting qualitative data* (2nd ed.). London: Sage.

Simpson, R., Hughes, J., Slutskaya, N., Balta, M. (2014a). Sacrifice and Distinction in Dirty Work: Men's Construction of Meaning in the Butcher Trade. *Work, Employment and Society*, 28(5), pp. 754–770.

Simpson, R., Slutskaya, N., Hughes, J. (2011). Emotional Dimensions of Dirty Work: Men's Encounters with Taint in the Butcher Trade. *International Journal of Work Organisation and Emotion*, 4(2), pp. 195–212.

Simpson, A., Slutskaya, N., Hughes, J. and Simpson, R., (2014b). The Use of Ethnography to Explore Meanings that Refuse Collectors Attach to Their Work. *Qualitative Research in Organizations and Management: An International Journal*, 9(3), pp. 183–200.

Slutskaya, N., Simpson, R., Hughes, J., Simpson, A. and Uygur, S. (2016). Masculinity and Class in the Context of Dirty Work. *Gender, Work & Organization*, 23(2), pp. 165–182.

Smith, C. and Pun, N. (2018). Class and Precarity: An Unhappy Coupling in China's Working-Class Formation. *Work, Employment and Society*, 32(3), pp. 599–615.

Soni-Sinha, U. and Yates, C. A. B. (2013). 'Dirty work?' Gender, Race and the Union in Industrial Cleaning. *Gender, Work & Organization*, 20(6), pp. 737–751.

Stacey, C. L. (2005). Finding Dignity in Dirty Work: The Constraints and Rewards of Low-wage Home Care Labour. *Sociology of Health and Illness*, 27(6), pp. 831–854.

Strauss, A. L., & Corbin, J. (1998). *Basics of Qualitative Research: Techniques and Procedures for Developing Grounded Theory.* (2nd ed.). Thousand Oaks, CA: Sage.

Taylor, C. (1989). *Sources of the Self: The Making of the Modern Identity.* Cambridge, MA: Harvard University Press.

Taylor, S. J. and Bogdan, R. (1984). *Introduction to Qualitative Research Methods: The Search for Meanings.* Michigan: Wiley-Interscience.

Thompson, S. (2006). *The Political Theory of Recognition: A Critical Introduction.* Cambridge: Polity Press.

Todd, S. (2021). *Snakes and Ladders: The Great British Social Mobility Myth.* New York: Random House.

Tomic, P; Trumper, R. and Dattwyler, R. H. (2006). Manufacturing Modernity: Cleaning, Dirt, and Neoliberalism in Chile. *Antipode*, 38(3), pp. 508–529.

Tracy, S. J. and Scott, C. (2006). Sexuality, Masculinity, and Taint Management Among Firefighters and Correctional Officers: Getting Down and Dirty With 'America's Heroes' and the 'Scum of Law Enforcement'. *Management Communication Quarterly*, 20(1), pp. 6–38.

Turgo, N. (2021). Manning the Waves: Masculinity Shift Amongst Filipino Seafarers in the Age of Precarity. *Gender, Work & Organization*, 28(4), pp. 1562–1578.

Vosko, L. (2010). *Managing the Margins: Gender, Citizenship, and the International Regulation of Precarious Employment.* Oxford: Oxford University Press.

Walkerdine, V. and Jimenez, L. (2012). *Gender, Work and Community after De-industrialisation: A Psychosocial Approach to Affect.* New York: Palgrave Macmillan.

Webber, G. and Williams, C. (2008). Mothers in 'Good' and 'Bad' Part-time Jobs: Different Problems, Same Results. *Gender & Society*, 22(6), pp. 752–777.

Willis, P. (1977). *Learning to Labour: How Working Class Kids get Working Class Jobs.* London: Hutchinson.

Zurn, C. (2015). *Axel Honneth*. London: Polity Press.

7 | Precarity and Diversity
The Intersectional Case of Female Christian Janitorial Workers

MARIAM MOHSIN AND JAWAD SYED

7.1 Introduction

Precarity, within sociological theory, transcends the boundaries of labor conditions. However, many scholars (e.g., Castel, 2003; Ross, 2009; Vosko, 2010) continue to see it as a primarily employment-related phenomenon. Precarity is understood in terms of precarious work, characterized by labor exploitation, insecure employment, low wages, and lack of employment benefits. Kalleberg (2009, p. 2) defines precarious work as 'employment that is uncertain, unpredictable, and risky from the point of view of the worker.'[1]

Focusing predominantly on postindustrial societies within the Western world, much of the extent literature on precarity links precarity to post-Fordism (e.g., Amin, 1994; Kalleberg, 2011; Ross, 2009). Mass-production systems and the consequent move to 'flexible accumulation' resulted in changing the structure of employment (Harvery, 1989). The new industrialized world, characterized by trade liberalization, redefined the structure of employment by dismantling organized labor and expectations in terms of employment benefits and protection for workers (Kalleberg, 2009). Precarity followed as a consequence. Thus, while precariousness of work has been part of history way before the post-Fordist world, the contemporary face of precarity is associated mainly with this era (Paraskevopoulou, 2020). While precarity has been considered a wider social, economic, and political problem (Paraskevopoulou, 2020), much of its academic treatment has been in three related terms: (1) precarious work (Vosko, 2010; Wilson & Ebert, 2013), (2) the changes in industrial relations (e.g.,

[1] The authors would like to thank Dr. Ayra Indrias Patras for her valuable comments on an earlier version of this chapter.

Pedaci, 2010), and (3) and analysis of structural mechanisms that contribute to precarity in the workplace (e.g., Wright, 2013).

Some studies (e.g., Betti, 2016; Chan, 2013; Young, 2010) have focused on how precarious work intersects with marginalized identities, such as social class or gender. These studies go on to argue that the neoliberal construction of work and employment, characterized by values such as individualistic goal-orientation, instrumentalism, and competitiveness, contribute to precarity, particularly for those who do not 'fit' into the neoliberal definitions of the ideal employee.

This chapter offers two interrelated case studies of female janitorial workers, working on a contractual basis, in a public sector organization in Pakistan where the typical employment format is full-time and permanent. This helps achieve three interconnected objectives: (1) to study the gendered aspect of precarious work in Pakistani organizations, (2) to identify the intersectionality of gender, social class and religion in relation to precarious work, and (3) and to understand the various dimensions of precarity in specific reference to intersectionality of gender and social class.

The rest of the chapter is divided into six sections. The next section discusses contemporary literature on precarity and precarious work and seeks to understand it in terms of diversity. The third section discusses the context and methodology of the study. Section four presents two case studies that illustrate the precarity of work for women working insecure and low-paid job within otherwise stable organizations owing to the intersectionality of gender, religion, and social class. Section five offers an in-depth discussion of the findings. Section six concludes the study, identifies limitations, and offers insights for practice and future research.

7.2 Literature Review

Precarity, in terms of work, or precarious work is best understood as the absence of the systems and structures that protect workers and decommodify labor (Ruberty et al., 2018). Decommodification is defined in terms of the presence of social protection program to offer immunity against market dependency (Huo et al., 2008). Precarious work, therefore, is defined as employment that is uncertain and unpredictable for the employee (Kalleberg, 2009). The effects of such an arrangement go beyond the boundaries of workplaces and work experiences and have multiple non-work outcomes (Kalleberg & Hewison, 2013).

It is pertinent to observe that while the broad contours of precarious work have been defined, there remains the need for a more nuanced understanding of the concept. One way of achieving such clarity is through identifying the multiple forms that precarious work can take, for instance, (1) precarity in terms of security and continuance of employment (e.g., Kalleberg, 2009; Kalleberg & Hewison, 2013), (2) precarity in terms of financial stability (e.g., Huo et al., 2008), and (3) systematic precarity that affects certain groups more than the others (e.g., Betti, 2016; Young, 2010). While there is a significant amount of research that focuses on the first two aspects, there remains the need to study precarity in specific reference to identities – for example, gender (Paraskevopoulou, 2020; Young, 2010) and social class (e.g., Han, 2018; Lazar & Sanchez, 2019) – that are most at risk of precarious employment.

7.2.1 Gender and Precarity

Gender and precarity, until recently, had remained a comparatively underexplored topic (Paraskevopoulou, 2020). The primary focus of earlier studies was the irregularity of employment for undocumented workers, migrant workers, low-wage employees, and so on. Some studies have focused on the particular relationship of gender and precarity. Young's (2010) study in the US context indicates a gender dimension of precarious employment in that women are more likely to work in low quality job settings. The study also highlights gender discrepancies in benefits and union protection. Moreover, it suggests that gender differences in wages and part-time work status are caused by workplace discrimination against women.

Hašková and Dudová's (2017) study of precarity and gender in the Czech Republic suggests that precarious or insecure jobs accepted by women with care responsibilities as a temporary strategy eventually become a trap excluding them from stable employment. Fudge's (2006) study of precarity in the Canadian context highlights the need to consider self-employment and unpaid caring labor in order to develop policies and laws that promote women's equality.

Similarly, in her study of the historical relationship between gender and precarious labor, Betti (2016) focuses on Italian women, and shows that different production modes and working conditions were simultaneously present in Fordist and post-Fordist societies, and women experienced a significant level of precariousness even during era of economic prosperity. The study identifies sexual division of labor and sex-based discrimination as the key reasons of the gendered nature of precarious work.

In their study of precarity and gender in a university context, O'Keefe and Courtois (2019) suggest that precarious female academics are 'non-citizens of the academy,' a status, which, they argue, is reproduced through exploitative gendered practices and evident in formal/legal recognition such as staff status, rights, and entitlements, as well as in informal dimensions such as social and decision-making power. The authors suggest that gender equality interventions in academia must start with a close examination of the state of the precarious academics.

7.2.2 An Intersectional Approach to Precarity

Scholars (e.g., Branch & Hanley, 2017;Tapia & Alberti, 2018) have focused on the intersection of multiple marginalized identities to understand precarity and those most frequently affected by it. Studies show that aspects of identity, such as gender, religion, social class, caste, and color of skin can create more complex situations that result in precarity of employment (Joy et al., 2015; Lawton, 2015; McDowell, 2018).

Studies on migrant workers in the United States show that informal employment owing to legal issues is a major determinant of precarity, specifically among women (Zou, 2015). The concept of legality is considered an important dimension in understanding precarity among migrant workers as it determines the worker's position in the labor market (Bloch et al., 2012). Research (e.g., Anderson, 2007; Triantafyllidou and Marcetti 2015) shows that when workers are forced to accept informal work contracts, they remain at the risk of being exploited. Women workers in similar situations face more irregularity owing to caregiving and additional familiar responsibilities. They also face added discrimination due to the additional household

Previous research suggests that religious identity, particularly of a minority group, may add to their feelings and experiences of precarity. For example, Shams's (2020) study of South Asian origin Muslim Americans suggests a collective precariousness felt by this group. Despite their professional success, their positionality as a racialized and stigmatized religious 'Other' gives them a feeling of insecurity and a fear t because of their race and religion. This anxiety, Shams suggests, affects their education and career choices. Similarly, Ahluwalia (2019) reveals how Sikh identities may be seen as precarious and vulnerable 'model minorities' in a post-Brexit/Trump era.

Previous studies on informal workers have explored several dimensions to the gendered aspect of precarity. Villegas (2019), for instance, noted that female domestic workers remain at risk of abuse and violence, with little or no legal protection, owing to the isolated work conditions and informality of work arrangements. The informal sector still remains an attractive choice for many individuals with marginalized identities, for instance, migrant workers working without legal work licenses and women workers looking for flexibility (Fantone, 2007). This shows that the flexible nature of precarious work allows individuals with marginalized identities to opt into irregular employment, which in turn may result in exploitation (Bloch & McKay, 2017). Fatone (2007), for instance, observed that many migrant women preferred irregular employment because it allowed them flexibility. Hašková and Dudová (2017) view the attractiveness of such flexibility as an exploitative trap that seeks out the ways in which these workers are excluded from mainstream employment and offer alternatives to the workers in form of precarious employment.

7.2.3 The Context of the Study

There is an increasing number of studies that call for conceptualizing precarity from non-US perspectives (e.g., Joy et al., 2015; Lee & Koffman, 2012). Research suggests that the concept of precarity within the Global South is inherently different from the Western perspectives for several reasons, such as (1) precarity is not only a corporate strategy but a policy response to conditions levied by international financial institutions, and (2) precarity in the global south goes beyond job quality and job insecurity and is a crisis of social reproduction (Lee & Koffman, 2012). Agarwala (2021) observes that in an attempt to globalize their economies, governments have enabled corporations to hire labor that is not bound by protective and regulatory legislation in order to reduce labor costs and reduce competition. The resultant precarity is not only a corporate strategy. It is by design and policy and attracts specific demographic and income groups and is therefore systematic. Similarly, in Pakistan, precarious work arrangements are highly prevalent, not only in the informal sector but also in the manufacturing sector (Ayaz et al., 2019). Ayaz et al. (2019) observe that specifically recruiting female factory workers is a norm across the garment manufacturing industry, because female workers consent to precarious work more easily than male workers.

In Pakistan, the issue of discrimination against non-Muslim minorities, particularly Christians, in terms of janitorial work has been highlighted locally (Shaukat, 2019) as well as internationally (The New York Times, 2020). This discrimination has its roots in the caste discrimination against lower caste Hindus, who converted to Christianity during colonial times. However, they could not rid themselves of the social stigma that was associated with their caste and remained associated with cleaning and janitorial work. In current times, Christians belonging to lower socio-economic classes are confined to cleaning jobs (The New York Times, 2020).

7.3 Methodology

Based on the premise that multiple aspects of identity may contribute to the precariousness of work, we identified cases where the intersection of gender, religion, and social class is most visible and in stark contrast to secure and protected employment. Among the most visible cases of intersectional precarity were females working in the manufacturing sector (Ayaz et al., 2019), female domestic workers (Agarwala, 2021), and female janitorial workers (Patras & Usman, 2019). We chose two case studies of religious-minority female janitorial workers from a public sector organization in Pakistan. These cases demonstrate and highlight instances of disproportionately precarious work for women working low-paid jobs. Both cases were selected for the following four reasons: (1) both the workers worked (or previously worked) at a public sector organization where most of the staff was hired on a permanent government contract as per law; however, some employees were hired on contractual basis and did not receive the benefits as those employed on permanent contracts. These benefits included job security, paid leaves, better compensation packages, better and more defined career trajectories, and opportunities for growth/ promotions, some medical benefits, and retirement benefits including provident funds and pensions. This gave us the opportunity to compare the precarity across permanent and contractual jobs. (2) There were different kinds of contracts within the organizations, however, those hired for lower-paid jobs, such as cleaning and janitorial staff, faced the most severe form of precarity. Their contracts were rarely revised and salaries rarely renegotiated; unlike those on contracts for higher positions. This allowed for comparison among different types of contractual jobs. (3) There were other female workers, across multiple levels of the organizational hierarchy on both permanent and contractual terms. This allowed some perspective into the precarity of women's jobs across different social classes. (4) There were other members of the janitorial staff who were hired on a permanent basis.

We conducted in-depth interviews with both respondents and analyzed the data through thematic analysis using Braun and Clark's (2012) method. Interviews were conducted bilingually in Urdu and Punjabi and then translated into English. Multiple interviews were conducted with each respondent. Each interview lasted for about an hour. Interviews were conducted at the workplace as well as at the residences of the respondents.

7.4 Results

The two case studies highlighted two major themes in women's precarious work – the intersection of gender and social class, and structural discrimination against women within organizational settings. Within both cases, particularly the first case, age (in terms of fertility), pregnancy, and childcare were observable sub-themes. For illustrative purposes while maintaining anonymity, Figures 7.1, 7.2, and 7.3 depict the social class and residential arrangements of the two respondents.

Case 1 – Women, Pregnancy, and Precarity – the Intersectionality Angle

Rachel[2] lives in a slum situated in Islamabad city. Majority of the population in the slums is of lower-class Christians, associated to janitorial work. Rachel is in her late thirties, is married, and has eight children. She currently works as a domestic worker in several homes. She has to walk several kilometers to reach bus stops in order to access public transport to move from one home to the other. The slum where she lives is situated next to an open sewerage drain and is therefore not

---

[2] All names have been changed to maintain confidentiality of the respondents.

Figure 7.1 Photograph of the entrance to a single-brick walled house

Figure 7.2 Photograph of an unplanned staircase structure

a legal settlement. The houses in the vicinity are unplanned and are structured with makeshift bathrooms and staircases (see Appendix 1).

Rachel used to work at a public sector organization in Islamabad where she was a member of the janitorial staff. She worked there for over seven years before being laid off. Her father used to work as a permanent staff member for the same organization before he retired at sixty years of age as per law. Her brother is also a janitorial worker

Figure 7.3 Photograph of water reserves in an illegal slum

in the same organization but has not been regularized as a permanent employee; he works as a contractual worker with no benefits or job security. Rachel was six months pregnant with her eighth child when her contract with the organization was terminated. She was verbally informed that the contract was being terminated because she was not a permanent staff member and could not be allowed maternity leave as per rules.

They assured me that I would be able to rejoin three months after the birth of my child. I told them I could not be without work for six months and that I would prefer to join earlier than that. They did not agree. I went to the office right after three months of giving birth. They had already hired another worker. I requested them to consider my case, but no one listened to me. It is easy to lay us off because we are poor. The men are still given some consideration, but women are fired very easily.

After several years, Rachel tried to regain her employment once again and submitted a written application with the help of some young female officers that she had befriended during her service in the organization.

There were some very nice young girls that I had become friends with. They were all officers, but they were kind to me and my children. Sometimes I had no choice but to take my children to work. They were very kind to my children. When I was pregnant with my seventh child, I couldn't work properly. I felt sick most of the time, but I knew if I complained, I would be terminated. I hid my pregnancy for six or seven months. I am not very slim, so it was easy for me to hide it. These girls knew and they supported me. Then after my child was born, all of them left the organization on study leave for further education. I got pregnant with my eighth child and was laid off. Many years later I came to know that some of them were back, so I went to them and asked for their help. One of them heard my case and drafted a letter. She pursued my case with the higher authorities, but nobody listened. Someone in the administration said that Rachel is lazy and useless. I am not lazy, I was pregnant. My father cleaned the floors and bathrooms of this place till he was sixty years old. My brother serves the place. Yet, I was tossed aside. It doesn't happen to those who aren't poor.

Rachel now works as a domestic worker for multiple families to meet her needs. She mentions that domestic work is extremely volatile and that she can be fired with so much as a 'don't come from tomorrow onwards'. Additionally, she faces multiple pressures pertaining to her faith, ranging from abusive behavior at the workplace to precarious employment:

'I named my son David (pseudonyms used), but we call him Dawood. Because I don't want him to face the same issues we do. I don't easily get domestic work because of my Christian name. When I do, many families hire me for cleaning work only. It is common. Many families don't allow us to work in their kitchens. There was a family I worked for. They had a separate helper for working in the kitchen and doing laundry; she was Muslim. I cleaned and mopped. Later, the other helper asked them for additional work. They fired me and handed my work to her. She was indispensable. I was fired easily'.

Case 2 – Intersectional Precarity – Structural Discrimination Against Women in Poverty

Alia has been working as a janitorial staff member at a public sector organization for over six years on a contractual basis. She receives a minimum wage, has no job security, and her contract can be terminated at any time. Moreover, if she is absent from work for more than once a month, it is deducted from her already small paycheck.

I live in a slum. I have to walk several kilometers to reach the bus stop where the office transport picks me up at 7 AM every day. I work every single day; I reach home after 5 PM. Sometimes I work on Saturdays too. I get a small over-time payment for working Saturday, but since the office transport doesn't run on Saturdays, the entire payment for the day goes to the taxi driver. I can't refuse, obviously. We can't refuse.

Several of her relatives also work in the same office. Some of the men from her family are members of the permanent staff.

Those with permanent jobs have benefits. They cannot be fired so easily. They have better pay. They have paid leaves too. But the women are all hired on a contractual basis.

Alia was aware of the fact that she had no option other than doing janitorial work, and that despite the contractual terms of service, working at a public sector organization was better than a private sector job. Many workers like Alia are employed under precarious conditions in the hope that one day, their jobs will be regularized.

What other option do I have? This is the only job I can get. Then it is better to work here and hope that one day I will be regularized. Do you know how it is for people who work private jobs? And those who work at people's homes? Many people don't even let us touch their utensils.

Alia did not fully understand the rules and regulations of public sector employment. The only difference she understood between contractual and permanent employment was job security, better pay, and paid leaves.

It is not like I will have children at this age. My children are all grown up. But they still do not regularize my employment. I have been working here for years now. I am clearly not going away either.

Alia was aware that younger women were discriminated against because of pregnancies, childbirths, younger children, and caregiving. She pointed out that she was not young anymore, so she should not be discriminated against. In response to questions about members of the permanent staff, female officers, getting benefits such as paid maternity leaves, Alia responded with a smile:

But those are officers. They have education and good jobs. Our jobs are not like theirs.

One other important observation among the residents of these slums was that the illegal status of their residences created problems in acquiring many citizen rights (Dawn, 2017). In some cases, children remained out of school because government-run public schools required a permanent address on the parent's CNIC (computerized national identity card). Similarly, many of these people could not land permanent jobs for the same reason.

The government officials say the slum is illegal. We paid money for our house, but it is illegal. So many people cannot get CNIC. The jobs require CNIC. Even domestic workers are required to submit a copy of CNIC to the house owners for security. I have a CNIC but many people don't.

7.5 Discussion

The two case studies suggest that gender's intersection with religion, social class, job profile, and personal situations such as pregnancy adds to precarity at work. In other words, precarity is an outcome of a complex interplay of multiple forms of identity, that is, gender, social class, and life cycle. It is important to note that many of the issues of precarity facing these two women may not be faced by those women who belong to the upper social class or those who have high-profile jobs. This reveals the diversity of experiences and issues facing women of different social classes and circumstances. The cases confirm findings from previous studies (e.g., Hašková & Dudová, 2017; Pedaci, 2010) that flexibility trap of precarious jobs attract those at the risk of poverty, facing legal issues such as registration into the national database due to illegal status of place of residence, or women who are unable to commit to extended durations of work due to caregiving duties at home.

The examples of Rachel and Alia illustrate that issues of precarity such as low wages, labor exploitation, insecure employment, and lack of employment benefits are attributable not only to their gender but also to their social identities like religion and class. As Paraskevopoulou (2020) observes, the interplay of marginalized identities, such as gender, minority status, and social class, creates a multiplicative effect that results in individuals being sucked into precarious work arrangements. In such cases, job security, stability, predictability, growth trajectory, and other employment benefits become secondary concerns and are treated as luxuries that the workers cannot afford. Figure 7.4 illustrates this intersectionality.

As we previously discussed in the literature review section, precarious employment can be taxonomized into three distinct but

Figure 7.4 Photograph of open garbage cans outside a slum entrance

interrelated categories: (1) precarity in terms of security and continuance of employment, (2) precarity in terms of financial stability,
and (3) systematic precarity that affects certain groups more than the
others. Our results show that not only are the three categories visible and identifiable, but there is also evidence to believe that each of
these categories has identifiably distinct effects on different categories of individuals. For instance, findings from previous studies (e.g.,
Ayaz et al., 2019) as well as the cases of Rachel and Alia, illustrate
that systematic precarity is clearly more of a gendered issue. The
patterns in both the case studies highlight that women are equally
affected by all three categories of precarity while social class as a distinct category of identity is more at risk of facing precarity in terms
of job security and financial stability. This also shows that women
belonging to lower-income groups remain at risk of facing an intensified form of precarity.

Figure 7.5 provides a conceptual illustration of intersectional taxonomy of precarious work. However, we recognize that there remains
a need for further empirical investigation to confirm this theoretical
connection. We call for further research to look into the contextually
distinct categories of precarious work and the specific implications it
has for different categories of workers. Through this contribution, this
chapter offers theoretical insight into conceptualizing precarity in a
more systematic way.

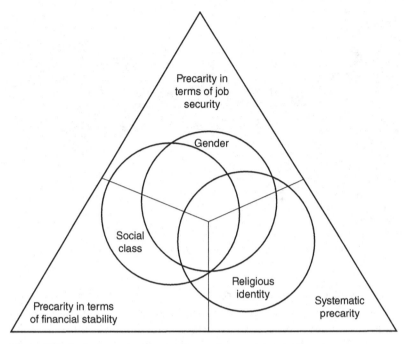

Figure 7.5 An intersectional taxonomy of precarious work

In addition to the above theoretical contributions, the study also initiates debate to inform policy on the informal sector, as well as systematic precarity within the formal, even public, sectors.

There are a few limitations that we find pertinent to discuss. First, while the case study method of research allows us to offer a deeper investigation of patterns within precarious employment situations, the small sample size does not leave room for generalization. Future research on intersectionality can use our model to design surveys or qualitative studies to confirm the proposition. Second, there remains the need for gender-disaggregated data, particularly in the informal sector, to inform policy.

7.6 Conclusion

Based on arguments from previous research, this chapter posits that we cannot understand precarity without taking into consideration the existing dimensions that produce and sustain inequalities (Jokela, 2017).

These dimensions include gender, religion, race/ethnicity, social class, and so on and reinforce existing inequalities in the labor market (Anderson, 2007). This study focuses on the gendered and intersectional consequences of precarity and posits that there are multiple categories within the larger idea of precarity which have different effects on different types of individuals.

References

Agarwala, R. (2021). An Intersection of Marxism and Feminism among India's Informal Workers: A Second Marriage? In L. Fernandez (ed.) *Routledge Handbook of Gender in South Asia* (pp. 263–275). Abingdon, Oxon: Routledge.

Ahluwalia, P. (2019). Precarious and model minorities: Sikh identities in the 'new' global politics of religion. *Sikh Formations*, 15(3–4), 332–342.

Amin, A. (1994). Post-Fordism: Models, fantasies and phantoms of transition. In A. Amin (Ed.), *Post-Fordism: A Reader* (pp. 1–39). Oxford: Blackwell.

Anderson B (2007) A very private business: exploring the demand for migrant domestic workers. *European Journal of Women's Studies, 14*(3), 247–264.

Ayaz, M., Ashraf, M. J., & Hopper, T. (2019). Precariousness, gender, resistance and consent in the face of global production network's 'reforms' of Pakistan's garment manufacturing industry. *Work, Employment and Society, 33*(6), 895–912.

Betti, E. (2016). Gender and precarious labor in a historical perspective: Italian women and precarious work between Fordism and post-Fordism. *International Labor and Working-Class History*, 89, 64–83.

Bloch, A. & McKay, S. (2017) *Living on the Margins: Undocumented Migrants in a Global City*. Bristol: Policy Press.

Bloch, A., Sigona, N. & Zetter, R. (2012). Migration routes and strategies of young undocumented migrants in England: a qualitative perspective. *Ethnic and Racial Studies* 34(8), 1286–1302.

Branch, E. H., & Hanley, C. (2017). A racial-gender lens on precarious nonstandard employment. *Res Sociological Work*, 31, 183–213.

Braun, V., & Clarke, V. (2012). Thematic analysis. In H. Cooper (Ed) *APA Handbook of Research Methods in Psychology, Vol 2: Research Designs*. Washington, D.C.: American Psychological Association, pp. 57–71.

Castel, R. (2003). *From manual workers to wage laborers: Transformation of the social question*. Trans. Richard Boyd. New Brunswick, NJ: Transaction Publishers.

Chan, S. (2013). 'I am king': Financialization and the paradox of precarious work. *The Economic and Labour Relations Review*, 24(3), 362–379.

Dawn (2017, Aug 1). Former residents visit Islamabad slum two years after it was razed. Available at: www.dawn.com/news/1348894/former-residents-visit-islamabad-slum-two-years-after-it-was-razed

Fantone, L. (2007). Precarious changes: gender and generational politics in contemporary Italy. *Feminist Review*, 87(1), 5–20.

Fudge, J. (2006). Self-employment, women, and precarious work: The scope of labour protection. *Precarious work, women and the new economy: The challenge to legal norms*, 201–222. https://ssrn.com/abstract=896170

Han, C. (2018). Precarity, precariousness, and vulnerability. *Annual Review of Anthropology*, 47, 331–343.

Harvey, D. (1989). *The Condition of Postmodernity: An Inquiry into the Origins of Cultural Change*. Oxford: Blackwell.

Hašková, H., & Dudová, R. (2017). Precarious work and care responsibilities in the economic crisis. *European Journal of Industrial Relations*, 23(1), 47–63.

Huo, J., Nelson, M., & Stephens, J. D. (2008). Decommodification and activation in social democratic policy: resolving the paradox. *Journal of European Social Policy*, 18(1), 5–20.

Jokela, M. (2017). The role of domestic employment policies in shaping precarious work. *Social Policy & Administration*, 51(2), 286–307.

Joy, A., Belk, R., & Bhardwaj, R. (2015). Judith Butler on performativity and precarity: Exploratory thoughts on gender and violence in India. *Journal of Marketing Management*, 31(15–16), 1739–1745.

Kalleberg, A. L. (2009). Precarious work, insecure workers: Employment relations in transition. *American Sociological Review*, 74(1), 1–22.

Kalleberg, A. L. (2011). *Good Jobs, Bad Jobs: The Rise of Polarized and Precarious Employment Systems in the United States, 1970s–2000s*. New York: Russell Sage Foundation.

Kalleberg, A. L., & Hewison, K. (2013). Precarious work and the challenge for Asia. *American Behavioral Scientist*, 57(3), 271–288.

Lawton, N. R., Calveley, M., & Forson, C. (2015). Untangling multiple inequalities: intersectionality, work and globalisation. *Work Organisation, Labour and Globalisation*, 9(2), 7–13.

Lazar, S., & Sanchez, A. (2019). Understanding labour politics in an age of precarity. *Dialectical Anthropology*, 43(1), 3–14.

Lee, C. K., & Kofman, Y. (2012). The politics of precarity: views beyond the United States. *Work and Occupations*, 39(4), 388–408.

McDowell, J. (2018). Men's Talk in Women's Work: 'Doing being a Nurse'. In B. Vine (Ed.) *The Handbook of Workplace Discourse*. London: Routledge.

Millar, K. M. (2017). Toward a critical politics of precarity. *Sociology Compass*, 11(6), 1–11.

O'Keefe, T., & Courtois, A. (2019). 'Not one of the family': Gender and precarious work in the neoliberal university. *Gender, Work & Organization*, 26(4), 463–479.

Paraskevopoulou, A. (2020). Gender and Precarious Work. In Klaus F. Zimmerman (Ed) *Handbook of Labor, Human Resources and Population Economics*, 1–18. New York: Springer.

Patras, A. I., & Usman, A. (2019). Intersection of Gender, Work and Caste: The Case of Christian Female Sweepers of Lahore. *Journal of the Research Society of Pakistan*, 56(2), 363–373.

Pedaci, M. (2010). The flexibility trap: Temporary jobs and precarity as a disciplinary mechanism. *Working USA: The Journal of Labor and Society*, 13, 245–262.

Ross, A. (2009). *Nice Work if You Can Get It: Life and Labor in Precarious Times*. New York: New York University Press.

Rubery, J., Grimshaw, D., Keizer, A., & Johnson, M. (2018). Challenges and contradictions in the 'normalising' of precarious work. *Work, Employment and Society*, 32(3), 509–527.

Shams, T. (2020). Successful yet precarious: South Asian Muslim Americans, Islamophobia, and the model minority myth. *Sociological Perspectives*, 63(4), 653–669.

Shaukat, Z. (2019). The faces of discrimination. Available at *The News* www.thenews.com.pk/tns/detail/592949-faces-of-discrimination

Tapia, M. & Alberti, G. (2018). Unpacking the Category of Migrant Workers in Trade Union Research: A Multi-Level Approach to Migrant Intersectionalities. *Work, Employment and Society*, 33(2), 314–325.

The New York Times (2020). Sewer Cleaners Wanted in Pakistan: Only Christians Need Apply. Available at: www.nytimes.com/2020/05/04/world/asia/pakistan-christians-sweepers.html

Triantafyllidou, A. & Marchetti, S. (2015). *Employers, Agencies and Immigration: Paying for Care*. Farnham: Ashgate.

Villegas, P. E. (2019). "I made myself small like a cat and ran away": workplace sexual harassment, precarious immigration status and legal violence. *Journal of Gender Studies*, 28(6), 674–686.

Vosko, L. F. (2010). *Managing the Margins: Gender, Citizenship, and the International Regulation of Precarious Employment*. Oxford: Oxford University Press.

Vosko, L. F. (Ed) (2006). *Precarious Employment: Understanding Labour Market Insecurity in Canada*. Montreal and Kingston: McGill-Queens University Press.

Wilson, S., & Ebert, N. (2013). Precarious work: Economic, sociological and political perspectives. *The Economic and Labour Relations Review*, 24(3), 263–278.

Wright, C. F. (2013). The response of unions to the rise of precarious work in Britain. *The Economic and Labour Relations Review*, 24(3), 279–296.

Young, M. C. (2010). Gender differences in precarious work settings. *Industrial Relations*, 65(1), 74–97.

Zou, M. (2015). The legal construction of hyper-dependence and hyper-precarity in migrant work relations. *International Journal of Comparative Labor Law and Industrial Relations*, 31(2), 141–162.

8 Precarious Work in the Gig Economy
Diversity, Race and Indigeneity Lenses

KURT APRIL

8.1 Precarity

The so-called gig-economy (McKinsey, 2016), built on digital platforms and ubiquitous access, has expanded globally and brings with it the promise of flatter and more participatory business models, as well as the promise to unite workers and make their services available to ever-expanding markets. As a result, today, and exacerbated by the COVID-19 pandemic, instead, markets and market conditions are uncertain and not guaranteed over long periods of time, different types of workplace-influencing technologies are changing at rapid and unpredictable rates, and individuals have, through their own choices or the choices of their employers, more loose connections to their work roles and operate more independently – mostly without the security and benefits associated with previous formal employment. The adoption of these latest neoliberal rationalities and scripts for economic development is no different in emerging economies, as many of the new approaches act as accelerants of precarity. The promise of the gig economy was of a break from the past, the excitement of progress, of things potentially being different than before, and a reconfigured capitalism. However for many in the gig economy, the future looks nothing like the promise and additionally does not come with the work securities of the past, therefore each day is filled with anxiety about work and 'their futures shadowed by pervasive terror' (Ridout & Schneider, 2012, p. 5). Some argue that all we have is *capitalism as usual* with its embedded inequities for many, particularly for those at the bottom of the working pyramid. The idiosyncratic governance of platforms have ensured that economic power remains concentrated with a few (new) elites, further embedding the class-race and local-foreign divides, while responsibility and control over economic transactions remain externalised to those deemed lower in the platform hierarchy, that is, typically black, African and foreign.

After the end of the world wars, organisations and management practice, in the Western world and Western-influenced world of work in general, sought to create relatively stable and secure jobs for workers – but since the 1970s, with the advent of radical workplace optimisation and capitalistically inspired efficiency initiatives, 'precarious work' has emerged as a primary concern for unions, politicians, the media, academics and non-governmental organisations (Kalleberg, 2009). Some, such as Standing (2011), even go as far as to write about a 'precariat' as a 'dangerous class-in-the making' (a new class landscape of 'bad precariat'), with robust critique by Seymour (2012) and Breman (2013) of this claim being a clear overstatement, and Munck (2013, p. 747) argued that 'the concept is highly questionable both as an adequate sociology of work in the North and insofar as it elides the experience of the South in an openly Eurocentric manner'. Standing (2011) defined seven forms of labour security – adequate opportunities, protection against dismissal, barriers to skill dilution, health and safety regulations, training, stable income, representation – all of which were being eroded in the new era; and, identified six components of 'social income' – direct production, wages, community support, company benefits, state provision, private/rentier income – each of which was shifting in different ways for different groups. Standing (2011) described the 'precariat' in terms of what it does not have in terms of labour security and social income, and argued for a new 'politics of paradise', underwritten by a universal basic-income grant for the 'good precariat' (Breman, 2013).

Even though Standing's book faced criticism from labour scholars, it opened up new and important discussions about precarity and precarious work under neoliberal capitalism. South Africa, for instance, is plagued by historic and recent structural socio-economic failures and inefficiencies, such as poverty, gender-based violence and gender marginalisation as a whole, social and human rights injustices, race-based workplace norms, income and wage inequalities, unequal historic wealth and assets, differential market and organisational access, inequality of access to quality education, unequal provincial services and service delivery, xenophobia and ethnocentrism, and very high levels of unemployment (particularly for South African youth and those from the lower-end working age groups, as well as for low- to unskilled foreigners) (Daya & April, 2021; April & Dharani, 2021; April & Syed, 2020; Stats SA, 2020; Stats SA, 2019).

Some forward-thinking organisations in South Africa have taken bold steps over the last number of years towards more progressive and developmental employment approaches, with the intention of growing the skills, capabilities, confidence, embeddedness and networks of employees throughout their employment journeys. However, this is not true for many organisations, where Western, neoliberal, bottom-line approaches dominate the thinking of management and policy makers. As a result, in South Africa, certain kinds of work (e.g., Uber, inDriver, Bolt, Didi, takeaway deliver cyclists and motorcyclists with dominant players such as MrD, call centre workers, domestic workers, cleaners, care workers, day labourers), certain conditions of work (e.g., independent work, zero-hour contracts, temporary contracts, temporary work permits, visas) and the targeting of particular employee groups (e.g., the already marginalised, immigrants, refugees, those who live in poverty or are from the lowest socio-economic classes) skirt the conditions of healthy employment and even basic human rights, with no real access to social justice – more broadly, this kind of work is known as 'precarious work', because of the tenuous natures of both the employment contracts and the work conditions of the employees. In short, precarity is a condition of necessary dependency for the under-resourced and less powerful in order to simply carry on. In South Africa, foreigner and refugee immigration – whether documented or undocumented – is a contentious issue, in relation to race, indigeneity and economic inclusion. As a result, this study sought to understand precarity as a way for understanding and therefore critiquing the current economic structures, and what it does to imbue ongoing social and economic inequities, and to assist scholars to rethink identity, class and group formations through the lens of precariousness. Jørgensen's (2016) article is instructive, as it draws on understandings that 'link the notion of the precariat (and processes of precarization) to practices and investigates links between immigration and precarity' (p. 959).

8.2 Methodology

This research took on an interpretivist ontological approach. From an ontological perspective, the interpretivist framework supports the view that there is more than one reality (Laverty, 2003; Searle, 1995). The interpretive paradigm has a subjectivist approach in its analysis of the social world (Ajjawi & Higgs, 2007; Deetz, 1996), and this paradigm assumes the research respondent's frame of reference as opposed to that of the observer (Burrell and Morgan, 1979). Additionally, Ajjawi and Higgs (2007) state that the interpretive research paradigm is rooted on the epistemology of idealism (in idealism, knowledge is considered to be socially constructed – and its main aim is to interpret the social world). The epistemological approach of this research was based on phenomenology. Phenomenology concerns itself with descriptions of the human, lived experiences of the respondents as it is lived within a particular context (Moustakas, 1994).

A qualitative strategy was used for this research, in which the industry was the unit of analysis (platform industry), and the unit of observation was at the level of the individual – as data was collected from individuals on three fronts: (a) a written, constructivist self-report approach for a relevant case study, with the respondent's permission to share his name (Yin, 2003; Schwarz, 1999), (b) a written perspective shared by way of a poem (with the respondent's permission to share her name) and (c) eight individuals engaged in precarious and platform work in South African work environments, who attended a university course, were asked to share their unique, socially constructed stories, perspectives/thoughts and feelings related to their lived experiences (Searle, 1995) – each of the respondents agreed to share their stories and perspectives, only if they could remain anonymous in the research. This non-probability, convenience sampling method was used because the platform industry population was too disperse, and random sampling was therefore not possible. Respondents shared stories of incidents and experiences of their struggles and triumphs working in the gig economy, which included elements that spoke to personal, interpersonal, organisational, institutional, and social factors shaping their worklives – it is important to remember that these stories were not removed from the contexts and spaces within which the respondents, and their work colleagues, lived out their experiences (Caxaj, 2015), and these experiences were described in their own words (Crabtree and Miller, 1999) – with some quotes taken verbatim out of longer responses by the individuals. Their insights and perspectives have been incorporated throughout the theoretical treatment of the topics under research. Due to the exploratory nature of the data gathered, the main limitation of the study was that it is merely indicative of the platform industry context.

8.3 Gig Disruption

For indigenous South Africans union membership, in the main, guards somewhat against the total exploitation of their labour. However, many who are unionised but do not have 'personal voice' or 'role status' in their organisations, are still exploited with long hours, go years without promotion or recognition of their contributions, have to hold down multiple jobs, have to sign unfavourable contracts to secure work, and face retrenchment by modern technology in the digital platform-economy. Most platforms feed off existing social and economic relations and merely bring efficiency to ongoing exploitation, therefore, collective union action for workers, such as striking and downing of tools, are their only means to have their voices heard and situations addressed. Respondent 6, a recent University graduate and working for three years, fears that the contract she signed and the continuous introduction of technology to replace humans in her workplace, has left her future uncertain and potentially part of what Wright (2015) calls 'futuristic feudalism' at the hands of what Pollio (2019) terms 'platform-capitalistic enterprises' (p. 762). Wright (2015) encourages us to ask who benefits from the gig disruption: the pampered in the back of the Uber or the driver in the front trying to scrap together enough money to make their car payment?; the Airbnb landlords or the rest of the people in a neighbourhood that has become a ghost town?; the rich business owner sifting out costs from their business or the worker who needs to be on call 365/24/7 for when their employer needs them? We have to ask: 'Is this really the promise of the so-called sharing economy, the gig economy?' Respondent 6 shared:

This so-called fourth industrial revolution has given my employers the power to mess me around and threaten me with easy replacement, just like the Apartheid bosses did to my parents and older black workers. I now want a living wage. I accepted a below-market package and no medical aid, just to secure a job when I first started. But now I am going to join the October strike that is planned. We will demand living wages and better contracts. I didn't think that I would ever be one of those, when I was still studying.

Similarly to Petriglieri et al.'s (2019) findings, we found that certain individuals who do not belong to formal organisational groups (e.g., unions) and do not have the backing of specific professional bodies (e.g., such as enjoyed by psychologists, social workers, engineers, accountants), some find great joy/comfort in their non-connection to such groups and bodies, while others suffer with continuous stress and anxiety from not having such connections and complementary support. Research Respondent 7 made it clear that he was not missing his previous stable, organisational work: 'Best thing I did was leave my organisation. They demanded too high a personal price from me. I didn't really have a life. I could never really be myself. I am pleased not to be a cog in their machine anylonger. It was my personal choice to work like this.'

Uber arrived in Cape Town in August 2013, in the form of a 'stealth launch' of 'secret Ubers,' a Twitter account, a blog and a marketing team (Studener, 2013). Research Respondent 3, a self-employed microentrepreneur, shared: 'I used to work in the formal, unionised taxi industry before. It was a bloody nightmare. I could only work certain hours, so my money was capped. Lots and lots of rules, which didn't make working lekker [nice].' These sentiments are similar to ones expressed in Pollio's (2019) study of Uber in Cape Town, and additional insights were shared in which a research respondent noted that in the formal taxi industry, the call centre which directed ride opportunities were often open to bribes and corruption: 'there's more justice. Call centres are so corrupt, but you cannot bribe the satellite [referring to Uber's geo-location system of allocating rides]' (p. 760). Pollio (2019) reported that call centre operators would ask for cigarettes and small tips to prioritise calls. Barchiesi's (2008) research however highlighted how, in precarious environments of weakened collective solidarity and unionised identities, marginalised groups with increasingly embattled employment security status tend to turn to defensive indentifications and privilege individual survival strategies of the self-entrepreneurial kind (p. 121). As urban immigrants and refugees increasingly become the norm in the global south, accompanied by self-settlement (with little to no assistance from authorities), we see local governments and businesses unable to offer formal employment (and the accompanying security and labour rights) ahead of their massively unemployed indigenous populations. As a result, many immigrants and refugees turn to the platform economy, the informal economy and entrepreneurialism for their livelihoods (April & Zolfaghari, 2021).

CASE STUDY

Henri Tshiamala, a refugee from the Democratic Republic of Congo, elaborates on this dilemma in a personal case study:

My Journey as a Refugee Entrepreneur in South Africa

I am a Congolese man, born 8th child of fourteen. My father was a polygamist who had three wives and my mother was the 3rd and the only one that he still lived with. My mother had seven children – six girls and one boy, me. I was born in the diamond rich province of Kasai. My experience as a refugee entrepreneur who came to South Africa – running away from the persecution, violence and abuses of the dictatorship of the late President Mobutu in what was then known as Zaire – brings a personal perspective to this chapter.

I arrived in South Africa in 1991, into a society that was socially and politically dysfunctional and marred by political and social violence. I was rejected by the white community because I was a black man and I was also rejected by the black South African community because I was a foreigner. For the white man I was a 'K-word' (an offensive designation legally banned in South Africa), and for the black man I was a 'makwerekwere' (one of the many derogatory appellations that could mean 'stupid stranger who speaks bizarre vernacular'). Despite these challenges of insecurity, hatred and institutional and societal exclusions (Zhou, 2004), I had to cultivate and learn new street-survival street skills away from the local communities.

I had no role model in my community, no reference point for how to succeed in an environment that was very hostile towards black Africans from outside the Republic of South Africa. There were and still are no comfort zones for refugees in South Africa (Kalitanyi & Visser, 2010). It is a 'make it or die', 'swim or sink' type of situation where one has no options but to navigate through life's waves. I did not have access to financial assistance for living, no scholarships for my studies, no permanent place to stay or any business incubation programme to rely upon. Police harassments were frequent, keeping me on the run almost all the time because I was without immigration permits. I had to learn new street survival skills that could help me overcome a variety of challenges to secure both my safety as well as build my future. I had no financial support on the streets of Johannesburg and Cape Town, but I aspired to be 'successful' just like some of the few Eastern and Western African businesses that seemed viable in South Africa. Street survival skills must have helped me to be resilient in entrepreneurship. Failure was not an option then, and is still not an option now, even though I have experienced sporadic xenophobic attacks resulting in the loss of a considerable amount of merchandise.

Through informal entrepreneurship as a refugee entrepreneur, I managed to complete my mostly self-funded studies in engineering at the Cape Peninsula University of Technology as well as my master's degree in business administration from the University of Cape Town. I initiated a successful small family retail and real estate enterprise without any financing from any government agencies or from the private sector, and I created employment for some locals. I am currently pursuing my PhD at the Graduate School of Business at the University of Cape Town and have found a way of paying back to the community through many years of pro bono entrepreneurship coaching, mentoring and lecturing at the Raymond Ackerman Academy of Entrepreneurship Development, at the TSIBA University and at many public engagements organised by community-based organisations, while my South African-born children are actively involved in tutoring in the some disadvantaged schools around Cape Town.

I have realised in the process of my own development as a refugee entrepreneur that I have incidentally become a role model for other refugees who are inspired and motivated by what they have observed in my progress; many of whom went on to achieve more than I could ever imagine. They have read my story in the *Succeed Magazine*, in the *Cape Argus newspaper*, and in the University of Cape Town's Graduate School of Business's *Breakwater Magazine*. Some of these refugees are working hard to achieve accomplishments in their studies and create their own business ventures as well. I assume that they think if one refugee can make it then nothing is impossible for all of them to achieve success. I was, and still am, invited to speak at motivational conferences and schools because some think that my career path and humble achievement is worth emulating.

Henri's voice and story are important, as it recognises the dynamism of refugee economics, highlights how some find avenues for opportunism amidst the ambiguity of precariousness, and can serve to help expand our ideas away from the narrow focus of immigrant and refugee marginal status and vulnerability – however, not all are as resilient and determined as he is, not all African communalist rationales bear out in practice, and we have to recognise his early (and still current) tough experiences and what he had to go through (and still goes through at times, particular with regard to his race and nationality).

8.4 Framing and the Racial Gaze

Race, social class and citizenship (who matters and who is deemed credible) are interlocked in interpretive processes, and form the bases for ongoing discriminatory engagement and embedded privilege. 'Frames' and 'framing', introduced by Burke (1937) and expanded upon by Goffman (1974, p. 21), are 'schemata of interpretation' that are continually in use and allow users 'to locate, perceive, identify, and label a seemingly infinite number of occurrences defined in its terms' (Klein & Amis, 2021). The framing term 'white gaze', in which black lives have no meaning and no depth without centralised, normative white standards, was popularised by critically acclaimed writer Toni Morrison (1994). Yancy (2008) describes the 'white gaze' as possessing power, which is drawn from whiteness, in which the black subject who wears their race on their face is objectified as morally defective, inferior sub-human, thus imposing 'coloniality of being' on the black subject (Maldonado-Torres, 2007). Coloniality (which is different to colonialism), according to Maldonado-Torres (2007, p. 243) is maintained in books, cultural patterns, in 'common sense', in the self-image of peoples, in aspirations, in labour, in intersubjective relations and so many other aspects of our modern day experiences. Thus, to gaze is to exercise power over the unknown [black] subject and in so doing bring their humanity into question and to continuously hold them at the end of racial subjection (Sithole, 2016). For Fanon (1967), the 'white gaze' is colonising, as the black subject continues to be in the existential predicament of having to survive. Anticolonial scholar and psychiatrist Frances Welsing (1991), building on the work of Fanon ([1964] 1967), suggested that the objectifying effect of the 'white gaze' on black people is tied to the systematic process of *inferiorisation* – which she defined as: 'the conscious, deliberate and systematic process utilised specifically by a white supremacy social system to mould [black people and other people of colour] within that system into "functional inferiors"' (p. 241). One could argue that the 'white gaze' fixed on foreign [black] and under-resourced indigenous workers functions to decentralise and locate the displaced, the migrant, the marginalised in positions where they feel unable to challenge both their economic and racial oppression, as well as their place in society, thus leaving intact 'coloniality of being' (discussed further in more detail). That being said, black South Africans too have thoroughly internalised the 'white gaze', particularly visible in relation to the race-blackness of other Africans in order to advance their relative social- and economic positions. Scapegoat theory suggests that some people from dominant racial groups (such as majority-population groups like black South Africans, but remain economic minorities with little economic power and influence) may displace their frustrations onto a 'scapegoat', which may happen to be a person or group of people from an ethnic minority (e.g., foreigners) or from a migrant background

(Zawadzki, 1948). Social- and therefore racialised frame/cognitive comparisons (Festinger, 1954) from indigenous white and black South Africans have persisted, and even been further embedded through the gig economy– the 'racial gaze' through television and social media which further reinforces their distinction from the 'under-classes' and 'poor blacks', as well as 'master–servant' interactions in the home with local black- and immigrant Africans acting as domestic maids and/ or gardeners. Workplace interactions that set-up or engender superior–inferior power relations further encourage authoritarian personalities and behaviours (the archetypical, dominant personality during apartheid) to view 'others' and minority ethnic groups as unconventional and threatening, and will act to degrade them and likely express their orientation to authoritarianism through discrimination toward them (Zastrow & Kirst-Ashman, 2010; Klein & Amis, 2021). As Fiske (2002, p. 123) so aptly reflected: 'Stereotyping, prejudice, and discrimination reflect, respectively, people's cognitive, affective, and behavioural reactions to people from other groups.' The racially 'othered' are perpetually placed outside the realms of consideration and compassion and, as Da Costa (2016, p. 475) asserts, are 'continually captive to their status of non- or less than human.'

According to Hoobler, Dowdeswell and Mahlatji (2021), Daya and April (2021), April and Syed (2020), and Durante and Fiske (2017), stereotypical social constructions and mental models continue to legitimise and perpetuate unequal systems of prejudice and power, and this is equally true in the gig economy where immigrants and refugees are afforded only certain job roles and economic opportunities (often the more insecure jobs). According to Respondent 1: 'This kind of work will always be handed to people like me – a foreigner, black, immigrant. I have family in other Western countries – it is the same for them.' Immigrant participants in the gig economy often comprehend their position and worth in the social and economic hierarchy, and can sometimes 'normalise' their lack of rights, as they perceive their economic- and social class locations as permanent or semi-permanent. According to Barchiesi (2008), in post-apartheid South Africa organised labour, who now occupy policy-making institutions with the national government and corporate business, saw indigenous South Africans enjoy fresh rights, safeguards, educational and skills development opportunities, institutional visibility and career mobility – shifting the working class (who are from the majority black population group) further away from social and economic vulnerability, and rendered them 'seen' by those in the middle- and upper classes of society. These sorts of rights and opportunities are, in the main, not fully available for immigrants, and less so for refugees, and the gig economy has exacerbated these inequalities. They often have to 'make their own way', 'rely on luck', 'be in the right place at the right time', 'self-fund their educational aspirations', 'take responsibility for their own development', and 'get closer to those who have access'. Immigrant and refugee Uber drivers in South Africa, in particular, enjoy marginal gains in the transactional asymmetries of ride-sharing (Pollio, 2019) and never fully experience the promised empowerment through micro-entrepreneurship of the gig economy but instead continue to suffer under racist neoliberal, capitalistic ideals (albeit, more efficient ideals).

8.5 Duality of Hope

We do know, from the work of Leigh and Melwani (2019), that societal and economic changes, as well as events (such as the onslaught of the COVID pandemic), can trigger cross-class comparisons, even when persons of different classes do not interact physically – however, even though the ordering of an Uber vehicle, or a restaurant-meal delivery service (such as UberEats, Mr Delivery or Bolt Food), happens digitally (thus ensuring 'distance'), the customer (often middle to upper class) still receives their car or meal engagement in person with the 'other', who is almost always black. In South Africa, that often means that there will be some form of physical interaction between previously isolated groups (middle to upper class indigenous South Africans) and foreigners – further embedding notions of cross-class comparisons, cross-race comparisons, intellectual-capability comparisons and certain levels of discomfort, and situating roles/certain work cognitively for certain race groups (robbing them of other potential capabilities and possibilities in the minds of those who often run or own businesses) – whether that be between white (mainly middle to upper class) and black groups, indigenous black groups and immigrants/refugees, or between immigrants with legal status in the country and undocumented refugees. Respondent 4 made the point that:

They [indigenous black South Africans] were previously downtrodden through Apartheid. This is the time for local black South Africans to move up in the world. As a foreigner, I am not even on the radar yet. Perhaps, if I am lucky, my children may be able to gain full working rights and proper employment in the future. But, this is not my time. I am stuck here, and I have to be grateful for that.

There is an acknowledgement that the precarity of their social situations and fragility of their economic situations are embedded in long-term, systemic, racial discriminatory practices in South Africa – particularly for people who look like them, and especially so for black African immigrants (compared to white, European immigrants who have different, often positive, engagements and interactions with, as well as job opportunities through, indigenous South Africans) – and that the road to full rights, better contracts and greater work security may never come, as the gig economy has changed the nature of employment forever.

Respondent 5 shared: 'I don't think that things will ever get to how it used to be, in terms of jobs and bosses personally looking out for workers. I hear some of the guys talking about such things [possibilities]. I think that it is a myth. We must accept how things are, because work and the world have changed forever.' Respondent 5 further added: 'You must just look at which foreigners mobilise and use the support that they have been offered – who seeks out support to survive and thrive. You must also check out how differently women and men mobilise support. The women are much better at it.' 'As a refugee, it is worse for me. I came here with nothing. The other immigrants came from nice jobs back home, with good educations. I don't have that. So I am even lower than them. I even feel a kind of loneliness at times. They eat in nice restaurants, and even own shops' (Respondent 2). What Respondent 2 is hinting at is the fact that, with the legal constraints that prohibited black South Africans from social and economic mobility being outlawed, opportunities now exist for those with good education and skills to climb the social and economic ladders – and that is even possible for immigrants with the right qualifications and access. Those from the working class and particularly without skills, though, receive messages and feedback that signal that the world is hierarchical, stigmatised, racist, rigid and lacking in economic networks for those who are like them, and that they have little influence over their limited futures – requiring that they need to either be docile and accepting of their current realities/unease (disassociate with their historical backgrounds and culture, and increase the value of their new realities) or remain continuously adaptable in the face of uncertainty and ambiguity – reflecting the hidden injuries of class (Sennet & Cobb, 1972) or cleft habitus (Bourdieu, 2007). This has led to social rifts between certain immigrant groups. There is, however, interaction across the groups, particularly at the lower end of economic opportunity as those from lower social class positions face significant barriers to gain admission to gateway institutions like professional companies and higher education organisations. Even with the felt-pressures and work insecurity which people experience in the onslaught of the exploitative, capitalist economic machine of the gig economy, and in a racialised South African society which is both rapidly integrating and dividing simultaneously, individuals (indigenous South Africans, immigrants and refugees) still yearn for significance and belonging – but find it hard to: (a) meaningfully engage others (particularly those with different strands of identity to themselves), (b) cross social, economic and emotional boundaries, (c) always, independently, find and have direction in work, and (d) confidently exhibit their authenticity, through traditional means and access to dialogue and positive engagement. According to Petriglieri, Ashford and Wrzesniewski (2019), identities give individuals 'cognitive, emotional, behavioural and social boundaries' (p. 3), and it is these identities that make people's inner worlds intelligible and manageable (Swann & Basson, 2010). People appropriate identities, negotiate and move between identities, and acquiesce to identities to reduce uncertainty (Petriglieri et al, 2019; Hogg & Terry, 2000) and in order to belong (Baumeister & Leary, 1995), because they wish to make sense of their translocational positionality (Anthias, 2009), relinquish their identities because of the restrictions it imposes on them and their engagements with others and for work (Collinson, 2003), or because specific identities cast those individuals in a negative light (Petriglieri, 2015).

8.6 Class and Mobility

In the study by Adut (2017), the interviewees did not reject nor try to disassociate themselves from their ethnic identity – and Adut defined 'ethnic identity' as the extent to which the interviewees spoke about a collective past and expressed a positive attitude toward their parental figures (Haybi-Barak & Shoshana, 2021, p. 238–329). Adut, though, did not distinguish between the mobility foundations of his interviewees, such as them having tertiary education and advanced degrees, or whether they worked in white-collar jobs, or in which suburbs/regions they lived, or the closeness of their social- and work lives to the central business district in a particular region (Lacy, 2004). Respondent 8, an immigrant from north-east Africa, spoke liberally about the negotiation between his old home-country culture and the embarrassment he felt when it was brought up (negatively) in conversation, and the joy of his new home country culture (in South Africa) but simultaneous disappointment of not being fully accepted in the new environment. He claims to have actually been part of the middle-class in his home country, having worked his way up to management level in an organisation (white-collar job) – with no formal, tertiary education – and, now, having to work as a low-level worker in a platform business and the concurrent pain, shame and future uncertainty he endures. Egla Ntumba originally from Mbuji Mayi in Central Africa, but who has been living in South Africa for a while now, reflects in a poem about the identity and belonging challenges of growing up in one country and, as a black female who moved to South Africa as a foreigner and never quite belonging where she is now (in South Africa) – additionally how, when she goes back to visit her home village and country, she also no longer quite belongs there either.

> I am from here, I am from there
> Central African origin, South African roots
> I live here but I don't belong here
> I am from here, I am from there
>
> I speak in language of the South
> And dream in the language of my ancestors
> But I am not foreign, I am African
>
> I am from here, I am from here
>
> My heart belongs to this continent
> I was raised here, I am here
> I am from here, I am from everywhere

Egla, a skilled professional today with a master's degree, represents what is known as a 'middleman' or is part of the 'middleman group' – a group of marginalised minority skilled people or entrepreneurs, from all gender identities, who openly deal, negotiate and navigate their way between two groups of people in a host society – the dominant (indigenous South Africans) and the subordinate groups (immigrants and refugees), or play an intermediary economic role between the economically/socially strong group (white South Africans) and the segregated weak groups (black South Africans, immigrants and refugees) with more fluid transitions between identities (Tshiamala, 2021; Bauman, 2000; Bonacich, 1973) and cultures (Schneider & Lang, 2014). 'Middleman' minority theory tends to suggest that societal trust, economical solidarities and reciprocal entrepreneurial favours are given and exchanged within a specific group of immigrants as a way of self-preservation as well as an economic emancipation strategy (Light, Sabagh, Bozorgmehr, & Der-Martirosian, 1994; Zhou, 2004). In South Africa, though, there is very little knowledge of the first-person lived experiences and insight into how middle[persons], other immigrants and refugees conceptualise their own integration into South African society, while 'travelling' back and forth between racio-spatial black and white neighbourhoods and workspaces. To better understand the organisational experiences of immigrants and refugees in order to create more inclusive and equitable contexts, these individuals must be allowed to give 'voice' to their racialised, precarious lived experiences via, what Detert, Burris, Harrison and Martin (2013) describes as, the discretionary provision of improvement-oriented information. Within organisational contexts, April, Dharani and April (2023), Fast, Burris and Bartel (2014), as well as Tangirala and Ramanujam (2012), argue the importance of managers' actively seeking and soliciting voice from employees, because doing so indicates leader openness and receptivity to input (Martin & Harrison, 2022), and a willingness to transform workspaces to being more inclusive (April, 2021). Martin and Harrison (2022) further recommend that managers actively counteract the tendency to rely on a history of elite cultural signals as indicators of quality, and consciously make a greater effort to solicit input from those who come from less prestigious backgrounds but have arrived at the same destination as others who may come from greater privilege – in doing so, they argue, may help with the necessary emancipation and rebalancing of disparity in opportunity. Nkomo et al. (2019) call for researchers and practitioners to extend their knowledge of workplace diversity and inclusion and place our dominant knowledge systems under critical examination, while Castilla (2008), Joshi et al. (2015)

and Gunn et al. (2021) argue that the evidence for traditionally linking skill supply, skill demand and productivity with fair remuneration
and labour protections (remuneration, health and well-being), particularly for those in precarious employment and racialised institutions,
should be rethought, since the current models and frameworks are
weak and dysfunctional.

The prevalent narratives of upward mobility, which encourage,
among other things, reflexivity about personal choice, meritocracy,
personal motivation, personal effort, individuality, and the dissocia-
tion from socio-political accounts, play a central role in the establishment and maintenance of the neoliberal discourse in contemporary
culture (Lamont, 2018). At the same time, researchers such as Lareau
(2015) have already pointed out that mobility rates are insignificant.
In other words, class remains one of the primary predictors of life
outcomes (Haybi-Barak & Shoshana, 2021, p. 327). More often than
not, members of the 'middle[persons] group' are part of an upwardly
mobile group who have professional skills and capabilities – however,
Martin and Harrison (2022), as well as Phillips, Martin and Belmi
(2020), claimed that upwardly mobile individuals experience cultural
mismatches and impaired performance in prestigious organisations
and in elite universities and, when seeking employment in prestigious
organisations, those evaluating applicants use signals of eliteness like
interviewees' leisure activities and self-preservation styles to select for
cultural/racial fit in ways that disadvantage those from lower-class
backgrounds. Additionally, women may not benefit from their class
advantage, and pay a penalty for their gender, as confirmed in research
conducted in the United States by Rivera and Tilcsik (2016). They
sent applications from fictitious students at selective, but non-elite,
law schools to 316 law firm offices in 14 cities, randomly assigning
signals of social class background and gender to otherwise identical
résumés (p. 1097). Their research results showed that higher-class
male applicants received significantly more callbacks than did higher-
class women, lower-class women and lower-class men. A survey
experiment and interviews with lawyers at large firms suggested that,
relative to lower-class applicants, higher-class candidates were seen as
better fits with the elite culture and clientele of large law firms – but,
although higher-class men received a corresponding overall boost in
evaluations, higher-class women did not, because they faced a com-
peting, negative stereotype that portrayed them as less committed to

full-time, intensive careers (p. 1125). This commitment penalty faced by higher-class women offsets class-based advantages these applicants may receive in evaluations and, consequently, signals of higher-class origin provide an advantage for men but not for women in elite labour markets (Rivera & Tilcsik, 2016, p. 1097). Upwardly mobile immigrant women face a 'triple whammy' though – not only the commitment penalty, the immigrant penalty, but also not having 'voice' in the appropriate spaces. Therefore, scholars and practitioners alike have a responsibility to disrupt and decolonise the normative narratives of precarious work and the people who engage in such work [foreigners and locals from lower social class environments] through continuously highlighting the lived experiences of penalties and suffering of many in the gig economy. Also, they have to deconstruct notions of indigenousness, and South African indigenousness in particular, as the only referent of progress, and challenge the centring narratives of others [foreigners] as deviants.

8.7 Identity and Anxiety

There are debates in the extant literature as to whether lower social class environments socialise inhabitants to a sticky 'habitus' (resistant to change), or a set of disposition or behaviours, that cultivates a reduced sense of personal initiative or self-efficacy (Martin & Harrison, 2022; Pitesa & Pillutla, 2019; Bordieu, 1984; Streib, 2015) as opposed to those researchers (Friedman, 2016) who argue against the stability of habitus through the changing of an individual's context and the concomitant high sense of efficacy, positive self-views, and engagement in 'voice' in the new context. Uber, Bolt, inDriver and MrD in South Africa offers the potential for economic emancipation, with supposed choice for its drivers regarding structure, as well as a community of trust (among drivers) and a container for people's existential anxieties about the insecurity of their futures – as such, it is appealing to many. On the other hand, with the absence of a traditional organisational holding environment, these drivers are confronted with the fact that their work and their constructed work identities are precarious. Similarly to Petriglieri et al.'s (2019) study of independent workers, we found that the drivers defined themselves through their work (productivity and accrued income) as opposed to, what we assumed might be the case, that is, belonging, with many expressing no need to 'belong' nor the need for 'feelings of belonging' – interestingly this was the case with both more skilled immigrants as well as skilled and unskilled refugees. In fact, immigrants and refugees respected each other for achieving work/productivity goals (a type of intersubjective solidarity). Academically, it is interesting to consider the nexus between solidarity and perceived injustice, which Tava (2023) contends to also trigger the emergence of solidarity. It is therefore important to understand both 'middle[person] minority' groups, 'upwardly mobile' groups, and 'refugee' groups not as separate entities but as dynamically interacting groups in labour provision and transitional justice in the gig economy. What unites our understanding (and framing) of these groups are their identities in relation to the precarious nature of the different work that they do, and the roles that they play within the South African economy. In society, as well as the workplace, multiple immigrant and refugee participants come together in an attempt to carry out individual- and organisational courses of action in concert with each other.

8.8 Conclusion

As shown in this study, the platform economy, which has perpetuated the racial inequalities and stereotypes in society, has done nothing to alleviate the plight of the most economically marginalised, and very little to shift the embedded inequalities in the class hierarchies of, and its players equitable and dignified access to, the ongoing neoliberal capitalist system – it remains deeply unfair and unequal, albeit more efficiently unequal. Additionally, this study highlights the intersectionalities between class, nationality and race, and its resulting experiences of oppressions and immobility. The study also shows how racio-economic issues are generally omitted in understanding the maintenance of platform-related structural inequalities, as well as how important issues to do with xenophobia and ethnocentrism are silenced and minimised in favour of the positive spin on the benefits of the gig economy. The question of 'who is central' and 'who matters' in this newly defined labour market and 'who is marginal' raises issues to do with power, dignity, status, opportunity and access, perceived and practiced justice, equity and democracy, living standards and virtues, and the value of all life in allegedly post-racial societies. Finally, the precarious work experiences of many in the study reveal patterns with respect to the psychological harm experienced by mainly black workers who are exposed to, and affected by, frequent race-related dilemmas and tensions in their daily interactions. It is important, though, to recognise that precarious workers contribute their efforts, time and skills to the modern economy with few protections, little reward, little recognition and, most importantly, with ongoing isolation and marginalisation by indigenous citizens and mainstream institutions. Given the global nature of platforms, we are encouraged to go beyond static conceptualisations of frames and gazes towards transnational frames through contact, interactions, narratives and emotions, and demonstrate how more dynamic, inclusive frames and gazes can emerge between framing agents (the powerful) and others (less powerful). The government- and workplace strategies, policies and efforts certainly must reflect this and even trade unions and professional bodies may want to broaden their scope and enrol a more diverse range of individuals into their membership and spheres of influence. Below are some potential, future research questions:

• In the gig economy, are we as humans just for sale (commodity capital), or are there more enriched ways in which to think about the changing nature of work and person-work engagement?
• How might the debates about precarious work be re-energised to contemporary regimes of racialisation?
• What are the ways in which race, indigeneity, and its intersections, need to be considered in international relations?
• What is the role of narratives and stories in deconstructing precarious work experiences and opening up enhanced lenses for its understanding?
• How important is a deeper understanding of the role of emotions in connecting 'belonging' and 'workplace precarity'?
• How might feminist critiques of institutional discrimination be brought to bear on our understanding of new participatory models?
• How might decolonial theories enhance our understanding of precarity?
• While precarity and precarious work has been brought to the fore in European activist circles, what might the perspectives be from Africa and other emerging economy environments?
• What the avenues for opportunism amidst the ambiguity of precariousness for the marginalised?

- In which ways do ethics and responsible leadership intersect with precarity at both the political- and organisational levels?

References

Adut, R. (2017). *'And All by Myself, Almost': Constructing Self-working Among Mobile Arabs and Mizrahim: Beit Safafa and Gilo as Case Studies [Unpublished doctoral dissertation]*. Ben Gurion University, Beer Sheva, Israel.

Ajjawi, R., & Higgs, J. (2007). Using hermeneutic phenomenology to investigate how experienced practitioners learn to communicate clinical reasoning. *The Qualitative Report, 12*(4), 612–638. https://doi .org/10.46743/2160-3715/2007.1616

Anthers, F. (2009). Translational belonging, identity and generation: Questions and problems in migration and ethnic studies. *Finnish Journal of Ethnicity and Migration,* 4(1), 6–15.

Anthias, F. (2008). Thinking through the lens of translocational positionality: An intersectionality frame for understanding identity and belonging. *Translocations: Migration and Social Change,* 4(1), 5–20.

April, K. (2021). The new diversity, equity and inclusion (DEI) realities and challenges. In P. Norman (Ed.), *HR: The New Agenda* (pp. 119–132). Randburg, SA: KR Publishing.

April, K., & April, A. (2009). Reactions to discrimination: Exclusive identity of foreign workers in South Africa. In M. F. Özbilgin (Ed.), *Equality, Diversity and Inclusion at Work: A Research Companion* (pp. 216–228). Cheltenham: Edward Elgar Press.

April, K., & Dharani, B. (2021). Diversity and entrepreneurship in South Africa: Intersections and purposive collaboration. In K. April, & B. Zolfaghari (Eds.), *Values-driven entrepreneurship and societal impact: Setting the agenda for entrepreneuring across (Southern) Africa* (pp. 241–254). Randburg: KR Publishing.

April, K., & Syed, J. (2020). Belonging: Race, intersectionality and exclusion. In J. Syed, & M. Özbilgin (Eds.), *Managing diversity and inclusion: An international perspective* (2nd ed., pp. 142–193). London, UK: SAGE Publications Ltd.

April, K., & Zolfaghari, B. (Eds.), *Values-driven Entrepreneurship and Societal Impact: Setting the Agenda for Entrepreneuring Across (Southern) Africa.* Randburg: KR Publishing.

April, K., Dharani, B, and April, (2023). A. Leadership for inclusivity. In K. April, B. Dharani & A. April (Eds.), *Lived Experiences of Exclusion in the Workplace: Psychological & Behavioural Effects* (pp. 169–195). Bingley: Emerald Publishing.

Barchiesi, F. (2008). Wage labor, precarious employment, and social inclusion in the making of South Africa's postapartheid transition. *African Studies Review*, *51*(2), 119–142. https://doi.org/10.1353/arw.0.0083

Bauman, Z. (2000). *Liquid modernity*. Cambridge: Polity.

Baumeister, R. F., & Leary, M. R. (1995). The need to belong: Desire for interpersonal attachments as a fundamental human motivation. *Psychological Bulletin*, *117*(3), 497–529. https://doi.org/10.1037/0033-2909.117.3.497

Bonacich, E. (1973). A theory of middleman minorities. *American Sociological Review*, *38*(5), 583–594. https://doi.org/10.2307/2094409

Bourdieu, P. (1984). *Distinction: A Social Critique of the Judgement of Taste*. Cambridge, MA: Harvard University Press.

Bourdieu, P. (2007). *Sketch for a Self-analysis*. Cambridge: Polity Press.

Breman, J. (2013). A bogus concept. *New Left Review*, *84*, 130–138.

Burke, K. (1937). *Attitudes Towards History*. New York, NY: New Republic.

Burrell, G., & Morgan, G. (1979). *Sociological Paradigms and Organisational Analysis*. London: Routledge. https://doi.org/10.4324/9781315242804

Burris, E. R., Detert, J. R., & Romney, A. C. (2013). Speaking up vs. being heard: The disagreement around and outcomes of employee voice. *Organization Science*, *24*(1), 22–38. https://doi.org/10.1287/orsc.1110.0732

Castilla, E. (2008). Gender, race, and meritocracy in organizational careers. *The American Journal of Sociology*, *113*(6), 1479–1526. https://doi.org/10.5465/AMBPP.2005.18778668

Caxaj, C. S. (2015). Indigenous storytelling and participatory action research: Allies toward decolonization? Reflections from the Peoples' International Health Tribunal. *Global Qualitative Nursing Research*, *2*. https://doi.org/10.1177/2333393615580764

Collinson, D. L. (2003). Identities and insecurities: Selves at work. *Organization*, *10*(3), 527–547. https://doi.org/10.1177/13505084030103010

Crabtree, B. F., & Miller, W. L. (1999). *Doing Qualitative Research* (2nd ed.). New York: SAGE Publications.

Da Costa, A. E. (2016). Thinking 'post-racial' ideology transnationally: The contemporary politics of race and indigeneity in the Americas. *Critical Sociology*, *42*(4–5), 475–490. https://doi.org/10.1177/0896920515591175

Daya, P., & April, K. (Eds.) (2021). *12 Lenses into Diversity in South Africa*. Randburg: KR Publishing.

Deetz, S. (1996). Crossroads – Describing differences in approaches to organization science: Rethinking Burrell and Morgan and their legacy, *Organization Science*, *7*(2), 191–207. https://doi.org/10.1287/orsc.7.2.191

De Stefano, V. (2016). The rise of the 'just-in-time workforce': On-demand work, crowd work and labour protection in the 'gig-economy'.

Comparative Labor Law and Policy Journal, *37*(3), 461–471. http:// dx.doi.org/10.2139/ssrn.2682602

Detert, J. R., Burris, E. R., Harrison, D. A., & Martin, S. R. (2013). Voice flows to and around leaders: Understanding when units are helped or hurt by employee voice. *Administrative Science Quarterly*, *58*(4), 624–668. https://doi.org/10.1177/0001839213510151

Durante, F., & Fiske, S. T. (2017). How social-class stereotypes maintain inequality. *Current Opinion in Psychology*, *18*, 43–48. https://doi .org/10.1016/j.copsyc.2017.07.033

Fanon, F. ([1964] 1967). *Toward the African Revolution* (H. Chevalier, Trans.). New York: Grove Press.

Fanon, F. (1967). *Black Skin, White Masks* (C. L. Markmann, Trans.) [Peau Noir, Masques Blancs]. New York: Grove Weidenfeld. (Original work published 1952)

Fast, N. J., Burris, E. R., & Bartel, C. A. (2014). Managing to stay in the dark: Managerial self-efficacy, ego defensiveness, and the aversion to employee voice. *Academy of Management Journal*, *57*(4), 1013–1034. https://doi.org/10.5465/amj.2012.0393

Festinger, L. (1954). A theory of social comparison processes. *Human Relations*, *7*(2), 117–140. https://doi.org/10.1177/001872675400700202

Fiske, S. T. (2002) What we know now about bias and inter-group conflict, the problem of the century. *Current Directions in Psychological Science*, *11*(4), 123–128. https://doi.org/10.1111/1467-8721.00183

Friedman, S. (2016). Habitus clivé and the emotional imprint of social mobility. *The Sociological Review*, *64*(1), 129–147. https://doi.org/10 .1111/1467-954X.12280

Goffman, E. (1974). *Frame Analysis: An Essay on the Organisation of Experience*. New York, NY: Harper & Row.

Gunn, V., Håkansta, C., Vignola, E. *et al.* (2021) Initiatives addressing precarious employment and its effects on workers' health and well-being: A protocol for a systematic review. *Systematic Reviews*, *10*(195). https:// doi.org/10.1186/s13643-021-01728-z

Haybi-Barak, M., & Shoshana, A. (2021). Ethnic mobility: Ethno-class identities and self-negation, *Social Identities*, *27*(3), 326–341. https://doi .org/10.1080/13504630.2020.1822796

Hogg, M. A., & Terry, D. I. (2000). Social identity and self-categorization processes in organizational contexts. *Academy of Management Review*, *25*(1), 121–140. https://doi.org/10.5465/amr.2000.2791606

Hoobler, J. M., Dowdeswell, K. E., & Mahlatji, L. (2021). Racialized social class work: Making sense of inequality in South Africa during the COVID-19 lockdown. *Africa Journal of Management*, *7*(1), 148–171. https://doi.org/10.1080/23322373.2021.1878812

Hunt, A., & Samman, E. (2019). Gender and the gig economy: Critical steps for evidence-based policy, Working Paper 546, Overseas Development Institute, London, January 2019, www.odi.org/sites/odi.org.uk/files/resource-documents/12586.pdf

Jørgensen, M. B. (2016). Precariat – What it is and isn't: Towards an understanding of what it does. *Critical Sociology*, 42(7–8), 959–974. https://doi.org/10.1177/0896920515608925

Joshi, A., Son, J., & Roh, H. (2015). When can women close the gap? A meta-analytic test of sex differences in performance and rewards. *Academy of Management Journal*, 58(5), 1516–1545. www.jstor.org/stable/24758232

Kalitanyi, V., & Visser, K. (2010). African immigrants in South Africa: Job takers or job creators ? *South African Journal of Economic and Management Sciences*, 13(4), 376–390. https://doi.org/10.4102/sajems.v13i4.91

Kalleberg, A. L. (2009). Precarious work, insecure workers: Employment relations in transition. *American Sociological Review*, 74(1), 1–22. https://doi.org/10.1177/000312240907400101

Klein, J., & Amis, J. M. (2021). The dynamics of framing: Image, emotion, and the European migration crises. *Academy of Management Journal*, 64(5), 1324–1354. https://doi.org/10.5465/amj.2017.0510

Lacy, K. (2004). Black spaces, black places: Strategic assimilation and identity construction in middleclass suburbia. *Ethnic and Racial Studies*, 27(6), 908–930. https://doi.org/10.1080/0141987042000268521

Lamont, M. (2018). Addressing recognition gaps: Destigmatization and the reduction of inequality. *American Sociological Review*, 83(3), 419–444. https://doi.org/10.1177/0003122418773775

Lareau, A. (2015). Cultural knowledge and social inequality. *American Sociological Review*, 80(1), 1–27. https://doi.org/10.1177/0003122414565814

Laverty, S. M. (2003). Hermeneutic phenomenology and phenomenology: A comparison of historical and methodological considerations. *International Journal of Qualitative Methods*, 2(3), 21–35. https://doi.org/10.1177/160940690300200303

Leigh, A., & Melwani, S. (2019). #BlackEmployeesMatter: Mega-threats, identity fusion, and enacting positive deviance in organizations. *Academy of Management Review*, 44(3), 564–591. https://doi.org/10.5465/amr.2017.0127

Light, I., Bhachu, P., & Stavros, K. (1989). Migration networks and immigrant entrepreneurship. *Immigration and Entrepreneurship: Culture, Capital, and Ethnic Networks*, V(April), 25–50. https://escholarship.org/uc/item/50g990sk

Light, I., Sabagh, G., Bozorgmehr, M., and Der-Martirosian, C. (1994). Beyond the ethnic enclave economy. *Social Problems*, 41(1), 65–80. https://doi.org/10.2307/3096842

Maldonado-Torres, N. (2007). On the coloniality of being. *Cultural Studies*, 21(2–3), 240–270. https://doi.org/10.1080/09502380601162548

Martin, S. R., & Harrison, S. H. (2022). Upward mobility, the cleft habitus, and speaking up: How class transitions relate to individual and organizational antecedents of voice. *Academy of Management Journal*, 65(3), 813–841. https://doi.org/10.5465/amj.2020.1550

McKinsey & Co. (2016). *Independent Work: Choice, Necessity, and the Gig Economy*. New York: McKinsey Global Institute. www.mckinsey.com/featured-insights/employment-and-growth/independent-work-choice-necessity-and-the-gig-economy

Morrison, T. (1994). *The Bluest Eye*. New York: Plume.

Moustakas, C. (1994). *Phenomenological Research Methods*. Thousand Oaks, CA: Sage Publications.

Munck, R. (2013). The precariat: A view from the South. *Third World Quarterly*, 34, 747–762. https://doi.org/10.1080/01436597.2013.800751

Nkomo, S. M., Bell, M. P., Roberts, L. M., Joshi, A., & Thatcher, S. M. B. (2019). Diversity at a critical juncture: New theories for a complex phenomenon. *Academy of Management Review*, 44(3), 498–517. https://doi.org/10.5465/amr.2019.0103

Petriglieri, G., Ashford, S. J., & Wrzesniewski, A. (2019). Agony and ecstasy in the gig economy: Cultivating holding environments for precarious and personalized work identities. *Administrative Science Quarterly*, 64(1), 124–170. https://doi.org/10.1177/0001839218759646

Petriglieri, J. L. (2015). Co-creating relationship repair: Pathways to reconstructing destabilized organizational identification. *Administrative Science Quarterly*, 60(3), 518–557. https://doi.org/10.1177/0001839215579234

Phillips, L. T., Martin, S. R., & Belmi, P. (2020). Social class transitions: Three guiding questions for moving the study of class to a dynamic perspective. *Social and Personality Psychology Compass*, 14(9), e12560. https://doi.org/10.1111/spc3.12560

Pitesa, M., & Pillutla, M. M. (2019). Socioeconomic mobility and talent utilization of workers from poorer backgrounds: The overlooked importance of within-organization dynamics. *Academy of Management Annals*, 13(2), 737–769. https://doi.org/10.5465/annals.2017.0115

Pollio, A. (2019). Forefronts of the sharing economy: Uber in Cape Town. *International Journal of Urban and Regional research*, 43(4), 760–775. https://doi.org/10.1111/1468-2427.12788

Ridout, N., & Schneider, R. (2012). Precarity and performance: An introduction. *TDR: The Drama Review*, 56(4), 5–9. www.jstor.org/stable/23362768

Rivera, L. A., & Tilcsik, A. (2016). Class advantage, commitment penalty: The gendered effect of social class signals in an elite labor market. *American Sociological Review*, *81*(6), 1097–1131. https://doi.org/10.1177/0003122416668154

Rubery, J., Grimshaw, D., Keizer, A., & Johnson, M. (2018). Challenges and contradictions in the 'normalising' of precarious work. *Work, Employment and Society*, *32*(3), 509–527. https://doi.org/10.1177/0950017017751790

Schneider, J., & Lang, C. (2014). Social mobility, habitus and identity formation in the Turkish German second generation. *New Diversities*, *16*(1), 89–105. https://newdiversities.mmg.mpg.de/wp-content/uploads/2014/11/2014_16-01_07_SchneiderLang.pdf

Schwarz, N. (1999). Self-reports: How the questions shape the answers. *American Psychologist*, *54*(2), 93–105. https://doi.org/10.1037/0003-066X.54.2.93

Searle, J. R. (1995). *The Construction of Social Reality*. New York: Free Press.

Sennett, R., & Cobb, J. (1972). *The Hidden Injuries of Class*. New York, NY: Vintage Books.

Seymour, R. (2012). We are all precarious: On the concept of the 'precariat' and its misuses. New Left Project, 10 February.

Sithole, T. (2016). The concept of the black subject in Fanon. *Journal of Black Studies*, *47*(1), 24–40. https://doi.org/10.1177/0021934715609913

Standing, G (2011). *The Precariat: The New Dangerous Class*. London: Bloomsbury Academic.

Stats SA (2019). Inequality trends in South Africa: A multidimensional diagnostic of inequality. Report No. 03-10-19. www.statssa.gov.za/publications/Report-03-10-19/Report-03-10-192017.pdf.

Stats SA (2020). Quarterly labour force survey: 1st Quarter 2020. Report No. P0211. www.statssa.gov.za/publications/P0211/P02111stQuarter2020.pdf

Streib, J. (2015). *The Power of the Past: Understanding Cross-class Marriages*. New York: Oxford University Press.

Studener, P. (August 28, 2013). Secret Ubers arriving in Cape Town now … lekker bru! http://blog.uber.com/capetown_secretubers (no longer available online).

Swann, W. B., Jr., & Bosson, J. K. (2010). Self and identity. In D. T. Gilbert, S. T. Fiske, & G. Lindzey (Eds.), *Handbook of Social Psychology* (5th ed., pp. 589–628), Hoboken, NJ: Wiley.

Tangirala, S., & Ramanujam, R. (2012). Ask and you shall hear (but not always): Examining the relationship between manager consultation and employee voice. *Personnel Psychology*, *65*(2), 251–282. https://doi.org/10.1111/j.1744-6570.2012.01248.x

Tava, F. (2023). Justice, emotions, and solidarity. *Critical review of International Social and Political Philosophy*, 26(1), 39–55. https://doi.org/10.1080/13698230.2021.1893251

Tshiamala, H. (2021). Challenging the odds: A critical analysis of refugee entrepreneurial resilience in South Africa. In K. April & B. Zolfaghari (Eds.), *Values-driven Entrepreneurship and Societal Impact: Setting the Agenda for Entrepreneuring Across (Southern) Africa* (pp. 255–268). Randburg: KR Publishing.

Welsing, F. C. (1991). *The Isis Papers: The Keys to the Colors*. Chicago: Third World Press.

Wright, M. (2015). The 'sharing' economy is just futuristic feudalism, talk more about the have-nots. The Next Web, 15th August. http://thenextweb.com/opinion/2015/08/15/i-didnt-know-we-had-a-king/

Yancy, G. (2008). *Black Bodies, White Gazes: The Continuing Significance of Race*. Lanham, Maryland: Rowman & Littlefield Publishers.

Yancy, G. (2013, September 1). Walking while black in the 'white gaze'. New York Times. https://opinionator.blogs.nytimes.com/2013/09/01/walking-while-black-in-the-white-gaze/

Yin, R. K. (2003). *Case Study Research: Design and Methods* (3rd ed.). Thousand Oaks, CA: Sage.

Zastrow, C., & Kirst-Ashman, K. K. (2010). *Understanding Human Behaviour and the Social Environment*. Boston: Cengage Learning.

Zawadzki, B. (1948). Limitations of the scapegoat theory of prejudice. *The Journal of Abnormal and Social Psychology*, 43(2), 127–141. https://doi.org/10.1037/h0063279

Zhou, M. (2004). Revisiting ethnic entrepreneurship: Convergencies, controversies, and conceptual advancements. *International Migration Review*, 38(3), 1040–1074. https://doi.org/10.1111/j.1747-7379.2004.tb00228.x

9 Refugees' Vulnerability towards Precarious Work
An Intersectionality Perspective

LENA KNAPPERT, BRIGITTE KROON, ANGELA
KORNAU, AND BASSANT ABDELMAGEED

9.1 Introduction

In 2020, more than thirty million people globally had to cross national borders to find protection from war, violence, or persecution. The top source country for refugees in recent years is Syria, with more than 6.5 million people who escaped the country since the war started in 2011 (UNHCR, 2020). While most of them stay in neighbouring countries like Turkey, Jordan, or Lebanon, a smaller section of Syrians succeeded in reaching European countries, such as Greece, Italy, Germany, or the Netherlands. Although host countries differ substantially in terms of policies and support for refugees, what unifies them is the need to find ways to integrate refugees into their societies as most refugees stay longer than just temporarily. Refugee employment has been identified as one of the key factors to facilitate societal integration (Ager & Strang, 2008; Lee et al., 2020). Yet, refugees are particularly vulnerable to under- and unemployment, are more likely to feel de-valued at work, and find themselves in precarious working conditions compared to host country residents (Cheung & Phillimore, 2013; Colic-Peisker, 2006; Ponzoni, Ghorashi, & van der Raad, 2017). For individuals on the intersection of multiple forms of discrimination (e.g., women refugees), these disadvantages are particularly pronounced (Tomlinson, 2010).

Existing studies report several reasons for refugees' vulnerability towards precarious work such as legal restrictions that prevent refugees from legal employment, health issues that disrupt regular employment, and non-recognition of qualifications which hampers appropriate wages (e.g., Baranik, Hurst & Eby, 2018; Cheung & Phillimore, 2013; Giri, 2018; Knappert, van Dijk & Ross, 2019).

Further, unlike other migrant groups, most refugees did not have time to prepare their departure from their home country, or their arrival in the host country, which further worsens their starting conditions (e.g., through lacking language knowledge or missing certificates) on the labour market (Ortlieb & Weiss, 2020). But also, employers play an important role in refugees' vulnerability towards precarious work. They frequently engage in "irresponsible behaviours" (Naccache & Al Ariss, 2018: 589) such as offering low-paying, dangerous and illegal jobs specifically to refugees (Lee et al., 2020), treat refugees as "interchangeable cheap labour" (Wehrle et al., 2018: 93) and hence, exploit and reinforce their vulnerability.

A smaller number of studies document the role of intersectionality for refugees' vulnerability towards precarious work. Most of these studies focus on how refugeehood intersects with gender (e.g., Dedeoglu, 2011; Tomlinson, 2010; Ünlütürk-Ulutaş & Akbaş, 2020). For instance, in their qualitative study, Ünlütürk-Ulutaş and Akbaş (2020) portray the struggles and burden for skilled Syrian women in the Turkish labour market and conclude that among the anyhow "invisible" group of refugees, women refugees are the "least visible", with high risks of exploitation and harsh working conditions. Scholarship in social work and clinical therapy has further advanced the understanding of how categories of discrimination overlap and how this affects refugees (e.g., Gangamma & Shipman, 2018; Lee & Brotman, 2013; Vervliet et al., 2014). One critical insight from this stream of research is that refugees' marginalization experiences based on social identity markers such as ethnicity, gender, or sexual orientation can vary at different stages and locations of their migration (i.e., premigration, during flight, and postmigration) (Anthias, 2008). For instance, women might be oppressed in their country of origin, under threat of physical violence and sexual assault during their escape, and with comparatively more legal protection and opportunities in the host country. Therefore, as refugees cross borders and contexts, the meaning of intersectionality for their experiences at work might involve more variations and contradictions, compared to non-transnational workers.

Drawing on the psychology of working theory (Duffy, Blustein, Diemer, & Autin, 2016) that postulates social class as the primary marker of access to social and economic resources, while acknowledging the intersections with gender and race or ethnicity, this chapter aims to explore how overlapping categories of discrimination shape refugees' vulnerability towards precarious work. By using the narrative accounts of four Syrian men and women refugees located in the Netherlands and Turkey, we illustrate how in particular the intersection of refugeehood with gender is further complicated by class (i.e., refugees' economic status in their home country) as well as by the societal expectations and protection in the host environment. With this chapter, we aim to make three contributions. First, case studies relating precarious work to refugee welfare provide insights in the interplay between individual agency and the economic, societal, and political context in their asylum destinations. Second, adopting an intersectional framework to the study of refugees' vulnerability towards precarious work allows us to simultaneously consider multiple structures of power, privilege, and oppression, while acknowledging their historical and national context. And third, using a narrative approach allowed us to present the personal stories and often dramatic situations of Syrian refugees. That way we put a spotlight on the individual voices of the humans behind the refugee label and the urgent need for humanitarian solutions.

The chapter is structured as follows: First, we will present the context of refugee employment in the Netherlands and Turkey, present some figures and policies in the two countries and present how precarity comes into play in these contexts. Second, a theoretical framework that integrates precarity and intersectionality is provided. Third, we present our sample and analysis as well as the four narrative accounts. This is followed by a discussion of the narratives, and their meaning for marginalization and agency on the intersection of refugeehood, gender, and class. In that section, we also present practical implications for policymakers, organizational decision-makers, and refugees and discuss their relevance during socio-economic upheaval. We conclude with a reflection and avenues for future research.

9.2 The Context of Refugee Precariousness in the Netherlands and Turkey

Turkey hosts the largest number of refugees worldwide. Most of them come from Syria, with 3.6 million refugees from the war-shaken neighbouring country currently being registered in Turkey (UNHCR, 2021). Being harder to reach geographically and enforcing the strict

European borders, the Netherlands hosts a comparably small number of refugees. In 2019, 94.430 refugees were registered in the country (UNHCR, 2019). Most asylum applications in recent years came from Syrian refugees, followed by people who had fled Nigeria, Iran, or Turkey (Asylum in Europe, 2021). Accordingly, the two countries differ in the socio-economic background of the Syrian refugee population, for instance with regard to the educational level and economic resources that refugees bring with them. Turkey, and in particular the bordering regions to Syria, are predominantly a refuge for people with less resources who barely reached the other side of the border. In contrast, people who flee from Syria to the Netherlands must be able to afford a flight ticket, show exceptional skills and qualifications that the country is seeking, or have to be very lucky to make the long journey or be chosen for resettlement (Muhanna-Matar, 2022; Knappert, van Dijk & Ross, 2019; van Haer, 2006).

The two countries also differ with regard to legal protection of refugees and labour market access policies. In the Netherlands, asylum seekers are not allowed to work for the first six months of their application. After that, they can start working, but they can keep only 25 per cent of their income and a maximum of €185 per month, as long as their asylum request is pending, and they receive basic social services. Once they obtain the legal refugee status, they have free access to the labour market and receive social welfare assistance during their job search. However, they are expected to apply for the vacancies offered and follow an integration course. The Migration Policy Index (MIPEX) traditionally placed the Netherlands on the higher ranks and considered it a good example for integration policy. However, due to the far-right's heavy influence on the public discourse, the Netherlands dropped drastically between the 2007 and the 2014 edition of MIPEX, pointing to several problems in integration policies also described as "policy of no policy" that leaves integration largely up to immigrants themselves. More recently however, for refugee labour market integration specifically, some programmes (for young migrants and women migrants) have been introduced and are evaluated as promising (MIPEX, 2021).

In contrast, since Turkey was at the bottom of MIPEX in 2010, the country has significantly improved with regard to integration policies in recent years. Yet, labour market integration policies for migrants and refugees are evaluated as unfavourable (MIPEX,

2021). More specifically, since 2016, Syrians can apply for a work permit for specific sectors and selected geographical areas under the Temporary Protection (UNHCR, 2021). Yet, Syrians in Turkey are mostly employed informally and in low-skilled occupations, mainly in the construction industry, restaurants, and factories (Baban et al., 2017; ILO, 2021; Kartal & Basci, 2014). One explanation is the likely overwhelmed labour market given the sheer number of more than two million Syrians in working age (ILO, 2021). Moreover, the actual numbers of issued working permits are rather low, such that for example, between 2011 and 2016 Turkey has issued only few (118 to 2,541 yearly) work permits for Syrian refugees, questioning their actual access to the Turkish labour market (Baban et al., 2017). These conditions particularly jeopardize the working conditions for women refugees who are more vulnerable to exclusion and exploitation (Dedeoglu, 2011; Ünlütürk-Ulutaş, & Akbaş, 2020), and less protected in light of a misogynous discourse that is put forward by the Turkish government (Kornau, Knappert & Acar Erdur, 2021).

9.3 Precarity and Intersectionality

Precarious work is work that is "uncertain, unstable, and insecure and in which employees bear the risks of work (as opposed to businesses or the government) and receive limited social benefits and statutory protections" (Kalleberg & Vallas, 2017, p. 1). Example work conditions include low wages, casual contracts, job insecurity, safety risks, poor regulatory protection, a lack of investments in employee training and development, no employee representation, leaving workers with little control over their wages, hours, and working conditions (Campbell & Price, 2016). The impact of precarious work conditions for individuals varies depending on their social context. A worker's individual circumstances present in the stage in life, the financial situation, the availability of alternative sources of income or opportunities for education can mitigate or amplify the consequences of precarious work for workers. For example, having a partner with a secure job, or using the job to finance university studies, or working just a few hours a week, can buffer the negative outcomes of precarious work. In addition, in response to globalization, technological change and the financialization of the economy, organizations have replaced the traditional internal labour market with flexible, open labour market approaches to achieve business results (Bidwell, Briscoe, Fernandez-Mateo, & Sterling, 2013). This has led to an increase of flexible labour, including part-time, on call and agency work (Cappelli & Keller, 2012). Especially for newcomers in the labour market, it has become more difficult to secure a permanent job as compared to some decades ago.

Over a life course, the duration of exposure to precarious work fortifies the vulnerability of certain groups to become precarious workers, who have little prospect to improve their situation (Wilson & Ebert, 2013). Intersectionality, the relative privilege, or marginalization of individuals based on the social constructions and economic status associated with their overlapping identities (Cole, 2009), significantly contributes to the vulnerability to become a precarious worker (Duffy, et al., 2016). The psychology of working theory points at the negative effects of marginalization and economic constraints for the ability to secure decent work (Duffy et al., 2016). It postulates social class as the primary marker of access to social and economic resources but acknowledges that, the intersections with gender and race or ethnicity create "a matrix of privilege and constraint in the process of career development and securing decent work" (Duffy et al., 2016; p. 131). The psychology of working theory further suggests that, once at the heart of factors accumulating to their marginalization, individuals find themselves in a negative spiral where they lack the support, energy, and economic means to break the loop. However, if individuals succeed in securing better work, over time they will experience less economic constraints and feel less marginalized. Breaking the negative spiral requires support in individual circumstances, together with personal agency factors such as career adaptability and a proactive personality.

9.4 Sample and Analysis

The cases presented in this chapter are based on interviews with four Syrian refugees: two in the Netherlands and two in Turkey. The semi-structured interviews were conducted as part of a larger project on refugees' workplace inclusion-exclusion across countries (see, e.g., Knappert, Kornau, Figengul, 2018). For this larger project, a purposive sampling strategy was applied to include participants who had a job at the time of interviewing and who varied in terms of gender. This allowed us to explore refugees' working conditions and effects of intersectionality. We used snowball techniques as well as personal and professional networks to identify and acquire suitable interview partners. In this book chapter, we present the narrative accounts of four refugees, two living in the Netherlands and two living Turkey (one woman and one man for each country). We selected four diverse accounts to illustrate refugees' vulnerability towards precarious work, highlighting different country-specific conditions as well as gender-related outcomes. Interviews were conducted in English, Arabic or Turkish (and later translated in English), recorded and transcribed. The interviews were paraphrased into short narrative accounts of four refugees struggling for a better life: Yara (woman, Turkey), Ahmed (man, Turkey), Amal (woman, the Netherlands), and Omar (man, the Netherlands).

9.5 Findings

Narrative 1: Yara – Bearing the Unbearable Spiral of Precarity

Yara is twenty-eight years old and flew from Syria to Turkey in 2014. Before, she lived with her husband and children in a house in Aleppo. She finished secondary school and never worked outside of their home before coming to Turkey. When the situation in Aleppo became too dangerous, the family had no choice but to leave their home and escaped across the border to settle down temporarily in Antakya, the capital of the province Hatay in southern Turkey.

Once in Turkey, the family did not receive any support such as food, basic accommodation, or health care from the state or non-governmental organizations. At the same time, Yara's husband did not find a job at their new place of residence, so that Yara had to earn money to ensure the survival of the family. Yara explained that it was easier for her as woman to find a job because "Syrian women are sweet and attractive [Laughing]. With their beauty they can attract more customers." Yet, women refugees not only get paid less than locals, but they also earn much lower salaries compared to men refugees: "They give 100 liras [about 10 Euros] each week. What can you do with 100 liras? If your rent is like 300–400?" In some instances, Yara's employers simply refused to pay her salary altogether.

Yara started with an informal, insecure job in a bakery, but lost it again quickly because she needed two days off to take care of her son who required a surgery. When she went back to her place of work, they had hired someone else in the meantime. This was followed by a job in a pastry shop that was not only underpaid but also physically very demanding with long working hours (10–11 hours a day) and no opportunity to rest. Yara proactively asked around to find a new job and now works in a private home, taking care of an elderly lady and cleaning the house. Although this job is tough and time-consuming, too, she at least receives some appreciation from the lady she works for: "The old lady loves me very much. I love her too. But sometimes I want to spend time with my children and husband, but because of my work I cannot do that."

Yara would like to learn the Turkish language and work as a translator, but she lacks the time and money to participate in costly language courses. This lack of support combined with short term economic pressure to earn money for her family leaves her in a negative spiral depriving her of the opportunity to develop herself and create a better future for herself and her family. Her advice for women still living in Syria is therefore clear-cut: Living in Turkey as a Syrian woman is hardly bearable, and you have to suffer a lot of pain and difficulties. Women who cannot withstand this, should better stay in Syria.

Narrative 2: Ahmed – Creating a Parallel Community in a Rightless Sphere

Ahmed is thirty-nine years old and flew with his wife and children from Syria to Antakya, Turkey, in 2012. In Syria, he had quit school before graduating and worked as a self-employed businessman in trade exporting raw materials. His hometown Aleppo was famous for trading, he said, but after the beginning of the war all trade was stopped, so that he couldn't earn a living anymore. "When the first events started in Syria, I moved to a place close to sea. In the cities close to the coast there was no such thing as war. When we had trouble finding raw materials, I took the decision to move to Turkey. In Turkey I have had many [business] partners."

Despite his contacts and previous work experience, he searched for a job without success and therefore decided to start his own business. Ahmed produces and sells kitchen counters made from marble and has three Syrian employees. He describes the relationship with his employees as very positive: "I am like their big brother. They listen to me, and they can comfortably say their opinion and if it is suitable, we may apply it." Although Ahmed is very satisfied with his personal work situation, he felt that Syrians have no rights and are viewed as fourth-class citizens in Turkey and treated accordingly. For instance, Syrians have no opportunity to take out a loan, they have no insurance, and wages are very low:

Assign them insurance and let the Syrians remain satisfied. While you give 1500 to a legal employee, Syrians get 700. I can live with that, but there are people with children who eat and have extra costs. Now, if you do not give them a credit, of course these men attack, of course they steal. He has to bring food to his family and children.

Ahmed's family also suffers from this general degradation of Syrians. For example, he bought a bicycle for his son, but other children stole it: "They said 'You are Syrian'. They both beat my child and took his bike. Thank God they did not take his eyes out. Children who were two to three years younger than him did this. Even the children are growing up like this. They learn this behavior from their parents." Also, Ahmed wanted to register his children to attend school, but they were not allowed because the family had apparently entered the country illegally.

Given these living conditions, it is not surprising that Ahmed and his family are only waiting for the war to be over, so that they can return to their home country. He recommends other Syrians not to leave their country,

even if they are starving. They can come to Turkey if they have money, in order to travel, but it is not a good place to work. (...) The words I want to say to people who come here to work is: Do not come, look for work in another country! Let them go to Europe, to Israel. It is way better. I say this from the bottom of my heart.

Narrative 3: Amal – Doing Her Best to Shine
Amal is thirty-five years old and flew from Syria to the Netherlands with her husband and two sons in 2017. In her home country, she had a diploma in assistant engineering and a degree in immediate translation from Arabic to English. She worked as an office manager for seven years in Syria. After relocation, Amal dedicated one and half years to studying the Dutch language. She believes that she could have found a job given her fluency in English, but she wanted to learn the language for better integration and better work opportunities. Meanwhile, she kept looking for opportunities through her social

network. Eventually, she found employment as the coordinator for a project by the Dutch government that a Dutch friend had recommended her. Most crucial for Amal's adjustment and opportunities in the Netherlands was the flexibility and support from her partner. "Still for women, it's always a hard choice to go working because you know you'll have double responsibility in work and house. So, I was lucky that he accepted to take care of the kids, to accept that I arrive home at 9 pm or maybe later."

Although the differences in culture between her home country and the Netherlands are clearly visible and not always comfortable for Amal, she makes a conscious effort to adapt and accept the differences. Some of these differences she even perceives as an advantage: "It's a safe place because you've all the kind of rules and policies to help women in their work, no one is allowed to be flirting or annoying to her." Amal appreciates that there are rules and policies in place that empower women, the Dutch's emphasis on "work-life balance", as well as women's freedom to choose their profession. "I've never felt free in Syria even before war, but here since my second year I started to understand we were never free, we had boundaries from traditions, families and needs, we've never had a choice in our country." In contrast, in the Netherlands, "[refugee] women are motivated because, for the first time, they are having attention and support, so they will do their best to shine". For similar reasons, Syrian men have trouble adapting to the new culture as it is hard for them to accept that they do not come first and should be equal to women.

Narrative 4: Omar – Starting and Starting Again under Better Conditions

Omar is twenty-six years old and flew from Syria with his parents to the Netherlands in 2017. He studied computer networking in Syria and worked as a teaching assistant for one year. Once he arrived in his host country, he started the journey of learning the language and searching for work. The first problem he faced was that the educational degrees from Syria weren't accredited by the Netherlands. To increase his chances on the labour market, he had to go back to university. "For me, going back to the university was a nightmare so this is something I didn't want to do." He started searching for alternatives until he found a non-profit organization that offers refugees a software development course in a six-month duration. He applied for this course, passed the selection process, studied hard, and learned new skills. After graduating from this course, the same organization helped him to find an internship to re-start his career. In this internship, Omar mentioned he was not feeling comfortable in the company and did not feel included at all. Omar described the environment as dominated by the Dutch working culture; everyone speaking Dutch that he couldn't cope with, and he felt isolated. Besides, the internship did not provide much structure. There was no specific development plan for interns, and support by supervisors and colleagues was lacking. Eventually, Omar decided to contact the non-profit organization to see if there are other opportunities for him. They helped him apply to another international company that has a tailored programme for refugees. Omar appreciated that the programme was very structured, the goals were well settled, and that he had a mentor who helped him throughout the internship. He felt included during collaborations and meetings, felt safe to share his opinion and ideas. He said that they gave him all the time and support he needed until he became fit for a permanent job with them.

Omar even felt that he was privileged because he was a refugee as he got this position through the company's refugee programme, while he might not have acquired a job in such a well-established company if he was not a refugee. He mentioned that, in Syria, people need to know someone from the board of directors or in high positions to even be able to have a chance for an interview at a company. "In The Netherlands, you just need to work hard to get to the next position. You'll get a result, and you don't need the sneaky way, just do your job and you'll get a result." He felt that the process is fairer in the Netherlands, which encouraged him to work hard.

As many refugees are struggling with traumas, Omar advised refugees to overcome their traumas and any psychological barriers first as these can easily get in the way of finding work. But he was positive that starting a new life in the Netherlands was possible.

9.6 Transnational Marginalization and Agency on the Intersection of Refugeehood, Gender, and Class

The narratives of Yara, Ahmed, Amal and Omar illustrate the matrix of privilege and constraint that refugees are faced with in the process of securing decent work and developing their careers (Duffy et al., 2016).

Yara's story confirms the psychology of working theory's proposition that, once at the heart of factors accumulating to their marginalization, individuals find themselves in a negative spiral where they lack the support, energy, and economic means to break the loop. The stories by Ahmed, Amal, and Omar show how personal agency such as career adaptability and a proactive personality in combination with support by other actors can break (the risk of) marginalization and a possibly negative spiral. Further, all four accounts highlight the importance of considering the different stages and locations of their migration (Anthias, 2008). While for Ahmed and Omar the work life was cut clearly in "before" and "after", they both navigated their careers and opportunities comparably well. Yara and Amal also both described a clear distinction in "before" and "after", yet while for Yara working outside of home was a new, postmigration experience that came with exploitation and unsafe working conditions, Amal experienced more freedom and more opportunities after the flight. This indicates how crucial the destination country is for women, especially the extent to which traditional gender roles prevail, as they are reflected in the treatment of women at work and relevant policies and support programmes (or the absence thereof). Moreover, whereas the differences in experiences are clearly following gender lines, these examples also mirror the crucial impact of class on refugees' vulnerability towards precarious work as belonging to a higher class comes with a higher likelihood of reaching a context with a better support structure (cf. van Hear, 2006). For women, reaching a context with more versus less legal protection and more versus less strict gender role expectations can have substantial consequences and further increase or reduce their vulnerability towards precarious work. In sum, this shows the variations and contradictions in meaning of intersectionality for refugees' experiences at work.

What could practical ways out of precarity look like? Our narratives indicate that individual level factors related to refugees' agency are crucial, hence support structures are needed, not only to help overcome traumata, but also to encourage self-confidence, flexibility, and proactivity when it comes to finding new job opportunities, for example, via volunteer mentoring programmes, language courses, and vocational trainings. In line with earlier research (Ortlieb et al., 2020) we further assume that these programmes might benefit women refugees as they are often confronted with stereotypes according to which women from the respective source countries do not work outside their homes. It is therefore likely that, by attending those programmes women refugees demonstrate to potential employers and other relevant actors that they are very well capable to work and adjust to the new environment.

Accordingly, practical recommendations follow for policy makers, employers and for refugees themselves. First, remove barriers to work by designing (international) policies underlining the right to work. By ensuring that registered refugees are entitled to the same employment terms and conditions as local workers, their vulnerability to precarious work will reduce. Second, employers should monitor and be monitored in offering inclusive workplaces, by adhering to non-discrimination law, providing opportunities for work to refugees, and by actively managing the inclusion of a diverse workforce. Finally, the psychology of working theory indicates how individuals with access to resources (e.g., financial resources, a career network, language skills, support in dealing with traumata's) manage to spiral out of precarity after their flight. This implies that support should be organized close to the refugees, in the communities where they are building and shaping their new lives.

Certainly, improving the living and working conditions of refugees in these times of socio-economic upheaval in a sustainable manner is a complex task. Societies are currently juggling various grand societal challenges simultaneously including climate change, growing income inequalities and – not least – the COVID-19 pandemic (Ferraro et al., 2015; George et al., 2016; Howard-Grenville, 2020). Such challenges are closely intertwined with the precarious situation refugees worldwide find themselves in. For instance, climate change-induced natural disasters such as droughts or floods are key drivers of forced migration (Gemenne, 2015). Disentangling and tackling such complex challenges cannot be done by single programmes or actors but need concerted efforts by various stakeholder groups (George et al., 2016; Hardy et al., 1994). Ferraro et al. (2015) recommend a participatory architecture, that is, "structure and rules of engagement that allow diverse and heterogeneous actors to interact constructively over prolonged timespans." (p. 373). While it is the responsibility of political decision makers and international organizations such as the United Nations to build such common grounds on a global scale, much can be done on a community level by, for example, identifying and mobilizing various actors involved in improving living and working conditions of refugees, including refugees themselves and develop context-specific support measures bottom-up.

9.7 Conclusion

Overall, we demonstrate how precarious work worsens the vulnerable position of refugees, while refugees who succeed in securing decent work manage to build a sustainable life in the country of destination. This resonates with the UN notion that decent work is key for securing socioeconomic development and wellbeing, which further provides support for the psychology of working theory.

We have tried our best to maintain critical distance to both country contexts and to present those in a balanced way. In fact, as women based in Europe's West (Germany and the Netherlands) and with working experience in Turkey (first and third author), our personal experiences about working in these two contexts are far more balanced than what our narratives in this chapter highlight, such that our own working conditions in Turkey were comparable to those in the Netherlands and Germany. At the same time, we are witnessing the stalled progress towards gender equity and equality across countries and in the Netherlands with worry (Alon et al., 2020; Gavett & Perry, 2019). However, as we are writing this from the privileged positions of highly educated, self-initiated migrants (first and fourth author), this supports our claim of the importance to consider class differences when studying refugees' vulnerability to precarious work. Further, others have observed the heavy impact of class differences on women employment and working conditions in Turkey specifically: "while professional women in Turkey have achieved better gender representation than their counterparts in advanced economies, their less well-educated sisters are effectively barred from [formal] employment in many low skilled jobs" (Özbilgin, Syed, Ali, & Torunoglu, 2012: 351). The fact that refugees "go as far as their money would take them" (van Hear, 2006) is also reflected in our refugee sample of the larger research project that consisted mainly of less educated individuals with comparatively few financial resources in Turkey, while our refugee sample in the Netherlands consisted of higher educated individuals with comparatively more financial resources. Of course, both groups also exist in the other country respectively and one limitation of this chapter is that we did not put more effort into finding those individuals. However, this would have meant much more effortful sample acquisition given the specific region in Turkey where we did our research and the general distribution of higher versus lower educated refugees in the two countries.

Despite these limitations, our chapter points into several fruitful research avenues that we structure along their level of analysis (cf. Syed & Özbilgin, 2009). With regard to the societal level, we noticed several differences between Turkey and the Netherlands. Next to differences in regulations for refugees, in Turkey, the wages, protection, and living conditions for lower-class workers are generally worse than in the Netherlands. Less social security and greater prevalence of precarious work may also affect domestic workers, which can fuel negative sentiments such as fear or competition towards refugees (Wilson & Ebert, 2013). These societal dynamics may cumulate into informal status hierarchies among precarious workers, especially affecting the protection of refugee workers in casual, low skilled jobs (Hopkins, 2011). Relevant questions for future research might therefore include comparisons across different groups of precarious workers (including refugees) within and across contexts. Moreover, evaluation studies of specific support programmes are needed (cf. Ortlieb et al., 2020), ideally in comparison with similar other programmes or contexts and with measurements for long-term outcomes.

Concerning the organizational level, we know that employers play a vital role for refugees' working conditions as they often exploit and reinforce their vulnerability by offering low-paying, dangerous and illegal jobs specifically to refugees (Lee et al., 2020). Yet, as Omar's story also shows, employers might also pay particular attention to recruiting and developing refugee employees, so much so that Omar felt privileged over other candidates and employees. What happens in organizations however as part of the decision making with regard to refugee working conditions largely remains a black box. Future research should therefore investigate how decent versus precarious working conditions for refugees materialize in organizations. One promising perspective to take here is the practice perspective (Janssens & Steyaert, 2019) that would also allow to analyse how intersectionalities are addressed in organizational practice.

On the individual level, each transition refugees go through before, during and after their flight disrupts individual identities and the associated status in both positive and negative ways. For example, differences in the position of women between the home and destination country may challenge previously accepted views about gender roles women ascribed to themselves. These changes in identity can contribute to individual volition, that is, the ability to break away from marginalization (Duffy et al., 2016). Hence, we call for more in-depth studies on how the different stages and locations shape these changes in identity and their consequences for the individual and their working conditions as well as for quantitative studies that capture individuals' experiences at the intersection of their identity dimensions.

Further, the here presented narratives exemplify differences in economic constraints (education, wealth, social class) as well as in psychological factors. Education, previous work experience, and wealth are enabling economic factors in promoting the agency of refugees to secure decent work. The notion that despite disruptions in social identity, pre-flight status differences persist and lead to unequal opportunities in securing stability in terms of decent work and social security, underlines the need to understand experiences of inclusion and exclusion in the workplace in relation to the structural relationships that exist among groups within their societies of origin. Accordingly, we see a particularly fruitful research avenue where these levels and different stages and locations of migration are considered simultaneously (Anthias, 2008; Purkayastha, 2012).

References

Acker, J. (2006). Inequality regimes: Gender, class, and race in organizations. *Gender & society, 20*(4), 441–464.

Ager, A., & Strang, A. (2008). Understanding integration: A conceptual framework. *Journal of Refugee Studies, 21*(2), 166–191.

Alon, T. M., Doepke, M., Olmstead-Rumsey, J., & Tertilt, M. (2020). *The Impact of COVID-19 on Gender Equality (No. w26947)*. National Bureau of Economic Research.

Anthias, F. (2008). Thinking through the lens of translocational positionality: An intersectionality frame for understanding identity and belonging. *Translocations: Migration and Social Change, 4*(1), 5–20.

Asylum in Europe. (2021). *Statistics – Asylum Information Database |* European Council on Refugees and Exiles. Retrieved 2 May 2021, from https://asylumineurope.org/reports/country/netherlands/statistics/.

Baban, F., Ilcan, S., & Rygiel, K. (2017). Syrian refugees in Turkey: Pathways to precarity, differential inclusion, and negotiated citizenship rights. *Journal of Ethnic and Migration Studies, 43*(1), 41–57

Baranik, L. E., Hurst, C. S., & Eby, L. T. (2018). The stigma of being a refugee: A mixed-method study of refugees' experiences of vocational stress. *Journal of Vocational Behavior, 105*, 116–130.

Bidwell, M., Briscoe, F., Fernandez-Mateo, I., & Sterling, A. (2013). The employment relationship and inequality: How and why changes in employment practices are reshaping rewards in organizations. *The Academy of Management Annals, 7*(1), 61–121. https://doi.org/10.1080/1941 6520.2013.761403.

Campbell, I., & Price, R. (2016). Precarious work and precarious workers: Towards an improved conceptualisation. *Economic and Labour Relations Review, 27*(3), 314–332. https://doi.org/10.1177/1035304 616652074.

Cappelli, P., & Keller, J. (2012). Classifying work in the new economy. *Academy of Management Review, 38*(4), 575–596. https://doi.org/10.5465/ amr.2011.0302.

Cheung, S. Y., & Phillimore, J. (2013). Refugees, social capital, and labour market integration in the UK. *Sociology*, 38038513491467. http://dx.doi .org/10.1177/0038038513491467.

Cole, E. R. (2009). Intersectionality and research in psychology. *American Psychologist, 64*(3), 170–180. https://doi.org/10.1037/a0014564.

Colic-Peisker, V. (2006). Employment niches for recent refugees: Segmented labour market in twenty-first century Australia. *Journal of Refugee Studies, 19*(2), 203–229. http://dx.doi.org/10.1093/jrs/fej016.

Davis, A. (1982). Women, race and class: An activist perspective. *Women's Studies Quarterly, 10*(4), 5.

De Vroome, T., & Van Tubergen, F. (2010). The employment experience of refugees in the Netherlands. *International Migration Review, 44*(2), 376–403.

Dedeoglu, S. (2011). Survival of the excluded: Azerbaijani immigrant women's survival strategies and industrial work in Istanbul. *Migration Letters.* 8(1), Retrieved from http://search.proquest.com/openview/45980f71ed4a a36e2ba616bfff674946/1?pq-origsite=gscholar&cbl=456300.

Duffy, R. D., Blustein, D. L., Diemer, M. A., & Autin, K. L. (2016). The Psychology of Working Theory. *Journal of Counseling Psychology, 63*(2), 127–148. https://doi.org/http://dx.doi.org/10.1037/cou0000140

Essers, C., Benschop, Y., & Doorewaard, H. (2010). Female ethnicity: Understanding Muslim immigrant businesswomen in the Netherlands. *Gender, Work and Organization, 17*(3), 320–339. http://dx.doi .org/10.1111/j.1468-0432.2008.00425.x.

Ferraro, F., Etzion, D., & Gehman, J. (2015). Tackling grand challenges pragmatically: Robust action revisited. *Organization Studies*, *36*(3), 363–390.

Gangamma, R., & Shipman, D. (2018). Transnational intersectionality in family therapy with resettled refugees. *Journal of marital and family therapy*, *44*(2), 206–219.

Gavett, G., & Perry, M. (2019, September 27). The Gender Gap in 6 Charts. Retrieved December 20, 2019, from *Harvard Business Review* website: https://hbr.org/2019/09/the-gender-gap-in-6-charts.

Gemenne, F. (2015). One good reason to speak of "climate refugees". *Forced Migration Review*, *49*, 70–71.

George, G., Howard-Grenville, J., Joshi, A., & Tihanyi, L. (2016). Understanding and tackling societal grand challenges through management research. *Academy of Management Journal*, *59*(6), 1880–1895.

Giri, A (2018) From refuge to riches? An analysis of refugees' wage assimilation in the United States. *International Migration Review, 52*(1), 125–158.

Hardy, C. (1994). Underorganized interorganizational domains: The case of refugee systems. *The journal of applied behavioral science*, *30*(3), 278–296.

Hopkins, B. (2011). Informal hierarchies among workers in low-skill food manufacturing jobs. *Industrial Relations Journal*, *42*(5), 486–499.

Howard-Grenville, J. (2020). Grand Challenges, Covid-19 and the Future of Organizational Scholarship. *Journal of Management Studies*, *58*(1), 254–258.

ILO. (2021). *Promoting Decent Work For Syrians Under Temporary Protection and Turkish Citizens*. Ilo.org. Retrieved 2 May 2021, from www .ilo.org/ankara/projects/WCMS_710959/lang--en/index.htm.

Janssens, M., & Steyaert, C. (2019). A practice-based theory of diversity: Respecifying (in) equality in organizations. *Academy of Management Review*, *44*(3), 518–537.

Kalleberg, A. L., & Vallas, S. P. (2017). Probing precarious work: Theory, research, and politics. *Research in the Sociology of Work*, *31*, 1–30. https://doi.org/10.1108/S0277-283320170000031017.

Kartal, B., & Basci, E. (2014). Türkiye'ye yönelik mülteci ve siginmaci hareketleri (asylum-seeker and refugee movement towards Turkey). CBÜ. *Journal of Social Sciences*, *12*(2), 275–299.

Knappert, L., Kornau, A., & Figengül, M. (2018). Refugees' exclusion at work and the intersection with gender: Insights from the Turkish-Syrian border. *Journal of Vocational Behavior*, *105*, 62–82.

Knappert, L., van Dijk, H., & Ross, V. (2019). Refugees' inclusion at work: a qualitative cross-level analysis. *Career Development International*.

Kornau, A., Knappert, L., & Erdur, D. A. (2021). Advertising, avoiding, disrupting, and tabooing: The discursive construction of diversity subjects in the Turkish context. *Scandinavian Journal of Management, 37*(2), 101151.

Lee, E. O. J., & Brotman, S. (2013). Speak out! Structural intersectionality and anti-oppressive practice with LGBTQ refugees in Canada. *Canadian Social Work Review/Revue Canadienne De Service Social, 30*(2), 157–183.

Lee, E. S., Szkudlarek, B., Nguyen, D. C., & Nardon, L. (2020). Unveiling the Canvas Ceiling: A multidisciplinary literature review of refugee employment and workforce integration. *International Journal of Management Reviews, 22*(2), 193–216.

MIPEX. (2021). Retrieved 2 May 2021, from www.mipex.eu/netherlands.

MIPEX. (2021). Retrieved 2 May 2021, from www.mipex.eu/turkey.

Muhanna-Matar, A. (2022). The emerging intersectional performative gender of displaced Syrian women in southeast Turkey. *Gender, Place & Culture, 29*(6), 772–792, DOI: 10.1080/0966369X.2021.1887091.

Naccache, P, Al Ariss, A (2018) The forced migration crisis and the role of European corporations: a point of view. *European Management Review* 15(4), 589–596.

Ortlieb, R., & Weiss, S. (2020). Job quality of refugees in Austria: Trade-offs between multiple workplace characteristics. *German Journal of Human Resource Management, 34*(4), 418–442.

Ortlieb, R., Eggenhofer-Rehart, P., Leitner, S., Hosner, R., & Landesmann, M. (2020). Do Austrian Programmes Facilitate Labour Market Integration of Refugees? *International Migration*, 1–21.

Özbilgin, M. F., Syed, J., Ali, F., & Torunoglu, D. (2012). International transfer of policies and practices of gender equality in employment to and among Muslim majority countries. *Gender, Work & Organization, 19*(4), 345–369.

Ponzoni, E, Ghorashi, H, Van der Raad, S (2017) Caught between norm and difference: narratives on refugees' inclusion in organizations. *Equality, Diversity and Inclusion* 36(3), 222–237.

Purkayastha, B. (2012). Intersectionality in a transnational world. *Gender & Society*, 26(1), 55–66. https://doi-org.vu-nl.idm.oclc.org/10.1177/0891243211426725.

Syed, J., & Özbilgin, M. (2009). A relational framework for international transfer of diversity management practices. *The International Journal of Human Resource Management, 20*(12), 2435–2453.

Tomlinson, F (2010) Marking difference and negotiating belonging: refugee women, volunteering and employment. *Gender, Work and Organization* 17(3), 278–296.

182 Lena Knappert et al.

UNHCR. (2019). *Global Trends report*. Retrieved 2 May 2021, from www.unhcr.org/be/wp-content/uploads/sites/46/2020/07/Global-Trends-Report-2019.pdf.
UNCHR. (2020). Figures at a Glance. UNHCR. Retrieved 2 May 2021, from www.unhcr.org/figures-at-a-glance.html.
UNCHR. (2021). *Livelihoods – UNHCR Turkey*. Retrieved 2 May 2021, from https://help.unhcr.org/turkey/information-for-syrians/livelihoods/.
UNHCR. (2021). *Refugees and Asylum Seekers in Turkey – UNHCR Turkey*. Retrieved 2 May 2021, from www.unhcr.org/tr/en/refugees-and-asylum-seekers-in-turkey.
Ünlütürk-Ulutaş, Ç., & Akbaş, S. (2020). The Most Invisible of the Invisibles: Skilled Syrian Women in the Turkish Labour Market. In *Women, Migration and Asylum in Turkey* (pp. 193–212). Palgrave Macmillan.
Van Hear, N. (2006). "I went as far as my money would take me": conflict, forced migration and class. *Forced migration and global processes: A view from forced migration studies*, 125–158.
Vervliet, M., De Mol, J., Broekaert, E., & Derluyn, I. (2014). "That I live, that's because of her": Intersectionality as framework for unaccompanied refugee mothers. *British Journal of Social Work*, 44(7), 2023–2041.
Wehrle, K., Klehe, U.-C., Kira, M., Zikic, J. (2018) "Can I Come as I am? Refugees' Vocational Identity Threats, Coping, and Growth", *Journal of Vocational Behavior* 105(1), 83–101.
Wilson, S., & Ebert, N. (2013). Precarious work: Economic, sociological and political perspectives. *Economic and Labour Relations Review*, 24(3), 263–278. https://doi.org/10.1177/1035304613500434.

10

Trapped in Precarious Work
The Case of Syrian Refugee
Workers in Turkey

DENIZ PALALAR ALKAN, RIFAT KAMASAK,
ESIN SAYIN, AND JOANA VASSILOPOULOU

10.1 Introduction

Precarious work has increased in many countries and has become a
global challenge (Foster, 2021; Vij, 2019). Numerous factors have
contributed to increasing precarity, such as macro-economic recession, neoliberal globalisation, increased organisational competition,
and economic integration that accelerated the adoption of work
outsourcing (Kalleberg, 2009; Standing, 2011). The existing literature suggests that as the labour market witnesses growth in self-
employment and zero-hour contracts to boost the economy and attain
profitability, it also increases precarious work globally (Harvey,
2005). However, previous studies demonstrated that certain groups
are far more vulnerable to precarious working conditions such as
young workers (Bradley & van Hoof, 2005; Kretsos, 2010), women
(Fudge & Owens, 2006; Jonsson & Nyberg, 2010) LGBTQ+ people (Kamasak, Özbilgin, Baykut & Yavuz, 2020), agency workers-
temporary employment (Elcioglu, 2010), older workers (D'Amours,
2010) and minority ethnic workers, migrants and refugees (Bhalla &
McCormick, 2009; Porthé et al., 2009), and Roma people (McKay,
Szymonek & Keles, 2012). In fact, McKay et al. (2012) argue that
undocumented migrants are the most vulnerable population of all the
mentioned categorisations since they attain limited opportunities to
land high-paying jobs and possibilities for upward mobility.

The conceptualisation of precariousness differs among scholars. For
instance, Ettlinger (2007) utilises the term to describe the generalised
condition of unpredictability in society, whereas Vasudevan (2015)
refers to the concept as an economic and political condition that arises
from "ambient insecurity" (p. 351). For some scholars, precariousness

is a multidimensional concept that occurs in five distinctive aspects of social life (Campbell & Price, 2016). The first level of precariousness is related to employment conditions, which is related to job specifications that are characterised by "insecurity" resulting in a low level of regulatory protection, minimum wages, high job insecurity, and low level of employee control over their work conditions (Vosko, 2010: 2; Vosko et al., 2009: 7). The second level referring to precarious work is related to "waged work" that encompasses several preciousness attributions (Standing, 2011). The third level of precariousness focuses on the "precarious worker" and on the experiences of individual lives (Anderson, 2010). The fourth level of precariousness is related to understanding a particular group, the so-called precariat, in a labour market (Standing, 2011). As Standing (2011) argues, this new social class, namely the "precariat," has arisen as a consequence of instability, insecurity, and unpredictability (Kalleberg & Vallas, 2018: 7) and provoked particular challenges like the "Occupy Movements" in Western societies. The fifth level of precariousness refers to a more generalised conceptualisation of precariousness in a social context, that is, housing, welfare, human geography, and personal relations (Anderson, 2010; Arnold & Bongiavi, 2013; Ali & Newbold, 2019). Although understanding precarity as a life condition resulting from unstable societal conditions (Bourdieu, 1999; Butler, 2004), the term is commonly used to explore the specific labour market condition (Dorre et al., 2006; Waite, 2009). As social and labour historians focused on understanding the structural conditions of precariousness within the domain of social life (Betti, 2018), precarious work conditions have increased steadily despite the commonly adopted "standard employment model" of the 1950–1970s. Herein the standard employment model refers to work arrangements characterised as "a stable, protected, full time that is regulated to a minimum level by collective agreement or by labour and social security law" (Bosch, 2004, pp. 618–619). Even though the standard work model is full-time employment, providing individual social protection via the employer and state support, precarious work is often related to short-term fixed contracts that are commonly found in hospitality, construction, agriculture, retail, care, and domestic work (Anderson, 2010; McKay, Szymonek & Keles, 2012).

Clement et al. (2009) argue that precariousness is contingent upon certain elements such as access to welfare services irrespective of labour market status. Due to a rise in transnational movements of the workforce globally, the immigrant population also increased substantially (Mcdowell et al., 2009). Immigrants and ethnic minorities face precarious work conditions as they are generally offered temporary contracts and seasonal work (Mcdowell et al., 2009). This condition is not surprising since Polanyi (1944) warned that allowing the market as the prevailing actor in society could be detrimental. Similarly, Kalleberg (2009) highlighted that there is an increased workforce vulnerability due to the unregulated labour market conditions. This circumstance resulted in limited rights to attain healthcare, welfare, and social benefits, inadequate employment rights, and difficulties such as acquiring essential education to gain relevant skills and competence to increase upward mobility (Bobek et al., 2018; Waite & Lewis, 2017) for the precariat. Although some of today's workforce has more flexibility and opportunities such as remote work and diverse work arrangements (Hoffman et al., 2020), the way immigrants and ethnic minorities experience precarious work may be distinctive, particularly since many immigrants and ethnic minorities work in professions that do not allow for remote work, such as cleaners.

Thus, this chapter focuses on the experience of the precarity of minority ethnic Syrians in Turkey. While minority ethnic Syrians entered the country as refugees, most of them have now settled permanently. As such, minority ethnic Syrians now form with nearly four million people one of the largest ethnic minority groups in Turkey. An ethnic minority is a group of people who differ in race or colour or in national, religious, or cultural origin from the dominant group, often the majority population, of the country in which they live. Accordingly, when referring to minority ethnic Syrians, we use both terms, refugees and ethnic minorities. However, only 15,000 Syrians have been granted a work permit, and they also lack access to vocational training, which has turned many Syrians, irrespective of their educational attainment, into precarious workers. Accordingly, the chapter starts by exploring how this group became a precarious workforce. We then describe the precariat context in Turkey from a historical perspective. Next, we present a qualitative study that illustrates the precariat experiences of minority ethnic Syrians in Turkey. Finally, we provide a chapter summary and discussion of possible ways to combat precarious work conditions.

10.2 Migrants and Refugees as Precarious Workforce

The employment conditions and relations of migrant and refugee workers in receiving countries have attracted the growing interest of management scholars (Wright & Clibborn, 2019; Zhang et al., 2021) as their working and living vulnerability has increased due to precarious work conditions (Anderson, 2007; Bloch et al., 2012; Triantafyllidou & Marcetti 2015). Anderson and Tipples (2014) have hinted at a link between segmented markets and migrant workers. Although the undesirability of the work conditions has created a demand for migrant workers, the circumstance also created poor employment terms and conditions. Since migrant and refugee workers face substantial mobility restrictions due to their legal status, they face increased precarious situations and are excluded from legal and social protection (ILO, 2012; UNDP, 2020). Although the categorisations of migrants and refugees and their status vary due to adopted national migration and refugee policies and discourses, the role of migrants and refugees in some economic landscapes may be vital. Various research on the migrant and refugee workforce and their precarious conditions have focused on their immigration/refugee status (McKay et al., 2009; Valentine, 2010), nationality (Kagan et al., 2011), and industry-specific attributes (Anderson & Rogaly, 2005; Bloch & McKay, 2017; Posch et al., 2020).

Previous research demonstrated that migrant and refugee workers are more likely to face unfavourable work treatment (Akinlade et al., 2020; Esses, 2021) and encounter greater difficulty integrating into the workforce (Ertorer et al., 2020; Amuedo-Hamrin, 2019). Amuedo-Dorantes and de la Rica (2007a, b) found that migrant workers often face discrimination based on their ethnic origin. The authors showed that undocumented migrants experience high job instability, disempowerment due to insufficient legal protection, and high vulnerability. Migrants and refugees often face limited job mobility and lack opportunities to obtain necessary skills and competence due to their unique conditions in the receiving country (Kamasak, Özbilgin, Yavuz & Akalın, 2020). Thus, migrant and refugee workers are frequently associated with precarious work characterised by minimum wages, high insecurity, undesirable working conditions and unfair treatment at work (Campbell & Price, 2016; Bloch & McKay, 2017). Especially undocumented migrants face precarious working conditions since they do not have the necessary permits, and lack knowledge of the host country and the regulative and legislative framework (McKay et al., 2012).

Zhang et al. (2021) outlined several factors contributing to migrants' precariousness in the labour market. These factors are categorised under three levels of analysis, namely micro (individual), meso (organisational), and macro (country or contextual) levels. The authors focused on various human resource management (HRM) practices utilised in managing a precarious workforce at the individual level. For example, Hopkins et al. (2016) identified that harsh HRM mechanisms, such as attendance control, are adopted to effectively manage the precarious workforce in an organisation. Researching the experiences of black, Asian, and asylum seekers they conclude that the individual experience of precarity varies across migrants, which must be understood as a heterogeneous group of migrant workers. This finding is relevant for the development of international human resource management literature, which often views migrant workers as a homogenous group. Campbell et al. (2019) conducted a study in Australia where an increasing level of precarity occurs. The study draws attention to so-called "wage theft," a practice known as intentional underpayment, which is a form of illegal employer practises implemented by organisations and tolerated by employees. The authors highlight employees' reluctance to complain about such practices and the rationales adopted by the precarious migrant workforce to do so. Esbenshade et al. (2019) examined the individual conditions of the precarious migrant workforce in the USA, exploring the ambiguities of the precarious workforce, such as lack of work protection and control.

Several studies have used a meso level of analysis, attempting to understand various organisational level aspects of migrant precarity, such as patterns of "vulnerabilisation" in organisations, and lack of representation by trade unions (Kirov & Hohnen, 2015). Several meso-level studies explored trade unions and employment agencies' responses to the changing labour market dynamics shaped by increasing precariousness. For instance, Heinrich et al. (2020) have considered the effects of trade union strategies to manage cross-border migrants' precarity in the European Union, arguing due to heightened competition among domestic and EU-migrant workers. The study adopted an actor-centred approach and tried to illuminate the perspective of trade union representatives. The study findings show that trade unions had inadequate knowledge of industrial relations among new and old member countries, adopted selective inclusive strategies, and lacked mechanisms to effectively manage conflict of interest.

At the macro level, authors argue that migrant and refugee workers' employment precarity is due to receiving countries' migration refugee and labour market policies. For example, Kushnirovich et al. (2018) has focused on identifying "bilateral agreements" (BLA) that establish the rights of the migrant precarity in Israel, specifically in the construction industry. The authors stated that BLA implementation in various countries has increased the vulnerability of migrant precarity and that BLA is effective only in the recruitment process and an ineffective macro-level mechanism to combat exacerbating conditions of migrant precarity such as protecting their social rights in the workplace. Additionally, Howe (2020) identified several governmental and legal interventions, such as a "new system of employer scheme" to combat the exploitation of migrant precarity in Ireland and New Zealand. The individual-level analysis of migrant precarity focuses on worker attributes such as employment experiences towards implemented HRM practices and mobility (Alberti, 2014; Premji, 2017). Finally, at the macro level, several authors examined the legal framework on migration policy and labour market regulation and investigated various adopted mechanisms in the receiving countries. There is a clear indication of several factors contributing to the heightened vulnerability of migrant precarity. Although these studies consistently indicate the exploitation of migrants in various contexts, much uncertainty exists in countries with "limited legal discourses and supportive measures" protecting the social rights of migrants and refugees (Küskü et al., 2020: 555).

10.3 Syrian Refugees in Turkey

Turkey is home to nearly four million Syrian refugees (UNHCR, 2020), which have become one of the largest minority ethnic groups in Turkey. In this chapter, we focus on the experience of the precarity of minority ethnic Syrians in the labour market in Turkey, who experience precarity in employment at a significantly larger scale compared to the majority population. Historically, irregular migration has not been a major issue in Turkey compared to other nations such as the United States and the EU countries (Boratav, 2006; Toksöz et al., 2012). Turkey has not been considered a popular destination for migrants until the 1990s because of its relatively unattractive economic and political conditions (Çelik, 2005).

In fact, it is the other way around, as a result of the neoliberal economic approaches of the government under the control of the Democrat Party (DP) which mainly adopted populist market policies with no social dimension and with the mechanisation of agriculture, many Turkish villagers became unemployed between the early 1950s and late 1970s (Kamasak & Yavuz, 2016; Boratav, 2006) and left the country. The harm in family farming in villages caused internal migration and emigration of Turkish people to other countries (Çelik, 2005; Akşit, 1993). In particular, the emigration activities which began in the early 1960s are conspicuous. Turkish workers systematically emigrated to Germany under the so-called guest workers agreement signed on October 30, 1961 (Akgündüz, 2018). Regular emigration continued until the mid of 1980s and its scope extended to other European countries, that is, Austria, Belgium, France, and the Netherlands. After the bilateral agreements between Turkey and the host countries, Turkey "turned into an emigration country" (Şenses, 2016). The systematic migration comprised nearly 1 million people of whom 800.000 went to Germany in 1973 (Deutsche Welle, 2021).

The popularity of Turkey for migrants only started increasing during the dissolution period of the Soviet Union between 1988 and 1991. People who were in desperate situations from Caucasian countries, that is, Azerbaijan, Turkmenistan, Kazakhstan, Uzbekistan, Georgia, and Armenia, and the former Eastern Bloc countries, that is, Moldavia, Romania, and Bulgaria, together with Ukraine arrived in Turkey as irregular migrants with no work permits (Toksöz et al., 2012). Irregular migration to Turkey did not come only from these countries but also from Pakistan and particularly Afghanistan which suffered from the Soviet occupation between 1979 and 1989.

Because of the lack of an optimal immigration policy and a low level of regulatory protection in work-life (Baykut et al., 2021), most of the migrants found themselves in an insecure work environment in Turkey, and they were considered unskilled workers irrespective of their actual skills (Şenses, 2016). Thus, while some migrants from certain nationalities were associated with the sex industry, others were positioned in housekeeping type of jobs and the others worked in industries such as construction, textile, hospitality which generally employ workers with low skills and pay minimum wages (Armağan & Lloyd, 2018). Although the position and social status of migrants in the labour market have changed over time, the basis of a toxic precarious environment has already been grounded. The precariat context has initially started to emerge after the arrival of the migrants from the countries mentioned above, yet the situation worsened in Turkey due to the civil wars in Iraq between 2006 and 2008 and particularly in Syria which has been continuing since 2011 as part of the wider 2011 Arab Spring protests (UNHCR, 2019). The civil war which is next to the south-eastern borders of Turkey made the country the home of millions of Syrian refugees. The upsurge in irregular migration resulting from the Syrian refugee crisis triggered the precarious conditions that are directed at the migrant population in Turkey.

According to the UNHCR (2020) report, as of October 2020, approximately 5 million migrants reside in Turkey of whom 3.9 million are descendants of Syrian nationality. In Turkey, "Law no. 6458 on Foreigners and International Protection" was approved in 2013 to provide a framework for the migration process (Migration Policy Institute, 2021). Although Law no. 6458 on immigration tries to eliminate undocumented migrants, approximately one million Syrian undocumented migrants are currently working in Turkey (Özvarış et al., 2020). The study by Tiryaki (2022) on migrant labour critically argues that 94 per cent of Syrian migrants are employed in the informal economy in Turkey. The informal economy is characterised by precarious work conditions from various perspectives (ILO, 2015). Thus, it is possible to argue that a substantial migrant workforce in Turkey faces precarious work. Although a considerable amount of research has focused on the precarious conditions of the migrant workforce in the Global North (Mcdowell, Batnitzky & Dyer, 2009; Milkman, 2011; Bloch & McKay, 2017; Hande, Akram, & Condratto, 2020), there are a limited number of studies (i.e., Parrenas et al., 2019; Wang, 2020) conducted in the Global South. Turkey hosts the highest number of migrants/refugees in the world and has been experiencing a surge of irregular migration movements since the Syrian conflict started. Therefore, it is important to explore the link between precarity and minority ethnic Syrian workers.

10.4 Methods

We have used an abductive methodology (Locke, 2011; Özbilgin & Erbil, 2019). Abductive research allows researchers the flexibility to move back and forth between data and the related literature to identify common patterns. Within the scope of this research, the data represents the participant migrant experiences concerning precarious work from a multilevel perspective. As part of an ethnic minority and migrant workforce, the experience of precarity rises from numerous sources, such as their belief system and attributes as consequences of micro-, meso-, and macro-level interactions of individuals. The researchers conducted in-depth interviews with fifteen Syrian refugees residing in Turkey. The participants' selection was based on their ability to provide researchers with obtaining an in-depth understanding of precarity. We have reached each participant through the contacts of one of the authors who works for the Small and Medium Enterprises Development Organisation of Turkey (KOSGEB) to which many migrants apply for business-related education, training, and funding. All interviews were conducted face-to-face, recorded, and transcribed verbatim. An average interview lasted approximately forty-five minutes and was conducted by one of the authors of the manuscript.

The demographics of the data reflect that the participants are between 25 and 46 years of age. The majority of the respondents are married with children. They have been residing in Turkey for an average of 5.2 years ranging from 2 to 8 years. All participants have fled Syria due to the civil war and conflicts in the country; thus, they all possess Syrian nationality. The migrants were from two Western cities of Turkey: Istanbul and Tekirdag. Both cities host many industries that offer high potential employment for job seekers. Only two of the participants were female, and the rest were male. The demographic data are presented in Table 10.1.

We have utilised semi-structured interviews to make participants associate their relevant experiences with precarity. The fully transcribed interview data including the precarious experiences of the migrants were analysed by a thematic analysis using the relational perspective.

10.4.1 Data Analysis

Three co-authors independently coded and thematically analysed the data in order to examine how the participants experience precarity in

Table 10.1 *Participants' demographic information*

Participant pseudonym	Age and gender	Marital status	Education level	Jobs in Syria	Jobs in Turkey	Arrival in Turkey	City of residence
Nubar	44 male	Divorced with 2 children	High school 2nd year dropout	Worker in the garment industry	Worker in the garment industry	2014	Tekirdag
Habib	46 male	Married with 3 children	Vocational school 1st year dropout	Grocer	Worker in textile, biscuits and agriculture	2015	Istanbul
Amine	28 female	Married with 3 children	Studying her final year in university	Not worked (she mentions that women should not work)	Not working	2016	Istanbul
Affan	26 male	Married	High school	Farmer and worker in construction	Worker in construction (not working since last month, could not find a job)	2014	Tekirdag
Secat	35 male	Married with 4 children	High school final year dropout	Electrician	Worker in a coal dealer	2018	Tekirdag
Benat	35 male	Married with 3 children	Theological school	Chauffeur	Cleaner in a mosque	2018	Istanbul
Arvin	30 male	Married with 3 children	Secondary school dropout	Egg dealer	Glassmaker	2019	Tekirdag

Name	Age/Gender	Marital status	Education	Previous job	Job in Turkey	Year	City
Furkat	28 male	Married with 1 child	Secondary school	Worker in construction	Worker in construction (not working, could not find a job because of the pandemic)	2019	Istanbul
Hafza	32 female	Divorced with 3 children	Secondary school dropout	Cleaning and housework	Cleaning and housework, and eldercare	2014	Tekirdag
Renas	32 male	Married with 2 children	Secondary school	Tailor	Sewer in a tailor shop	2018	Istanbul
Omar	31 male	Single (his wife is pregnant)	Unknown	Police officer in the department of homicide	Worker in construction	2015	Tekirdag
Othman	Unknown male	Married with 1 child	Unknown	Worker in women's shoe manufacturing	Worker in construction	2014	Tekirdag
Menduh	28 male	Married with 1 child	Tailoring education	Worker in textile	Worker in textile	2019	Tekirdag
Hubeyb	36 male	Single	Law school 3rd year dropout	Jobless	Worked in ironing, construction, aluminium and has been working in knitting for 4 years	2014	Tekirdag
Sufi	25 male	Married	High school	Farmer	Worker in construction (not working, could not find a job because of the pandemic)	2014	Tekirdag

the Turkish labour market. The common procedure in thematic analysis requires methodological categorisation of the empirical data. This procedure involves encoding qualitative data through explicit codes, leading to emerging patterns (Braun & Clarke, 2006). Furthermore, the identified themes were evaluated on their overall significance in shaping the thematic analysis by the co-authors. Lincoln and Guba (1985) identified several factors in achieving trustworthiness of qualitative data of the explored construct, known as credibility, dependability, conformability, and transferability. The researchers have observed the same phenomenon across various individuals and examined common underlying factors contributing to experiences of precarity to attain the study's credibility. We have enriched multiple iterations and emphasised vital factors contributing to migrants' precarious experiences to achieve the study's dependability. For conformability, after the first author collected the raw data, the data was codified and shared among two co-authors who conducted the analysis and coding and selected illustrative codes independently. Then common and significant themes were discussed among the researchers. When authors could not reach common ground on specific themes, the theme was omitted or reconstructed until consensus among the researchers was reached. The study provides valuable insights into migrants' precarity in developing nations with limited regulative discourses in terms of transferability of the study.

We have adopted a relational perspective in this study, in which micro (individual), meso (organisational), and macro (labour market, government) levels are incorporated that impact migrant workers' experience of precarity (Özbilgin & Vassilopoulou, 2018; Kamaşak, Özbilgin, & Yavuz, 2020) (Figure 10.1). The study's key focus on identifying themes of migrants' precarity experiences in Turkey contributes to understanding the mechanisms that drive an individual to accept such adverse conditions. The constructed thematic analyses allowed researchers to identify categories of themes to discuss some of the prominent reasoning that lead to precarity acceptance. This research critically analyses the precarious migrants' conditions in a context that has high migration levels and is characterised by a limited and durable migrant policy. Figure 10.1 outlines how intersectional encounters can be viewed from the perspective of multilevel relationality.

As depicted in Figure 10.1, within this study, we have identified various intersectional factors contributing to the acceptance of precarious conditions of migrants in Turkey. For the macro-level encounters, we

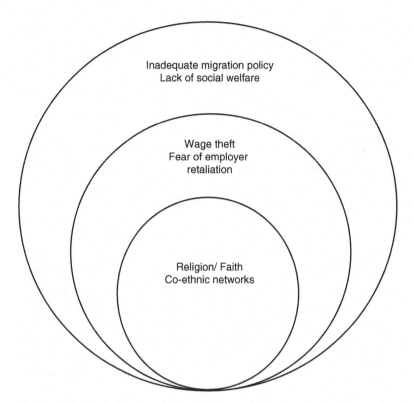

Figure 10.1 A relational multilevel framework for intersectional encounters and intersectional analysis

have observed a lack of inadequate migration policy and lack of social welfare highly contribute to the acceptance of vulnerability. In the study, we have discovered wage theft and fear of employer retaliation are some of the salient causes that lead to migrant precariousness in Turkey for meso-level analysis. The micro-level factors contributing to migrants' acceptance of adverse work conditions stem from their religious affiliation and belief system in addition to co-ethnic employment attachment.

10.5 Findings and Discussion

In this section, we present the findings of our study across the three levels of analysis, namely the micro, meso and macro levels. Starting with the macro level of analysis, we examine how inadequate migration policy exacerbates the conditions of the precariousness of migrants. Next, on the meso level, we analyse how precarity manifests on the organisational level. Lastly, on the micro level of analysis, we focus on how individuals experience precarity in the labour market in Turkey.

Currently, there are three distinctive immigration categorisations in Turkey: (i) irregular/undocumented labour migrants and transit migrants, (ii) asylum seekers and refugees, and (iii) documented/regular migrants (İçduygu & Aksel, 2012). Respective of the categorisation, the irregular/undocumented migrants comprise those considered either as "transit" that use Turkey as a transit state to immigrate to another country or those who stay and work without legal documentation. Furthermore, asylum seekers and refugees are given temporary protection from an emergency humanitarian situation. Lastly, regular migrants immigrated to Turkey for employment, education, settlement, and long-term or recreational purposes. Although various groups are facing an increased vulnerability of precarity including women, young workers, students and the disabled workforce, the majority of the precarious workforce consists of undocumented migrants (Mckay et al., 2012). In the study, the majority of the participants are also undocumented migrants, who migrated to Turkey due to the Syrian conflict.

10.5.1 Macro-level Encounters: How Inadequate Migration Policy Exacerbates the Conditions of the Precariousness of Migrants

Turkey is one of the countries with the highest Syrian migrant population, currently unable to provide adequate policy and social welfare to its irregular migrants. The high absorption rate of migrants in Turkey created various challenges, such as increased inter-communal hostility. This is partially due to the migrant's acceptance of precarious work in metropolitan areas, that is, Istanbul and Ankara, and industrial cities such as Tekirdag and Gaziantep where the conditions create a conflict of economic interest (International Crisis Group, 2018) among migrants. Even though the Turkish government demonstrated constructive efforts in managing migration, due to limited migration policy, the majority of the migrants currently work in the informal economy with limited social welfare. According to the report by International Crisis Group (2018), approximately 750,000–950,000

Syrian migrants currently reside in Turkey. However, only 15,000 out of the Syrian migrant population have obtained a work permit, are highly illiterate, and lack access to vocational training. Since one of the salient attributes of precarious work is related to its unpredictability of working conditions irrespective of the industry, we have identified that inadequate migration policy exacerbates the conditions of the precariousness of migrants. One of the participants, Amine, who experienced the challenge of getting employment opportunities through state-supported institutions said:

I was looking for a job and applied to ISKUR (Turkish employment Agency), but they told me that 'you are Syrian and you will not be able to get a job through us'.... In the end, no institution helps us to get a job.

Also, the majority of the participants attained job opportunities through the imams of mosques. This is partially due to insufficient treasury allocation of the Turkish Government to municipalities, as these are designed irrespective of the migrant population (International Crisis Group, 2018). The claim of Hubeyb supports this as he stated:

The state could not manage the refugees well from the beginning, opened the borders, and left them in chaos. If Turkey needed the workforce, if it had obtained a residence permit legally, it would have given a work permit, etc. Both political and economic barriers prevent refugees from working. Opposition parties want to rule the state and talk about refugees in every election to win elections.

Although the participants possessed various occupational backgrounds prior to migration to Turkey, ranging from education, textile, accounting, participant migrant workers have attained short-term jobs that lack standard rights and entitlement (Campbell & Price, 2016). Participant Habib commented:

In my county, I used to work as an accountant. Here I have been working in the denim industry in spinning and weaving. Before this, I worked in a food manufacturing factory; however, they have closed the factory, and when I first arrived in Turkey, I worked in plantation agriculture.

Additionally, participant migrants have substantial limitations attaining several social benefits such as educational attainment, food, and household goods assistance to effectively transition into the living standards of the receiving country. The participant migrant, Hafza, who experienced a lack of social welfare, claimed:

I looked to get a job but I could only find it through a close friend, I did not have any chance to get vocational training, and I do not think I will ever get any training as well.

Since the migrant workforce in Turkey fills low-skilled job vacancies, they also lack necessary adjustment and integration support such as language training, assistance in housing and education, and accessing government services such as healthcare (Davas, 2018).

10.5.2 Meso-level Encounters: How Inadequate Organisational Level Interventions Exacerbates the Conditions of the Precariousness of Migrants.

For the most part, employers operating in low-skilled industries only employ migrant workers because such jobs are not attractive to the majority population (McKay & Markova, 2010); the low cost of the migrant workforce (MacKenzie & Forde, 2009), and their flexibility (Thompson et al., 2013), which often is a necessity for migrants to get work, rather than a mindset or choice. Forde and Mackenzie's (2009) study has shown that employers of migrant workers adopt a "low wage and long hours" approach predominantly to maintain low labour costs to remain competitive in the marketplace. For example, a study by Bloch and McKay (2017) has shown that the migrant workforce is generally employed in temporal/seasonal conditions such as construction, agriculture, the hospitality industry, care, and cleaning industries. In a similar vein, the majority of migrants attain employment opportunities in labour-intensive and hazardous industries such as construction, textile (mainly denim industry), and manufacturing (Davas, 2018) in Turkey.

One of the common challenges that the migrant workers face in the receiving country is known as wage theft, as numerous studies identify the issue as being systematic and widespread in various cultures (Berg & Farbenblum, 2017; Clibborn & Wright, 2018; Weil, 2018; Cambell et al., 2019). Scholars argue several rationales behind the acceptance of wage theft, including implementing state policies favouring employers that potentially increase the vulnerability of the migrant workforce (Clibborn & Wright, 2018; Befort and Budd, 2009). The migrant workforce frequently encounters wage theft since there is a limited collective representation and employment opportunities (Fudge, 2014; Holgate, 2005). In the study, we have observed a similar challenge. The participants indicated that their employers are non-compliant with the minimum wage laws and are poorly compensated relative to Turkish citizens conducting the same job. One of the participants, Othman expressed:

Although we generally do the same job, Syrians are paid far less than Turkish. We accept this circumstance since we do not have any other employment opportunities. For example, we do the same job, but a Turkish employee earns 200 TL, I get 100 TL, and they give my brother 80 TL.

Undocumented migrants face structural barriers to collective representation as governments embrace employer-friendly imperatives, resulting in the heightened vulnerability of the workforce. Moreover, the lack of collective representation of the migrant workforce leads to an exclusive regulatory system that allows employers to breach employment regulations (Clibborn & Wright, 2018). This circumstance intensifies the current adverse conditions of migrants residing in Turkey since the state regulation on migration policy is relatively new. Additionally, in the context of a toxic triangle (Küskü et al., 2021), where employment laws and a lack of adequate legal measuring mechanisms occur, the likelihood of precariousness of the migrant workforce increases. Interestingly, although the employers exploit the fundamental rights such as earning a minimum wage, the migrant workforce is reluctant to voice their complaints out of employer retaliation fear (Campbell et al., 2019). One participant, Menduh, states the unequal treatment to the local and migrant workers in the workplace:

There is a big difference between a Turkish and a Syrian in terms of compensation. Even though we did the same job in my previous workplace, they paid me very little money, so I asked for a raise. The Turks laughed at me for asking for a raise. I did not know why the Turks laughed at me or why it was so interesting. They usually made fun of me because I do not speak Turkish and only speak Arabic. They used to tell me, "shut up, we speak Turkish here. The boss misbehaves towards us at work. Everyone was afraid of him anyway, I mean, he was not mean to everyone, but he was to those he felt overpowered."

Migrants' reluctance to challenge mistreatment and employment violations in organisations is driven by specific rationales such as lack of employment opportunities due to undocumented status and perception of power imbalance in the employment relation (Weil, 2018; Campbell et al., 2016). One limitation for the migrants on the way of reaching employment opportunities is the existence of unique traditions and ethos in relation to accommodation of migrants in state institutions such as police and military services. The state is an employer as well as a service provider to the whole society. However, state employment is rather difficult for the migrants. Omar who was a police officer in the department of homicide in Syria provides support to this argument:

I was an officer in the department of homicide, yet it was impossible for me to do my job as an immigrant here.... Therefore, I started to work with some other friends in the construction business. This is not a contemporary job. We sometimes work one day a week and wait for another week.

In addition to the various claims of participants above, the participants live under financial pressures without access to social security and welfare benefits. As immigration policies amplify employers' power over migrants', their adverse conditions may even further exacerbate, especially when exposed to immediate deportation.

10.5.3 Micro-level Encounters: How Experiences of Individuals Exacerbate the Conditions of the Precariousness of Migrants

The literature emphasises the political economy of migrant precariousness as they are subjected to exclusion due to their legal and social status in the receiving country (MPI, 2021; International Crisis Group, 2018; Campbell et al., 2016; McDowell et al., 2009). Furthermore, within the social fragmentation that they experience in their new residency, the migrant precarity also creates their new sense of self through mechanisms such as religion to cope and increase resiliency. Religion can be interpreted as an agency to minimise the adversity of migrant precariousness as it can help create a positive stance within a society and increase interconnectedness by attaining reliability and candour (Nijhawan, 2019). In the interviews we have conducted within the scope of this study, religious affiliation was the focal point of attaining employment opportunities for the majority of the participants. As one of the participants, Omar's, claim illustrates this:

Being Muslim is a privilege in Turkey. This is one of the salient characteristics and reasons we are accepted in this country. The conditions in Europe are far better, but they are not Muslims.

The claim of Benat further supports the fact that migrants need to search for other means of mechanisms such as religious affiliations to attain employment opportunities in Turkey.

I think they help Muslims to find jobs in Turkey, I found my job through the local Imam Ahmet like many of my friends.

Faith and religion are the underexplored aspect of migrant precariousness (Nyamnjoh et al., 2022). They provide essential survival support and minimise economic challenges. As the illustrated quotes above suggest, in the lack of state support, religious affiliation becomes a primary source of employment. However, as the participants indicate, it also creates an increasing precarity since the Islamic faith religiosity values gratitude, the migrants' will to negotiate to ameliorate work conditions diminishes.

Additionally, co-ethnic networks provide employment opportunities specifically in the first year of arrival to the receiving country for many migrants (Battisti et al., 2018). Since Syrian migrants in Turkey face challenges in attaining social support such as access to education (Baban, IIcan, and Rygiel, 2017), health services, and the language barrier; they rely on the co-ethnic social networks to survive (Oner et al., 2020). Participant Nubar explains how he experienced the help of co-ethnic networks in finding employment opportunities:

I found my job with the help of my friends and people I met. They had friends from the refugee camp, looking for employment as well. Since I do not have any relatives in Turkey, I get help from the Syrians.

The above quote highlights that attaining jobs via co-ethnic social networks expedites the employment process, but it also creates limitations such as obtaining necessary skills to increase employability. Thus, co-ethnic networks may also intensify and contribute to migrant precarity.

10.6 Conclusion

This chapter has analysed how Syrian workers in Turkey experience precarity in the labour market from a multilevel perspective, namely the micro, meso, and macro levels of analyses. We have identified a number of challenges for Syrian workers on all three levels of analysis and at the same time, we identified coping strategies that Syrian workers deploy to minimise the negative impact of precarious work on their lives. In the following, we summarise what we view as the most important factors exacerbating precarity for Syrian workers in Turkey. Finally, we will offer policy recommendations for breaking the link between precarity and being a minority ethnic worker in Turkey.

On the macro level we identified that there is a low level of regulatory protection such as a lack of adequate migration policy and employment laws that could prevent Syrian workers from being exploited in the labour market, ultimately leading to precarity in employment. Additionally, we identified a lack of political support for Syrian workers in Turkey, which partially explains the willingness to implement regulatory protections for Syrian and other minority ethnic workers. A lack of unionisation in Turkey contributes further to the precarity of Syrian workers and rising economic inequality. Overall, the absence of effective policy aiming to integrate refugees into the labour market and into wider society, make it difficult for Syrian refugees to live and work in Turkey.

On the meso level of analysis, we highlight that employers, at the expense of migrants, often deploy precarious working conditions for migrants in order to remain competitive in the marketplace. Such conditions are, for example, long working hours, but also low pay and in extreme even cases wage theft. Several studies have identified wage theft as being systematic and widespread in many countries (Berg & Farbenblum, 2017; Clibborn & Wright, 2018; Weil, 2018; Cambell et al., 2019) and so is the case in Turkey. There are little Syrian migrants can do against wage theft, since there is limited collective representation, and/or other employment opportunities and a lack of employment laws providing protection for Syrian workers. Resultantly, the only agency Syrian workers are left with when experiencing wage theft is acceptance. Lastly, the micro level of analysis has provided us with an understanding of the rationale behind accepting precarious working conditions in Turkey, with the main factor being that this is actually not a matter of choice, but rather a matter of necessity since there is a lack of alternatives in dealing with precarity at work and there is not much choice in terms of finding better employment that offers secure working conditions. Instead, many Syrians grapple for survival on a daily basis. A further finding points to the importance of networks held by an individual. Although attaining jobs via co-ethnic social networks expedites the employment process, it also creates limitations such as obtaining the necessary skills to increase employ-ability. Thus, co-ethnic networks may also intensify and contribute to migrant precarity.

Lastly, our study shows that on the micro-/individual-level religion and religious faith constitute an important part of Syrian work-ers coping strategies with precarity, in that it is used to minimise the individual experience of adversity by creating a positive stance within Turkish society and a sense of belonging through the Islamic faith, which is the dominant religion in Turkey. However, as the participants indicate, it also creates an increasing precarity since the Islamic faith religiosity values gratitude, the migrants' will to negotiate to amelio-rate work conditions diminishes. Additionally, religious affiliation is viewed by the majority of participants of this study as helping with finding employment opportunities. Faith and religion are the under-explored aspect of migrant precariousness (Nyamnjoh et al., 2022). They provide essential survival support and minimise economic chal-lenges. The relevance of religion and religious faith for not only coping with precarity but also for the development of belongingness in the host country is a very interesting finding and something that should be studied further since it constitutes a major difference in the context of other major refugee receiving countries, such as for example Germany, where the majority population is predominantly of Christian faith. Also, many studies pertaining to the integration of immigrants in Germany and other countries discuss the religion of migrants, in par-ticular, if they are of Muslim faith, as hindering their integration into the host country, instead of questioning how the host country receives Muslims to their shores and what stigmatists are attached to Muslims that leads to for example discrimination.

The firm stance of the nation-state as the manifestation of the sov-ereign identity is fragmented through a heightened level of migration, curtailing the concept of cultural singularity and creating challenges. Traditionally Turkey has been a country of emigration, particularly in the 1960s and 1970s. Only recently Turkey has become a country of immigration and hence immigration, as well as integration policy and equality and inclusion measures, remains underdeveloped, leav-ing many migrant workers at the mercy of employers who have little interest to provide secure employment to them, without legal enforce-ment. Like many other countries before, Turkey will have to come to terms with being an immigration country and with the fact that the majority of its migrant and refugee population will remain in Turkey and become part of Turkey's population. Having a large minority ethnic population requires a regulatory framework that provides protection from precarity as well as a long-term labour market integration policy that fosters equality and inclusion. Migrants in Turkey experience hardships such as working in hazardous jobs, earning less, and being subjected to social exclusion. The Turkish "Law on Foreigner and International Protection" tries to alleviate the adverse conditions, yet the growing evidence of inter-communal hostility exacerbates migrants' grapple of survival. It will require political will to implement legislation that not only protects minority ethnic workers from precarity but also creates equality and inclusion in the labour market, which is required for the successful labour market integration of minority ethnic workers.

References

Akgündüz, A. (2018). *Labour Migration from Turkey to Western Europe, 1960–1974. A Multidisciplinary Analysis.* London: Routledge.

Akinlade, E. Y., Lambert, J. R. and Zhang, P. (2020). Mechanisms for hiring discrimination of immigrant applicants in the United States. *Equality, Diversity and Inclusion: An International Journal, 39*(4), 395–417.

Akşit, B. (1993). Studies in Rural Transformation in Turkey 1950–1990. In *Culture and Economy in Turkish Villages*, ed. P. Stirling, 187–200. London: Eothen Press.

Alberti, G. (2014). Mobility strategies, "mobility differentials" and "transnational exit": the experiences of precarious migrants in London's hospitality jobs. *Work, Employment and Society, 28*(6), 865–881.

Ali, W. K. & Newbold, K. B. (2019). Geographic Variations in Precarious Employment Outcomes Between Immigrant and Canadian-Born Populations. *Papers in Regional Science, 99*, 1185–1213.

Ali, W. K. & Newbold, K. B. (2020). Geographic variations in precarious employment outcomes between immigrant and Canadian-born populations. *Regional Science, 99*(5), 1185–1213.

Amuedo-Dorantes, C. & de la Rica, S. (2007a). Labor Market Assimilation of Recent Immigrants in Spain. IZA Discussion Paper No. 2104, doi.10.2139/ssrn.900382.

Amuedo-Dorantes, C. & de la Rica, S. (2007b). Labour Market Assimilation of Recent Immigrants in Spain. *British Journal of Industrial Relations, 45*(2), 257–284. doi:10.1111/j.1467-8543.2007.00614.x

Anderson, B. (2010). Migration, immigration controls and the fashioning of precarious workers. *Work, Employment and Society* 24(2), 300–317.

Anderson, B. & Rogaly, B. (2005). *Forced Labour and Migration to the UK*. London: Trades Union Congress.

Anderson, B., Ruhs, M., Rogaly, B., and Spencer, S. (2007) *Fair Enough? Central and East European Migrants in Low-Wage Employment in the UK*. York: Joseph Rowntree Foundation.

Anderson, D. & Tipples, R. (2014). Are vulnerable workers really protected in New Zealand? *New Zealand Journal of Employment Relations, 39*(1), 52–67.

Armağan, F. & Lloyd, T. (2018). Beyond illegality: The gendered (in-) securities of illegal Armenian care workers in Turkey/Yasadışılığın ötesi: Ermeni kadınların toplumsal cinsiyet temelli güvencesizlikleri. *Fe Dergi, 10*(1), 79–93.

Arnold, D. & Bongiovi, J. (2013). Precarious, informalizing, and flexible work: transforming concepts and understandings. *American Behavioral Scientist, 57*(3), 289–308.

Baban, F., Ilican, S. & Rygiel, K. (2017). Syrian Refugees in Turkey: Pathways to Precarity Differential Inclusion, and Negotiated Citizenship Rights. *Journal of Ethnic and Migration Studies, 43* (1), 41–57.

Battisti, M., Peri, G. & Romiti, A. (2018). *Dynamic Effects of Co-Ethnic Networks on Immigrants' Economic Success*. NBER Working Paper 22389.

Baykut, S., Özbilgin, M. F., Erbil, C., Kamasak, R., & Baglama, S. (2021). The impact of hidden curriculum on international students in the context of a toxic triangle of diversity. *The Curriculum Journal, 33*(2), 156–177. https://doi.org/10.1002/curj.135

Befort, S. F. & Budd, J. W. (2009). *Invisible Hands, Invisible Objectives: Bringing Workplace Law and Public Policy into Focus*. Stanford, CA: Stanford University Press.

Berg L. & Farbenblum, B. (2017). Wage theft report. Migrant Worker Justice Initiative.

Betti, E. (2018). Historicizing Precarious Work: Forty Years of Research in the Social Sciences and Humanities. *International Review of Social History, 63*(2), 273–319.

Bhalla, A. McCormick, P. (2009) *Poverty Among Immigrant Children in Europe*. London: Palgrave Macmillan.

Bloch, A., & McKay, S. (2017). *Living on the Margins: Undocumented Migrants in a Global City*. Bristol: Policy Press.

Bloch, A., Sigona, N., Zetter, R. (2012). Migration routes and strategies of young undocumented migrants in England: a qualitative perspective. *Ethnic and Racial Studies* 34(8), 1286–1302.

Bobek, A., Pembroke, S. & Wickham, J. (2018). *Social Implications of Precarious Work*. Dublin: TASC.

Boratav, K. (2006). *Türkiye İktisat Tarihi [Economic history of Turkey]*. Ankara: İmge Kitabevi.

Bosch, G. (2004). Towards a New Standard Employment Relationship in Western Europe. *British Journal of Industrial Relations*, 42(4), 617–636.

Bourdieu, P. (1999). Job insecurity is everywhere now. In *Acts of Resistance: Against the Tyranny of the Market*. New York: New Press.

Bradley, H. & J. van Hoof (2005). Fractured Transitions: The Changing Context of Young Peoples' Labour Market Situations in Europe, in H. Bradley and J. van Hoof (eds) *Young People in Europe*, (pp. 99–113). Bristol: The Policy Press.

Braun, V. & Clarke, V. (2006) Using Thematic Analysis in Psychology. *Qualitative Research in Psychology*, 3, 77–101.

Butler, J. (2004). *Precarious Life: The Powers of Mourning and Violence*. London: Verso.

Campbell, I. & Price, R. (2016). Precarious work and precarious workers: Towards an improved conceptualisation. *The Economic and Labour Relations Review*, 27(3), 314–332.

Campbell, I., Tranfaglia, M.A., Tham, J.-C. & Boese, M. (2019). Precarious work and the reluctance to complain: Italian temporary migrant workers in Australia. *Labour and Industry: A Journal of the Social and Economic Relations of Work*, 29(1), 98–117.

Çelik, A. B. (2005) "I miss my village!": Forced Kurdish migrants in İstanbul and their representation in associations. *New Perspectives on Turkey, 32*, 137–163.

Clement, W., Mathieu, S., Prus, S. & Uckardesier, E. (2009) *Precarious lives in the new economy: Comparative intersectional analysis*. GWD/CPD Working Paper Series.

Clibborn, S. & Wright, C. F. (2018). Employer theft of temporary migrant workers wages in Australia: Why has the state failed to act? *The Economic and Labour Relations Review*, 29(2), 207–227.

D'Amours, M. (2010). Employment after age 50: How precarious is it? *Relations Industrielles/Industrial Relations*, 64(2), 209–229.

Davas, A. (2018). What determines the health of migrant workers? *Toplum ve Hekim, 33*(5), 327–336.

Deutsche Welle. (2021). The German-Turkish Recruitment Agreement 60 years on. Retrieved from. www.dw.com/en/the-german-turkish-recruitment-agreement-60-years-on/a-59398455

Dorre, K., Kraemer, K. & Speidel, F. (2006). *The increasing precariousness of the employment society – driving force for a new right-wing populism?* 15th Conference of Europeanists, Chicago, IL.

Elcioglu, E. F. (2010). Producing Precarity: The Temporary Staffing Agency in the Labor Market. *Qualitative sociology*, 33(2), 117–136.

Ertorer, S. E., Long, J., Fellin, M. & Esses, V. M. (2020). Immigrant perceptions of integration in the Canadian workplace. Equality, Diversity and Inclusion: An International Journal, Vol. ahead-of- print No. ahead-of-print. doi: 10.1108/EDI-02-2019-0086.

Esbenshade, J., Shifrin, E. & Rider, K. (2019). Leveraging liminality: how San Diego taxi drivers used their precarious status to win reform. *Labor History*, 60(2), 79–95.

Esses, V. M. (2021). Prejudice and discrimination toward immigrants. *Annual Review of Psychology*, 72(1), 503–531.

Ettlinger, N. (2007). Precarity unbound. *Alternatives*, 32, 319–340.

Forde, C. & Mackenzie, R. (2009). Employers' use of low-skilled migrant workers: assessing the implications for human resource management. *International Journal of Manpower*, 30(5), 437–452.

Foster, J. (2021). Tracking Precarity: Employment Pathways of Precarious Status migrant Workers in Canada. *Canadian Journal of Sociology*, 46(3), 257–278.

Fudge, J. (2014). Making claims for migrant workers: human rights and citizenship. *Citizenship Studies*, 18(1), 29–45.

Fudge, J. & Owens, J. (2006) *Precarious Work, Women and the New Economy: The Challenge to Legal Norms*, Oxford, UK: Hart Publishing.

Graneheim, U. H., Lindgren, B. & Lundman, B. (2017). Methodological challenges in qualitative content analysis: A discussion paper. *Nurse Education Today*, 56, 29–34.

Hamrin, S. B. A. (2019) Constructions of inclusion at two senior nursing home units in Sweden: immigrants' perspectives. *Equality, Diversity and Inclusion: An International Journal*, 38(4), 462–476.

Han, C. (2018). Precariousness, precarity and vulnerability. *Annual Review of Anthropology*, 47(1), 331–343.

Hande, M. J., Mian Akram, A. and Condratto, S. (2020). "All of this happens here?": Diminishing perceptions of Canada through immigrants' precarious work in Ontario. *Journal of International Migration and Integration, 21*, 711–729.

Harvey, D. (2005). *A Brief History of Neoliberalism*. Oxford: Oxford University Press.

Heinrich, S., Shire, K., & Mottweiler, H. (2020). Fighting (for) the margins: Trade union responses to the emergence of cross-border temporary agency work in the European Union. *Journal of Industrial Relations*, 62(2), 210–234. https://doi.org/10.1177/0022185619900649.

Hoffman, B. J., Shoss, M. K. & Wegman, L. A. (2020). *The Cambridge Handbook of the Changing Nature of Work*. Cambridge: Cambridge University Press.

Holgate, J. (2005). Organizing migrant workers: a case study of working conditions and unionization in a London sandwich factory. *Work, Employment & Society, 19*(3), 463–480.

Hopkins, B., Dawson, C. & Veliziotis, M. (2016). Absence management of migrant agency workers in the food manufacturing sector. *International Journal of Human Resource Management,* 27(10), 1082–1100.

Howe, J. (2020). How effective are legal interventions for addressing precarious work? The case of temporary migrants in the Australian horticulture industry. *New Zealand Journal of Employment Relations, 44*(2), 35–50.

İçduygu, A. & ve Aksel, D. B. (2012). *Türkiye'de Düzensiz Göç.* Türkiye: Uluslararası Göç Örgütü.

ILO. (2012). *From precarious work to decent work. Outcome document to the workers' symposium on policies and regulations to combat precarious employment.* Geneva: International Labour Organisation.

ILO. (2015). Informal Economy. Retrieved from www.ilo.org/global/topics/dw4sd/themes/informal-economy/lang--en/index.htm

International Crisis Group. (2018). Turkey's Syrian Refugees: Defusing Metropolitan Tensions. Retrieved from Turkey's Syrian Refugees: Defusing Metropolitan Tensions | Crisis Group.

Jonsson, I. & Nyberg, A. (2010). Sweden: precarious work and precarious unemployment, In Leah F. Vosko, Martha MacDonald and Iain Campbell, (Eds.) *Gender and the Contours of Precarious Employment, in: Gender and the Contours of Precarious Employment.* London & New York: Routledge, 2009, p. 194–210.

Kagan, C., Lo, S., Mok, L., Lawthom, R., Sham, S., Greenwood, M. & Baines, S. (2011). *Experiences of Forced Labour among Chinese Migrant Workers.* York: Joseph Rowntree Foundation.

Kalleberg, A. & Vallas, S. (2018). Probing Precarious Work: Theory, Research, and Politics. In Kalleberg, A.L., Vallas, S.P., Kalleberg, A.L. and Vallas, S.P. (Eds.) *Precarious Work* (Research in the Sociology of Work, Vol. 31), Bingley: Emerald Publishing Limited, pp. 1–30. https://doi.org/10.1108/S0277-283320170000031017.

Kalleberg, A. L. (2009). Precarious work, insecure workers: Employment relations in transition. *American Sociological Review,* 74(1), 1–22. https://doi.org/10.1177/000312240907400101

Kamaşak, R., & Yavuz, M. (2016). Economic development, market characteristics and current business conditions in Turkey: A guide for successful operations, In Christiansen, B. and Erdogdu, M. M. (Eds.), *Comparative Economics and Regional Development in Turkey* (pp. 336–354), Michigan, USA: IGI Global Publications.

Kamasak, R., Özbilgin, M. F., Baykut, S., & Yavuz, M. (2020). Moving from individual intersections to institutional intersections: Insights from

LGBTQ individuals in Turkey. *Journal of Organizational Change Management*, *33*(3), 456–476.

Kamaşak, R., Özbilgin, M.F., & Yavuz, M. (2020). Understanding intersectional analyses. In: King, E., Roberson, Q. and Hebl, M. (eds.), *Research on Social Issues in Management on Pushing Understanding of Diversity in Organizations* (pp. 93–115). Charlotte, USA: Information Age Publishing.

Kamaşak, R., Özbilgin, M.F., Yavuz, M., & Akalin, C. (2020). Race discrimination at work in the UK. In: Vassilopoulou, J., Brabet, J., Kyriakidou, O. and Shovunmi, V. (eds.), *Race Discrimination and the Management of Ethnic Diversity at Work: European Countries Perspective* (pp. 107–127). Bingley, UK: Emerald Publishing.

Kirov, V. & Hohnen, P. (2015). Trade unions strategies to address inclusion of vulnerable employees in "anchored" services in Europe. *International Journal of Manpower*, *36*(6), 848–873.

Kretsos, L. (2010) The persistent pandemic of precariousness: young people at work. In: Tremmel J (ed) *A Young Generation Under Pressure?* New York: Springer.

Kushnirovich, N., Heilbrunn, S. & Davidovich, L. (2018). Diversity of Entrepreneurial Perceptions: Immigrants vs. Native Population: Entrepreneurial Perceptions of Immigrants. *European Management Review*, *15*(3). DOI: 10.1111/emre.12105.

Kushnirovich, N., Raijman, R. & Barak-Bianco, A. (2019). The impact of government regulation on recruitment process, rights, wages and working conditions of labor migrants in the Israeli construction sector. *European Management Review*, *16*(4), 909–922.

Küskü, F., Araci, O. & Ozbilgin, M. (2020). What happens to diversity at work in the context of a toxic triangle? Accounting for the gap between discourses and practices of diversity management. *Human Resource Management Journal*, *31*(2), 553–574.

Küskü, F., Aracı, Ö. & Ozbilgin, M. (2021). What happens to diversity at work in the context of a toxic triangle? Accounting for the gap between discourses and practices of diversity management. *Human Resource Management Journal*, *31*(2), 553–574.

Lincoln, Y. S., & Guba, E. G. (1985). *Naturalistic inquiry*. Beverly Hills, CA: Sage Publications.

Locke, K. (2011). Field research practice in management and organization studies: Reclaiming its tradition of discovery. *Academy of Management Annals*, *5*(1), 613–652. https://doi.org/10.5465/19416520.2011.593319

MacKenzie, R. & Forde, C. (2009).The rhetoric of the "good worker" versus the realities of employers' use and the experiences of migrant workers. *Work, Employment and Society*, *23*(1), 142–159.

McDowell, L., Batnitzky, A. & Dyer, S. (2008). Internationalization and the spaces of temporary labor: the global assembly of a local workforce. *British Journal of Industrial Relations*, 46(4), 750–770.

McDowell, L., Batnitzky, A., & Dyer, S. (2009). Precarious work and economic migration: Emerging immigrant divisions of labour in Greater London's service sector. *International Journal of Urban and Regional Research*, 33(1), 3–25.

McKay, S. & Markova, E. (2010). The operation and management of agency workers in conditions of vulnerability. *Industrial Relations Journal*, 41(5), 446–460.

McKay, S., Szymonek, J. & Keles, J.Y. (2012). *Study on Precarious Work and Social Rights (Report for the European Commission (VT/2010/084))*. London: Working Lives Research Institute, London Metropolitan University.

Migration Policy Institute, MPI. (2018). Retrieved from www.migration policy.org/programs/data-hub/international-migration-statistics

Migration Policy Institute (MPI). (2021). *The EU-Turkey Deal, Five Years On: A Frayed and Controversial but Enduring Blueprint*. Retrieved from www.migrationpolicy.org/article/eu-turkey-deal-five-years-on.

Milkman, R. (2011). Immigrant workers, precarious work, and the US Labor Movement. *Globalizations*, 8(3), 361–372.

Nijhawan, M. (2019). Migrant precarity and religious individualisation. In M. Fuchs, A. Linkenbach, M. Mulsow, B.-C. Otto, R. B. Parson, & J. Rüpke (Eds.), *Religious individualisation: Historical dimensions and comparative perspectives* (Vol. 1, pp. 737–758). De Gruyter.

Nyamnjoh, H., Hall, S. & Cirolia, L.R. (2022). Precarity, Permits, and Prayers: "Working Practices" of Congolese Asylum-Seeking Women in Cape Town. *Africa Spectrum*, 57(1), 30–49.

Oner, A. C., Durmaz-Drinkwater B. & Grant, R. J. (2020). Precarity of refugees: the case of Basmane-İzmir, Turkey, *Journal of Ethnic and Migration Studies, 1469–9451*. DOI: 10.1080/1369183X.2020.17 32591.

Özbilgin, M., & Erbil, C. (2019). Yönetim Çalışmaları Alanındaki Kısır Yöntem İkilemlerini Dışaçekimsel ve Geçmişsel Yaklaşım ve Eleştirel Gerçekçilikle Yöntem Yelpazesine Dönüştürmek. *Yönetim ve Çalışma Dergisi*, 3(1), 1–24.

Özbilgin, M. & Vassilopoulou, J. (2018). Relational Methods in Organization Studies: A Critical Overview. In: Ciesielska, M., Jemielniak, D. (eds) *Qualitative Methodologies in Organization Studies*. Cham: Palgrave Macmillan. https://doi.org/10.1007/978-3-319-65442-3_7.

Özvarış, Ş. B., Kayı, İ, Mardin, D., Sakarya, S., Ekhayez, Meagher, K. & Patel, P. (2020). COVID-19 barriers and response strategies for refugees and undocumented migrants in Turkey. *Journal of Migration and Health*, 1–2, 100012. https://doi.org/10.1016/j.jmh.2020.100012

Parrenas, R. S., Silvey, R., Hwang, M. C., 6 Choi, C. A. (2019). Serial labor migration: Precarity and itinerancy among Filipino and Indonesian domestic workers. *International Migration Review*, 53(4), 1230–1258.

Polanyi, K. (1944). *The Great Transformation: The Political and Economic Origins of Our Time*. Boston: Beacon Press.

Porthé, V., Ahonen, E., Vázquez, M.L., Pope, C., Agudelo, A., García, A., Amable, M., Benavides, F., & Benach, J. (2010). Extending a model of precarious employment: the case of Spain. *American journal of industrial medicine*, 53(4), 417–424.

Posch, K., Scott, S., Cockbain, E. & Bradford, B. (2020). *Scale and nature of precarious work in the UK*. Retrieved from https://assets.publishing .service.gov.uk/government/uploads/system/uploads/attachment_data/ file/1040243/scale-and-nature-of-precarious-work-in-the-UK.pdf.

Premji, S. (2017). Precarious employment and difficult daily commutes. *Industrial Relations*, 72(1), 77–98.

Republic of Turkey Directorate General of Migration Management. (2021). *Law on foreigners and international protection*. Retrieved from https:// en.goc.gov.tr/kurumlar/en.goc/Ingilizce-kanun/Law-on-Foreigners-and-International-Protection.pdf.

Sapkal, R. S. & Sundar, K. R. S. (2017). Determinants Of Precarious Employment In India: An Empirical Analysis. Kalleberg, A.L. and Vallas, S.P. (Ed.) *Precarious Work (Research in the Sociology of Work, Vol. 31)*, Bingley: Emerald Publishing Limited, pp. 335–361. https://doi .org/10.1108/S0277-283320170000031011.

Şenses, N. (2016). Rethinking Migration in the Context of Precarity: The Case of Turkey. *Critical Sociology*, Vol(⅞), 975–987.

Standing, G. (2011). *The Precariat: The New Dangerous Class*. London: Bloomsbury Academic.

Thompson, P., Newsome, K. & Commander, J. (2013). "Good when they want to be": migrant workers in the supermarket supply chain. *Human Resource Management Journal*, 23(2), 129–143.

Tiryaki, S. (2022). Türk Basınında Göçmen, Sığınmacı ve Mülteci Haberleri Üzerine Bir İnceleme. *Kültür Araştırmaları Dergisi*, 15, 124–156. DOI: 10.46250/kulturder.1188891.

Toksöz, G., Erdoğdu, S. & Kaşka. (2012) *Irregular Labour Migration in Turkey and Situation of Migrant Workers in the Labour Market*. Ankara: International Organisation for Migration.

Triantafyllidou A. & Marchetti, S. (2015). *Employers, Agencies and Immigration: Paying for Care*. Farnham: Ashgate

UNDP. (2020). Charting pathways out of multidimensional poverty: Achieving the SDGs. Retrieved from http://hdr.undp.org/sites/default/ files/2020_mpi_report_en.pdf.

The United Nations High Commission for Refugees (UNHCR). (2019, October). UNHCR Turkey – Fact Sheet October 2019. https://reliefweb .int/report/turkey/unhcr-turkey-fact-sheet-october-2019

UNHCR. (2020). Refugees and Asylum Seekers in Turkey. Retrieved from www.unhcr.org/tr/en/refugees-and-asylum-seekers-in-turkey.

Valentine, R. (2010). *Hope Costs Nothing: The Lives of Undocumented Migrants in the UK*. London: Migrants Resource Centre and Barrow Cadbury Trust.

Vassilopoulou, J. and Ozbilgin, M. (2018). Relational Methods in Organization Studies: a critical overview, in Ciesielska, M. and Jemielniak, D. (eds.) *Qualitative Research in Organization Studies: New Approaches, Methods and Possibilities*. Volume 2: Methods and Possibilities. Palgrave., II. pp. 151–179. ISBN 13: 9783319654416.

Vasudevan, A. (2015). The makeshift city: Towards a global geography of squatting. *Progress in Human Geography, 39*(3), 338–259.

Vij, R. (2019) The global subject of precarity, *Globalizations*, 16(4), 506–524.

Vosko, L., MacDonald, M. & Campbell, I. (2009). *Gender and the Contours of Precarious Employment*. London: Routledge.

Vosko, L. F. (2010). *Managing the Margins: Gender, Citizenship and the International Regulation of Precarious Employment*. New York, NY: Oxford University Press.

Waite, L. (2009). A place and space for a critical geo-graphy of precarity? *Geography Compass* 3(1), 412–433.

Waite, L. & Lewis, H. (2017). Precarious Irregular Migrants and Their Sharing Economies: A Spectrum of Transactional Laboring Experiences. *Annals of the American Association of Geographers*, 107(4), 964–978. https://doi.org/10.1080/24694452.2016.1270188.

Wang, B. (2020). Time in migration: temporariness, precarity and temporal labour amongst Chinese scholars returning from the Global North to South. *Journal of Ethnic and Migration Studies*, 46(11), 2127–2144.

Weil, D. (2018). Creating a Strategic Enforcement Approach to Address Wage Theft: One Academic's Journey in Organizational Change. *Journal of Industrial Relations*, 60 (3), 437–460. doi:10.1177/0022185618765551.

Wright, C. F. & Clibborn, S. (2019). Migrant labour and low-quality work: a persistent relationship. *Journal of Industrial Relations*, 61(2), 157–175.

Zhang, H., Nardon, L. & Sears, G. J. (2021). Migrant workers in precarious employment. Equality, Diversity and Inclusion: *An International Journal*, Vol. ahead-of-print No. ahead-of-print. https://doi.org/10.1108/ EDI-01-2021-0018.

11 How Precarity Is Threaded into Migration Rules
The Cases of the UK, Germany, and Australia

DIMITRIA GROUTSIS, SHIREEN KANJI,
AND JOANA VASSILOPOULOU

11.1 Introduction, Background, and Context

This chapter aims to show how precarious workplace/worker and societal arrangements have been woven into a system of migration management (Paret and Gleeson, 2016; Vosko, 2010). Accordingly, we examine the rules underscoring how migrants as workers are accepted, settle, and integrate in a new land and labour market across three different country contexts over time: the UK, Germany, and Australia.

While the notion of precarity and precarious employment is contested with no single definition (Ahmad, 2008; Betti, 2018), migrant workers have been theorised as experiencing amplified precarity by nature of their migration status (e.g., newly settled, non-citizen, temporary settlement, undocumented status); and, their labour market status (e.g., entering a segmented labour market; becoming part of a labour reserve; exploitation; wage theft; being denied their rights) (Anderson, 2010; Alberti, 2014). While they may well be subject to precarious employment and precarity in their social participation and standing, migrants make choices and have agency in the decisions they make to build their lives even in instances where agency is severely restricted such as in the case of forced migration (Alberti et al., 2018).

Vosko (2010, 2) notes precarity "is shaped by the relationship between employment status (e.g., self – or paid employment), form of employment (e.g., part-time or full-time), and dimensions of labour market insecurity, as well as social context (e.g., occupation, industry and geography) and social location (or the interaction between social relations), such as gender, or legal and political categories, such as citizenship". Clearly power, choice, access, and equity infuse definitions

213

of precarity and precarious employment which guide our explanation and understanding of how migrants have been attracted to and have settled in different destination country contexts.

To speak of migrants as a homogenous group is problematic: they differ in terms of the sending country and race/ethnicity, forced and voluntary migration. These differences are key dimensions in the precarious social and employment arrangements experienced by migrants, where racial hierarchies operate around visa status; entry pathways into the country and into the labour market; access to knowledge and information; and access to power and influence (Joseph, 2020).

The story of migration has twists and turns which are rarely linear; comprising trials, tribulations, and triumphs. Even within the trials we can see triumphs which highlight the complexity around the concept of precarity. In the same moment one is marginalised, they may make a choice to free themselves by exiting the situation; they may be compromised in a specific moment in time and emerge stronger over time; they may be excluded as an individual yet find inclusion as a group and vice versa; they may experience precarity in the initial years of migration but feel freedom from poverty, war, and persecution from their homeland, diluting the effects of precarity. How precarious arrangements play out for migrant workers is certainly context- and time-specific (Ahmad, 2008), and it is for this reason that delving into three distinct country contexts is a useful point of departure.

Our chapter adopts a comparative and historical perspective which allows us to capture points and patterns of convergence and divergence in migration histories. In doing so, we bring 'contemporary events into clearer focus' around migration arrangements and the precarity which is threaded into these arrangements; and, as it affects the experience of migrant workers (Lawrence, 1984, 307–308; Paret and Gleeson, 2016). Accordingly, we distil how precarity plays out for migrant workers whose agency is guided, and some would argue determined by destination country migration policies. The question guiding this chapter is: *how do macro level policies embed precarity into the labour market and social structures in which migrants settle and labour?* We challenge the social science community which tends to 'search for general and abstracted laws', resulting in 'universalist and presentist' explorations and findings which are cut 'off from history' (Zald, 2002, 381). Instead, we adopt a distinct, locally specific, and comparative analysis which captures analyses "sensitive to the subjective, irrational and volatile nature of human behaviour and the crucial role of perception" (Keulen and Kroeze, 2012, 173–174).

We begin our discussion with an examination of the context of migration and history of migration rules in the UK, before turning to Germany and then Australia. Following our examination of each of these contexts we draw out some key points of similarity and difference while providing a critical treatment of the precarity that is etched into the systems and processes and outcomes of migration for particular groups of migrant workers. We conclude the chapter with a list of research questions for future consideration.

11.2 History of Migration Rules: The UK

Two major social and political issues have driven much of the debate around immigration in Britain in the period after World War II. The first relates to migration from Britain's former colonies while the second, and more recent issue, relates to migration from the European Union (EU). The connections between these two eras while not obvious is based on a long history of opposition to non-white migration from Britain's former colonies, which preceded fears over the free movement of labour, a key facet of the desire for Brexit (Thompson, 2017). Race and racism have been instrumental in reconciling tensions between working class and elite interests in the UK. Against this backdrop it is hardly surprising that migrants have faced multiple points of discrimination at all levels in the UK labour market through the racialisation of labour, in continuity with previous colonial practices (Virdee, 2019). The different routes to migration have channelled migrants into particular labour market segments which are associated with distinct characteristics in terms of job quality, such as care work (Demireva, 2011). The vulnerability and precarious position of migrants to the UK is evident in multiple ways: through pay gaps (ILO, 2020) employment rates and wage discrimination (Clark and Drinkwater, 2008) and ethnic penalties relating to overeducation and underemployment (Rafferty, 2012).

Opposition to non-white migration had been evident in Britain since the late 1940s, crossing Conservative and Labour party political lines (Hansen, 1999a). A race-based approach was in evidence at the outset of colonial migration into the UK but was in operation long before this time. It was not confined to Britain, according to Hannah Arendt

(1944), who noted that race-thinking emerged during the nineteenth century in all European countries. It takes little investigation to reveal some of the many links between Vote Leave and the appeal to Britain's colonial past. As El-Enany (2020) draws to our attention two of the most used slogans in the campaign were about "taking back control of our borders" and "making Britain great again". Paul Gilroy considers that the very need for Brexit came from "an unhealthy and destructive post-imperial hungering for renewed greatness". Indeed, restoring Britain's place in the world was an on-going preoccupation, which was not only fundamental to Brexit but also formed part of the argument for Britain to join the EEC in the first place so that Britain could realise its "power pretensions" through membership of the larger economic block (Bulpitt, 1992). Harking back to a golden era in Britain's past has partly been about reinforcing racial hierarchies in the UK which also affect the living conditions and possibilities for those who are labelled as 'other' in this quest to restore the mythical past.

It is perhaps somewhat surprising, and a mark of the strength of the ideology of "empire", that the British Nationality Act (BNA) of 1948 granted all British subjects in the empire the right to reside in the UK. It was part of the ideology of empire that all those who lived under the British Empire as British subjects (a classification that has rarely been applied since 1983 – www.gov.uk/types-of-british-nationality/british-subject) were entitled to live in Britain and were free to move between parts of the British Empire. In this vein, Olusoga (2016) writes that the intention of the 1948 BNA was to extend cooperation between Britain's "white dominions" rather than facilitate the migration of racialised non-white people into Britain. In practice, while there had always been the right to free movement across the empire, Britain was forced to reformulate and make explicit its new policy when, in 1947, the Canadian government set up a new system which ended reciprocal rights for British citizens to settle in Canada.

Migration of racialised minorities was not anticipated, in part because in the period before the legislation was enacted, administrative controls were able de facto to limit the extent of immigration of racialised minorities. Both Conservative and Labour governments tried to restrict access to the rights made evident in the BNA to white citizens (Hansen, 1999). "Whitewashing" of migration in Britain is well documented. In accordance with this view, few opposed restricting non-white migration but some members of parliament, across party lines, bitterly opposed the Macmillan government's 1962 Commonwealth Immigrants Act because it marked a decisive end to the ideology of the British Empire in taking away the right of Commonwealth citizens to settle in the UK (McKay, 2008). Under the new act, migration to the UK was now evaluated in three categories: category A for people holding a job offer, category B for those with skills in demand in the UK, and category C for unskilled workers which was capped (McKay, 2008). The introduction of this Act immediately diminished the numbers of non-white migrants coming into Britain. The 1968 Commonwealth Immigrants Act, introduced by the Labour home secretary James Callaghan, considerably further closed the possibilities for migration from the Commonwealth. The Act specifically aimed to prevent the entry of Asians from Kenya by adding a new requirement that British citizens had to have a qualifying connection to the UK in the form of a parent or grandparent born in the UK or if they could satisfy the requirement that they were born in the UK, a specification that made a mockery of the British citizenship of East-African Asians. Unable to obtain Kenyan citizenship because of the Kenyatta government, they were rendered de facto stateless (Hansen, 1999).

Tomlinson (2018) considers that the Immigration Act (1971) definitively marked the end to a long process of blocking free movement from the Commonwealth, further tightening up limitations on immigration from the non-white Commonwealth. This legislation provides the Secretary of State a high degree of discretion to set immigration policy, granting almost unlimited powers. The relatedness of migration from Britain's colonies and migration from Europe again became apparent in what Consterdine (2017) terms a "numbers game": where the desire to limit non-white migration was reinforced by the perceived need to restrict other types of migration, as joining the EEC would bring about further migration through the free movement of labour (Consterdine, 2017).

The tension between EU and non-EU migration was at its most evident under New Labour in 2004 when Britain granted unrestricted rights to members of the newly acceded states (i.e., Cyprus, Czech Republic, Estonia, Hungary, Latvia, Lithuania, Malta, Poland, Slovakia, and Slovenia) to work in the UK, in contrast to many other EU countries such as Austria and Germany which applied the right, accorded to all EU states to limit such migration from 2004 until 2011. During New Labour's thirteen years in office, migration increased substantially. The proportion of immigrants in the working age population rose from just over 8 per cent in 1997 to over 16 per cent in 2013, three years after New Labour left power (Wadsworth, 2014), although similar changes were also taking place in some other European countries. New Labour brought in many new items of legislation on immigration (Mulvey, 2010). Some of this legislation aimed to make the environment more unwelcoming, particularly for refugees. The groundwork was laid, although in a more tempered form, for the later hostile environment. Labour's Points Based System, which was introduced in 2008 through secondary legislation, required 'sponsors' such as employers and education providers to monitor foreign employees and students and report any violations of their conditions of stay to the Home Office. This policy move could be seen as a precursor to the hostile environment, although it was not until 2014 that heavy penalties were to be exacted from employers who were in breach of the new rules (Griffiths and Yeo, 2021).

Using the uncontrolled powers provided in the Immigration Act (1971) and trying to counter New Labour's expansive immigration policy, the conservative government sought to decrease immigration and in particular the seeking of asylum in a set of policies, collectively termed "the hostile environment". Any subtlety in previous policies that had created a precarious environment for migrants was abandoned; in fact, creating precarity for certain groups of migrants had become an explicit objective. Theresa May, the then home secretary in 2012, proudly announced the aim was to "create here in Britain a really hostile environment for illegal immigrants". But it was not just "illegal" migrants who suffered as we will go on to see. The new policies and in particular the Immigration Act of 2014 and 2016 turned swathes of the working population into border guards through the checks that doctors and nurses in the health service, landlords, letting agents, and employers were required to make. The bordering function significantly ramped up the external control that had already started under Labour's Points Based System which, as stated, shifted the responsibility for implementing controls to employers and educational institutions (Consterdine, 2020).

The hostile environment unleashed a range of new industries sustained by government funding and directed towards implementing the policies that are part of making the environment hostile. Specifically in relation to refugees and asylum seekers who make up only a small percentage of migrants overall, the second most discussed issue for both Labour and the Conservatives is the removal of failed asylum seekers, after the first ranked issue which is the need for reform of the existing system (Chaney, 2020). The conditions for asylum seekers had been changing since the 1990s when three laws on asylum and immigration restricted their access to welfare benefits and services: the Asylum and Immigration Appeals Act 1993; the Asylum and Immigration Act 1996 (Conservative) government; and the Immigration and Asylum Act 1999 (Labour) (Guentner et al, 2016).

In the more explicitly stated criteria brought in under New Labour, economic (un)worthiness distinguished refugees and asylum seekers from more worthy economic migrants (Anderson, 2013). Consterdine (2020) argues that the new points-based system was in accord with the rhetoric of flexibilisation, achieved by granting subsequent governments flexibility to loosen or tighten the restrictions as they saw fit.

Parmar (2020) draws attention to how the criminality which results from the implementation of the removal policies and race-thinking are intertwined facets of the migration scheme. Police action in dealing with the criminality associated with transgressing border controls perpetuates colonial genealogies. As Parmar (2020) explains, all groups are racialised on the basis of visual differences. The result is that migration becomes a key aspect of identifying and defining particular groups as "other", even those who have no recent migration history. Migration and the hostile environment have become a means of maintaining the racial state which, as has been discussed, has been a defining feature of Britain's inward migration, founded on its colonial history. Through its practices the racial state makes conditions, in particular for those who are not white, but more recently also for some groups of eastern European migrants.

11.3 History of Migration Rules: Germany

Germany has struggled to accept that it has become an immigration country since the unintentional settlement of its so-called guest workers who had been recruited to help reconstruct post-war Germany, from the 1960s onwards (Vassilopoulou, 2011). The term migration background is a term which itself is contested since it implies that a person has a migration history even if born in Germany. This term goes as far back as to consider the birthplace of one's grandparents. Currently the government is debating to change this term to "immigrants and their descendants". The change would finally categorise citizens born to immigrants in Germany as simply Germans and thereby drop the label that classifies them as having a migration history, which many who fall under this category factually do not have. This proposed change has been widely welcomed and is seen as a positive step towards social cohesion (Fachkommission Integrationsfähigkeit, 2021).

Migrants were recruited to post-war Germany initially only from neighbouring European countries and later, when the supply of Christian European workers dried up, they turned to Turkey and North-Africa (Vassilopoulou, 2011). As a result, 7.5 million people with a migration background in Germany hail from another European country. However, at present, ethnic Turkish people form the largest ethnic minority group, with numbers estimated at 3–7 million; followed by Poles and Russians respectively. Other ethnic groups include 4.6 million people from Asia, 3.2 million people from the Middle East, just under 1 million people of African descent and a little over half a million come from North, Central and South America and Australia (Deutsche Welle, 2020). The recent war in the Ukraine has created the largest post-war movement of refugees, with nearly 400,000 Ukrainian refugees arriving in Germany to date. It is expected that this number will continue to grow over the coming months. Taken together, these figures highlight the diversity comprising German society and its defining characteristics as an immigration country.

In recent years, Germany has built an image to the outside world of being not only welcoming to migrants, but also to refugees and, over the last five years, Germany has ranked as one of the five most popular destination countries for immigrants in the world. Immigration is indeed welcomed by some parts of the population as well as by many employers in industries that are facing labour shortages, and by some politicians who recognise that Germany, with its ageing population and low birth rate, relies on continuous migration to sustain economic growth. However, this positive image fails to capture the fact that racism and discrimination against ethnic minorities, migrants and refugees have increased considerably in recent years (InfoMigrants, 2020). Fuelled by various right-wing groups, these movements have added to pronouncements to restrict immigration (Deutsche Welle, 2021).

In 2015 the German Chancellor Angela Merkel welcomed some one million refugees and famously asserted: "Wir schaffen das" (we will manage it). Later that year she defended her position in a TV interview saying that it was her "damned duty" to help refugees (Paterson, 2015). Her strong support may have come as a surprise to some, considering that only five years earlier she told a gathering of younger members of her conservative Christian Democratic Union (CDU) that "the approach [to build] a multicultural [society] and to live side-by-side and to enjoy each other ... has failed, utterly failed" (BBC 2010a, b). An assimilationist approach has dominated migration management in Germany for well over sixty years (Vassilopoulou, 2011; Tatli et al., 2012; Vassilopoulou et al., 2014). Correspondingly, concepts such as equal opportunities and race equality have been mostly overlooked, as possible measures for the better integration of migrants and refugees into the German labour market (Vassilopoulou et al., 2019).

A political and public consensus frames ethnic minorities as failing to integrate in Germany (Esser, 2002). This is particularly seen to be the case for ethnic minority Turks and Muslims more generally, who are viewed to be exceptionally difficult to integrate. Moreover, ethnic minorities, are cast as solely responsible for their alleged "failure" to build the human capital needed for success in the labour market (Berlin Institut für Bevölkerung und Entwicklung, 2009; Vassilopoulou, 2011). Labour market integration is viewed as a key indicator for the successful integration of immigrants in Germany (Esser, 2006). However, people with a migration background are historically over-represented in precarious and underpaid occupations, starting with the first generation of guest workers, who predominantly worked in manufacturing, mining and cleaning; in jobs that the majority population did not want to do. Similarly, today migrant workers are found in cleaning industry, food production, care work, particularly elder care, in warehousing and delivery jobs. The same applies to asylum seekers and refugees.

The concept of precarity emphasises temporary, informal, underpaid, and insecure work, in its numerous manifestations (Bourdieu, 1998): defining characteristics of migrant and refugee workers in Germany. For instance, almost 36 per cent of people with a migration background, but born in Germany, earn below the minimum wage as compared to 15.9 per cent people without a migration background (Lukas, 2011). In terms of labour market location, migrants have historically largely been excluded from working for the two largest employers in the Germany. The German state provides a broad range of civil services and is staffed by some five million employees (Destatis.de, 2021). Yet becoming a civil servant requires holding German citizenship, which automatically excludes a large part of the German population. This is particularly problematic in the context of restrictions around dual citizenship for German nationals where if the second nationality is from outside the EU, this blocks one's ability to also hold German citizenship. The law that only entitles German citizens to work as civil servants is a relic of Germany's Nazi-past and was part of the first major law restricting the rights of Jewish citizens in Nazi-Germany. The Law for the Restoration of the Professional Civil Service of April 7, 1933, had the goal to remove so-called "alien" persons from civil service and as such excluded Jews and those considered as "politically unreliable" civil servants and employees from state service. This law was part of the so-called Aryan Paragraph, which excluded Jews and other "non-Aryans" from various organisations, professions, and other aspects of public life (Mayer, 2003).

The church is the second largest employer, staffed by some 1.3 million. The Protestant and Catholic Churches and their associated welfare organisations (Diacony and Caritas) are subject to church employment law, as are their employees who must comply with the principles of the faith of their employer and must behave accordingly both at work and privately. By law (article 137 paragraph 3 of the Weimar Reich Constitution (WRV)), all religious societies are therefore entitled to make their own decisions – independently and without state supervision, governed by what is known as the "Third Way", in labour law. When Germany finally adopted the EU General Equal Treatment Act (Allgemeine Gleichbehandlungsgesetz, AGG) in 2006, article 9 was added to the new bill in response to yearlong protests surrounding the implementation of the new bill by churches. Article 9 ensured that religious organisations irrespective of their legal form and facilities associated with them may discriminate based on religion. This has meant that Muslim, Greek, or Russian Orthodox workers could be denied work based on their religion. Consequently, this large labour market has remained inaccessible for these groups of workers. Some minor changes have been made in recent years, with judges ruling that churches have to abide by the General Equal Treatment Act; however, article 9 has still not been removed (www.arbeitsrechte.de/kirchliches-arbeitsrecht/).

It is safe to say that migrants and their descendants have predominantly been used to fill unattractive jobs and skilled jobs where home grown skills are scarce. One of the historical failures has been that the government has never truly enforced equal opportunities for these groups. This has meant that even highly skilled minority ethnic and migrant workers have experienced labour market marginalisation, often working below their qualifications (Al Ariss et al., 2013).

Since the arrival of large numbers of refugees in 2015, history is repeating itself. Initially, Germany responded relatively quickly to their arrival by adapting the government's integration framework to facilitate the integration of refugees. The German state re-orientated its refugee policies by emphasising their role as potential labour market participants, in the hope that they fill existent labour gaps (Degler & Liebig, 2017). And indeed, many humanitarian entrants have found work since 2015. The success was declared in 2018 by Annette Widmann-Mauz (government integration commissioner), who noted that the labour market integration of refugees had been more successful than anticipated over the last four years (Reliefweb, 2019). However, this assessment which is mostly based on numbers of employed migrants omits the fact that as with the former guest workers, refugees have been channelled into precarious work, with 67 per cent of refugees earning below minimum wage in 2018 and facing higher unemployment rates compared to ethnic Germans (Reliefweb, 2019; Bundesagentur für Arbeit, 2021).

The precarity of their labour market integration has been highlighted since the start of the COVID-19 pandemic, which saw many refugees and migrants not only lose their jobs but also contract the virus at a higher rate than ethnic Germans (mediendienst-integration, 2021). For example, the unemployment rate for migrants from non-EU countries rose by 17 per cent in January 2021 (Bundesagentur für Arbeit, 2021). Moreover, new figures show that only around 35 per cent of Syrians of working age in Germany can make a living from their work (MacGregor, 2021).

On the one hand, some argue that the pandemic has interrupted the integration of migrants and refugees. Others state that the pandemic has placed the spotlight on the failings of government policies which have amplified risks and dignity injuries for migrants and refugees. There is still time to address this failure. Germany, the reluctant migration country, needs to now accept that equal opportunities and anti-discrimination are important tools for the sustainable labour market integration of migrants and refugees.

Lastly, by the end of April 2022, almost 400,000 Ukrainian refugees have arrived in Germany and similar to the arrival of Syrian-conflict refugees have been framed as an opportunity to fill labour shortages (Statista, 2022). On the surface, it is argued that the labour market and social integration of Ukrainians will be easier, particularly when compared to Syrian refugees since they have access to preexisting refugee integration structures, created since the 2015 arrival of the Syrian-conflict intake. It will, however, be interesting to see if Ukrainians will also be integrated into precarious employment as experienced by Syrian refugees. One of the main differences between these two groups, which will be relevant for their labour market integration, is that Syrian refugees were mostly male, while Ukrainian refugees arriving in Germany are mostly women and children. Another point of difference is that Ukrainian refugee settlers have so far not generated any backlash in the population, with some arguing that this is because Ukrainians are white and Christian and, as such, closer to the majority population culture in Germany, highlighting a racialised hierarchy to the migrant and refugee intake and, as such, a racialised hierarchy to precarious conditions.

11.4 History of Migration Rules: Australia

Throughout Australia's post-colonial history, the country has relied on migrant workers. This reliance has been characterised by a pecking order of selection and a variance in the settlement services available to migrants based on country of origin, while the state apparatus has enacted different responsibilities to facilitate migration and settlement in Australia. While the majority of the early waves of migration hailed from the UK and more specifically Britain, smaller groups of migrants entered from other parts of the world. Australian immigration policy in the immediate post-war period did not welcome non-British immigrants. The very protectionist policy originated during the gold rush of the 1850s when the population trebled with a significant increase in non-British settlers. The migration of a large number of Chinese fuelled hostility exacerbated by the media reaction. Stereotypes of Chinese migrants highlighted the "differences" in appearance, the eating habits, and religious practices (Evans et al., 1975). Legislation responding to the resulting social "problems" invoked restrictive practices on migration with the introduction of a residence tax for Asian immigrants (Markus,1979). A social Darwinist mentality resonated throughout early colonial society, shaping the attitudes of the early white invaders/settlers towards non-Europeans and the Indigenous people.

The Chinese Restriction Bill reinforced anti-Asian sentiment throughout the Australian society. As Sir Henry Parke's put it in 1888, "I maintain that ... it is our duty to preserve the type of the British nation, and that we ought not ... detract from, or in any appreciable degree lower that admirable nationality" (quoted in Willis, 1982: 62). This tradition was supported by the White Australia Policy and the Immigration Restriction Act (1901) (Keating, 1994). Such policies created a national culture underpinned by a narrow ideological position towards other "races", cultures, and ethnic groups entering Australia. Temporary workers were unwelcome and were expected to leave following their short stay period of work. Their work and settlement status was precarious; they were simply migrant labouring hands, excluded by and from the broader society.

Patmore (1991) points out that "racist" ideologies have prevailed throughout the course of white invasion/settlement in Australia. Non-Europeans were considered "racially" inferior and capable of only mundane work, much like the dominant perception of Aboriginal labour. The so-called "coloured brothers" entering Australia – Melanesian, Kanaka, and Chinese immigrants – were targeted as the "unwelcome" groups. The union movement reinforced this ideological position, generating a tradition of suspicion towards non-British migrants as well as towards non-Europeans. This position was reproduced in the early post-war years with "new" target groups – European immigrants, especially those from the Communist bloc (Patmore, 1991).

Only after World War II when the migration policy was changed was such overt racism challenged. A population shortage posed problems for the Australian nation in the late 1940s, affecting both national economic growth and the labour market (Collins, 1991; Jayasuriya et al., 1988). In 1945 Australia established the first immigration portfolio and set about expanding the population by embarking on an aggressive migration growth strategy, targeting a broader set of non-British countries. The Government's commitment to the White Australia Policy continued as they espoused to largely keep the immigration fabric intact by also maintaining British immigration (Collins, 1984). Unions were most suspicious of the government's immigration policy fearing a threat to their employment, wages, and conditions. These "fears" were allayed as immigrants and refugees who landed in Australia filled areas that were weakly staffed by Australian labour, illustrating that overseas settler arrivals had a role to play in the Australian labour market that no one else was willing to fill. They filled jobs that came to be known as dirty, dangerous, and difficult jobs. The focus on a permanent settler drawn to Australia to fulfil labour market needs and to be reunited with their family furnished the migration policy through to the 1990s (Groutsis, 2006b; Taksa and Groutsis, 2010).

In 1966 the White Australia Policy was modified and disbanded in 1973 and thus followed the assent of the Multicultural Policy. This policy acted as a guiding philosophy for migrant settlement and integration with a focus on permanent settlers (Jayasuriya and Cook, 1988, 171). The policy has been contested and disputed from its inception with critics noting it lacks "substance and precision" (Koleth 2010, 2). Koleth (2010) highlights that the policy of multiculturalism has shifted beyond settlement and nation building for newly arrived migrants raising questions about the impact of the policy for the multiple generations living and working in Australia, a position fuelled by the shifts in migration policy towards temporary migrant workers.

Migration policy turned in the mid-1990s to temporary migration, liberalised to make way for a temporary pathway beyond the high-end business executive. The labour pool was broadened to include temporary entrants to address immediate workforce needs (Khoo et al., 2003). Since the late 1990s the temporary migration pathway has continued to grow in terms of the number of entrants and in the diversity of categories and criteria determining their temporary stay (Khoo et al., 2003; CEDA, 2019).

The policy of multiculturalism within the Australian context has and continues to be inextricably linked to integration marking a departure from a racist, divisive, and exclusionary approach to settlement which dominated the earlier part of Australia's migration history (Jupp, 1996). Both multiculturalism and integration, however, remain ill-defined, context-specific, and contested as concepts and policies (Modood, 2007; Castles et al., 2001). For example, according to scholars, integration places the onus of adjustment on the immigrant who must "assimilate" and foster the reproduction of the dominant ethnic culture, propagating the ideal that it is up to "them" to be like 'us' (Jayasuriya and Cook, 1988:171; see also Schinkel, 2018). Alternatively, multiculturalism is seen as a two-way process of adjustment and settlement: an evolving and dynamic process that cuts across diverse generations and groups. There is also an ever-present tension in the broader Australian society between being open to multiculturalism, and enjoying the diversity it offers, while at the same time expecting immigrants to do better at integrating by adopting "Australian" values in spite of rather than because of the supports offered to new arrivals (Scanlon Foundation, 2020).

Overwhelmingly, Australian multiculturalism is citizenship- and permanent resident–centred. Mares (2016) captures this paradox by noting Australia's unique position on migration when compared to Europe, where the latter's guest worker program discourages its migrants from citizenship and residency which accordingly threatens social cohesion. In drawing on a speech by Minister Bowen, Mares states that Australia is spared such threats because it is "not a guest worker society". Rather, "people who share respect for our democratic beliefs, laws and rights are welcome to join us as full partners with equal rights" (see also Mares, 2012). Markus et al. (2009) extend on this by showing that temporary migrants remain outside discussions surrounding multiculturalism and integration, and the protections associated with these policies. They remain an invisible and powerless entity. Little regard is given to their contribution to the workforce and the economy; the role they play in shaping and reshaping the broader social milieu of the Australian society; and the rights they are afforded, and obligations expected of them.

The policies surrounding multiculturalism and integration have largely neglected temporary migrant who is seen as a convenient and viable source of labour. Their position remains acutely precarious in the workplace, as they are bonded to their employer, and they are treated as a short-term convenience rather than a long-term investment, in spite of the fact that more than 50 per cent of migrants who arrive on temporary visas seek permanent residency. Overwhelmingly, their limited residency rights and restricted freedoms to move between employers amplifies the risks faced by temporary migrants living and working in Australia and many find themselves in precarious situations (Anderson, 2010; Underhill et al.,

2020; Boucher, 2019). Failing to see temporary visa holders as worthy of protection reinforces the acute structural inequality of the Australian society, and undermines belonging, settlement and cohesion. These tensions have been amplified in the COVID-19 context (Wright, Groutsis and Kaabel, 2022).

For humanitarian entrants, the conditions of entry into the country and into the labour market have been historically more challenging than other migration pathways. While only a small proportion of the entrants into Australia comprise refugees, it is perhaps the most controversial of the visa pathways. For instance, while Australia receives around 200,000 permanent immigrant arrivals and over 700,000 temporary immigrant arrivals each year, the humanitarian program comprises a meagre 1.7 per cent of the total immigration intake. There is a chorus of research which suggests that those arriving under the humanitarian program experience greater challenges when it comes to settlement and labour market entry, found to be key to successful settlement. A lack of paperwork/documentation, experience of torture and trauma combine to amplify the challenges experienced by humanitarian entrants with the vast majority channelled into the secondary labour market irrespective of pre-migration skills and qualifications (Colic-Peisker and Tilbury 2007; Colic-Peisker 2009; Refugee Council of Australia, 2010). Overall, the approach to and process of accepting humanitarian entrants has been fraught underscored by what is a false binary between voluntary and involuntary migration pathways and the treatment of those entering under each pathway (Koser, 2017).

Privileging particular groups of visa entrants as somehow more worthy and relegating other groups to precarity means that we are overlooking the individual needs of migrants and refugees (UNHCR, 2015; Zetter, 2012). Irrespective of migration status, migrant and refugee workers are, in the main, found to labour in precarious areas of the labour market, largely channelled into the secondary sphere as determined by a pecking order of access based on country of origin, skills, education and qualifications and the visa pathway through which the individual arrives into the country (Groutsis, 2006a and 2006b; CEDA, 2019; Sherrell, 2019). Taken together, such policy levers have shaped the settlement and labour market

experience of these entrants; and their lived experience in the destination society more broadly.

11.5 Conclusion, Reflection, and Questions for Future Research

This chapter has investigated the precarious arrangements embedded in the systems and processes of migration management across three different country contexts: the UK, Germany, and Australia. The examination has employed an historical methodology to show how approaches to migration management create a hierarchical racialised precarity in the destination country generally; and more specifically in the destination country labour market where different groups of migrant workers are channelled into and toil in the least favourable areas of the labour market.

A historical perspective of the three country contexts has shown that the experience of migration, settlement and labour market entry is influenced by the countries from which one has emigrated, the visa pathway through which they enter the destination country, destination country settlement and labour market policies, how difference and "otherness" becomes inscribed to facilitate precarious social and workplace arrangements. Precarious arrangements materialise in the systems, structures, and process of migration management and are both visible and invisible and as such difficult to address and dismantle: that is, it is difficult to disentangle where the precarity begins and how to unpick it.

Our historical overview across three very different systems of migration management captures the origins and degrees of precarity institutionalised in the process manifesting in inclusionary/exclusionary outcomes for different groups of migrants. Our discussion of locally specific examples captured what we see as a spectrum of precarity embedded in the societal and labour market structures.

Visibility is evident in the types of the work migrants are enabled to take up. In all three countries, the position of migrants, particularly from countries of the Global South, is precarious because only certain sectors of the labour market are de facto open to migrants. This is in part because of racialised boundaries around work, which migrants and refugees in these country contexts have and continue to find themselves bounded by and trapped in. In the case of Germany for instance, it is no accident that migrants are disproportionately represented in low-wage work in specific sectors of the labour market. Similarly, within Australia, racialised determinants have shaped who has been allowed in and where they have been channelled in the labour market.

For many migrants the possibility to advance to higher quality work is missing. Access to better and more secure work is indeed a ticket out of precarity. In all three countries there is some sense that migrants provide a useful source of labour that the majority population does not want to do. Having said that acceptance co-exists with political opposition, for example with regard to the far right in Germany or the Brexit movement in the UK. In the UK, it is only post-Brexit that attention has been forced to the valuable contribution that many Eastern European migrant workers have made, particularly in terms of their workplace location, in food processing, agriculture, transport, and care.

We drew on a historical perspective which has allowed us to explain and understand the ways in which race thinking manifests in the current period – albeit in different ways as typified in the three countries discussed. The similarities elucidated show that race or cultural background cast particular groups of migrants and refugees as not only the outsider, but also puts them on a path of life long precarious work. In the UK, New Labour built on pre-existing sentiment to position refugees and asylum seekers as bad migrants in comparison to the good migrants who fill labour shortages. Similarly in Australia, the right to seek asylum has been fraught with challenges informed by a public discourse of queue jumping and rorting the welfare system. The juxtaposition of good with bad migrants further manifests in attitudes to integration, particularly as seen in Germany and Australia: the good migrant wholly adopts and accepts the host country's rules and regulations; those who do not integrate are personally deficient and blamed for this failure rather than being listened to or helped. In the case of asylum seekers and refugees many have undergone significant trauma, exposed to the "injury, violence and death" that Butler speaks of. Rapid adjustment to the receiving country's norms is unrealistic, even if it were desirable. On the contrary, humanitarian assistance is required.

The outsider treatment can be traced back largely to colonial histories in Australia and the UK which continued, and were also contested, in the post-WWII period. Germany has been a reluctant migration nation until recent decades when it became more open, particularly to refugees. Furthermore, it has become more actively engaged in integrating refugees into the German labour market. While these efforts need to be acknowledged, we also need to highlight that similar to previous migrant and refugee generations, this new generation, experiences precarious social integration by means of precarious work.

Many migrants in the UK, Australia, and Germany have been classed as key workers, particularly since the start of the COVID-19 pandemic. While this has led to what in the UK became known as "clap for carers", which was a social movement created as a gesture of appreciation for the workers of the NHS, or other key workers, it has not been met with a similar movement to dismantle the precarious working conditions of many of these migrant key workers. Instead, the precarity faced by migrants workers, which has been only exacerbated since the start of the pandemic, remains unaddressed by many employers and governments.

11.5.1 Research Questions for Future Consideration

- How does race intersect with other diversity dimensions to shape precarious social and labour market arrangements?
- In a race-based hierarchy of migration, what can be done at a macro, meso, and micro level to "level" the field of migration pathways?
- The story of migration is about freedom from a past and freedom to experience a new future: how does precarity shape a newfound freedom?
- Whiteness has figured in both British and Australian migration history as a key dimension of selection and exclusion; how has this shaped migration policies today?
- Are there examples of excluded ethnic minority groups/individuals who have gained access to a powerful position and as such have changed the perceptions of the stigma such marginalised groups of migrants face?
- Is it possible to lose the stigma associated with coming from an excluded ethnic minority group by gaining a powerful position or through labour market success?
- Will the experience and labour market integration of Ukrainians differ from Syrian refugees, in countries such as Germany, the UK, and Australia? Will precarious work feature in the same way?

References

Adamy, W. (2012). Vollzeitbeschäftigte mit Berufsausbildung im Niedriglohnsektor. Hg. v. DGB. Online verfügbar unter www.dgb.de/themen/++co++ad7aedf2-33c1-11e2-ab3a-00188b4dc422, zuletzt aktualisiert am, 21, 2012.

Ahmad, A. (2008). Dead men working: time and space in London's ('illegal') migrant economy. *Work Employment and Society*, 22(2): 301–318.

Al Ariss A., Vassilopoulou J., Groutsis D., & Özbilgin M. (2012). A multilevel understanding of the careers of minority ethnic elites. In: *Global Elites. The Opaque Nature of Transnational Policy Determination.* Basingstoke, Palgrave (Eds Kakabadse & Kakabadse).

Al Ariss A., Vassilopoulou J., Özbilgin, M., & Game, A. (2013). Understanding career experiences of skilled minority ethnic workers in France & Germany. *International Journal of Human Resource Management*, 24(6): 1236–1256.

Alberti, G. (2014). Mobility strategies, 'mobility differentials' and 'transnational exit': the experiences of precarious migrants in London's hospitality jobs. *Work Employment and Society*, 28(6): 865–881.

Alberti, G., Bessa, I., Trappmann, V. Umney, C. (2018). In, Against and Beyond Precarity: Work in Insecure Times. *Work Employment and Society*, 32(3): 447–457.

Anderson, B. (2010). 'Migration, Immigration Controls and the Fashioning of Precarious Workers'. *Work, Employment and Society*, 24(2): 300–317.

Anderson, B. (2013). *Us and Them? The Dangerous Politics of Immigration Control.* Oxford: Oxford University Press.

Arendt, H. (1944). Race-Thinking before Racism. *The Review of Politics*, 6(1): 36–73. Retrieved July 1, 2021, from www.jstor.org/stable/140 4080.

BBC. (2010a). Merkel says German multicultural society has failed. Available at: www.bbc.co.uk/news/world-europe-11559451 (August 2020).

BBC. (2010b). Germany's charged immigration debate. Available at: www .bbc.co.uk/news/world-europe-11532699 (August 2020).

Berlin-Institute für Bevölkerung und Entwicklung (Hrsg.). (2009). *Ungenutzte Potenziale. Zur Lage der Integration in Deutschland.* Berlin: Berlin-Institute für Bevölkerung und Entwicklung.

Betti, E. (2018). Historicizing Precarious Work: Forty Years of Research in the Social Sciences and Humanities. *IRSH*, 63(2018): 273–319

Boucher, A. (2019). Measuring Migrant Worker Rights Violations in Practice: The Example of Temporary Skilled Visas in Australia. *Journal of Industrial Relations*, 61(2): 277–301. https://doi.org/10.1177/0022185618783001.

Bourdieu, P. (1998). *Acts of Resistance: Against the New Myths of Our Time.* Cambridge: Polity Press.

Bulpitt, J. (1992). Conservative leaders and the 'Euro-ratchet': Five doses of scepticism. *Political Quarterly*, 63(3): 258–275.

Bundesagentur für Arbeit. (2021). *Berichte: Arbeitsmarkt kompakt: Auswirkungen der Migration auf den deutschen Arbeitsmarkt (Monatszahlen)*. Bundesagentur für Arbeit Statistik/Arbeitsmarktberichterstattung.

Butler, J. (2009). *Frames of War* London: Verso.

Castles, S., Korac, M., Vasta, E., and Vertovec, S. (2001). *Integration: Mapping the Field*. Report, Centre for Migration and Policy Research and Refugee Studies Centre, University of Oxford.

CEDA. (2019). *Effects of Temporary Migration: Shaping Australia's Society and Economy*. Melbourne: Committee for Economic Development of Australia.

Chaney, P. (2020). Examining Political Parties' Record on Refugees and Asylum Seekers in UK Party Manifestos 1964–2019: The Rise of Territorial Approaches to Welfare? *Journal of Immigrant & Refugee Studies*, 0(0): 1–23.

Clark, K, Drinkwater, S. (2008). The labour market performance of recent migrants. *Oxford Review of Economic Policy*, 24: 495–516.

Colic-Peisker, V. (2009). Visibility, settlement success and life satisfaction in three refugee communities in Australia. *Ethnicities*, 9(2): 175–1999.

Colic-Peisker, V. and Tilbury, F. (2003). 'Active' and 'passive' resettlement: the influence of support services and refugees' own resources on resettlement style. *International Migration*, 41(50): 61–92.

Colic-Peisker, V. and Tilbury, F. (2007). *Refugees and Employment: The Effect of Visible Difference on Discrimination: Final Report*. Murdoch University, Western Australia. www.cscr.murdoch.edu.au/_docs/refugees andemployment.pdf.

Collins, J. (1984). 'Immigration and class: The Australian experience', In G. Bottomley and M. de Lepervanche (eds), *Ethnicity, Class and Gender in Australia*, Sydney: Allen and Unwin.

Collins, J. (1991). *Migrant Hands in a Distant Land, Australia's Post-War Immigration*, Sydney London: Pluto Press, Second Edition.

Consterdine, E. (2017). Community Versus Commonwealth: Reappraising the 1971 Immigration Act. *Immigrants & Minorities*, 35(1): 1–20, DOI: 10.1080/02619288.2016.1241712.

Consterdine E. (2020). Parties matter but institutions live on: Labour's legacy on Conservative immigration policy and the neoliberal consensus. *The British Journal of Politics and International Relations*, 22(2): 182–201. doi:10.1177/1369148119890253.

Consterdine, E. & Hampshire, J. (2014) Immigration policy under New Labour: Exploring a critical juncture. *Br Polit*, 9: 275–296. https://doi.org/10.1057/bp.2013.19.

Deakin, N. (1969). The British Nationality Act of 1948: A brief study in the political mythology of race relations. *Race*, 11(1): 77–83. doi:10.1177/030639686901100106.

Degler, E. & Liebig, T. (2017). *Finding their Way. Labour Market Integration of Refugees in Germany.* OECD. www.oecd.org/migration. Accessed, 17, 11–28.

Demireva, N. V. (2011). New Migrants in the UK: Employment Patterns and Occupational Attainment. *Journal of Ethnic and Migration Studies,* 37(4): 637–655

Deutsche Welle. (2020). German population of migrant background rises to 21 million. Available at: www.dw.com/en/german-population-of-migrant-background-rises-to-21-million/a-54356773 (August 2021).

Deutsche Welle. (2021). Meet Germany's 'Querdenker' COVID protest movement. Available at: www.dw.com/en/meet-germanys-querdenker-covid-protest-movement/a-57049985, (accessed April, 2023)

El-Enany, N. (2020). *(B)ordering Britain: Law, Race and Empire.* Manchester, UK: Manchester University Press. ISBN 9781526145420.

Esser H. (2002). Kulturelle Pluralisierung und strukturelle Assimilation. Das Proble der ethnischen Schichtung. *Schweizerische Zeitschrift für Politikwissenschaft,* 7(2): 97–108.

Esser H. (2006). Migration, language and integration. AKI Research Review 4 Arbeitsstelle Interkulturelle Konflikte und gesellschaftliche Integration (AKI), Wissenschaftszentrum Berlin für Sozialforschung (WZB).

Evans, R., Saunders, K., and Cronin. K. (1975). *Exclusion, Exploitation and Extermination,* Sydney: ANZ Books.

Fachkommission Integrationsfähigkeit. (2021). Bericht der Fachkommission der Bundesregierung zu den Rahmenbedingungen der Integrationsfähigkeit. Available at: www.fachkommission-integrationsfaehigkeit.de/resource/blob/1786706/1787474/5a5d62f9636b87f10fd0e271ba326471/bericht-de-data.pdf?download=1 (September 2021).

Fozdar, F. E. (2014). 'Aussie Cows and Asylum Seekers: Cartooning About Two Key Political Issues' In Renate Brosch and Kylie Crane (eds.) *Visualising Australia: Images, Icons, Imaginations* (pp. 135–149). Germany: WVT Wissenschaftlicher Verlag Trier.

Griffiths, M., Yeo, C. (2021). The UK's hostile environment: Deputising immigration control. *Critical Social Policy,* 41(4): 521–674. doi:10.1177/0261018320980653.

Groutsis, D. (2006a). 'Globalisation and labour mobility: Migrants making spaces, migrants changing spaces' In M Hearn and G Michelson (eds.) *Rethinking Work: Time, space and discourse* (pp. 144–164). Melbourne, VIC: Cambridge University Press.

Groutsis, D. (2006b). Geography and credentialism: the assessment and accreditation of overseas-trained doctors. *Health Sociology Review,* 15(1): 59–70.

Guentner, S., Lukes, S., Stanton, R., Vollmer, B. A., Wilding, J. (2016). Bordering practices in the UK welfare system. *Critical Social Policy*, 36(3):391–411. doi:10.1177/0261018315622609.

Hansen, R. (1968). *The Historical Journal*, 42(3): 809–834. Retrieved July 4, 2021, from www.jstor.org/stable/3020922.

Hansen, R. (1999a). The Kenyan Asians, British Politics, and the Commonwealth Immigrants Act.

Hansen, R. (1999b). The Politics of Citizenship in 1940s Britain: The British Nationality Act. *Twentieth Century British History*, 10(1): 76.

Hansen, R. (2014). *Paradigm and policy shifts: British immigration policy*, 1997–2011. In: Hollifield.

ILO. (2020). The migrant pay gap: Understanding wage differences between migrants and nationals. www.ilo.org/wcmsp5/groups/public/---ed_protect/---protrav/---migrant/documents/briefingnote/wcms_7637 96.pdf

InfoMigrants. (2020). Racism on the rise in Germany. Available at: www.infomigrants.net/en/post/25252/racism-on-the-rise-in-germany (August 2021).

Jayasuriya, L., and Cook, J. (1988). A struggle for equality In V. Burgmann and J. Lee, (eds.) *Making a Life: A People's History of Australia Since 1788*. Fitzroy Victoria: McPhee Gribble/Penguin.

Joseph, E. (2020). *Critical Race Theory and Inequality in the Labour Market: Racial Stratification in Ireland*. Manchester: Manchester University Press

Jupp, J. (1996). Understanding Australian Multiculturalism, Centre for Immigration and Multicultural Studies Australian National University/ Department of Immigration and Multicultural Affairs, ACT.

Keating, C. (1994). *Race and Sex Discrimination in Employment and Training*, ANESBWA Policy Paper 3, Prepared for, and presented at the Association of Non-English Speaking Background Women of Australia conference, ANESBWA (April) 1994.

Ker-Lindsay, J. (2018). Turkey's EU accession as a factor in the 2016 Brexit referendum. *Turkish Studies*, 19(1): 1–22. DOI: 10.1080/14683 849.2017.1366860.

Keulen, S., and Kroeze, R. (2012). Understanding Management Gurus and Historical Narratives: The benefits of a historic turn in management and organization studies. *Management and Organizational History*, 7(2): 171–189.

Khoo, S. E., Voigt-Graf, C. Hugo, G. and McDonald, P. (2003). Temporary Skilled migration to Australia: The 457 Visa Sub-class. *People and Place*, 11(4): 27–40.

Koleth, E. (2010). *Multiculturalism: a review of Australian policy statements and recent debates in Australia and overseas*, Research Paper No. 6, 2010–11, Parliament of Australia, Department of Parliamentary Services.

Koser, K. (2017). *A Global Compact on Refugees: The Role of Australia (August 2017)*. Australia: Lowy Institute.

Lawrence, B. S. (1984). Historical Perspective: Using the Past to Study the Present. *The Academy of Management Review*, 9/2: 307–312.

Lukas, W. (2011). Migranten im Niedriglohnsektor unter besonderer Berücksichtigung der Geduldeten und Bleibeberechtigten.

MacGregor, M. (2021). Germany: Two-thirds of Syrian refugees unable to support themselves. Available at: www.infomigrants.net/en/post/33597/germany-twothirds-of-syrian-refugees-unable-to-support-themselves (September 2021).

Mares, P. (2012). *Temporary migration and its implications for Australia*, www.aph.gov.au/About_Parliament/Senate/Powers_practice_n_proced ures/~/~/link.aspx?_id=06B96F584FD0483D9F369F0B5186C6A9&_z=z

Mares, P. 2016. *Not Quite Australian: How Temporary Migration is Changing the Nation* (pp. 207–257). Melbourne, VIC: Text Publishing Company

Markus, A., McDonald, P.F., and Jupp. J. (2009). *Australia's Immigration Revolution*. Crows Nest, N.S.W: Allen & Unwin.

Markus, M. (1979). *Fear and Hatred: Purifying Australian and California 1850–1901*, Sydney: Hale and Iremonger.

Martin, J. P. L., Orrenius, P. (eds.) *Controlling Immigration: A Global Perspective* (pp. 199–220). Stanford, CA: Stanford University Press.

Mayer D. (2003). *Non-Germans under the Third Reich. The Nazi Judicial and Administrative System in Germany and Occupied Eastern Europe, with Special Regard to Occupied Poland, 1939–1945*. John Hopkins University Press, Baltimore.

McKay, J. (2008). The Passage of the 1962 Commonwealth Immigrants Act, a Case-Study of Backbench Power. *Observatoire de la société britannique*, 6: 89–108.

Mediendienste Integration. (2021). Corona-Pandemie und Migration. Available at: https://mediendienst-integration.de/migration/corona-pandemie.html (September 2021).

Modood, T. (2007). *Multiculturalism: A Civic Idea*. Cambridge: Polity Press.

Mulvey, G. (2010). When Policy Creates Politics: the Problematizing of Immigration and the Consequences for Refugee Integration in the UK, *Journal of Refugee Studies*, 23(4): 437–462. https://doi.org/10.1093/jrs/feq045

OECD. (2016). *Making Integration Work: Refugees and Others in Need of Protection*. Paris: OECD Publishing.

Olusoga, D. (2016). *Black and British A Forgotten History*. London: Macmillan.

Parekh B. (2000). The Future of Multi- Ethnic Britain. *The Commission on the Future of Multi-Ethnic Britain*. London: Runnymede Trust/Profile Books.

Paret,M., and Gleeson, S. (2016). Precarity and agency through a migration lens. *Citizenship Studies*, 20(3–4): 277–294.

Parmar, A. (2020). Borders as Mirrors: Racial Hierarchies and Policing Migration. *Critical Criminology*, 28, 175–192.

Paterson, T. (2015). Angela Merkel: 'It's our damned duty to help refugees'. Available at: www.independent.co.uk/news/world/europe/angela-merkel-it-s-our-damned-dutyhelp-refugees-a6686631.html (August 2021).

Patmore, G. (1991). *Australian Labour History*, Cheshire Melbourne: Longman.

Phillips, N. and Hardy C. (1997). Managing Multiple Identities: Discourse, Legitimacy and Resources in the UK Refugee System. *Organization* [May 1997], 4(2): 159–185.

Pilgrim, D. (2000). www.ferris.edu/HTMLS/news/jimcrow/antiblack/picaninny/homepage.htm.

Rafferty, A. (2012). Ethnic Penalties in Graduate Level Over-education, Unemployment and Wages: Evidence from Britain. *Work, Employment and Society*, 26(6): 987–1006. https://doi.org/10.1177/0950017012458021

Refugee Council of Australia. (2010). *Economic, Civic and Social Contributions of Refugees and Humanitarian Entrants: A Literature Review*. Canberra: Department of Immigration and Citizenship.

Reliefweb. (2019). *Germany. Integration of Refugees into Labour Market Deemed Success – with Limitations*. Available at: https://reliefweb.int/report/germany/germany-integration-refugees-labour-market-deemed-success-limitations (September 2021).

Scanlon Foundation. (2020). Social Cohesion Index, Accessed January 20, 2021.

Schaffer, G. (2006). Re-Thinking the History of Blame: Britain and Minorities during the Second World War. *National Identities*, 8(4): 401–419, DOI: 10.1080/14608940601052065.

Schinkel, W. 2018. Against 'Immigrant Integration': For an End to Neocolonial Knowledge Production. *Comparative Migration Studies*, 6(1): 31. https://doi.org/10.1186/s40878-018-0095-1.

Sherrell, H. (2019). '*Migration – Permanent and Temporary Visa Trends'. In Briefing Book: Key Issues for the 46th Parliament* (pp. 128–131). Canberra, ACT: Parliament of Australia.

Statista. (2022). Gesamtzahl der offiziell gezählten Kriegsflüchtlinge aus der Ukraine in Deutschland im April 2022 (Stand: 29. April) Available at: https://de.statista.com/statistik/daten/studie/1294820/umfrage/kriegs fluechtlinge-aus-der-ukraine-in-deutschland/ Accessed May 2, 2022.

Taksa, L. & Groutsis, D. (2010). Managing Diverse Commodities: From Factory Fodder to Business Asset. *The Economic and Labour Relations Review*, 20(2): 77–98.

Tatli A., Vassilopoulou J., Ariss A. & Özbilgin M. (2012). The role of regulatory and temporal context in the construction of diversity discourses: the case of the UK. *France and Germany. European Journal of Industrial Relations*, 18/4: 293–308.

Thompson, H. (2017). Inevitability and contingency: The political economy of Brexit. *The British Journal of Politics and International Relations* 19(3): 434–449.

Tomlinson, S. (2018) Enoch Powell, empires, immigrants and education. *Race Ethnicity and Education*, 21(1): 1–14, DOI: 10.1080/13613324 .2017.1365055.

Underhill, E., Groutsis, D., van den Broek, D., Rimmer, M. (2020). Organising Across Borders: Mobilising temporary migrant labour in Australian Food Production. *Journal of Industrial Relations*.

UNHCR. (2015). *The Sea Route to Europe: The Mediterranean Passage in the Age of Refugees*. Geneva.

Vassilopoulou, J. (2011). *Understanding the habitus of managing ethnic diversity in Germany*. A multilevel relational study (Doctoral dissertation, University of East Anglia).

Vassilopoulou, J., Merx, A. & Bruchhagen, V. (2019). An overview of diversity policies in the public and private sector that seek to increase the representation of migrants and ethnic minorities in the workplace: the case of Germany. In: *Race discrimination and the management of ethnic diversity at work*. European countries perspectives. Emerald Publisher.

Vassilopoulou, J., Özbilgin, M., Tatli, A. & Jonsen, K. (2014). Multiculturalism in organizations. In: *Diversity ideologies in organizations*. Taylor-Francis (Eds Thomas, Plaut & Tran.).

Virdee, S. (2019). Racialized capitalism: An account of its contested origins and consolidation. *The Sociological Review*. 67(1): 3–27. doi:10.1177/0038026118820293

Vosko, L. (2010). *Managing the Margins: Gender, Citizenship, and the International Regulation of Precarious Employment*. Oxford: Oxford University Press.

Wadsworth, J. (2014). Immigration, the European Union and the UK Labour Market. Centre for Economic Performance Policy Paper

Number CEPPA015. https://cep.lse.ac.uk/_new/publications/abstract.asp?
index=4437

Willis, R. (1982). *Issues in Australian History*. Melbourne: Longman
Cheshire.

Wright, C. F., Groutsis, D. and Kaabel, A. (forthcoming). Regulating
Migrant Worker Temporariness in Australia: The Role of Employment
and Post-Arrival Support Policies. *Journal of Ethnic and Migration
Studies*.

Zald, M. (2002). Spinning Disciplines: Critical Management Studies in the
Context of the Transformation of Management Education. *Organization*,
9: 365–385.

Zetter, R. (2012). Are refugees an economic burden or benefit? *Forced
Migration Review*, 41(1): 50–52.

Zou, M. (2015). The legal construction of hyper-dependence and hyper-
precarity in migrant work relations. *International Journal of Comparative Labour Law and Industrial Relations*, 31(2): 141–162.

12 Culture, Precarity, and Dignity

RAMASWAMI MAHALINGAM

12.1 Introduction

Decades ago, calling home was an ordeal when I came to the United States from India. International calls were prohibitively expensive ($2.95 per minute) in the daytime, and could call only at midnight (between 11 PM and 7 AM was the economy rate, $1.75/minute). As an immigrant and a first-generation student from a lower-middle-class family, I still supported my family back home. To make ends meet, I used to do several jobs paid both under and over the table. Working as a janitor and dishwasher was my most extended gig. Although the term "gig economy" did not exist then, I lived through that. Globalization as a phenomenon – outsourcing manufacturing jobs to developing countries and the gigification of cleaning and service jobs just began.

Decades later, communication technologies have evolved, and the process of globalization is in full flow. I can call home on WhatsApp for free anytime and do Facetime with my mother. Most of the cleaning and service industry jobs are outsourced, and the gigification of work is complete and normalized with the arrival of Uber and Lyft. Our lives face a Janus-faced reality. Sherry Turkel found that the more time we spend on social media, the more we feel disconnected and lonely. We are hyperconnected yet socially disconnected, with growing disparities between rich and poor and between the West and the global south.

The gig economy fragments our identities and our connections to work and family. Precarious working conditions have become part of our social and organizational life worldwide (Hewison & Kalleberg, 2012). In the United States, at least 25 percent of the courses in Universities are taught by lecturers, who teach at least at 2–3 places to make ends meet. Following the US lead, many private educational institutions in India hire teachers (at high schools and colleges) on contracts. In this chapter, I explore the cultural psychology of precarity at the intersections of caste, class, and "dirty work." Specifically, I focus on the production, reification, and consequences of embodying precarity with a specific focus on dignity injuries. I propose a radical magnanimity perspective foregrounding social justice-inspired mindfulness to preserve the dignity of workers. The rest of the chapter is structured as follows. In the first section, I will present the background and theoretical perspective for my approach to precarity, followed by a case study of janitors in India. In the final section, I outline a mindfulness perspective to protect the dignity of precarious workers for a caring organizational culture (Tronto, 2013). I have included quotes from scholars and readers from India. As part of my methodological reflexivity to authentically represent the voices and a commitment to decolonizing linguistic hegemony in research language, I have not edited them. I hope the readers pardon my discretion.

12.2 Theorizing Precarity and Dignity

There is a growing body of research on precarity from sociological and critical theory perspectives. Many studies examining the precarious working conditions and the psychological precarity of being vulnerable due to uncertain working conditions have also garnered scholarly attention. Although these approaches provide valuable insights about precarity, the cultural specificity of precarity is largely underexplored. Specifically, the cultural psychology of precarity, the embedded and situated nature of precarity (i.e., its production, endurance, and circulation) in reproducing social inequalities, is largely unexplored. The cultural specificity of precarity is shaped by various cultural practices and beliefs that work synergistically to legitimize structural conditions that perpetuate inequalities. Using caste as an essential cultural lens, I will examine the contours of the cultural specificity of precarity in India. Specifically, I focus on the precarious working conditions of Dalit janitors in India to illustrate how intersections of caste, occupational status, and social class undergird the production, perpetuation, and reproduction of precarity and social inequalities (Bapuji & Chrispal, in press).

12.3 Cultural Psychology of Caste: An Intersectionality Perspective

Caste is defined in various ways (see Mahalingam, 2007, for a review). Natrajan (2011) identified four different modes of representation of caste. Caste is a cultural identity, the ethnicization of caste, with specific practices and rituals. Caste is used as a tool to maintain group boundaries through endogamous marriage practices. Caste as social capital provides opportunities for networking and social mobility. Caste is also viewed as a biological category (i.e., caste is biologically transmitted) where caste groups are positioned in a hierarchy with Brahmins at the top and Dalits (formerly treated as untouchables) at the bottom. Mahalingam (2007) found that essentialist beliefs about caste were positively related to the hierarchical positioning and status of the caste groups (Parish, 1996). For example, more than Dalits, Brahmins believed in the biological transmission of caste identity. Various intersections of caste locations and gender shape beliefs about caste identity.

Emerging scholarship on intersectionality has underscored the need to look at how various intersections of identities (e.g., race, class, gender, age, caste, ethnicity) shape how we make sense of our lives (Crenshaw, 1989). There is a growing body of research on intersectionality in various disciplines (for a review, see Cho, Crenshaw, and McCall, 2013; Tatli & Özbilgin, 2012). For example, Walby, Armstrong, and Strid (2012) identified the following six dilemmas or tensions in using the concept of intersectionality: (a) tension between political and structural intersectionality; (b) tension between "categories" and "inequalities"; (c) the significance of class; (d) the balance between stability and fluidity; (e) varying degree of competitive, cooperative, hierarchical and hegemonic relationships between inequalities; and (f) the issue of "visibility" in the tension between "mutual shaping" and "mutual constitution" of inequalities. The critical issues raised by Walby et al. (2012) underscore the role of power differentials in producing systems of inequalities of different valance and the hegemonic relationship between inequalities.

Intersectional approaches in cultural psychology examine how intersections of power, gender, social class, and caste shape ideologies, practices, and the phenomenology of everyday experiences (Mahalingam, Jagannathan & Selvaraj, 2019). Mahalingam and Rabelo (2013) proposed three approaches to using an intersectional framework in cultural psychological research. Intersectional approaches can focus on how embodying intersecting identities shape our attitudes, behaviors, and emotions. For example, one can study how caste, gender, and social class shape experiences of discrimination in urban India.

Intersectional approaches could focus on how intersecting cultural-ecological contexts shape psychological processes in a community. For example, Mahalingam, Haritatos, and Jackson (2007) studied how gender attitudes, including female infanticide, are shaped in landowning and warrior caste groups. Agricultural communities prefer sons to preserve the land resources because daughters will fragment their land resources as dowry. By contrast, warrior caste groups prefer sons because protecting daughters' honor is a source of stress. The situated and fluid nature of identities is a core tenet of an intersectional approach to research. Intersectional awareness refers to our cognizance of various privileges and marginalities associated with our identities and social class.

Social positioning and caste hierarchy affect the experience of precarity at different locations. Dalits have been historically forced to do janitorial work in India. More than 90 percent of the janitors in India are Dalits (Mahalingam, Jagannathan & Selvaraj, 2019). While most of the precarity research in India focuses on economic precarity, the role of caste and culture in the production of precarity has only gained attention recently (Mahalingam, Jagannathan & Selvaraj, 2019; Mahalingam & Selvaraj, in press). Dalit janitors experience two essentialized precarities. A precarity based on their belonging to a "polluted caste" and a precarity based on doing "dirty work." Embodying these two essentialized precarities have existential and health consequences. Epistemic rigging and epistemic violence result in ethical loneliness, undermining their sense of belonging. The dignity injuries they experience are normalized and rendered invisible, affecting their psychological and physical well-being. In the following sections, I review relevant research on narratives, ethical loneliness, recognition, invisibility, dignity, and "dirty work" before presenting the case study of janitors in India.

12.4 Narratives, Ethical Loneliness, and Invisibility: The Phenomenology of Precarity

Fricker (2007) defines phenomenology as "what it is like" to experience something instead of the phenomenological methods developed by Edmund Husserl and others. Fricker calls to our attention not only perceptions, feelings, and bodily processes but the very structures that structure the very process of how to feel, think and understand our sensory experiences. Butler (2007) argues that precarity produces and reifies "ungrievable" subjectivities by dehumanizing the narratives of suffering. aster organizational narratives marginalize the narratives of precarious subjectivities, a process Nelson (2001) calls epistemic rigging.

Any master narrative- even a benign one- possesses the Borg-like capacity to assimilate resistance by wrapping a narrative tendril people or facts that call the master narratives into question. But oppressive master narratives, in particular, tend to meet the problem of opposition by stopping it before it starts. Rather than absorb resistance, they keep it from rising in the first place. (Nelson, 2001, p. 162)

Such epistemic rigging fails to recognize the suffering and dehuman-ization of oppressive working conditions. By silencing and absorb-ing narratives, epistemic rigging perpetuates inequalities. For Nelson (2001), narratives call for social recognition, a fundamental aspect of human existence. Epistemic rigging disrupts our capacity to *recognize* – a precursor to relate and empathize with – the everyday struggles of embodying precarity. According to Honneth (2007), recognition is the ethical core of any human interaction.

It seeks to draw attention to practices of humiliation or degradation that deprive subjects of a justified form of social recognition and, thus, of a deci-sive condition for the formation of their autonomy., On the other hand, this way of formulating the issue makes clear that "recognition" was always treated as representing the opposite of practices of domination or subjec-tion. Such forms of exercising power were to be regarded as phenomena of withheld recognition, intentional disrespect, or humiliation, such that rec-ognition itself could never come under suspicion of functioning as a means of domination. (Honneth, 2007, p. 325)

Stauffer (2015) points out that the lack of recognition of the suffer-ings and humiliations experienced by refugees and asylum contributes to *ethical loneliness* (Stauffer, 2015).

Ethical loneliness is the isolation one feels when one, as a violated person or as one member of a persecuted group, has been abandoned by humanity or by those who have power over one's life's possibilities. It is a condition undergone by persons who have been unjustly treated and dehumanized by human beings and political structures, who emerge from that injustice only to find that the surrounding world will not listen to or cannot properly hear their testimony – their claims about what they suffered and about what is now owed them – on their own terms. So ethical loneliness is the experience of being abandoned by humanity compounded by the experience of not being heard. Such loneliness is so named because it is a form of social abandonment that can be imposed only by multiple ethical lapses on the part of human beings residing in the surrounding world. (Stauffer, 2015, pp. 1–2)

Lack of all forms of recognition (love, rights, solidarity, and epistemic) undergirds ethical loneliness. Organizations also fail to respond to alleviate their pain and suffering. Epistemic rigging furthers their "ungrievable" state of intensifying their ethical loneliness, perpetuating invisibility.

12.4.1 Invisibility

A growing body of research on invisibility underscores the destructive nature of invisibilities in undermining a sense of belonging and organizational commitment (for a review, see Hatton, 2017). Early research on invisibility was spearheaded by researchers who studied domestic labor, especially undervalued women's work. Hatton (2017) has identified three sources of invisible work. Naturalization of work, especially women's domestic work, renders women's labor invisible. Work that fell outside the traditional definition of work (e.g., sex workers) was also considered invisible. Finally, spatial segregation of work, such as virtual work, also perpetuates the invisibility of labor. The invisibility of labor at the bottom of the supply chain in developing countries is another example of invisibility perpetuated by spatial separation of consumption and production (e.g., Donaghey, Reinecke, Niforou, & Lawson, 2014). The spatial separation is a core reason why their work and their exploitative conditions go unnoticed by Western stakeholders.

Bartel, Wrzesniewski, and Wiesenfeld (2012) found that work invisibility was positively related to a lack of respect. Rabelo and Mahalingam (2019) studied the invisibility of janitorial workers in a university setting. Their participants share their stories of invisibility at work and a lack of recognition and under-appreciation of their labor from students, staff, and faculty. They made sense of their invisibility and lack of recognition in myriad ways. A range of themes includes a sense of shame, fear, anxiety, sadness, and resignation. In a review of research on social isolation at work, Bentein, Garcia, Guerrero, and Herrbach (2017) found that perceived social isolation affects one's ability to develop coping strategies at work. Brink and Eurich (2006) categorized several kinds of social exclusion resulting from invisibilities in the corporate context. Cultural exclusion in the form of a clash of civilizations, communicative exclusion, such as bullying and harassment, exclusion from decision-making, exclusion from success, and exclusion from the opportunity for success undermines the ethical-existential recognition of a person in their community. The converging evidence from research on invisibility and exclusion (an intentional act to perpetuate invisibility) shows that invisibility in the workplace adversely affects workers' well-being, resiliency, sense of belonging, and dignity.

12.4.2 *"Dirty Work" and Dignity*

Walzer (2008) observes that most cultures delegate marginalized communities to jobs requiring physical and hard labor (e.g., janitorial work, crematorium work, Jagannathan, Selvaraj, & Joseph, 2016). Many such jobs are viewed as "dirty work" (Ackroyd, 2007; Ashforth & Kreiner, 1999; Hughes, 1951, 1958) because they are physically tainted (i.e., involving dirt or blood or dead bodies) or morally tainted (i.e., sex work, prison guards). Most of the "dirty work" is performed by those from marginalized communities (e.g., Dalits, immigrants, refugees), and they lack social acceptance and respect (Goffman, 1963; Hughes, 1962). Gaining respect and recognition is always a struggle for janitors (Mahalingam, Jagannathan & Selvaraj, 2019) and butchers (Simpson, Slutskaya & Hughes, 2011). The jobs labeled "dirty work" also have low dignity (Thomas & Lucas, 2019). In a study of narratives of garbage workers, Hamilton, Redman, and McMurray (2019) documented discursive constructions of dignity narratives. Deguchi and Chie (2020) found that sanitation workers in Japan also construct discursive narratives of dignity, highlighting their critical role in ensuring public safety during COVID. In their study of slaughterhouse workers, Baran, Rogelberg, and Clausen (2016) found that doing work labeled as "dirty work" affects workers' well-being.

Dignity at the workplace was spearheaded by Hodson's (2001) groundbreaking work on organizational practices that undermine the dignity of workers. Hodson (2001) identified four factors in the workplace that undermine the dignity of workers: (a) mismanagement and abuse; (b) overwork; (c) limits on autonomy; (d) contradictions of employee involvement. Bolton (2007) highlighted the inherent dignity accorded to certain kinds of professions (e.g., doctors, firefighters) and the dignity as an opportunity to gain expertise and professional self-esteem (also see Jacobson, 2009). I define dignity as an embodied praxis – a constellation of processes we embody to recognize, intervene, preserve, and cherish the very core of what makes us human. When such processes are trampled and systemically violated will result in a culture of oppressive and pernicious working conditions full of dignity injuries (Lucas, Kang, & Li, 2013).

12.4.3 Dalit Janitors and Precarity: A Case Study

In Indian culture, due to centuries of practice of untouchability, Dalits have been exploited and forced to do all the menial jobs (e.g., cleaning and crematorium work). Dalits are viewed as ritually "polluted" because they are born into a caste that was forced to do the "dirty work," and Dalits who engage in "dirty work" are viewed as polluted. Such circular cultural logic reproduces caste hierarchy and inequality by forcing Dalits to work in precarious working conditions. By keeping Dalits doing the janitorial work, the social life caste short-circuits the empathic compassionate responses of dominant caste members toward the sufferings of Dalits.

In their provocative paper on urban sanitation imaginary, Morales, Harris, and Oberg proclaim, "urban life means your shit is not your problem" (p. 2816). I argue that in urban imaginary, is not only the shit invisible but also those who clean the shit, normalizing their suffering. Dalit janitors embody two essentialized precarious identities (being a Dalit and a janitor). The dominant caste groups reason that the ritualized polluted nature of Dalit caste identity justifies their delegated status to remove the sewers or manually carry human excreta.

Although Dalit is a broad umbrella term to denote caste groups treated as "untouchables" by the dominant caste, there is also a hierarchy among Dalit caste groups where Dalits who work as sanitation workers are at the lowest end the social stratum. In her book *Unseen*, journalist Bhasha Singh documents the humiliation women janitors, in particular, feel when they work as manual scavengers and are not given enough soap to wash off the stench. At the end of their workday, the women are afraid to give their children hugs, fearing the smell might turn them away. They feel ashamed of their low status and never talk to their children about their work and the dignity injuries they experience on the job. They want to protect their children from becoming manual scavengers but feel powerless to do so. Cultural beliefs about bad karma from a previous life haunt them in this life, and they are often resigned to their fate. One mother lamented:

I have spent a whole lifetime doing manual scavenging. It stinks ... I remember how terrible my first day was. By the time I returned home, I had thrown up at least ten times. I had never thought that I would have to do such filthy work. But this was what fate had in store for me ... the punishment for being born in this caste. (Sharada, female janitor, Singh, 2014, p. 38)

The exploitation against Dalits has continued even after globalization. In truth, globalization has made their lives worse (Ram, 2012). Due to intense competition post-globalization, the neoliberal economy demands abundant cheap labor to improve or consolidate profit (Connell & Dados, 2014). Hence, destructive labor policies are created, such as labor flexibilization, which included schemes like "labor-only contracting, subcontracting, hiring of casuals and contractual, and the hiring of apprentices" (Lindio-McGovern, 2007, p. 23). Contractualization of the labor force leads to labor exploitation, increased unemployment rate, job insecurity, and preventing employees from collectivizing (i.e., joining trade unions that would increase collective bargaining power). Most of the public sectors and private sectors outsource cleaning work. Dalit janitors work on the streets and malls as contract laborers without benefits (Mahalingam & Selvaraj, in press).

Intersections of gender, social class, and caste together shape the precarious working conditions of Dalit women janitors in the mall. In a study of mall women janitors, Mahalingam and Selvaraj (in press) noted many dignity injuries experienced by women janitors. Although the mall has become the poster child for the neoliberal economy, only the wealthy can afford to shop in these malls. The mall customers, primarily from the privileged class, yelled and abused the cleaners. Some customers spoke to the woman in English, knowing that the janitors would not understand them since most janitors did not finish middle school (Mahalingam & Selvaraj, in press).

12.4.4 Chennai Floods and Overworked Janitors

In 2015, an unprecedented downpour of torrential rain resulted in massive flooding in Chennai, India. The middle-class volunteers worked very hard to deliver medicine to the needy. Media covered the power of social media and the power of people coming together to help each other. Although there were so many volunteers from the middle class to distribute food, sanitary napkins, water, and medicine, when it came to cleaning the city, which included removing dead animals and cleaning the sewers, no one wanted to volunteer. The city government went to neighboring provinces to gather Dalit janitors to work as contract laborers to clean the city (Mahalingam, Jaganathan & Selvaraj, 2019).

The Dalit janitors were forced to overwork during the Chennai floods in 2015 under denigrating working conditions. The following are examples of their ethical loneliness.

When we were cleaning the city, we were still regarded as untouchables. Nobody welcomed us in their homes. Even when some of them gave us food, it was not on their plates, but they wrapped it in newspapers and plastic bags and gave us. As if we were dogs who could not eat on the plates of human beings. People will give things without touching, will not notice us, and will not see us as humans. They do not call me by my name. They call me thotti (a derogatory term for sanitation worker). They forget that I am human, too, with a name. People treat me like this because we are born as Dalits. (Mahalingam, Jagannathan & Selvaraj, 2019, p. 224)

The lack of recognition of the sufferings of Dalit labor in social media was criticized by progressive nongovernmental agencies and Dalit intellectuals and activists (for a review see Mahalingam, Jagannathan & Selvaraj, 2019). They acted as pneumonic communities to document the degrading treatments of Dalit janitors during the cleaning of the city.

Misusing power to withhold recognition deprives opportunities for growth and a sense of belonging. Lack of recognition, augmented by chronic mistreatment, disrespect, and humiliation, also negatively affects workers' physical and psychological well-being. Due to chronic exposure to dignity injuries, janitors who do the cleaning in appalling working conditions have a low life expectancy. Dalit janitors have one of the worst health outcomes and a high rate of alcoholism. Even when they die, the organizations take their sweet time to pay the workers' compensation. Mahalingam, Jagannathan, and Selvaraj (2019) observed that more than 70 percent of janitors were addicted to alcohol. Unequal exposure to risk and injury dehumanizes marginalized workers by treating them as "ungrievable" (Butler, 2009; Mahalingam, Jagannathan & Selvaraj, 2019). Dalit janitors' working conditions are rife with humiliation and mistreatment (Mahalingam, Jagannathan & Selvaraj, 2019). Considering the death rates of janitors at work, the institutional apathy toward their working conditions reifies their status as "ungrievable" subjects.

12.4.5 *Public Perceptions of Dalit Janitors' Cleaning Work*

While following the social media responses to the disaster, I observed many instances of communities coming together to help each other across class, caste, and religion. There were also reports of price gouging and black marketeering of essential goods like milk. As we mentioned earlier, while the distribution of relief supplies and food drew more volunteers from the middle class, the city cleaning was delegated to janitors who were hired temporarily from outside the district. They were transported in lorries like cattle for a twelve-hour journey on the road. Several media outlets have reported the mistreatment of the workers. For a *Hindustan Times* article on the abuse of city cleaners, there were forty-two readers' comments.

I downloaded the comments to identify some key themes. I classified them into four major categories. One category of response was readers' acknowledgment of the mistreatment of janitors with a recognition that something systemic needs to change to improve the lives of janitors.

First of all, the whole sanitation and sewage system needs to be remodeled to be easily accessed without somebody taking a dip in the dirty fluids. Urban spaces need to remodel the sewage system completely. The state government needs to subsidize the sanitation worker equipment and bring in more educational institutions that can help design better equipment. More than anything, they should also be paid a little better with full health benefits, So everyone wanting to do this job will join, not just one weak community.

Another category of responses was to offer technical solutions like giving proper equipment and safety training for janitors and a call for more professionalization of janitorial services.

More than their caste or religion, society needs to look into their working conditions, such as protective gear, fair wages, employment conditions, automated tools for cleaning, and proper healthcare for working in hazardous situations.

Some readers viewed that problem as a caste-blind issue and wanted to focus on improving the janitorial work without acknowledging that almost all cleaners are Dalits because that would divide society.

This news is another conniving attack to communalize and castecize society. In the rain, many people suffered. Why one has to pin it on Dalits, this shows how the journalists don't want peace in the country.

Some called the reporter a communist sympathizer who did not believe in the meritocracy of the system; janitors should be responsible for their situation. They reasoned that if janitors were smart, they would have gotten a better job and that no one was preventing them from doing that.

Why don't you go and do it? Who is stopping you? You can join the Dalits and help them instead of showing false sympathy here. Somebody has to clean the shit. It is not as if they are looking at caste certificates before appointing people to these jobs. Dalits are welcome to get an education and use the reservation and get good jobs. If they choose to clean shit, they can do so too.

The above comment is emblematic of a worldview that the world is without discrimination. It also elides modern slavery-like working conditions of Dalits where physical and structural coercion keep them from doing the cleaning work for generations. Educational institutions are filled with casteist practices that are often implicit and invisible.

Although the readers' responses were not representative, they captured typical middle-class attitudes toward janitors, ranging from resigned helplessness to utter contempt for janitors. Their lack of concern and care about the cleaners' safety and indignities underscores the power of the association fallacy that those who work with dirt are dirty. Such naturalization of occupation and caste prevents non-Dalits from developing an empathic understanding of the sufferings and the inherent dignity of Dalit janitors. Medina (2013) characterizes such insensitivity to the privileged group as epistemic vice. Medina (2013) defines epistemic vice as "a set of corrupted attitudes and dispositions that gets in the way of knowledge" (p. 30). Meta-blindness, arrogance, and a privileged attitude of *needing-not-to* know are characteristics of epistemic vice – a mental process that is systemically closed or unwilling to open to certain experiences and knowledge (Medina, 2013). White fragility or Brahmin/upper caste fragility (in the Indian context) is an example of discomfort in engaging with one's meta-blindness, an epistemic vice. At the micro-level, cultivating mindfulness could help overcome meta-blindness with compassion and openness to recognize the dignity of others.

The general public's meta-blindness to the sufferings overlooks janitors' appalling and dangerous working conditions. Exposure to perennial dignity injuries (psychological and physical) affects Dalit janitors' sense of agency and mental and physical health. Dalit janitors have a low life expectancy due to harsh working conditions and high alcohol addiction rates (Mahalingam, Jagannathan & Selvaraj, 2019). The cost of the unrecognized suffering of the janitors is not insignificant. Every year, around 200 janitors die while cleaning the sewers in India. Dalit janitors' lives illustrate how an insidious cultural logic of precaritizing caste and occupational identities (Dalit and "dirty work") perpetuates precarious material and working conditions affecting their physical and mental well-being.

12.5 General Discussion

Mahalingam and Selvaraj (2022) called for a radical interdependence perspective drawing on Dr. Ambedkar, an engaged Buddhist and a pioneering Indian intellectual who spearheaded the writing of the Indian Constitution). For Ambedkar, caste is not about the division of labor but about the division of laborers based on their birth, not their occupation (Ambedkar, 1991).

In India, a man is not a scavenger because of his work. He is a scavenger because of his birth, irrespective of the question whether he does scavenging or not. (Ambedkar, 1991, p. 292)

The caste system provides the trope for oppressing Dalits, forcing them to embody psychological and material precarity. To address precarity in organizations at the macro level, we need caring leadership that protects the dignity of the workers. At the micro-level, we need to cultivate a holistic mindfulness perspective with a commitment to recognize and preserve the dignity of the workers who toil in the gig economy.

Caritative Leadership
Caritative leadership emerged from caring science and is primarily concerned with alleviating suffering and preventing dignity injuries

in healthcare settings (Eriksson, 2002; Watson, 1997). Caring science calls for a holistic approach to recognize people's sufferings, not just as a symptom of a disease but as a process of embodied and active engagement with their unfolding life story. Caritative leadership is based on dignity, human relationships, love, and caring ethos, where the caregiver and the receiver's dignities are preserved (Bondas, 2003).

Extending the caritative leadership model to other organizational settings call for an ontological approach to ethics where ethics is about the ethos of valuing love, dignity, and mercy (Ostman, Nasman & Ericksson, 2019). Caritative leadership is grounded in the philosophy of "human love and mercy and a humanistic view of the human being" (Nasman, 2018, p. 518). Caritative leadership is about the recognition of suffering. It is based on the recognition of love, rights, and solidarity emanating from an epistemic recognition of a person's life circumstances. A caritative leader is nonegotistic and caring and creates an organizational ethos where recognition and alleviation of suffering is an edified virtue.

Hospital patients, janitors, immigrants, and refugee workers share a common existential predicament: visible invisibility. Their suffering and dignity injuries are normalized through several institutional practices (Jacobson, 2009). Doctors objectify patients while making a diagnosis and often fail to recognize the intersubjective elements of care. Dalit janitors' humiliation and degradation are erased due to the cultural logic that they are "born polluted" and that it is "natural" for them to work with pollution, which lacks all forms of recognition, a precursor to caring and dignified work. Immigrants and refugees had to fight for recognition to preserve their dignity. Paradoxically, precarity naturalizes invisibility and objectification. Patient objectification follows a scientific logic, whereas Dalit objectification follows a cultural logic. Immigrant and refugee discrimination follows a bureaucratic logic. Organizational practices governed by these logics create conditions for a monological, not a dialogical, form of recognition. A caritative leadership calls for opening the heart with a commitment to thwart the institutional logics and practices that render the sufferings and dignity injuries invisible. Caritative leadership highlights the need for love, mercy, dignity, and the recognition of suffering in the workplace. Sustaining the commitment to be a caritative leader and cultivating the skills to be nonegoistic and caring is a demanding task.

12.5.1 Mindful Mindset and Dignity

Drawing from Buddhist psychology and social justice research, I developed a mindful mindset framework that fosters interconnectedness with a commitment to preserve personal, intersubjective, and processual dignities. Personal dignity refers to the inherent dignity, the defining quality of being human, with a capacity to exercise our agency. Intersubjective dignity refers to our commitment to recognize the dignity of others in our social interactions. Processual dignity refers to our commitment to preserving a dignity culture around us (e.g., work, home). My mindful mindset framework provides tools to cultivate our capacity to recognize the sufferings and dignity injuries of those whose sufferings and labor are invisible.

Understanding that our lives are interconnected and interdependent is necessary for respect for others, a critical condition for dialogical modes of recognition. A mindful mindset demands a commitment to engage with our lives and communities to make the visibly invisible visible by disrupting the processes that naturalize their sufferings. A mindful mindset has seven features: compassion, sympathetic joy, wonder, situated intersectional awareness, generosity, negative capability, and cultural humility. Compassion and sympathetic joy refer to our ability to alleviate others' suffering and our ability to rejoice with others' happiness, respectively. Situated intersectional awareness refers to an understanding that our identities are fluid, situational, and located in different axes of privilege and marginality (Mahalingam, 2019). For Keats (1817, cited in Cornish, 2011), negative capability is our ability to reside in a situation with an open mind, "when a man is capable of being in uncertainties, mysteries, doubts, without any irritable reaching after fact and reason" (emphasis added, Keats, 1817, p. 43). In the organizational context, Cornish (2011) defined negative capability with the following three characteristics: (a) capacity to be open, (b) attentiveness to diversity, and (c) suspension of ego. Ortega and Faller (2011) argued that cultural humility is necessary to suspend our ego.

Ortega and Faller (2011) argued that any helping profession, such as social work and disaster management, requires cultural humility and cultural sensitivity when working with people from diverse social and cultural backgrounds. According to Ortega and Faller (2011),

a cultural humility approach advocates for incorporating a multicultural and intersectional understanding and analysis to improve practice since together these concepts draw attention to the diversity of the whole person, to power differences in relationships (especially between workers and families), to different past and present life experiences including microaggressions and potential resources or gaps. (Ortega & Faller, 2011, p. 32)

Ortega and Faller's cultural humility perspective highlights the need to be open to learning from people who are different. Wonder refers to accepting others who are different (La Caze, 2013), and generosity refers to our ability to help (e.g., material, emotional and intellectual) while keeping the self-respect of the recipient of our help intact (Mahalingam, 2019). Buddhism emphasizes generosity because of the interconnected nature of our lives. Thus, the mindful mindset framework helps us engage with others with awakened attention, openness to realizing interdependence, and commitment to preserving the dignity of those laboring in the gig economy.

12.5.2 Personal Reflections: Toward a Decent Society

Work consumes an enormous amount of our lives. We are at our most vulnerable at work because our survival depends on our livelihoods for most of us. Dependency on employers for basic needs often results in harmful and demeaning working conditions, including humiliation and invisibility. Dignity injuries are humiliating, and their invisibilities undermine our ability to build a decent and just society (Margalit, 1996). Cultural logic, such as caste, perpetuates meta-blindness to humiliation and invisibility. A globalized gig economy perpetuates precarious working conditions. Precarious working conditions and lack of workplace health benefits compound workers' vulnerability. Specifically, for those who perform "dirty" work (e.g., janitors, sex workers), precarious working conditions normalize their suffering and humiliation, adding another layer to their invisibilities (Hatton, 2017; Mahalingam, Jagannathan & Selvaraj, 2019; Rabelo & Mahalingam, 2019). The emerging body of research on modern slavery (Crane, 2013; Kara, 2009) also highlights the appalling working conditions and exploitation of workers in the Global South.

I call for a critical cultural psychology framework for a decent workplace for meaningful work without humiliation and invisibility with an explicit discussion of the mechanisms for allocating hard and bad jobs or tasks (Walzer, 2008). Often precarity is framed as an inevitable consequence of a globalized economy. For example, an economist might argue whether a decent workplace is necessary for making a profit (Akerlof & Yellen, 1988) even if the standard economy tends to defend more intense forms of division of labor and continues to take a restrictive view of the costs of using the labor force without paying attention to the disproportionate concentration of precarity in marginalized communities. Although there is a substantial body of research on mistreatment and incivility in the workplace, it focuses on individual experiences. In contrast, the invisibility I like to mobilize is part of a collective framework: the humiliation experienced does not need people who deliberately humiliate but result from a humiliating social structure (Memmi (2013).

The idea of a decent society is one of the central features of our perspective (Margalit, 1996). In decent societies, people can participate in institutional life free of humiliation. Yet, organizations systemically deprive people of dignity, and a mindful mindset perspective will help us interrogate. Engaged Buddhists like Ambedkar and Thich Naht Hanh have called for a praxis – engaged mindfulness – to challenge social marginality and humiliation based on intersecting oppressions (Mahalingam, 2019). Feminist philosopher Nel Noddings (2013) proposed a caring perspective delineating the two primary human motives – our desire to care and be cared for. Drawing from research on caring science (Erikson, 2002), Bondas (2003) outlined a Caritative Leadership perspective anchored on love, compassion, and grace (Nasman, 2018). We need to rethink organizational practices and diversity to open new possibilities for a decent workplace where mindful engagement and caritative caring are the core values to ensure decent work.

12.6 Future Directions and Conclusions

Precarity is situated, embodied, and a multilayered phenomenon. Intersections of identity and social contexts shape how we make sense of precarity. It has *economic, spatial, social, cultural, psychological,* and *phenomenological* dimensions. Justifiably economic precarity has gained considerable scholarly attention, particularly the gig economy and the production of economic precarity. The gig economy perpetuates job insecurity and substantial psychological stress. Dignity injuries proliferate in the gig economy, and their psychological impact is largely underexplored. We need to explore the relationship between the globalization of capital and the spread of the gig economy around the world. Doing two jobs is becoming a norm across the globe resulting in a new regime of marginality (Wacquant, 2016).

The paramount material attribute of the emerging regime of marginality is that it is fed by the fragmentation of wage labor, that is, the diffusion of unstable, part-time, short-term, low-pay, and dead-end employment at the bottom of the occupational structure– a master trend that has accelerated and solidified across advanced nations over the past two decades. (Wacquant, 2016, pp. 1081–1082)

The gig economy contributes to a new regime of social marginality where economic precarity is touted as the freedom to innovate, explore, or be one's boss. However, the reality is that economic precarity undermines physical and psychological well-being (Kalleberg & Vallas, 2018). Spatial precarity refers to the spatial segregation of marginalized communities, which is a barrier to the social mobility of Dalits, ethnic minorities, such as African immigrants, and African American communities (Mahalingam, 2007). In the United States, spatial precarity adversely affects access to education, job, personal and community health, and a sense of belonging (Wagmiller, 2007; Williams & Collins, 2001). Essentialist cultural beliefs about social groups (Mahalingam, 2007) embedded in cultural practices legitimize and perpetuate social and cultural precarity normalizing the sufferings of members of marginalized groups (e.g., Dalits, transgender, and Muslims in India).

We also need to identify conditions under which precarity and dignity injuries proliferate. For Jacobson (2009), an order of inequality, an uncaring environment, a position of vulnerability, and harsh circumstances promote dignity injuries and psychological precarity. Jacobson (2009) also founds that compassion, a position of confidence, solidarity, humane circumstances, and an order of justice promote dignity by lowering psychological precarity. Stauffer (2015) reminds us of the power of narratives as a window to the phenomenology of precarity. We must pay attention to the sufferings of those who embody precarity as part of their everyday existence. For example, immigrants, refugees, trafficked women, and asylum seekers experience ethical loneliness because they often embody economic, spatial, social, and cultural precarities that shape their phenomenological precarity. Research on precarity needs to explore the complex relationship between ethical loneliness and embodied narratives of precarity. I suggest an *inter-sectional precarity* framework to explore how intersections of race, ethnicity, caste, class, gender, sexuality, religion, and immigrant or refugee and different kinds of precarity shape the production and perpetuation of inequality and their impact on well-being.

Cultural logic provides the ideological trope to reify and reproduce precarity in complex forms at various intersections. It also rationalizes suffering by perpetuating meta-blindness and invisibility. Caritative leadership, including a mindful mindset with a commitment to dignity, is essential to alleviate the sufferings of Dalits who experience spatial, economic, social, cultural, psychological, and phenomenological precarity because of their status of "perpetual outsider" who lives at the margins of the society – both figuratively and literally since most of the Dalit colonies at the outskirts of the village or city. Such a perspective is critical to thwarting the normalization of humiliation and invisibility at work and imagining new organizational and societal transformation possibilities to improve the dignity of workers at various intersections of culture-specific precarious working conditions.

References

Ackroyd, S. (2007). Dirt, work, and dignity. In S. C. Bolton (Ed.), *Dimensions of Dignity at Work* (pp. 30–49). Oxford, UK: Butterworth-Heinemann.

Agarwal, S., & Levien, M. (2020). Dalits and Dispossession: A Comparison. *Journal of Contemporary Asia, 50*(5), 696–722.

Akerlof, G. A., & Yellen, J. L. (1988). Fairness and unemployment. *The American Economic Review, 78*(2), 44–49

Ambedkar, B. R. (1991). What Congress and Gandhi have done to the Untouchables In Vasant Moon (ed.) *Dr. Babasaheb Ambedkar: Writings and Speeches v 9. Bombay, India: The Education Department,* Government of Maharashtra (reprint).

Ashforth, B. E., & Kreiner, G. E. (1999). "How can you do it?": Dirty work and the challenge of constructing a positive identity. *Academy of Management Review, 24*(3), 413–434.

Banerjee, A., & Sabharwal, N. (2013). Nature and forms of discrimination experienced by Dalit Women in the urban labour market in Delhi. IIDS-IDRC Report Series No. 60.

Bapuji, H. (2015). Individuals, interactions and institutions: How economic inequality affects organizations. *Human Relations, 68*(7), 1059–1083.

Bapuji, H., & Chrispal, S. (forthcoming). Understanding economic inequality through the lens of caste. *Journal of Business Ethics, 162*(3), 533–551.

Baran, B. E., Rogelberg, S. G., & Clausen, T. (2016). Routinized killing of animals: Going beyond dirty work and prestige to understand the well-being of slaughterhouse workers. *Organization, 23*(3), 351–369.

Bardia, M. (2009). Dr. B. R. Ambedkar: His ideas about religion and conversion to Buddhism. *Indian Journal of Political Science, 70*(3), 737–749.

Bartel, C. A., Wrzesniewski, A., & Wiesenfeld, B. M. (2012). Knowing where you stand: Physical isolation, perceived respect, and organizational identification among virtual employees. *Organization Science, 23*(3), 743–757.

Bentein, K., Garcia, A., Guerrero, S., & Herrbach, O. (2017). How does social isolation in a context of dirty work increase emotional exhaustion and inhibit work engagement? A process model. *Personnel Review, 46*(8), 1620–1634.

Bolton, S. C. (2007). Dignity in and at work: Why it matters? In S. C. Bolton (ed.). *Dimensions of Dignity at Work* (pp. 1–16). Oxford: Elsevier.

Bondas, T. E. (2003). Caritative leadership: ministering to the patients. *Nursing Administration Quarterly, 27*(3), 249–253.

Bourdieu, P. (1984). *Distinction: A Social Critique of the Judgment of Taste.* Cambridge, MA: Harvard University Press.

Brink, A., & Eurich, J. (2006). Recognition based upon the vitality criterion: A key to sustainable economic success. *Journal of Business Ethics, 67*, 155–164.

Butler, J. (2007). *Frames of War: When is Life Grievable?* New York: Verso.

Butler, J. (2009). *Frames of War. When Is Life Grievable?* London: Verso.

Cho, S., Crenshaw, K., & McCall, L. (2013). Toward a field of intersectionality studies: Theory, applications, and praxis. *Signs, 38*(4), 785–810. doi:10.1086/669608

Connell, R., & Dados, N. (2014). Where in the world does neoliberalism come from? The market agenda in a southern perspective. *Theory and Society, 43*(2), 117–138.

Cornish, S. (2011). Negative capability and social work: Insights from Keats, Bion and business. *Journal of Social Work Practice, 25*(02), 135–148.

Crane, A. (2013). Modern slavery as a management practice: Exploring the conditions and capabilities for human exploitation. *Academy of Management Review, 38*(1), 49–69.

Crenshaw, K. (1989). Demarginalizing the intersection of race and sex: A black feminist critique of antidiscrimination doctrine, feminist theory, and antiracist politics. *University of Chicago Legal Forum, 1*, 139–167.

Deguchi, M., & Chie, M. (2020). Voices of sanitation workers in Japan amidst the COVID-19 pandemic. *Asia Pacific Journal, 18*(15), 1–12.

Donaghey, J., Reinecke, J., Niforou, C., & Lawson, B. (2014). From employment relations to consumption relations: Balancing labor governance in global supply chains. *Human Resource Management, 53*(2), 229–252.

Dreze, J. & Sen, A. (2002). Democratic practice and social inequality in India. *Journal of Asian and African Studies, 37*(2), 6–37.

Eriksson, K. (2002). Caring science in a new key. *Nursing Science Quarterly, 15*(1), 61–65.

Fricker, M. (2007). *Epistemic Injustice: Power and the Ethics of Knowing.* New York: Oxford University Press.

Goffman, E. (1963). *Stigma-Notes on the Management of Spoiled Identity.* Englewood Cliffs, NJ: Prentice-Hall

Guru, G. (1995). Dalit women talk differently. *Economic and Political Weekly, 30*(41/42), 2548–2550.

Hamilton, P., Redman, T., & McMurray, R. (2019). "Lower than a Snake's Belly": Discursive Constructions of Dignity and Heroism in Low-Status Garbage Work. *Journal of Business Ethics, 156*, 889–901.

Hatton, E. (2017). Mechanisms of invisibility: rethinking the concept of invisible work. *Work, Employment and Society, 31*(2), 336–351.

Hewison, K., & Kalleberg, A. L. (2012). Precarious work and flexibilization in the south and southeast Asia. *American Behavioral Scientist, 57*(4), 395–402.

Hodson, R.(2001). *Dignity at Work.* Cambridge, UK: Cambridge University Press.

Honneth, A. (1995). *The Struggle for Recognition: The Moral Grammar of Social Conflicts.* Cambridge, MA: Polity Press.

Honneth, A. (2007). Recognition as ideology. In B. van den Brink & D. Owen (eds.). *Recognition and Power: Axel Honneth and the Tradition of Critical Social Theory* (pp. 323–348). New York: Cambridge University Press.

Hughes, E. C. (1951). Work and the self. In J.H. Rohrer & M. Sherif (Eds.), *Social Psychology at the Crossroads: The University of Oklahoma Lectures in Social Psychology* (pp. 313–323). Oxford, UK: Harper.

Hughes, E. C. (1958). *Men and their Work.* Glencoe, IL: Free Press.

Hughes, E. C. (1962). Good people and dirty work. *Social Problems, 10*(1), 3–11.

Jacobson, N. (2009). Dignity violation in health care. *Qualitative health research, 19*(11), 1536–1547.

Jagannathan, S., Selvaraj, P., & Joseph, J. (2016). The funeralesque as the experience of workers at the margins of international business: Seven Indian narratives. *Critical Perspectives on International Business, 12*(3), 282–305.

Kalleberg, A. L., & Vallas, S. P. (2018). Probing precarious work: Theory, research, and politics. *Research in the Sociology of Work, 31*(1), 1–30.

Kara, S. (2009). *Sex Trafficking: Inside the Business of Modern Slavery.* New York: Columbia University Press.

La Caze, M. (2013). *Wonder and Generosity: Their role in ethics and politics.* New York: SUNNY press.

Lindio-McGovern, L. (2007). Neo-liberal globalization in the Philippines: Its impact on Filipino women and their forms of resistance. *Journal of Developing Societies, 23*(1–2), 15–35.

Lucas, K., Kang, D., & Li, Z. (2013). Workplace dignity in a total institution: Examining the experiences of Foxconn's migrant workforce. *Journal of business ethics, 114*(1), 91–106.

Mahalingam, R. (2007). Essentialism, power and the representation of social categories: A folk sociology perspective. *Human Development, 50*(6), 300–319.

Mahalingam, R. (2019). Mindful Mindset, Interconnectedness, and Dignity. *Global Youth, 1,* 230–253.

Mahalingam, R., & Rabelo, V. (2013). Theoretical, methodological, and ethical challenges to the study of immigrants: Perils and possibilities. *New Directions for Child and Adolescent Development, 141,* 25–41.

Mahalingam, R., & Selvaraj, P. (2022). Ambedkar, radical interdependence and dignity: A study of women mall janitors in India. *Journal of Business Ethics, 177*(4), 813–828.

Mahalingam, R., Jagannathan, S., & Selvaraj, P. (2019). Decasticization, dignity, and "dirty work" at the intersections of caste, memory, and disaster. *Business Ethics Quarterly, 29*(2), 213–239.

Mandal, B. C. (2014). Globalization and its Impact on Dalits. *Contemporary Voice of Dalit, 7*(2), 147–162.

Margalit, A. (1996). *The Decent Society.* Boston, MA: Harvard University Press.

McMurray, R., & Ward, J. (2014). "Why would you want to do that?": Defining emotional dirty work. *Human Relations, 67*(9), 1123–1143.

Medina, J. (2013). *The Epistemology of Resistance: Gender and Racial Oppression, Epistemic Injustice, and Resistant Imagination.* New York: Oxford University Press.

Memmi, A. (2013). *The Colonizer and the Colonized.* Routledge: New York.

Morales, M. D. C., Harris, L., & Öberg, G. (2014). Citizenshit: the right to flush and the urban sanitation imaginary. *Environment and Planning A, 46*(12), 2816–2833.

Näsman, Y. (2018). The theory of caritative leadership applied to education. *International Journal of Leadership in Education, 21*(4), 518–529.

Natrajan, B. (2011). *The Culturalization of Caste in India: Identity and Inequality in a Multicultural Age.* New York: Routledge.

Nelson, H. L. (2001). *Damaged Identities, Narrative Repair*. Ithaca, NY: Cornell University Press.

Noddings, N. (2013). *Caring: A Relational Approach to Ethics and Moral Education*. Berkeley, CA: University of California Press.

Ortega, R. M., & Faller, K. (2011). Training child welfare workers from an intersectional cultural humility perspective: A paradigm shift. *Child Welfare, 90*(5), pp. 27–49.

Östman, L., Näsman, Y., Eriksson, K., & Nyström, L. (2019). Ethos: The heart of ethics and health. *Nursing Ethics, 26*(1), 26–36.

Parish, S. M. (1996). *Hierarchy and its Discontents: Culture and the Politics of Consciousness in a Caste Society*. Philadelphia, PA: University of Pennsylvania Press.

Purser, R. E. (2019). *McMindfulness: How Mindfulness became the New Capitalist Spirituality*. London: Repeater.

Queen, C. S. (1996). Introduction: The shapes and sources of engaged Buddhism. In. C.S. Queen., & S.B. King (eds.) *Engaged Buddhism: Buddhist Liberation Movements in Asia* (pp. 1–44). New York: SUNY Press.

Queen, C. S., & King, S. B. (1996). *Engaged Buddhism: Buddhist Liberation Movements in Asia*. New York: SUNY Press.

Rabelo, V. C., & Mahalingam, R. (2019). "They really don't want to see us": How cleaners experience invisible "dirty" work. *Journal of Vocational Behavior, 113*, 103–114.

Ram, R. (2012). Reading neoliberal market economy with Jawaharlal Nehru: Dalits and the dilemma of social democracy in India. *South Asian Survey, 19*(2), 221–241.

Rivera, K. D. (2015). Emotional taint: Making sense of emotional dirty work at the U.S. Border Patrol. *Management Communication Quarterly, 29*(2), 198–228.

Roberts, D. E. (1997). Spiritual and menial housework. *Yale Journal of Law and Feminism, 9*(1), 51–80.

Simpson, R., Slutskaya, N., & Hughes, J. (2011). Emotional dimensions of dirty work: men's encounter with taint in the butcher trade. *International Journal of Work Organisation and Emotion, 4*(2), 195–212.

Singh, B. (2014). *Unseen: The Truth about India's Manual Scavengers*. New York: Penguin.

Stauffer, J. (2015). *Ethical Loneliness: The Injustice of Not Being Heard*. New York: Columbia University Press.

Tatli, A., & Özbilgin, M. F. (2012). An emic approach to the intersectional study of diversity at work: A Bourdieuan framing. *International Journal of Management Reviews, 14*(2), 180–200. doi:10.1111/j.1468-2370.2011.00326.x

Thomas, B., & Lucas, K. (2019). Development and validation of the workplace dignity scale. *Group & Organization Management, 44*(1), 72–111.

Thorat, S. (2009). *Dalits in India: Search for a Common Destiny*. New Delhi: Sage

Tronto, J. C. (2013). *Caring Democracy: Markets, quality, and Justice*. New York: New York University Press.

Wacquant, L. (2016). Revisiting territories of relegation: Class, ethnicity and state in the making of advanced marginality. *Urban Studies*, *53*(6), 1077–1088.

Wagmiller, R. L. (2007). Race and the Spatial Segregation of Jobless Men in Urban America. *Demography*, *44*(3), 539–562. www.jstor.org/stable/30053101

Walby, S., Armstrong J., & Strid, S. (2012). Intersectionality: Multiple inequalities in social theory. *Sociology*, *46*(2), 224–240. doi:10.1177/0038038511416164

Waldron, J. (2015). *Dignity, Rank, and Rights*. New York: Oxford University Press.

Walzer, M. (2008). *Spheres of Justice: A Defense of Pluralism and Equality*. Basic Books.

Watson, J. (1997). The theory of human caring: Retrospective and prospective. *Nursing Science Quarterly*, *10*(1), 49–52.

Williams, D. R., & Collins, C. (2001). Racial residential segregation: a fundamental cause of racial health disparities. *Public Health Reports*, *116*(5), 404.

13 Transforming Humanitarianism Precarities at Work in the New Activist Volunteer Sector

SUE CLAYTON

13.1 The Crises Driving New Social Movements

In recent years, a number of social and political crises have required large-scale civic responses that have proved uniquely challenging in their scale and complexity, and in the demands they have placed on those who committed to act – and whose commitment may have begun as voluntary, but for many ended as a full-time, unpaid, long-term labour (Clayton, 2020). Here, I argue that such events as the 2015–2020 European 'Refugee Crisis' that left hundreds of thousands abandoned in Europe with no support; the 2017 London Grenfell Tower fire which left hundreds homeless and inadequately supported by government; and the 2019–2021 COVID-19 pandemic which has caused severe poverty and hardship: all of these have all required civic responders to engage in very different kinds of care humanitarian values, politics, and action. While this mobilisation by many thousands of new 'humanitarians' who felt compelled to intervene has been positive in many ways in terms of widened social awareness, and the skilling up of many into new roles, it has also pushed many of these actors into positions of economic and personal precarity.

Referencing in particular those volunteers working in context of refugee aid, I will look at the already compromised backgrounds and contexts from which many came, and which almost all went on to face, in financial, legal and societal, and personal psychological frameworks. I will consider how this new humanitarian workforce, which began as emergency aid and has developed into a permanent de facto care army, continues to operate at some cost to those who were caught up in this historic social change (Hughes et al., 2020). And at a broader level I will argue that while theorists of 'the precariat' such as Standing and others have indeed considered that volunteerism in its conventional sense 'should be called work and be built into our sense of occupation' (Standing, 2021), there has not as yet been a full understanding of the unprecedented role that the new generation of activists volunteers has filled, and how they have now become defined as part of what Standing calls the 'dangerous' precariat – not only performing key functions outside the established workforce, but also as I will describe here, in the process laying foundations for a radical shift in alliances between a number of other disenfranchised cohorts and communities.

13.2 A New Definition of Humanitarianism

Humanitarian aid as a term has tended to be historically associated with the operation of western NGOs and charitable organisations in the global south. More recent scholars (Agier, 2011; Fassin, 2011) have argued that much of its underlying rhetoric – the 'us and them' and other notions it embodies of separation and difference – have their roots in neo-colonialist attitudes. Robin Vandevoordt argues:

No matter how benevolent its intentions, [traditional] humanitarian support always carried with it an element of repression. As benefactors are assumed to have the resources and expertise those receiving aid are lacking, the latter tend to be reduced to bodies that need to be fed, cared for or represented by others. (Vandevoordt 2019, p. 246)

By implication, while poorer or war-ravaged countries have been seen as suitable recipients of this kind of aid, the inhabitants of affluent western donor countries have been considered to be 'above' the need for this kind of intervention (hence the reluctance of Europe to allow INGOs to set up 'camps', with the word's seemingly shameful connotations, within its own borders). But in recent years as western governments have signally failed to fully respond to crises at home, and traditional aid agencies more used to operating in the global south struggled to adapt and function in their home states (Borton, 2016), it was left to a mass mobilisation of ordinary citizens to step in – and the manner in which they did this, I argue, has changed the values of the term: because these new humanitarians not only provided aid, but equally sought to question the establishment on its failures, and act, as Vandevoordt describes (ibid.) in solidarity with those they sought to help – hence he calls them 'subversive volunteers', and in my recent study (Clayton, 2020) I call them 'activist volunteers'. As I will detail below, their innovative approaches to humanitarian work expanded the base of civic volunteering to include more diverse groups and communities – but at the same time, increased the precariousness of the task. While these factors can be seen at play in all the events cited above, they are particularly clear in the case of the 'Refugee Crisis' where nearly two million people reached Europe to face in many cases extreme neglect and abuse by state actors, and would have perished if this humanitarian force had not exerted itself in radical new ways.

13.3 The European Refugee Crisis

From the summer of 2015 to spring 2020 (when the COVID-19 pandemic slowed numbers), conflicts in Syria and crises in Afghanistan, Iraq, Sudan, Eritrea, and elsewhere brought almost two million asylum seekers on perilous journeys to a Europe which, far from offering them safety and security, in large part proved unwilling or unable to accommodate them. With the main exception of Angela Merkel's Germany, the official line of many other European states ranged from indifference to open hostility. The new arrivals, having in many cases already faced war and violence, abuse by traffickers, and near-drowning at sea, were met on arrival by closed borders, police aggression, the abuse of many of their human rights, and lack of the most basic food or shelter. Subsequent EU deals with Turkey and Libya, along with the peremptory closing of borders to refugees in many Balkan states and between, for instance, Italy and France, led to hundreds of thousands of forced migrants remaining trapped to this day at European borders or in city ghettos without support.

But set against this harsh (and frequently unlawful) regime, and against a great deal of mass media and party-political hostility, there was in equal measure a broad public reaction of concern, triggered particularly by media images of mass shipwrecks in the Mediterranean, and of children such as three-year-old Alan Kurdi, who drowned off the coast of Turkey in September 2016. This concern translated into an extraordinary mobilisation, described in my book *The New Internationalists: Activist Volunteers in the European Refugee Crisis* (2020) as the largest civic mobilisation since the Second World War. The mobilisation embraced a wide spectrum of individuals, breakaway groups from existing organisations, and new grassroots formations, and included initiatives by many of the new arrivals themselves.

As an example, mobilisations in the UK included self-organised faith groups from local churches, Quaker and Jewish communities, and mosques; it included those from professional groups who formed their own breakaway organisations like Doctors without Borders and Social Workers without Borders. Trades Unions such as NEU (National Education Union) formed refugee support groups, many under the banner of Stand Up to Racism, an organisation active in many unions. There were groups based on specific political ideologies like the anarchist group No Borders. Other initiatives formed out of solidarity movements with particular countries, like Are you Syrious which was concerned with issues faced by Syrian refugees. Some were at the intersection of several concerns – like Dirty Girls of Lesvos, a UK women's group that also focussed on environmental issues (witnessing UNHCR distributing single-use blankets to those sleeping outdoors on Lesvos, Dirty Girls set up laundries to re-use such a vital supply, and minimise waste in the makeshift camps). Beyond hundreds of such collective initiatives, tens of thousands of UK individuals, like their European counterparts, simply showed up and found their way into actions on the ground, or formed their own associations via the burgeoning social media networks that sprang up, like People to People Solidarity, Donate4Refugees and Mobile Refugee Support. It is estimated (Clayton, 2020) that over two hundred thousand European citizens organised to rescue those at sea abandoned by official EU Frontex 'rescue forces'; or to greet the new arrivals, provide emergency medical care, and find or make them shelter and food – often dealing with thousands of new arrivals a day. They fundraised at home, sourced food, tents, medical aid and supplies, and ferried these to the camps and borders. They built whole settlements, medical centres, schools and creches, and set up legal advice centres and many more support services and activities. And increasingly they campaigned along with the new arrivals to secure their rights and a sustainable future, when none seemed possible. Researching this topic, I gathered hundreds of volunteer testimonies which provide insight into the precarity of their work. I was able to elicit particularly nuanced and considered responses because I myself was also engaged in volunteer practice, and that connection fostered a sense of trust and solidarity. Below I quote from these testimonies, as well as my own direct experience of the camps, focusing not so much on what their stories tell us about the refugees themselves, but on the volunteers' own practices – looking at what this unique social mix of people generated, what challenges they faced, and how exploring these challenges and dangers, might help us better understand this movement and might consolidate its work to remain sustainable in the longer term.

13.3.1 First Responders: Facing the Unknown

The suddenness of the crisis – its intensity and scale, and the way it was instantly politicised by European governments and media – meant that from the beginning, those 'giving aid', whether in person or by donating, had to operate in a different frame of reference: one that was considerably more complex and demanding than the conventional donating or joining established groups. The first wave of volunteers were local citizens who responded to those arriving quite literally on their doorsteps. Greek island resident Yannis translates the contribution of his mother Katina, who lived in a village on the island of Samos, a popular crossing point from Turkey. Like many of the of these early responders Katina was an older person, living a very isolated rural life and without emergency aid infrastructure, but as a former refugee herself (her military father had sought sanctuary for his family in Syria in the years after the 1948 Greek civil war) she considered herself compelled to respond. Katina went daily to the beach to find greet the arrivals, she did first aid, she cooked, she had people stay in her home. She had to process a great deal of death and distress, but was shunned by many in her community, and her work went all but unrecognised by local authorities.

In 2015, 2016, it was a lot of people. One time, 22 boats came in one day. My mother Katina always had an open heart, and would offer welcome to whoever came. When they would come in the night-time, the boats would overturn coming in, they were crying for help, so it was also traumatic. One night in a storm, a small boat came in and many died. One little girl was left alone, calling for her mother, who never came. Eleven people survived the wreck but thirteen died, most of them women and children ... Katina would go down to the beach every day and bring the new arrivals whatever she could – milk, water, cake, biscuits. In the beginning she would try the police, the Coastguard, but they usually never came. Nobody asked her, 'Do you need help?', nobody asked her anything. Since Doctors Without

Borders came to the island, she got their number and she called them to pick up people. She doesn't get any other support, so she always helps alone, not from the neighbours either because they are afraid.

On the small remote Italian island of Lampedusa – nearer the shores of North Africa than to Italy itself – Lillo Maggiore had a similar experience of being disregarded by Italian authorities as he offered aid.

I will tell you about Bakeri. I met him on the main road of Lampedusa. He was alone, he was ten years old and came from Eritrea. He had a throat infection and struggled to speak. I said 'Come home with me, you need warm liquids, my wife will make you tea and a soup.' He accepted right away. For about 20 days, he came daily to our house. He was showing affection and the feelings were mutual; so we asked him whether he would consider staying to live with us. He was thrilled; a life with a family and the possibility to go back to school.... We contacted social services to become his foster family; we presented our case to the Tribunal of Minors of Agrigento. We managed to stall his transfer from the Hotspot [holding-place for new arrivals] to the mainland to buy time, while waiting for the court to process our application. But one morning he was forced to board a ship; witnesses reported his resistance and desperation. The authorities ignored his protests. He was taken away from us without a word; we never knew what went wrong or where he was taken.

Local responders on the Greek and Italian islands were later nominated for numerous humanitarian awards (UNHCR, 2016; Africanews 2017), but such citations rarely acknowledged the overwhelming commitment local people had made in terms of their working time and physical resources, and the hostility they experienced from both within their own communities, and from state authorities.

Those at distance from the points of arrival of arrivals also encountered political opposition as they struggled to find their modus operandi. Jess and her family began a large-scale donations operation from South West England.

My mum and I decided to get some donations together to send to Lesvos. We ended up sending containers out, my mum raising funds and me setting up our social media, and arranging donation collection and shipping. We send containers to Lesvos and to Syria. The word 'volunteering' doesn't quite encompass the nose-to-the-grindstone graft that went on. And the backlash from British people towards us on social media was horrific – complete hatred directed at us through Facebook and on our message board.

We were accused of funding terrorism, of being responsible for deaths that occur because of terrorism and (as far as I can gather) the downfall of British society.... Later I went to Lesvos with more aid and visited the Moria camp. That was very difficult because of how hopeful everyone is when they arrive, how happy they are to be in Europe. As by then I had seen people at the other end of their journey in Calais, how they had been battered by our European nations, and I really struggled knowing what was in store for everyone. I found the whole situation extremely challenging.

As we shall see, the challenges were not only structural and physical, but psychological too.

13.3.2 New Organisations: On the Front Line

Countless new unofficial organisations – like Sea of Solidarity, Peope2People, the Pipka camp on Lesvos and Lighthouse Relief – formed in great haste to meet the overwhelming demand as thousands upon thousands arrived to the Greek islands during this period. Further north, national borders became congested along the Balkan route as borders began closing; and the impromptu, officially unrecognised, Calais camp – known as 'the Jungle' – was at its height in 2016–17 home to 10,000 displaced people. Some heard about groups like Refugee Youth Service (RYS), Refugee Community Kitchen (RCK), and Refugee Women's Centre in Calais through social media, and went to join. Others headed to these places of danger alone. Shakir, himself originally a refugee, talks about the vital but entirely unofficial and unregulated role he chose to fill as an independent volunteer in the Jungle:

I am a nurse from Pakistan with eight years of professional experience. I was living in the Calais Jungle and providing a medical service for the people who were living there. There were several medical charities, including Médecins Sans Frontières, who provided services for refugees from 9 am until 5 pm. After they had finished their working day, there was no one available to help during an emergency and so this is when I was most needed. I normally did this work alone, without professional assistance. Regarding the police, there were many occasions when they used tear-gas against the refugees, and even rubber bullets. Tear-gas is indiscriminate and spreads over hundreds of metres. Every time it is used, it affects many people in the vicinity, including families with children. This was an unacceptable use of force against innocent people. If the wind had blown the tear- gas partly away, rubber bullets would be fired … I have treated people who have been injured in the head and in the face, and who have been beaten with sticks by the police, who have been pepper-sprayed, and who have been bitten by police dogs. The police and the CRS (French riot police) have become hardened and are blind to the suffering of the refugees, and behave with aggression and force as a routine. The injuries I have seen are not part of peacekeeping, crowd control or self-defence: I would describe them as grievous bodily harm. I was at personal risk when I helped people in these situations, and I often had to move through the gas myself. I was also hit with a rubber bullet in my chest.

I will discuss later how state forces came to target the volunteers themselves as they stood increasingly in solidarity with the new arrivals. Meanwhile we see how the new grassroots organisations developed the best they could, as volunteers struggled with the numbers and the seeming impossible scale of their task. Pru Waldorf arrived in Samos in 2015:

Samos had thousands of people arriving each month and the there was no official provision of anything; a small team of local women had been doing their best to feed and clothe everyone, but the situation had escalated beyond their control. We arrived in the midst of this. Thousands were being forced to sleep on the concrete floor of the ferry port. Many had no coats or shoes, and the temperatures were dropping and there was torrential rain most nights. It was filthy and completely shocking. Small children slept on the hard concrete with no shelter. There was no government-funded provision of food, water, or shelter, and no medical care. Just a handful of volunteers, some who stayed for months, others who came for a matter of days or weeks. I was in a team co-ordinating distributions of clothing and essential items to people arriving on the island. Numbers were building up as the ferry failed to leave and arrivals kept coming. We also helped with food distribution: thousands of people queued in the worsening weather long into the night to receive a bowl of stew and bread. It was a truly terrifying time. My initial two-week 'recce' became three months before I had even realised that the time had passed. I arrived in September and reluctantly went back home for a break in December to organise a large collection of aid. By January 2016 I was back on Samos again and I was there for the rest of that year.

Waldorf's commitment – she has now completed years of further work since that first Samos visit – is a common pattern in this new sector (Berry-Hart, 2018). There is no doubt that many shared moments – cooking and eating together; engaging the children in play and games; the sense of achievement in collectively building shelters and bringing some normality and hope to people who sorely needed it – has had huge rewards and a sense of collective achievement for all who committed to do this work. Spirits were often high, and there was a constant adrenalised rush of activity around aiding survival, that became to many of us almost addictive. But in the context of our topic here, it is also important to reflect on the drawbacks, the dangers, and the precarity of the work, to ensure that it can be more sustainable in the future.

13.3.3 The Long Haul: Economic, Domestic, and Psychological Challenges

For those who committed be permanently based or do regular stints at borders and in unofficial makeshift camps, living and working conditions were, and remain, extremely irregular. Firstly there was a lack of basic accommodation, with many sleeping in tents and trailers through all weathers. Most volunteers heavily subsidised their own travel and living costs, and lacked any level of pay, and especially the early years, training or structured work conditions. Many were also juggling family and other commitments back at home – particularly as it was estimated that around 80 per cent of volunteers were women, likely to have greater childcare responsibilities and less long-term career security (New Humanitarian, 2019). In addition, as I have discussed elsewhere (Clayton, 2017), women tend to be regarded especially by the younger arrivals as mother figures or mother substitutes, and so they feel an additional burden of responsibility – one that is hard to discharge given the constant flux and chaos of the unofficial camps. All these tensions inflected the development of the new volunteer work in complex ways, both social and psychological. Sarah, who went to volunteer at the Grande-Synthe camp near Dunkerque, says:

> You have to understand, I am no one special – no real skillset, quite a judgemental and very bad-tempered person! ... but I do believe in right and wrong. When not physically at Grande-Synthe I was permanently attached to my phone organising aid, donations, meetings, volunteers, sorting food aid, packs of toiletries and so on. My entire family was being neglected but not deliberately ... my kids were proud of me but resentful too. They were quite young but I felt guilt when I wasn't at Grand-Synthe. The people's lives in camp became mine – their despair, their joy, their pain – all became

mine. I stopped sleeping. Mild panic attacks started – immense guilt and the feeling I was not good enough. Not a good enough mum, wife, daughter, friend, volunteer, translator ... it started to get worse. My family were getting cross. Old neighbours in France who I thought were friends, unfriended me on Facebook – cute dog stories were fine, but real pain and anguish in northern France – oh no! I was living and breathing the worst situations I couldn't even imagine happening to human beings in Europe. When the Grand-Synthe camp was moved from Basroch to La Linière [and a local French grassroots organisation formally appointed to run it], I made the decision to take a step back. It was the hardest decision of my life. One of my girls was presenting with serious mental health issues, we were broke, and my youngest started to get separation anxiety.

Sandra Uselli, working with the Italy Refugee Crisis Database, talks about the effect of income insecurity and how it began to undermine her. Clearly with huge regret, she writes:

I can't spend any more time on unpaid activities. If we, the volunteers, become as hopeless as the refugees we support, we can't be of any help any more. Most independent volunteers work full-time, not just eight hours a day but a lot more, so they don't have time to do other work to cover their costs. As nation states and NGOs step back, we now represent the new humanitarian stakeholders, and we have for several years now – those who get involved no matter what, who totally dedicate themselves, are not afraid of stepping on important people's toes, but also those who inevitably will end up like me.

Those who kept going faced high levels of stress. D.E, a young woman volunteering independently in the Calais Jungle, describes many moments of achievement and comradeship, but she also emphasises how conditions affected her ability to function:

Last night a volunteer's van was broken into during the night. This van was parked exactly where I usually park my van ... I realise quite a continuous feeling I have here, is feeling trapped in my breathing. I don't know if this is something environmental, because of the unhealthy air (plastic burning, asbestos in the ground, factories on either side and regular tear-gas showers), or because it is something emotional and internal – I feel anxious a lot of the time here.

Polly Martin, a volunteer from Denmark who has worked with many groups including Calais Action and A Home For Winter, further considers issues of mental and physical vulnerability, and the need for internal support within the new organisations:

There is a lot of emphasis put on the fact that we're working 'for a greater good'. To that end, many people keep on working in situations that are mentally damaging to them and lack the support of senior staff or from mental health professionals. There is a sense that one should not complain if one is struggling, as the refugees and asylum seekers we are helping have it worse than we do. This is an overarching theme that I have seen time and time again whilst working in London, Calais and Athens with various different organisations. Many volunteers push themselves, both mentally and physically, meaning they then render themselves ill and unable to do their jobs to their full capacity. It is very rare that volunteers have a mental health support worker to whom they can turn to in times of need. I have found this to be the biggest challenge within this field and ultimately many volunteers suffer from anxiety, depression, PTSD and other illnesses. Many go untreated for long periods of time and many self-medicate with alcohol and drugs amongst others. I realise this is a very bleak outlook, however for grassroots organisations to function there needs to be better support for its volunteers. If we are unable to help ourselves we are not best placed to help others and it leads to a psychological vicious circle which is difficult to escape.

As the initial 2015 mobilisation consolidated over the following five years, some grassroots groups did respond to the need for better working conditions, volunteer training, and welfare. For example, Calais Action developed a 'buddying' system where volunteers talked and listened to each other every day. The Auberge des Migrants appointed a volunteer welfare support worker, and pioneered sessions with the Refugee Resilience Collective, a group of volunteer therapists who visited Calais on a rota basis from the UK. But the reality remained that the 'rescue' task put onto these volunteers – or the task they elected for ideological and moral reasons to take on – was so large that it always threatened to take priority over self-care and support. This level of public crisis, with nearly two million new arrivals in five years, was historically unique; and not only did the established large NGOs find themselves unable to operate by their old rules (due to lack of nation states' support; overwhelming numbers, and increasing police violence), but also the guidelines their sector had established around wellbeing and sustainable practices, could not always be embraced or applied by these newer mobilisations. For instance, the traditional overseas NGO practice of regular paid respite time off was not an option for those in Europe not paid at all; and the collective nature of most of these new ventures meant that many volunteers also bore the constant burdens and risks of shared management, as well as fulfilling demanding daily work or 'employee' functions. But more than that, as Tess Berry-Hart writes (Berry-Hart, 2020), the new solidarity to which I referred earlier, has changed the landscape of inter-volunteer, and volunteer-refugee relationships, and blurred many traditional working boundaries. For instance, as Berry-Hart describes, in the Calais Jungle some volunteer aid groups chose to wear tabards to make themselves recognisable in camp, and possibly protect their own safety, while others thought wearing a uniform of any kind contributed to an unhelpful 'us and them', a sense of 'othering' the new arrivals. She also discusses how many volunteers thought it was 'othering' to keep a professional distance and to decline to be involved in personal relationships with the arrivals. And she describes how many, as we shall see in the next section, took larger political actions in support of the arrivals, contravening old laws and challenging new ones: they chose to expose themselves to extreme precarity in ways that no traditional governmental or NGO paid employee would or could ever do. So we see that the collapsing of many traditional boundaries between 'us and them' helped set the stage for broader and very necessary political change, and a re-appraisal of some 'first-world' values around aid. But it also brought about difficulty and confusion in finding new working practices, and in protecting both the new arrivals and those on whom they came to depend for care and support.

13.3.4 The Context of Trauma, and Finding Resilience

A novel insight I discovered during my research – something also echoed in Good Chance Theatre's *verbatim* play The Jungle (Murphy and Robertson, 2018) which was the result of grounded research in the camp – was an understanding of just how many of those who responded to the refugee crisis, did so from a position of being themselves marginalised in some way: including those who were or had been refugees themselves, or who had unsecure citizen status; those who identified with trauma and suffering because they had parallel experiences; or had suffered discrimination on the grounds of gender, religion or race. Sarah Mardini, discussed further late in this chapter, is one of the most celebrated volunteers. A Syrian refugee-turned-rescuer, she is celebrated because of her bravery both in the rescues she effected (Al-Jazeera, 2021), and in her decision to return to the Greek islands as a volunteer rather than enjoy settled status and a University education in Germany. Mardini exemplifies this drive for many who have been through precarious and traumatic stages in their own lives, to work through their own feelings of vulnerability and powerlessness as they come to the aid of others, and fight to resist the brutality they all suffered.

Like Mardini, Majida was also a refugee from Syria who then became a volunteer. She arrived first in Samos and lived in the newly established Vathy camp, where she began to volunteer with the group Friendly Human and later the Red Cross. Majida was inspired by collective moments and the coming together of diverse groups. She says:

Every day is challenge for me, to learn how I can became stronger and I don't lose my mind or my life, for my mother's sake, before everything in my life…. The worst challenge was in Syria when I was taken to the jail and I met somebody who was torturing prisoners; he was absolutely unforgettable. What made me want to help was my craving to heal from what I had been through when I was in Syria. Pain, grief, scarcity … to feel that I even still had a life. When no one and nothing can help me, only myself, then giving the others what they need helped me to carry on living. Because I identify myself with them. We came from the same pain, the same wars. We are mirror of each other.

It is clear how vital the human-contact side of volunteering was to Majida's own sense of survival, as well as others' – and how the dissolved boundaries between volunteers and refugees was for her extremely important and liberating. Majida goes on:

I offered translation services, and to teach the children in the camp, and I did entertainment for children…. My best activity was coffee night where all people sat and talked to each other in a friendly way, with a cup of tea or coffee. They listened to their favourite music. We made a creative project with Max, an artist from America. That was very amazing and creative experience for me, because I was equal to them and we gave to the people some power.

Again we see the importance here for those with little to anchor their lives, in forming these bonds; where they may risk re-traumatisation, but despite this, opt for a continued attempt to engage with the very conditions that cause their own trauma. Majida, like Sarah Mardini and a number of other refugees after they finally get status, chose to stay on the islands and continue the work she began there when still an asylum-seeker; she works as a translator and supports refugee families. From her and others' wisdom, many of us working as volunteers learned to focus not on the victimhood and suffering of the new arrivals, but on their resilience and their deeper understanding of the significance of their journeys. So while volunteering may have exacerbated the trauma many had already faced in whatever form, perhaps the seeds of resilience, and hope for a more sustainable future can be found in this practice too. Initiatives such as the Refugee Solidarity Summit (2020), which in January 2020 brought together over 800 international volunteers who had worked across Europe during the previous five years, made a long-term commitment to prioritise not only self-care for volunteers, but also to find ways where refugee voices and views can be given greater authority in steering volunteer activities and processes. Marta Lodola, who has worked across Europe and particularly in Athens, describes her progress of marginality as follows:

> The biggest challenge for me was with myself. On multiple occasions what I heard and saw upset me deeply, and I had to learnt to listen and at the same time to be able to process this information without wounding my spirit. Wounding indeed, because every time I listened to certain experiences of inhumanity it was as if part of me could not accept that men could do this to fellow men. The other side of me was totally wrathful, unable to think … I believe that the first year forced me to confront this shortcoming, this sensitivity of mine which then turned to strength, witnessing in the activation of the project something unique and unrepeatable. To be able to create a more heterogeneous community of people who can share these things, was for me a great victory.

13.3.5 State Violence: The Price Paid by Volunteer Communities

As well as facing the challenges outlined above, the volunteer workforce has found itself subject to increasingly harsh legal penalties for its activities saving lives at sea and at borders, or offering food, shelter, and support to people on the move (Amnesty, 2020). A report by the Institute of Race Relations cited over 250 cases across Europe of the criminalisation of volunteers, the majority being cited as human smuggling crimes (IRR, 2018). Perhaps the most concerning of these from a legal and human rights perspective is the issue of sea rescues. In 2014 the EU's maritime rescue force Mare Nostrum was replaced by the more punitive Frontex mission, whose job was more to repel arriving boats than to rescue those in distress (Heller and Pezzani, 2017). In response, fleets of volunteer rescue boats run by groups like Jugend Rettet and Médecins Sans Frontières began patrolling the Mediterranean coast, and have since been responsible for saving many thousands of lives, while fighting off legal attacks by European states (The Guardian, 2020). In 2019 Carola Rackete, captain of the volunteer ship *Sea-Watch-3*, was refused permission to land in Italy with forty rescuees on board. As the ship ran short of water and supplies she feared for the survival of her passengers, and docked at Lampedusa, where she was convicted of people-smuggling and faced a twenty-year jail sentence. (This was ultimately overturned on appeal.) Two further cases are currently being brought – in Italy against the crew of the *Iuventa,* another volunteer rescue mission, and in Greece against volunteers Sean Binder and Sara Mardini (discussed earlier in this chapter) – all of whom face up to twenty years in prison for effecting rescues at sea (Reuters, 2021). EU and national European laws are meant to uphold the United Nations' 'Declaration on Human Rights Defenders' adopted in 1998, but many EU states have sought to make an example of the sea-rescue missions, calling them the 'Libyan taxi service' as they're accused of aiding the passage of those leaving the torture camps of Libya. Volunteer ships are now frequently impounded in Italy, Spain, and Malta, while the Frontex ships remain in port.

Land-borders within Europe have also become sites of precarity for both refugees and their volunteer supporters, as many European states closed their borders to migrants – several in breach of EU protocols – which led to people attempting highly dangerous crossings. The support group La Roya Citoyennes have been regularly harassed by police and arrested for leading people safely through the lethal Alpine mountain passes, where many had previously got lost and died of exposure (Al-Jazeera, 2017). In 2017, local farmer Cedric Herrou was arrested in and heavily fined for leading eight people to safety and shelter, though as in Rackete's case, the court upheld his appeal, claiming that the principle of fraternity in the French constitution specifically 'confers the freedom to help others, for humanitarian purposes, regardless of the legality of their presence on national territory' (New York Times, 2018). In Calais, UK volunteer 'M' was concerned that many refugee minors had a legal claim to UK protection, but paradoxically their case could only be heard if they were present in the UK, which would involve them making the perilous illegal crossing by stowing away, or by sea, risking injury and death. He made the decision to transport several young people when he travelled back to the UK by car. He faces a jury trial and likely long jail sentence in the UK in 2021 for trafficking charges 'for gain', even though the evidence shows he was clearly not exploiting the young people or benefitting financially.

As well as effecting rescues, the new movement has what in the end may turn out to be its most significant role – but again one hedged with danger from a legal and human rights point of view. This involves their role in witnessing and reporting day-to-day abuses and using these to challenge the law. Grassroots evidence has time and again reported the regular abuse of human rights principles and obligations that are supposed binding upon European states (Guardian, 2021). In Greece, the volunteer group Disinafux documented state's failure to provide food or shelter after a fire destroyed the Moria camp on Lesvos in 2020, when thousands of families including young children were banned from the town and forced to sleep for days outdoors in a graveyard: In this process thirty-three NGO workers and independent volunteers were indicted for supporting a the protest against this (BBC, 2020). In the Balkan states, volunteers also monitor illegal border pushbacks, where police and army forces in Croatia, Serbia, and Bosnia and Herzegovina use extreme violence on refugees. Volunteers are prevented from recording these incidents, are attacked by police, and have had cameras destroyed. In Calais, the aggressive regime used against refugees by the town's Mayor Natacha Bouchart, and the French riot police (CRS) was extended to volunteers: in 2017 Bouchart made it a criminal offence to offer food or shelter to an undocumented migrant, and the CRS and local police have both attacked volunteers and held them in detention for recording this violence. The fact that the UK government part-funds this security operation at Calais should be of particular concern. Volunteer protests against increasingly draconian asylum policies in the UK have been met with harsh sentencing – as in the case of the 'Stansted 15' whose peaceful anti-deportation airport protest resulted in them being found guilty in 2018 of a terrorist change that carried a maximum of twenty years in jail. It took over two years for their sentences to be commuted and their appeal to be upheld in the High Court (Amnesty, 2021).

13.4 Facing the Future: The Need for Intra-Community Support and Care

In sum, the refugee volunteer community – which intersects and has much in common with other new forms of humanitarian activism – has faced challenges which are not widely evidenced by the European governments or populist mainstream media: it has suited both to continue 'othering' the 'foreign invasion' of refugees (Baker, 2020) and render invisible, or play down the vital and challenging support role that the volunteers fulfil – a role that many argue should have been assumed by governments themselves. I hope here I have begun to identify some of the characteristics of this new kind of care that volunteers both offer, but ultimately need to provide for themselves too, in order to sustain both communities. I have also indicated that many involved in such caring movements, already had vulnerabilities themselves, whether around legal statis, past trauma, or economic or political discrimination on grounds of their gender or ethnicity.

While such work has had in many cases critical effects on many as individuals (and on their families and dependents), there is no doubt that many benefitted from the challenges, the learning of new skills and creating of new organisations – some of which, like Help Refugees, have now become established as large-scale institutions. And there has since the initial crisis been a period of reflection and re-grouping, where lessons about personal precarity are, as far as is feasible, being applied. Thus the notion of self-care, and claiming respect and recognition for this work as a 'job' (– a job that, after all, many argue that nation states should have been doing –) is now more widely acknowledged in this movement, and will greatly aid its long-term sustainability. And the taking on board of a notion of collective resilience (Hughes et al., 2020) which I argue here was learnt in many ways from the new arrivals themselves, has been a positive force for change. In addition, while groups have been geographically very separated and isolated, online platforms such as Volunteer Support Group and People2People Solidarity have provided valuable support and discussion, which has helped de-stigmatise commonly held feelings of survivor guilt, vicarious trauma, stress and burnout that has dogged this mobilisation. In these practices, there are important connections and parallels with movements I mentioned at the beginning of this chapter.

For instance, the 'refugee volunteers' were among the first to respond to the London's 2017 Grenfell Tower fire, and provided holistic support for survivors – including immediate material aid, and listening, and support in the ensuing campaigns for an investigation. The climate change movement Extinction Rebellion has also shown concern for the well-being of those involved in effectively full time activity (Clayton, 2021). Concerns around survival and sustainability have also been raised in the Black Lives Matter movement, and in those protesting the UK government's COVID-19 policies and providing vital voluntary services during the COVID crisis. Perhaps as a result of all these initiatives of the last five years, 'care' as a critical term has been widely taken up in new contexts, as evidenced in a spate of new critical writing (Care Collective, 2020; Santos, 2020). It is clear that this wider attention to the concept of care, in both the personal and societal sense, has been both informed by – and informs – the future of real social change, and needs further work and critical investigation. In the context of the wider political framework, the volunteers' challenges to state and EU immigration policies have a better chance of success as these diverse new movements increasingly work together, to establish common interests and goals around race, ethnicity, environment, asylum, human rights, and progress towards a fairer and more robust democracy where all, including marginalised, voices can be amplified and heard.

References

Africanews (2017) *Italy: Lampedusa mayor wins top UNESCO prize for welcoming migrants.* www.africanews.com/2017/04/20/italy-lampedusa-mayor-wins-top-unesco-prize-for-welcoming-migrants// Accessed 25.05 .2021

Agier, M. (2011). Managing the Undesirables. *Refugee Camps and Humanitarian Government.* London: Polity Press.

Al-Jazeera (2017) *France Prosecuting Citizens for Crimes of Solidarity.* www.aljazeera.com/features/2017/1/25/france-prosecuting-citizens-for-crimes-of-solidarity Accessed 04. 06. 2021.

Al-Jazeera (2021) Syrian 'Hero' Swimmer among Dozens Facing Trial in Greece. www.aljazeera.com/news/2021/11/17/activists-in-greece-face-charges-for-assisting-incoming-refugees

Amnesty (2020) *Europe: People helping refugees and migrants risk jail as authorities misuse anti-smuggling laws.* www.amnesty.org/en/latest/

news/2020/03/europe-people-helping-refugees-and-migrants-risk-jail-as-authorities-misuse-anti-smuggling-laws/ Accessed 25.05.2021.

Amnesty (2021) *Stansted 15 tell their Story through Film.* www.amnesty.org.uk/stansted-15-tell-their-story-through-film

Baker, T. A (2020). The Othering of Migrants has Negative Consequences for Society at Large in https://blogs.lse.ac.uk/brexit/2020/08/19/the-othering-of-migrants-has-negative-consequences-for-society-at-large/

BBC (2020) Moria migrants: Fire destroys Greek camp leaving 13,000 without shelter. www.bbc.co.uk/news/world-europe-54082201 Accessed 25.05.2021.

Berry-Hart, T. (2018). People to People: The Volunteer Phenomenon in Refugee History. http://refugeehistory.org/blog/2018/6/19/people-to-people-the-volunteer-phenomenon

Berry-Hart, T. (2020). Flashpoint: Calais In Clayton, S (ed) *The New Internationalists: Activist Volunteers in the European Refugee Crisis.* London: Goldsmiths Press.

Borton, J. (2016). The Humanitarian Impulse: Alive and Well among the Citizens of Europe. *Humanitarian Exchange*, 67. London: Overseas Development Institute.

Burck, C., Corrie, J. and Hughes, G. (2020). The Endeavour Towards Wellbeing In Clayton, S (ed) *The New Internationalists: Activist Volunteers in the European Refugee Crisis.* London: Goldsmiths Press.

Care Collective (2020) *Care Manifesto: The Politics of Interdependence.* London: Verso.

Clayton, S. (2017). Narrating the Young Migrant Journey: Themes of Self-Representation In Clayton, S, Gupta, A and Willis, K (eds.) *Unaccompanied Child Migrants: Identity, Care and Justice.* UK: Policy Press.

Clayton, S. (2020). *The New Internationalists: Activist Volunteers in the European Refugee Crisis.* London: Goldsmiths Press.

Clayton, S. (2021). The Future of Protest: How Smartphones and Digital Apps are Transforming Activist Movements In Zylinska, J (ed) *The Future Of Media.* London: Goldsmiths Press. (upcoming September 2021).

Fassin, D. (2011). *Humanitarian Reason: A Moral History of the Present.* Los Angeles: University of California Press.

The Guardian (2020) *How Rescuing drowning Migrants Became a Crime* www.theguardian.com/news/2020/sep/22/how-rescuing-drowning-migrants-became-a-crime-iuventa-salvini-italy 22nd Sept 2020.

The Guardian (2021) *Refugee rights 'under attack' at Europe's borders, UN Warns.* www.theguardian.com/global-development/2021/jan/28/refugee-rights-under-attack-at-europes-borders-un-warns Accesses 04.06.2021.

Heller, C. and Pezzani, L. (2017). Liquid Traces: Investigating the Deaths of Migrants at the EU's Maritime Frontier In De Genova, N (ed) *The*

Borders of 'Europe': Autonomy of Migration, Tactics of Bordering. USA: Duke University Press.

Hughes, G., Burck, C., and Roncin, L. (2020). Therapeutic activism: Supporting emotional resilience of volunteers working in a refugee camp In *Psychotherapy and Politics International* (vol. 18 issue 1). USA: Wiley Online Journals.

Institute of Race Relations (2018) *Investigations and prosecutions for crimes of solidarity escalate in 2018* https://irr.org.uk/article/investigations-and-prosecutions-for-crimes-of-solidarity-escalate-in-2018/ Accessed 25.05 .2021.

Murphy, J. and Robertson, J. (2018). *The Jungle (play transcript)*. London: Faber and Faber.

New Humanitarian (2019) *Celebrating women in aid: 10 stories for World Humanitarian Day*. www.thenewhumanitarian.org/news/2019/08/19/aid-women-gender-world-humanitarian-day Accessed 25. 05. 2021.

New York Times (2018) www.nytimes.com/2018/07/06/world/europe/france-migrants-farmer-fraternity.html

Refugee Solidarity Summit (2020) https://refugeesolidaritysummit.org/

Reuters (2021) *Italian magistrates set to level charges against sea rescuers, NGOs*. www.reuters.com/article/europe-migrants-italy-idUSL5N2L16NM 3rd March 2021.

Santos, F. G. (2020). Social movements and the politics of care: empathy, solidarity and eviction blockades. *Social Movement Studies,* 19(2) 125–143 London: Taylor and Francis.

Standing, G. (2021). *The Precariat: The New Dangerous Class (Covid-19 Special Edition)*. London: IB Tauris.

UNHCR (2016) *Greek volunteers receive UNHCR Nansen Refugee Award*. www.unhcr.org/uk/news/latest/2016/10/57ee19bc4/greek-volunteers-receive-unhcr-nansen-refugee-award.html Accessed 25.05.2021.

Vandevoordt, R. (2019). Subversive Humanitarianism: Rethinking Refugee Solidarity through Grass-Roots Initiatives in: *Refugee Survey Quarterly*. Oxford vol. 38.

14 | Artificial Intelligence, the Gig Economy, and Precarity

MUSTAFA F. ÖZBILGIN, NUR GUNDOGDU,
AND JAN AKALIN

14.1 Introduction

Technological changes have always transformed social, economic, and political structures and lives. Technology has been used as an instrument serving interests of different stakeholders across all contexts. There is an interplay between technological advancements and the sociopolitical context, which cogenerates unique outcomes and significant impacts on different communities and possibilities of technological innovation (Schwartz and Thompson 1990; Pfaffenberger 1992). Internet technology was introduced in the United States in the Cold War era in the early 1960s as a military research technology in competition against the Russian military infrastructure (Castells 2002). Since its introduction, internet technology has evolved to permeate every aspect of social, political, and economic life internationally. Notably, in the last four decades, we are going through such significant changes, partly due to the emergence and advent of internet technology–enabled businesses (Gomez-Uranga et al. 2014). Despite the widespread impact of internet technology in the social domain, the internet technology has started having a marked impact on domains of careers, employment, and work in the last two decades (Webster and Ivanov 2020), and an even more intensified impact on these domains with the mass adoption of artificial intelligence (AI), which supported emergence and unprecedented growth in AI-led industries, for example, AI-led gig economy, in the last decade. In this chapter, we refer to the gig economy as an economy which is enabled by technology such as the internet technology, artificial intelligence (AI), and digital platforms.

The global COVID-19 pandemic has seen both the growth and the strains of excessive demand in the digital economy (Pandey and Pal 2020). Some multinational corporations and individuals who invested in the digital economy have seen meteoric business success in this period. For example, Amazon achieved stellar growth of business and Jeff Bezos of Amazon has become the richest person in the world (Mergen and Ozbilgin 2021). However, the expansion of the digital economy has not been so lucrative for everyone involved. Some commentators reflect on the uneven nature of the impact of COVID-19 pandemic, suggesting that billionaires were the only ones who benefited from the pandemic, when the poor have gotten poorer (Kelly 2020). In fact, the explosive expansion of the artificial intelligence–enabled gig economy, the gig economy where the work process is controlled by AI systems, had an uneven impact internationally and among different groups of workers, particularly in the context of the pandemic (Umar et al. 2020; Devakumar et al. 2020). We consider the COVID-19 pandemic as a significant milestone for the growth and strain of the digital economy as national economies strive for recovery (Brewis and Ozbilgin 2013) with investment on technology-enabled platforms of the gig economy after the pandemic. In this chapter, we capture both the dark and the light side of these asymmetrical impacts that the growth of artificial intelligence and the gig economy had on different groups of workers and communities.

Previous research has been critical of the corrosive impact of internet technologies and artificial intelligence on careers, terms and conditions of work and employment across many industries, and in the gig economy in particular (Harari 2018; Frey and Osborne 2017). Most of the research to date on the interplay of technology and the socio-economic context takes a view on the precarity experienced at the individual level. In this chapter we take a structural perspective, and argue that artificial intelligence merely accentuates conditions of precarity that are inherent in systems and structures, rather than being the original source of those woes. In particular, in a national context, where there is a strong welfare system that shields individuals against precarity, AI would lead to less precarity than in a system which has no safety nets. Yet, James and Whelan (2021) argue that even in a welfare state the use of technology and ethical applications need to be monitored through accountability structures. AI is not the only cause of any precarity in the digital economy. It reproduces current precarity in the traditional working environment. In a less regulated context, AI technology could accentuate the inherent precarities, exploitative and discriminatory work practices. Therefore, AI technology–based platforms which are used in the gig economy do not have either positive or negative outcomes by themselves but show both positive and negative consequences and lead to multifaceted outcomes depending on the systems in which they are embedded. We recognise that unidirectional treatment of the impact of AI merely leads to polarisation of arguments on its impact across ideological fault lines, between defenders of technology-enabled business (Verhoef et al. 2021) and those who want to combat precarious work induced by technological advancements. We argue that precarity is only partly a condition of the AI technology–based platforms but it is also a result of the sociopolitical choices and institutional arrangements that are available for international, national, societal, organisational regulation of AI technologies and their varied impacts.

While the technology-enabled change has opened up new opportunities of work and career, it has rendered many jobs and forms of work obsolete. For example, AI-enabled taxi services, such as Uber, have opened up job opportunities for minority ethnic drivers who were excluded by traditional taxi companies (Kamasak et al. 2019, See also Chapter 8 for a detailed analysis). However, many depots of companies, such as Amazon, are now fully automated with AI technology and robotised, causing loss of jobs for the same group of workers. Resultantly, AI-led automation is predicted to cause over twenty million workers who traditionally have done the sorting, lifting and storing jobs to be replaced by robots by 2030 in international context (Cellan-Jones 2019). Transcending the duality of outcomes of AI-enabled advances in the gig economy, we offer suggestions for effective regulation in order to combat the precarity in the sector.

In this chapter, we first frame the dualistic nature of the consequences of the gig economy in terms of inclusion of atypical workers on the one hand and the rise of precarity on the other in the introduction. We provide a contextual view of the gig economy, diversity, and precarity, providing definitions of terms, and empirical evidence of the interplay between the gig economy, diversity and precarity in their particular geographic and historical contexts. In particular we focus on the way atypical workers are drawn into the gig economy in large numbers and their inclusion came at a cost to them, which lessens the impact of their exclusion from economic participation on the one hand and yet retains their precarious position in labour markets on the other. The section on theoretical framework focuses on the role of regulation in combating precarity and fostering inclusion. In the case study, we explore the interplay between AI-enabled gig economy and the logistic sector with transportation and delivery of goods, services, and food in particular. Exploring the issue in advanced economies with strong safety nets against precarity and in countries with limited measures against precarity. We provide a roadmap in which we propose a multilevel framework for better regulation of the AI-enabled gig economy in order to promote inclusion and to tackle precarity.

14.2 Background to the AI-Enabled Gig Economy, Diversity, and Precarity: A Contextual View

In this chapter, we mobilise three concepts: the AI-enabled gig economy, diversity and precarity. We provide here their definitions and present our vision of a contextual view in exploring the relationship between these three concepts. Gig economy, which is also known as "platform economy" and "sharing economy", has been defined by the UK Department for Business, Energy and Industrial Strategy Report (Lepanjuuri et al. 2018, p. 9) as "involving exchange of labour for money between individuals or companies via digital platforms that actively facilitate matching between providers and customers, on a short-term and payment by task basis". In this chapter, we focus on the AI-enabled gig economy in particular. In the context of the AI-enabled gig economy, we explore two particular outcomes: precarity and inclusion of atypical workers. Precarity and precariousness are defined as general conditions of insecurity in life, work, employment, and pay that individuals experience. Campbell and Price (2016) defined precarious work as work which subjects workers to high levels of insecurity and precariat as a class of workers who experience entrenched forms of precarity. Atypical workers are defined as individuals who come from traditionally disenfranchised, discriminated against, excluded and underrepresented groups such as women, minority ethnic, disabled, LGBT+, religious and political minorities, younger or older workers, among others (Alter 2018; Samdanis and Ozbilgin 2020). There are also typical and prototypical workers, the former are the individuals coming from relatively privileged backgrounds such as white, middle-class men. Prototypical workers are the ones who are idealised for the jobs that they do. For example, upper-class white men are often considered ideal candidates for leadership positions. Inclusion of atypical workers has been a particular achievement of the gig economy and their continued precarity remains a concern for the regulation of the gig economy.

Gig economy is a broad term which includes artists, writers, professional service workers, IT workers and drivers, couriers among others. Therefore there is marked demographic diversity among workers in the gig economy, even though the gig economy has provided inroads for a larger number of workers who were previously discouraged, excluded or kept away from economic participation. Depending on what segment of the gig economy a study is predicated on shapes the consequences of the gig economy on that particular group. For example, Petriglieri et al. (2019) study the artists, IT workers and writers, whereas Kamasak et al. (2019) examined the Uber drivers, who are predominantly minority ethnic Muslims of working class background in the UK, in their case study. The issues which were revealed in these studies reveal different insights into gig economy by ethnicity, religion, and class in particular. We, therefore, would like to caution the readers to the choice of sample in terms of socio-demographic profiles as the outcomes of studies on the impact of the gig economy is highly context-dependent.

Gig economy has both positive and negative impacts at the individual, organisational and system levels in terms of precarity and inclusion of atypical workers. Multifaceted impacts of the gig economy from the dark and the light sides vary based on what the gig economy is, timeframe, and the particular context. Below, we present the interplay of the gig economy, precarity and diversity from a multilevel contextual perspective, drawing on the relational model of Syed and Ozbilgin (2009): at the micro level, we explore the consequences of the gig economy on individual actors. At the meso level, we explore the role of organisations in the way the gig economy interfaces with precarity and diversity. The macro level elaborations focus on the national and international context, which regulates the interface of the gig economy in terms of precarity and diversity.

14.2.1 The Micro-Individual Context

The dark and the light sides of the gig economy have been discussed mostly at the individual level. The costs and benefits of gig economy on an individual working life are in the focus of discussions. Scholars have different perspectives and there is not any consensus about the impacts. In fact, most of the discussions are conceptual and empirical studies of workers in the gig economy across national contexts are limited. According to the Department of Business, Energy and Industrial Strategy report (National Audit Office, 2018), there are approximately 2.8 million gig workers in the UK. Most of these workers work as a courier, driver, and food-delivery workers.

Gig workers are often categorised in two distinct groups: gig only and gig plus. Gig only workers do not have any other job apart from their gig economy work. They do not hold any part-time and full-time organisational affiliation. While gig plus workers hold organisational affiliations as full-time- or part-time-based and use the gig economy for additional income and to develop their skills (Prudential, 2017). A US-based study among 1,491 gig economy workers, 721 of whom are gig only, indicated that gig workers have less working hours than other workers (approximately 25 hours per week) (Prudential, 2017). Therefore gig economy only workers earn less compared to full-time non-gig economy employees (approximately forty hours per week). The average annual salary of gig workers was $36,500 versus $62,700 of full-time employees in 2016. Gig only workers had less access to employer-based benefits, such as different kinds of insurance. The average age of gig only workers was forty-seven, and they were less satisfied than full-time employees; however, they had less intention to change their jobs and to switch to full-time mode of work. The report disclosed that gig workers wanted to have control over their job and not give up work flexibility. What they needed was regulating their working conditions in order to improve them. The report further highlighted that the main motivation of gig workers, who were older than fifty-six years of age, was financial; however gig workers, who were between thirty-six and fifty-five years of age, wanted to change work in the future.

Although independent professionals often enjoy autonomy in their work, content, and conditions (Pichault and McKeown 2019), absence of facilities and benefits associated with traditional working environments in the gig economy causes some emotional tensions and loss of autonomy among workers. Petriglieri et al. (2019) argue that workers experience both anxiety and satisfaction when they work in the gig economy. They craft strategies to deal with these forms of cognitive dissonance by rationalising their choices or making alternative arrangements. Gig economy workers need routines, places, social connections and meanings for the work when calculating the cost and benefits of their situations. Overall, the micro-individual context of workers in the gig economy suggests that the gig economy offers a divergent range of experiences and possibilities to workers. Depending on the particular circumstances, backgrounds and needs of individual workers, the gig economy shows divergent impacts.

14.2.2 The Meso-Organisational Context

The organisational context of the gig economy as it interfaces with precarity and diversity shows that there is a dearth of regulatory pressure on organisations. The global COVID-19 pandemic has also created conditions, which forced an expansion of the gig economy. Food and goods delivery services have grown to capture the increased demand for service as lockdowns, curfews, and quarantine arrangements prevented public travel and forced large groups of customers to turn to the gig economy for essential supplies (Almeida et al. 2020). While the dark side of the gig economy on precarity is heavily felt, some studies suggest that the impact of the pandemic led, in some cases, as expansion of job opportunities (Polkowska 2021). Studies of organisations conducted during the pandemic period show that the conditions of precarity among gig economy workers have exacerbated as they lacked the requisite institutional affiliations to qualify for furlough arrangements offered by the state and institutions. Furthermore, their terms and conditions have deteriorated in terms of health and safety due to increased traffic and demand during the pandemic and because they were often the key workers which faced customers (Rani and Dhir 2020). Jerg et al.' s (2021) comparative study between the UK, Denmark, and Germany demonstrates that the pandemic created conditions of multiple job holding in the gig economy for a large number of workers, as the demand increased but both the supply of workers and the terms and conditions of each gig position remained limited.

Yummy is a Sweden-based start-up. Its aim is to create access to economic participation for highly educated immigrant women to serve their home-cooked food to customers (Webster and Zhang 2020). The results of interviews with six highly educated immigrant women living in Sweden highlighted the importance of the gig economy in terms of intersectional labour perspective. The study reveals how the gig economy provides entrepreneurial opportunities to new immigrants. Producing at home and serving is not a new concept historically but doing this by using AI-based platforms provides opportunities to groups of workers who were excluded by traditional labour market structures. The case is not new and unique in the high-tech industry, many AI-based platforms such as Amazon, Apple, Google, and Facebook are founded by individuals, and they offer work and employment to first-, second-, or third-generation immigrants (CNBC 2018). The meso-organisational context of the gig economy illustrates that there is a strong interface between organisations in the gig economy and atypical workforce as both a possibilities of work and employment and emergent forms of precarity. Social changes create a pressure on gig platforms. Uber recently announced that the company will guarantee a minimum wage, holiday pay and pensions to its 70,000 UK drivers (BBC 2021). Although it is a significant improvement and may affect other platforms, comparative to traditional working environments, the risk of precarity still continues.

14.2.3 The Macro-Systems Context

At the macro level, the gig economy emerges as a source of precarity and inclusion for atypical workers at the nexus of economic, political, and social contexts. In particular, the interface between the welfare regimes, democratic traditions of nation states, technological advancements, structures, and resources of the gig economy and the way these are prioritised in each country shapes the way gig economy impacts on precarity and inclusion of atypical workers. Studying the gig economy across the 1980s and the 1990s in the United States, Davis and Hoyt (2020) provide evidence to show that the traditionally disadvantaged groups such as women, minority and low income workers fared poorly in the performance-related pay system in terms of health and precarity outcomes. The study calls for better regulation of the performance-related pay system in the gig economy and suggests that atypical workers are more vulnerable in a national context where the social welfare provision remains weak.

Generally unemployed or underemployed people use AI-based platforms to get income and these trends alleviate entrepreneurial activities (Burtch et al. 2018). Yet as underemployment and unemployment are structural problems which are induced by socio-economic choices and regulatory arrangements that nation states make, it is possible to question the move from unemployment and underemployment into the gig economy, with conditions of precarity, as a trend which hides the systemic nature of inequality and precarity.

During the COVID-19 pandemic, many gig economy companies have generated extensive income as the global and national level emergencies required them to expand their businesses to cover essential services. For example, Getir from Turkey is a platform-based delivery company that serves household goods and products from nearby retail outlets as well as their own outlets. Getir secured a round of funds that elevated the valuation of the firm to $850 million. Building on its success at the cost of employee precarity in Turkey, Getir recently started operations in central London (Financial Times 2021). Getir has a service provision to make deliveries in around ten minutes (Getir 2021) Getir and other Turkish delivery companies are now facing a national controversy for the precarious conditions, such as ten-minute delivery time limit that puts drivers at risk of speeding and accident, under which they employ drivers who had fatal traffic accidents in line of service, largely due to the excessive time demands that the work imposes on them. Deaths of drivers in service have increased tenfold during the COVID-19 pandemic (Gazete Vatan 2021; New York Times 2021). While the precarity of the workers is not addressed, Getir now launched a branch in London to expand its operations internationally, building on its commercial success in Turkey. In the same way, Mergen and Ozbilgin (2021) explain that in the case of Amazon and its extensive globalisation project, what remains invisible is the precariousness that Amazon subjects its workers in its value chain.

At the macro systemic level precarity in the AI-enabled gig economy remains almost hidden behind stories of global and national organisations making inroads in business and serving the revival of the economy. Therefore, we suggest that there is a need for a responsible and inclusive supply chain to involve all workforce (Koberg and Longoni 2019).

Gig economy is predominantly studied in terms of winners and losers of technological innovation and business capture. Most studies of the gig economy and precarity emanate from the North American and Western European context. Big tech companies have been at the forefront of technological changes that fostered the platform economies. In the Global North, GAFAM (Google, Amazon, Facebook, Apple and Microsoft) and in the Global South, BATX (Baidu, Alibaba, Tencent, Xiaomi) have been over-explored in terms of their work and employment practices. This over-exploration ignores the contribution and the challenges which young tech start-ups face and leaves them unattended in studies and public policy. The dominant nature of such studies of the Global North has recently generated new interest in studies of the Global South, suggesting a polarisation of experiences between countries with developed and developing systems of industrial democracy, worker, and social welfare, where the former set of countries are able to offer some degree of protection to workers in the gig economy against precarity, when compared to the latter group of countries. Without international regulation, the toxic nature of the gig economy and its precarious impacts may be entrenched deeper. Lack of institutional regulation leads to normalisation of precarity in the sector, as the sector does not experience international and national normative pressures to change towards inclusive, democratic, and equality-based practices.

14.3 Theorising Precarity and Diversity (Gender, Migration, Disability, Class) in the AI-Enabled Gig Economy

Hardin's classical work, which he refined recently (1998), on the tragedy of the commons stipulates the importance of optimum regulation of the common good for sustainability and longevity of a socio-economic and political system. Hardin argues that with no regulation and everyone holding full freedom to use the common good based on self-interest alone, the common good would soon perish. Drawing on this idea, Jonsen et al. (2013) related the tragedy of the commons theory to the management of diversity. The authors argue that effective regulation of diversity is required for sustainability of the common good. Building on the theory of the tragedy of the commons, we propose a multilevel regulatory framework that can push the agenda for better and optimum regulation of the common good which in this case is the gig economy and its extensive impact on public good. We explore regulation from multiple levels: micro-individual, meso-institutional, and meso-national and international. At the individual level, we turn to the social identity theory to explore the identity effects of both the AI and the individual identities of the atypical workers who are drawn to the gig economy. Social identity theory (Tajfel 2010) suggests that individuals are drawn to the groups, which they identify with. For atypical workers, who were excluded from traditional forms of employment, the gig economy provided a home where they could retain their social identities and seek an escape route away from discrimination (Kamasak et al. 2019). This also involves an individual responsibilisation which considers the precarity of workers. For example, there are calls for individuals not to order food of too small value during peak times to avoid death of drivers. Yet, at the individual level, the AI technology is considered often in a moral vacuum, due to its supposedly objective structure. For example, Smith et al.'s (2021) study reveals that Australian consumers were less aware of the working conditions of gig workers in the food-delivery sector, and they had less intention to improve the conditions of these gig workers. Further scrutiny of AI and digital platforms suggests that their design and implementation is imbued with traditional forms of public neglect, bias by gender, ethnicity, sexual orientation, and other categories.

One of the methodological concerns that we have regarding the micro-level treatment of precarity and gig workers is one of representation of research subjects. We note that middle-class white scholars often lead the debate on precarity of gig workers who come from different backgrounds to researchers. We caution that the sociodemographic differences between the researcher and the research subject could present a blindness to other's experience. One manifestation of such blindness occurs when academics who study precarity launch a critique of precarity and call for protests of gig economy companies on this basis, but forget that the gig economy despite its exploitative potential still offers atypical workers a chance to work, which is denied to them by traditional industries. Such blanket rejection of gig economy would merely serve to cut a lifeline of work, even if lowly paid and precarious, to atypical workers who would otherwise be excluded, underemployed, and unemployed in discriminatory labour markets. Untapped talent potential of atypical workers is exploited through the gig economy. So the debate on the exploitative potential of the gig economy should also acknowledge the problematic nature of the exclusionary and discriminatory approaches in the traditional labour market which keeps the atypical worker out.

At the meso organisational level, organisational/sectoral regulation is required if precarity is to be tackled and inclusion of workers to be achieved. Studies on diversity and inclusion suggest that voluntarism does not yield effective outcomes (Ozbilgin and Slutskaya 2017) as organisations need normative pressure from social movements (Ozbilgin and Erbil 2021) and coercive pressure from law (Tatli et al. 2012) in order to assume responsibility for most of their interventions and practices. Responsibilisation of gig economy businesses remains largely at the mercy of national-level regulations. Therefore, as we outlined above, countries where there is strong regulation against precarity and exclusion are more likely to regulate their gig economies in terms of their precarity impact. Yet, we caution that structures of equality and inclusion and combating of precarity will not necessarily be resolved through hyper-formalisation of such issues as often envisaged. Authors such as Healy and Pekerak (2020) suggest that there is a high road to dealing with precarity in the gig economy for organisations if they adopt the high road approaches that are developed for high-performance human resource management.

At the macro, national, and international levels, there is an expansion of the debate on the potential regulation for the gig economy (Novitz 2020). These debates focus on how existing universal international labour standards, fundamental principles and rights for decent work can be applied for gig workers. However, the current potential for international regulation and responsibilisation of the gig economy remains rather weak at the United Nations and other international agencies provide limited voluntary encouragement for industries to take up of democratic, progressive, and sustainable approaches. Although decent work is one of the sustainable development goals, there is limited discussion about how decent work conditions should include gig workers.

14.4 Case Study: The AI-Enabled Gig Economy and Precarity in the Food Delivery Sector

Over its brief history, the gig economy has increased the reach and opportunities both in the supply and in the demand of goods and services. In fact, the growth of the gig economy in the last ten years and with the COVID-19 pandemic could be described as meteoric; that is, while many sectors shrunk in size the gig economy grew in a spectacular way internationally. However, the unprecedented growth of the gig economy also enabled the commodification of gig economy workers at worrying levels (Katta et al. 2020). For instance, in the case of a restaurant working with Uber Eats, the supply side has increased its possible market size, while the customers have a vast choice of cuisine in reach of their thumb. The restaurant may view the platform provider as an unfair fee earner in this setting. Simultaneously, the delivery worker has emerged as nothing but a transport tool that shows up in the restaurant with a code, waiting in line with many other delivery workers. Katta et al. (2020) explain that gig workers face the challenge of dehumanisation as their work is often not fully protected by employment regulation and welfare arrangements In terms of the service provider, the delivery worker is often viewed as a commodity with an optimum level of service with strict regulation of time and service standard.

The closest worker to this atypical delivery person in the traditional economic systems would be a delivery driver for a courier company or a postal service, who has a fixed salary and a fixed route with a predetermined list of deliveries. The work has a structure and a known location and time for the end of the day. The gig economy delivery worker in the new systems has none of the above. They have to deal with the uncertainty of any decision they make because they get paid by their performance, absorbing some of the risk associated with low demand. A worker may not choose their destination and they may end up in a location that can be in an irrelevant part of town with poor demand, which offers them little income for the rest of the day. Even though Uber has the option for drivers and workers to end the day with a relevant job that will take them closer to their home, or their neighbourhood, they still have to wait for that job given to them by the AI system. So, the choice that the gig economy offers is constrained by the demand and the demand side risks are absorbed by the workers, under the illusion of worker choice.

The absence of a workday structure is only a small part of an atypical gig worker's challenge. If we also consider the security in terms of statutory workplace regulations, the uncertainty is even deeper. Any typical worker in transport or delivery could take sick leave and the employer must ensure their health and safety. But in the case of gig economy delivery workers, they are in the streets of metropolitans proven not to be safe for cyclists or motorists. The Royal Society for the Prevention of Accidents suggests that, on average, we lose 100 cyclists a year, and most injuries are not even reported (ROSPA 2020).

Even though AI-enabled gig economy companies are more efficient and have extensive transportation and logistics arms, drivers' conditions for delivery services are now raising concerns in the developed world and developing countries such as Turkey. Turkey reported that the food delivery companies such as Getir, Yemek Sepeti, and others are losing motorised staff to traffic accidents in large numbers (Evrensel 2020). With the challenges of delivering in a big city and key performance indicators like rapid delivery, the delivery workers and environment and people on their path will undoubtedly be put in danger during their commute from point A to B. In their study on delivery service gig workers, Christie and Ward (2019) found out that 42 per cent of their interview and survey participants had been involved in a collusion in the UK in traffic. The relationship between profitability of the sector and the precarity experienced by the workforce presents a contrast. There are growing concerns over how income is generated and how the income is distributed to workers and shareholders. For example, Butler (2021) identified that the Deliveroo workers could earn as small as 2 pounds per hour, which is a quarter of the national minimum hourly wage in the UK.

The AI-enabled gig economy in the food delivery service offers employment to a large number of workers, mainly from non-traditional and atypical backgrounds. At first sight, the sector appears to offer access and opportunities to individuals who are kept out of employment due to biases, discriminatory patterns, and inflexible organisation of the traditional employment and economic paths. Yet, a closer inspection of the sector reveals that most of the income generated by the AI-enabled gig economy does not return to workers and comes at a cost of precarity in the workforce.

14.5 A Roadmap: Better Regulation of the AI-Enabled Gig Economy

There are three distinct values in the gig economy enabled by AI. These are openness in terms of entry to the sector, competition with traditional sectors, and flexibility in terms of workplace practices. First value is openness and supposedly independent of location, and socio-demographic background, every member of the platform is free to join with a low barrier of entry. For instance, in the UK, low entry means that migrants with work permits could have similar chances of entry as local residents. While this openness could allow people from atypical backgrounds to join the gig economy, the individual worker is often commodified and downgraded to be a number. Anwar and Graham (2020) explain that in the case of African countries discourses of openness are actually not in benefit of the individual gig workers, but for the purposes of the company which generate a constant supply of cheaply resourced and poorly paid and treated labour.

Second, the gig economy is built on the value of internal and external competition. In this context competition is a burden carried mainly by the seller or the delivery worker. For example, a service promised in a fixed delivery time or with a refund option impacts both the seller and the delivery workers but not the platform. In essence, competition in the day-to-day operations doesn't affect the service provider in a direct manner, but only in terms of the bottom line financial gains to a certain extent. Graham and Anwar (2019) explain that workers in the African gig economy are left to look after themselves and compete against each other.

Third, flexibility is another value which supposedly drives the gig economy. However, flexibility may not be as innocuous as advertised. We need to ask the question of flexibility for whom? The main focus is the gig worker who looks for a top-up income through freelancer platforms or an individual doing his/her on-time delivery job for a couple of hours a day (Prudential 2017). However, in reality, there is another side to the story. Companies use gig workers as agency workers while the service provider is acting as a human resources agency rather than purely undertaking activities of a food provider or a restaurateur. Temporary staffing agencies, which act in a similar manner. are observed to initially increase transitional employment; however, they are also observed to exploit and reproduce structural vulnerabilities (Elcioglu 2020).

The gig economy supposedly enables openness, competition, easy entrance to the system, autonomy, and flexibility but with a considerable cost to workers as precarity. The adverse outcomes in the case of gig economy workers as delivery workers accentuated versions of precarity conditions inherited from the industry's existing structures. The precarious conditions of agency or temporary workers are amplified by so-called Food Delivery providers or freelancer platforms. Gig economy creates structural long-term problems and obstacles when they provide micro level benefits and access to their workers. Below we outline a roadmap to better regulate the AI-enabled gig economy with a view to counteract its tendency to create precarity.

AI-enabled gig economy is expanding rapidly across the globe. The impact of the gig economy is multifaceted in that it allows workers from traditionally excluded backgrounds to enjoy economic participation, when such participation often comes with precarious terms and conditions. We stipulated that better regulation could help improve the positive consequences of the gig economy and help combat the precarity it may cause. Regulation comes in multilevel and multifaceted forms, ranging from self-regulation to organisational/sectoral, societal, national, and international regulation, each of which is intricately connected to other levels. We propose regulatory measures for a roadmap as the effective regulation of the gig economy has already shown positive signs of dealing with precarity in different contexts.

We explore regulation in terms of self-regulation of the AI with values of human rights, decent work, inclusion, industrial democracy, and job security for workers at the micro level. As outlined in the earlier section, the gig economy is fast developing on values of openness, flexibility, autonomy, and inclusion, among others. However, we still need to question the real impact of these practices and add more humanising values such as industrial democracy, worker safety, equality, and fight with precarity in order to develop self-regulation of the AI-based gig economy. AI technology is criticised for destroying traditional work environments, reducing work opportunities, and requiring new skills and knowledge. One of the main points is that the cover and reach of current range of national and international regulations don't meet the needs induced by AI-based innovative disruptions. Therefore, it is important for the AI technology which leads the gig economy to have humanistic values ingrained in it so that it can regulate its own impact on workers.

At the meso level, we propose that the impact of the gig economy could be regulated by works councils, trade unions, organisational mechanisms, and identity groups at work. For example, in response to the death of almost one driver/courier per day in internet-based food delivery companies in Turkey, workers have started unionising to tackle their precarious working conditions. They are now in negotiation with the employers to demand better working conditions including extended rest times, and speed restrictions for deliveries (Evrensel 2020). We are likely to see emergence of self-organising meso-level initiatives for effective regulation of the gig economy and its likely toxic consequences.

At the macro level, we argue that the industrial relations partners such as trade unions, international bodies, the government, and employers have a role in regulating the gig economy. Furthermore, sector-specific forums and interventions could also help improve the conditions and terms for workers in the gig economy. For global companies which use extensive networks of gig economy workers across national borders, we also call for regulatory measures to curb the exploitative practices which are particularly problematic for national contexts with weak regulations against precarity at work. For example, international labour standards and principles have not been regulated to involve gig workers.

14.6 Conclusion

The gig economy presents opportunities for inclusion of atypical workers, but often at a cost of precarity for them. In this chapter we examined the complexity of this duality and provided a contextual view of the gig economy, diversity, and precarity, illustrating how the context shapes the duality of outcomes of the gig economy. As they are often excluded, discriminated against, and demarcated in the traditional sectors of work, atypical workers are drawn in the gig economy with relative ease and in large numbers. We examined in the theory section the role of welfare regimes and legal regulation in combating precarity and fostering inclusion. The case study turns to the logistic sector with transportation and delivery of goods, services, and food in particular and suggests how the sector provides access for atypical workers and yet offers precarious conditions. We provide a roadmap in which we propose a multilevel framework for better regulation of the AI-enabled gig economy in order to promote inclusion and to tackle precarity. Centrally, we argue that exploration of the gig economy, precarity, and inclusion requires an examination of the welfare regimes and regulatory systems, organisational practices, and individual experiences. Notably the nexus of welfare regimes and industrial democracy traditions of countries plays a significant role in shaping the levels of precarity that may be experienced in the gig economy.

Future research could examine the interplay of welfare regimes, industrial democracy approaches, and anti-precarity measures taken in different countries and assess their varied levels of effectiveness in inculcating inclusion of atypical workers. Most of the AI-based platforms are produced in developed countries and are used internationally. Working with the same platforms but in different countries and contexts may cause different working experiences, and challenges for workers. Future research may focus on cross-cultural comparative analysis to explore precarity and international diversity in the gig economy in this way.

References

Almeida, F., Santos, J. D., & Monteiro, J. A. (2020). The Challenges and Opportunities in the Digitalization of Companies in a Post-COVID-19 World. *IEEE Engineering Management Review*, 48(3), 97–103.

Alter, N. (2018). *The Strength of Difference: Itineraries of Atypical Bosses.* Emerald Group Publishing.

Anwar, M. A., & Graham, M. (2020). *Between a Rock and a Hard Place: Freedom, Flexibility, Precarity and Vulnerability in the gig Economy in Africa.* Competition & Change, 1024529420914473.

BBC (2021). Uber "willing to change" as drivers get minimum wage, holiday pay and pensions www.bbc.co.uk/news/business-56412397 17 March 2021; accessed at 28 March 2021

Brewis, J., & Özbilgin, M. (2013). Introducing recovery and organization. *Culture and Organization*, 19(5), 371–376.

Burgess, J., & Campbell, I. (1998). The nature and dimensions of precarious employment in Australia. *Labour & Industry: A Journal of the Social and Economic Relations of Work*, 8(3), 5–21.

Burtch, G., Carnahan, S., & Greenwood, B. N. (2018). Can you gig it? An empirical examination of the gig economy and entrepreneurial activity. *Management Science*, 64(12), 5497–5520.

Butler, S. (2021). UK Deliveroo riders can earn as little as £2 an hour, survey finds www.theguardian.com/business/2021/mar/25/some-uk-deliveroo-riders-earning-just-2-an-hour-survey-finds#:~:text=Deliveroo%20has%20said%20riders%20are,were%20paid%20less%20than%20that. March 25, 2021; accessed 5 April 2021.

Campbell, I., & Price, R. (2016). Precarious work and precarious workers: Towards an improved conceptualisation. *The Economic and Labour Relations Review*, 27(3), 314–332.

Castells, M. (2002). *The Internet Galaxy: Reflections on the Internet, Business, and Society.* Oxford University Press on Demand.

Cellan-Jones, R. (2019). Robots "to replace up to 20 million factory jobs" by 2030. URL: www.bbc.com/news/business-48760799, accessed on 28 March 2021.

Christie, N., & Ward, H. (2019). The health and safety risks for people who drive for work in the gig economy. *Journal of Transport & Health*, *13*, 115–127.

CNBC (2018). More than half of the top American tech companies were founded by immigrants or the children of immigrants www.cnbc.com/2018/05/30/us-tech-companies-founded-by-immigrants-or-the-children-of-immigrants.html May 28, 2018; accessed March 5, 2021.

Davis, M. E., & Hoyt, E. (2020). A longitudinal study of piece rate and health: evidence and implications for workers in the US gig economy. *Public Health*, *180*, 1–9.

Devakumar, D., Bhopal, S. S., & Shannon, G. (2020). COVID-19: the great unequaliser. *Journal of the Royal Society of Medicine*, 113(6), 234–235.

Elcioglu, E. F. (2020). Producing Precarity: The Temporary Staffing Agency in the Labor Market. *Qualitative Sociology*, 33, 117–136. https://doi.org/10.1007/s11133-010-9149-x

Evrensel (2020) Pandemide 160'tan fazla kurye hayatını kaybetti www.evrensel.net/haber/421490/pandemide-160tan-fazla-kurye-hayatini-kaybetti

Financial Times (2021). Turkish start-up Getir launches grocery delivery service in London. www.ft.com/content/bdb43495-fadf-4217-bc33-bc52e6f0fdd4 (Accessed at 26 March 2021)

Frey, C. B., & Osborne, M. A. (2017). The future of employment: How susceptible are jobs to computerisation? *Technological forecasting and social change*, 114, 254–280.

Getir (2021) https://getir.uk/ (Accessed at 28 March 2021)

Gómez-Uranga, M., Miguel, J. C., & Zabala-Iturriagagoitia, J. M. (2014). Epigenetic economic dynamics: The evolution of big internet business ecosystems, evidence for patents. *Technovation*, 34(3), 177–189. Chicago.

Graham, M and Anwar, M. A. (2019). The Global Gig Economy: Towards a Planetary Labour Market, *First Monday*, 24(4) doi: http://dx.doi.org/10.5210/fm.v24i4.9913.

Harari, Y. N. (2018). Why technology favors tyranny. *The Atlantic*, 322(3), 1–17.

Hardin, G. (1998). Extensions of "The tragedy of the commons". *Science*, 280(5364), 682–683.

Healy, J., & Pekarek, A. (2020). Work and wages in the gig economy: Can there be a High Road? In *The future of work and employment*. Edward Elgar Publishing.

James, A., & Whelan, A. (2021). "Ethical" artificial intelligence in the welfare state: Discourse and discrepancy in Australian social services. Critical Social Policy, 0261018320985463.

Jerg, L., O'Reilly, J., & Buschoff, K. S. (2021). Adapting social protection to the needs of multiple jobholders in Denmark, the United Kingdom and Germany. Transfer: European Review of Labour and Research, 1024258921991039.

Jonsen, K., Tatli, A., Özbilgin, M. F., & Bell, M. P. (2013). The tragedy of the uncommons: Reframing workforce diversity. *Human Relations*, 66(2), 271–294.

Kamasak, R., Özbilgin, M. F., Yavuz, M., & Akalin, C. (2019). Race discrimination at work in the United Kingdom. In *Race Discrimination and Management of Ethnic Diversity and Migration at Work*. Emerald Publishing Limited.

Katta, S., Badger, A., Graham, M., Howson, K., Ustek-Spilda, F. and Bertolini, A. (2020). (Dis)embeddedness and (de)commodification: COVID-19, Uber, and the unravelling logics of the gig economy. *Dialogues in Human Geography*, 10(2), 203–207.

Kelly, J. (2020). Billionaires Are Getting Richer During The COVID-19 Pandemic While Most Americans Suffer www.forbes.com/sites/jackkelly/2020/04/27/billionaires-are-getting-richer-during-the-covid-19-pandemic-while-most-americans-suffer/

Koberg, E., & Longoni, A. (2019). A systematic review of sustainable supply chain management in global supply chains. *Journal of Cleaner Production*, 207, 1084–1098.

Lepanjuuri, K., Wishart, R., & Cornick, P. (2018). The characteristics of those in the gig economy. Department for Business, Energy and Industrial Strategy. https://assets.publishing.service.gov.uk/government/uploads/system/uploads/attachment_data/file/687553/The_characteristics_of_those_in_the_gig_economy.pdf.

Mergen, A., & Ozbilgin, M. F. (2021). Understanding the followers of toxic leaders: Toxic illusio and personal uncertainty. *International Journal of Management Reviews*, 23(1), 45–63.

National Audit Office (2018). *Department for Business, Energy & Industrial Strategy*, www.nao.org.uk/wp-content/uploads/2018/09/BEIS-Overview-2017-18.pdf

New York Times (2021). Delivery Workers in South Korea Say They're Dying of "Overwork". www.nytimes.com/2020/12/15/world/asia/korea-couriers-dead-overwork.html accessed at 28 March 2021

Novitz, T. (2020). The Potential for International Regulation of Gig Economy Issues. *King's Law Journal*, 31(2), 275–286.

Özbilgin, M. F., & Erbil, C. (2021). *Social movements and wellbeing in organizations from multilevel and intersectional perspectives: The case of the# blacklivesmatter movement*. The SAGE handbook of organisational wellbeing.

Özbilgin, M. F., & Slutskaya, N. (2017). Consequences of neo-liberal politics on equality and diversity at work in Britain: Is resistance futile?

In Chanlat, J.-F. and Özbligin, M.F. (Eds.) *Management and Diversity* (International Perspectives on Equality, Diversity and Inclusion, Vol. 4, pp. 319–334). Bingley: Emerald Publishing Limited. https://doi.org/10.1108/S2051-233320160000004015

Pandey, N., & Pal, A. (2020). Impact of digital surge during Covid-19 pandemic: A viewpoint on research and practice. *International Journal of Information Management*, 55, 102171.

Petriglieri, G., Ashford, S. J., & Wrzesniewski, A. (2019). Agony and ecstasy in the gig economy: Cultivating holding environments for precarious and personalized work identities. *Administrative Science Quarterly*, 64(1), 124–170.

Pfaffenberger, Bryan (1992). "Social anthropology of technology." *Annual review of Anthropology*, 21(1), 491–516.

Pichault, F., & McKeown, T. (2019). Autonomy at work in the gig economy: analysing work status, work content and working conditions of independent professionals. *New Technology, Work and Employment*, 34(1), 59–72.

Polkowska, D. (2021). Platform work during the COVID-19 pandemic: a case study of Glovo couriers in Poland. *European Societies*, 23(sup1), S321–S331.

Prudential (2017). Gig Workers in America. www.prudential.com/wps/wcm/connect/4c7de648-54fb-4ba7-98de-9f0ce03810e8/gig-workers-in-america.pdf?MOD=AJPERES&CVID=mD-yCXo, accessed 28 March 2021

Rani, U., & Dhir, R. K. (2020). Platform Work and the COVID-19 Pandemic. *The Indian Journal of Labour Economics*, 63(1), 163–171.

ROSPA (The Royal Society for the Prevention of Accidents) (2020). "Road Safety Factsheet" Available at: www.rospa.com/media/documents/road-safety/cycling-accidents-factsheet.pdf (Accessed at 25 March 2021)

Samdanis, M., & Özbilgin, M. (2020). The duality of an atypical leader in diversity management: The legitimization and delegitimization of diversity beliefs in organizations. *International Journal of Management Reviews*, 22(2), 101–119.

Schwarz, M., & Thompson, M. (1990). *Divided We Stand: Redefining Politics, Technology, and Social Choice*. Philadelphia, PA: University of Pennsylvania Press.

Smith, B., Goods, C., Barratt, T., & Veen, A. (2021). Consumer "app-etite" for workers' rights in the Australian "gig economy". *Journal of choice modelling*, 38, 100254.

Syed, J., & Özbilgin, M. (2009). A relational framework for international transfer of diversity management practices. *The International Journal of Human Resource Management*, 20(12), 2435–2453.

Tajfel, H. (Ed.). (2010). *Social Identity and Intergroup Relations* (Vol. 7). Cambridge, UK: Cambridge University Press.

Tatli, A., Vassilopoulou, J., Ariss, A. A., & Özbilgin, M. (2012). The role of regulatory and temporal context in the construction of diversity discourses: The case of the UK, France and Germany. *European Journal of Industrial Relations*, 18(4), 293–308.

Umar, M., Xu, Y., & Mirza, S. S. (2020). The impact of Covid-19 on the Gig economy. *Economic Research-Ekonomska Istraživanja*, 33(1), 1–13.

Vatan, G. (2021). Bir yılda motokurye ölümleri 10 kat arttı www.gazetevatan .com/bir-yilda-motokurye-olumleri-10-kat-artti-1377037-gundem/ accessed at 28 March 2021

Verhoef, P. C., Broekhuizen, T., Bart, Y., Bhattacharya, A., Dong, J. Q., Fabian, N., & Haenlein, M. (2021). Digital transformation: A multidisciplinary reflection and research agenda. *Journal of Business Research*, 122, 889–901.

Webster, C., & Ivanov, S. (2020). Robotics, artificial intelligence, and the evolving nature of work. In George, B., Paul, J. (eds) *Digital Transformation in Business and Society* (pp. 127–143). Cham: Palgrave Macmillan. https://doi.org/10.1007/978-3-030-08277-2_8

Webster, N. A., & Zhang, Q. (2020). Careers delivered from the kitchen? Immigrant women small-scale entrepreneurs working in the growing Nordic platform economy. *NORA-Nordic Journal of Feminist and Gender Research*, 28(2), 113–125.

Index

Printed in the United States
by Baker & Taylor Publisher Services